With Best Wishes
For Good Reading

To: _Gwen Lowey_

From: _Larry & Bonnie Malone_

Hab 2:2 :)

The
Believer's
Way
of
Life

VOLUME 2
Loewen's Selections
of Bible Readings
for Daily Devotions

HERITAGECLASSICS

Library of Congress Catalog Card Number: 94-75580

ISBN: 0-9640876-1-8

Cover design by Gwen Stamm

Printed in the United States of America

FOREWORD

The preparation of these two volumes of Bible readings grew out of a long tradition of family devotions. My wife Elfrieda's father and grandfather were farmers and preachers in the American west. Daily devotional readings were a matter of course. My own forebears on the prairies of western Canada were entrepreneurs with threshing crews, sawmills and construction gangs, yet they had time for Bible reading and prayer.

It was therefore natural that in our own growing family with six children we maintained that happy tradition of family devotions. Yet, even good habits can become routine and perfunctory. We tried a variety of devotional materials to keep the attention of several age-groups: Bible verses assembled on a theme, comments on short passages, and, of course, the popularized Bible stories, mainly about Old Testament heroes. All were useful at certain periods of the family's development. Essentially, these readings needed to attract attention and provoke discussion, then move to reflection and prayer. Morning devotions were short and brisk as the family dashed off to school and work. Evening readings - between supper's main dish and dessert - were more paced, prompting comments and personal resolve.

Reading the entire Bible cannot be improved upon, for God's word is the believer's ultimate guideline for faith and practice. But for families with children, even for adults in their private readings, long genealogies, reenforcing repetitions, and the symbolisms of some prophecies can become wearying. We began to wonder whether a series of Bible readings could be related to a theme (or themes) and gathered into a meaningful sequence. Could perhaps a one-page selection for a day tell of an incident or relate an event with consequent impact on life? Could those teachings be tied together for 365 pages and become a year's daily readings? Could we be selective yet offer an introduction to each of the sixty-six books of the Bible? Hopefully, the readings would draw the reader to the Bible itself for a fuller study of God's revelation.

So we set the following guidelines in choosing the selections:
    i) A reading would not be more than one page in length;
    ii) Though some verses might be skipped in a reading, the narrative had to stand by itself; there would be no backtracking or rearranging of verses;

iii) The sequence of readings would be progressive, i.e. move in the direction of the Books in the Bible from Genesis to Revelation;

iv) When all the selections had been read, the reader would have read something from each book of the Bible.

We eventually selected 660 passages. Many remained intact as in the original text; some retained a natural flow even when verses needed to be deleted; a few, unfortunately, were held together more for convenience than by logic. For these latter, we beg the reader's understanding. But each reading has enough material to sketch an event, to relay a teaching; something on which to meditate, to pray and to act.

What about the overriding themes? Are there major threads that weave through the Scriptures? We found two, and used them for the two volumes. First, God's Way of Salvation traces the creation of man to his ultimate redemption from the Fall via the choosing of a people who were to be models and who were to present the Savior, a people at once obedient and rebellious. Throughout, God is preparing the way of salvation for all mankind through His Son Jesus.

The other theme is a corollary to the first. Having accepted THE WAY what then will be the Believer's Way of Life? Are there not many examples of how faithful men and women walked with God? How did this earlier cloud of witnesses handle their situations? We read with joy their magnificent psalms of victory. Alas, we see also the torment of their souls as they agonized in defeat and sought forgiveness and restoration with the Father.

It was not always easy to separate these two streams. Indeed, seventy readings of the first volume also relate to the theme of the second volume.

We hope that as you meditate on these pages from God's word you will catch the majesty of His ways in the believer's life.

Melvin J. Loewen
at Old Oaks
Easter Sunday, 1994

CONTENTS

Bible Readings Found in the Two Volumes of Loewen's Selections of Bible Readings

		Volume 1	Volume 2
		God's Way of Salvation	The Believer's Way of Life
		Page	Page
Genesis 1:1-23	God Creates The Heavens And The Earth	1	
Gen 1:24-2:3	And God Made Man	2	1
Gen 2:15-3:7	"Did God Really Say You Must Not Eat Of The Fruit?"	3	
Gen 3:8-24	So God Banished Them From The Garden	4	
Gen 4:1-15;5:3-5	Cain Kills Abel	5	2
Gen 6:9-7:6	Noah Was A Righteous Man		3
Gen 7:7-8:4	The Floods Covered The Earth		4
Gen 8:21-9:17	God Gives The Rainbow		5
Gen 11:1-9	The Tower Of Babel		
11:27-32	Terah, Father Of Abram	6	
Gen 12:1-8a;13:1-12	Abram And Lot	7	
Gen 15:1-21	Abram's Descendants Will Have A Land	8	6
Gen 16:1-16	Sarai Gives Hagar To Be Abram's Wife	9	
Gen 17:1-20a	No Longer Abram, Your Name Will Be Abraham		7
Gen 18:1-19	Sarah Is Promised A Son	10	8
Gen 18:20-33;19:15-17	Abraham Pleads For Sodom And Gomorrah	11	
Gen 21:1-21	Isaac Is Born, Ishmael Sent Away	12	9
Gen 22:1-18	Abraham Told To Sacrifice Isaac	13	
Gen 23:1-20	Sarah Dies	14	

		Vol. 1	Vol. 2
Gen 24:10-26	Rebekah Waters The Camels	15	
Gen 24:50-67	Isaac Marries Rebekah	16	
Gen 25:1-18a	Abraham Dies		
	And Is Buried By Isaac And Ishmael	17	10
Gen 25:19-34;26:34-35	Jacob And Esau	18	11
Gen 27:1-24	Deception By Rebekah and Jacob	19	
Gen 27:25-40	Isaac Blesses Jacob	20	12
Gen 27:41-28:9	Jacob Leaves Home	21	
Gen 28:10-29:6	Jacob Has A Dream	22	
Gen 29:13-28	Jacob Marries Leah And Rachel	23	
Gen 31:17-36	Jacob Leaves For Canaan	24	13
Gen 31:38-55	Laban And Jacob Separate In Peace	25	
Gen 32:8-28	Jacob's Name Changed To Israel	26	
Gen 33:1-18	Jacob And Esau Meet In Peace	27	14
Gen 35:9-20,22c-29	Rachel Dies		
	Isaac Dies And Is Buried By Esau And Jacob	28	15
Gen 36:2-14,40-43	Esau's Descendants	29	
Gen 37:2b-18	Young Joseph Has Dreams	30	16
Gen 37:19-36	Joseph Is Sold To Traders	31	17
Gen 39:1-21	Joseph Is Bought By Potiphar	32	
Gen 40:1-22a			
Gen 41:1-24	Pharaoh Has A Dream	34	
Gen 41:26-46	Joseph Becomes Prime Minister	35	18
Gen 42:1-21	Joseph's Brothers Seek Food In Egypt	36	
Gen 42:35-43:14			
	Joseph's Brothers Prepare Second Trip To Egypt	37	
Gen 43:15-33	Benjamin Goes Along To Egypt	38	
Gen 44:10-31	Silver Cup Found In Benjamin's Bag	39	
Gen 45:1-20	Joseph Reveals Himself To His Brothers	40	
Gen 46:1-6,26-47:3			
	Jacob And His Descendants Move To Egypt	41	19
Gen 47:28-48:9;49:29-33	Jacob Dies	42	20
Gen 50:2-20	Joseph And His Brothers Bury Jacob	43	21
Exodus 1:6-22	A New King Oppresses The Israelites	44	22
Exo 2:1-21	Moses Is Born; Later Flees To Midian	45	
Exo 3:1-17a			
	Moses Is Called To Lead Israel Out Of Egypt	46	23
Exo 4:1-20	Moses Returns To Egypt	47	
Exo 5:1-21a	Moses' Appeal Rejected By Pharaoh	48	24
Exo 6:28-7:13;11:1-3	Aaron Helps Moses	49	25

		Vol. 1	Vol. 2
Exo 12:21-36,50-51	Passover And Exodus	50	26
Exo 13:17-22;14:5-14	Pharaoh Pursues The Israelites	51	
Exo 14:19-31;15:19-21	Crossing The Red Sea	52	
Exo 15:27-16:15	Water And Bread	53	
Exo 17:1-15	Moses Strikes Rock For Water, And Raises Hands For Victory	54	
Exo 18:6-24	Moses Accepts Advice From His Father-in-law	55	
Exo 19:3-19	Moses Meets God On Mt.Sinai	56	27
Exo 20:1-19	The Ten Commandments	57	28
Exo 24:3-25:2;25:8-9	God Confirms His Covenant	58	
Exo 32:1-7,15-24	The Israelites Build The Golden Calf	59	
Exo 34:1-16	Moses Chisels Two Stone Tablets	60	29
Exo 36:2-6;37:1-9,25-29	Building the Tabernacle, The Ark And The Altar Of Incense	61	
Exo 40:1-17,34-38	Moses Sets Up The Tabernacle And The Tent Of Meeting	62	
Leviticus 4:5-21	The Sin Offering	63	30
Lev 8:1-21	Aaron And His Sons Anointed As Priests	64	
Lev 9:5-23	The Priests Begin Their Ministry	65	31
Lev 19:1-4,9-18,30-37	Rules For Daily Living	66	32
Lev 25:3-23	The Sabbatical Year; The Year Of Jubilee	67	33
Lev 26:3-21	The Rewards Of Obedience, And The Punishments For Disobedience	68	34
Lev 27:16-28,30-34	A Tithe Belongs To The Lord	69	35
Numbers 1:20,21,23,25,27,29,31, 33,35,37,39,41,43,45-50	A Census Of Israel	70	
Num 3:1-16,39-43	Aaron And Sons Appointed As Priests	71	
Num 8:5-25	Levites Set Apart	72	
Num 10:11-17,29-36	Israelites Leave Sinai	73	
Num 11:11-17	Seventy Elders Appointed		
11:31-34	The People Complain And Get Quail	74	36
Num 12:1-15	Miriam And Aaron Talk Against Moses	75	
Num 13:1-2,17-33	Scouts Look At Canaan	76	
Num 14:7-24	Again The People Grumble	77	37
Num 20:2-12	Moses Strikes Rock For Water		
20:15-21	Edom Refuses Passage To Israel	78	

		Vol. 1	Vol. 2
Num 20:22-29	Aaron Dies		
21:4-9	Bronze Snake On A Pole	79	
Num 22:21-38	Balaam Is Asked To Prophecy	80	
Num 23:7-12;24:1-9	Balaam Blesses Israel	81	
Num 26:1-4,51-56,62-65	Another Census Before Entering Canaan	82	
Num 27:18-23	Joshua Succeeds Moses As Leader		
32:6-17	Reuben And Gad Stay East Of Jordan	83	
Num 33:51b-56	Instructions On How To Take Canaan		
35:2-14	Towns For Levites And Cities Of Refuge	84	38
Deuteronomy 4:23-38	God Makes For Himself One Nation	85	
Deu 5:4-22	The Ten Commandments	86	
Deu 6:3-25	Fear The Lord And Serve Him Only	87	39
Deu 7:7-19,25-26	A Special People Loved Of God	88	
Deu 14:22-23,27-29;15:1-11	Give A Tithe; Help The Poor	89	40
Deu 23:7-8	Respect Edomites And Egyptians		
24:5	Newly-Married Should Stay At Home		
24:10-15,19-22;25:13-16	Loans, Weights, Measures	90	41
Deu 28:1-14,20-24	Blessings And Curses	91	42
Deu 30:1-18a	Prosperity When You Obey The Lord	92	43
Deu 31:1-8,19-26a	Joshua Succeeds Moses	93	
Deu 32:48-52;34:1-12	Moses Dies	94	
Joshua 1:1-18	Instructions To Joshua	95	
Josh 2:1-18	Spies Make A Deal With Rahab	96	
Josh 3:1-17	Israelites Cross The Jordan Into Canaan	97	
Josh 6:10-23	The Fall Of Jericho	98	
Josh 9:3-21	The Gibeonites Deceive The Israelites	99	
Josh 10:1-15	The Sun Stands Still At Gibeon	100	
Josh 21:43-45	All Of Canaan Given To Israelites;		
22:1-9	Reuben, Gad And Manasseh Return To East Of Jordan	101	
Josh 24:19-24,29-33	Death Of Joshua And Of Eleazar	102	
Judges 1:1-3,8-18,27-29	Israel Fights The Canaanite Tribes	103	

		Vol. 1	Vol. 2
Judg 2:1-3,14-23;3:5-6	Israel Lives With The Canaanites	104	
Judg 4:1-16;5:1-3	Deborah Leads Israel	105	
Judg 6:14-23,33-40	Gideon Puts Out A Fleece	106	44
Judg 7:5b-20	Gideon's Three Hundred Fight Midian	107	45
Judg 8:22-35	Gideon Dies	108	
Judg 11:1-6,9-10,29-39a	Jephthah Sacrifices His Daughter	109	
Judg 13:6-24	Samson Is Born	110	
Judg 14:1-3,10-20	Samson Marries A Philistine Woman	111	
Judg 16:8-22	Delilah Betrays Samson	112	
Judg 16:23-31	Death of Samson	113	
Ruth 1:1-19	Ruth Migrates With Naomi	114	46
Ruth 2:8-20a	Ruth Meets Boaz	115	
Ruth 3:1-18	Boaz Promises To Find A Husband For Ruth	116	
Ruth 4:2-17	Boaz Marries Ruth	117	
1 Samuel 1:3-20	Birth Of Samuel	118	
1 Sam 1:21-28;2:19-21,26	Samuel Is Dedicated To The Lord	119	47
1 Sam 2:22-36	The Sons Of Eli Are Wicked	120	
1 Sam 3:1-21	The Lord Calls Samuel	121	48
1 Sam 4:5-21	Eli's Sons Are Killed And Eli Dies	122	
1 Sam 5:10b-6:12	Philistines Return The Ark Of The Covenant	123	
1 Sam 7:2-17	Peace In Israel While Samuel Is Judge	124	49
1 Sam 8:1-22	Israel Asks For A King	125	
1 Sam 9:1-17	Samuel Looks For A King	126	
1 Sam 9:22-10:8	Samuel Anoints Saul As King	127	
1 Sam 10:11-27;13:1	Saul Becomes King Of Israel	128	
1 Sam 14:4-15,20-23	Jonathan Attacks The Philistines	129	
1 Sam 15:10-26	Saul Rejected As King	130	
1 Sam 16:5b-23	Samuel Anoints David As The New King Yet David Serves Saul	131	50
1 Sam 17:4-10,32,41-50	David And Goliath	132	
1 Sam 18:9-16,20-30	David Marries Saul's Daughter	133	
1 Sam 19:1b-20	Saul Pursues David	134	
1 Sam 20:24-42a	David And Jonathan	135	51

		Vol. 1	Vol. 2
1 Sam 24:7-22	David Could Have Killed Saul		
25:1	Samuel Dies	136	
1 Sam 28:3-20	Saul Consults A Witch	137	
1 Sam 31:1-13	Saul Takes His Own Life	138	
2 Sam 2:1-17	David Becomes King Of Judah	139	
2 Sam 3:12-27			
	Abner Joins David And Is Murdered By Joab	140	
2 Sam 4:5-5:5	David Becomes King of Israel	141	52
2 Sam 5:6-12,17-25			
	Jerusalem Becomes City Of David	142	
2 Sam 6:2-19			
	David Returns Ark Of The Lord To Jerusalem	143	
2 Sam 7:1-17			
	David's Son To Build A House For The Lord	144	
2 Sam 9:1-13	David Shows Kindness To Jonathan's Son	145	53
2 Sam 11:2b-21	David, Bathsheba And Uriah	146	
2 Sam 12:1-18a	David Repents	147	54
2 Sam 15:1-17a			
	Absalom Leads A Rebellion And David Flees	148	
2 Sam 17:1-16			
	Ahitophel And Hushai Davise Absalom	149	
2 Sam 18:1-17	Absalom Dies	150	
2 Sam 18:32b-19:14	David Returns To Jerusalem	151	
2 Sam 20:1-15a	Sheba Leads A Rebellion	152	
2 Sam 22:31-51	David's Song Of Praise	153	
2 Sam 24:1-4,8-17			
	God Punishes David For Counting His Forces	154	
1 Kings 1:11-30a	Adonijah Usurps The Throne	155	
1 King 1:36-53	Solomon Is Anointed King	156	
1 King 2:1-11	David's Final Instructions To Solomon	157	55
1 King 2:30-46			
	Solomon Establishes His Own Administration	158	
1 King 3:11-28	Solomon The Wise	159	56
1 King 5:1-18			
	Solomon Prepares To Build The Temple	160	
1 King 6:11-18	Solomon Builds The Temple	161	
1 King 7:1-11	Solomon Builds His Palace	162	
1 King 8:15-30	Dedication Of The Temple	163	
1 King 9:1-14,24-25	God's Promise To Solomon	164	57

	Vol. 1	Vol. 2
1 King 10:1-10,23-29		
Solomon Is Rich, Visited By The Queen Of Sheba	165	
1 King 11:1-18		
Solomon's Many Wives Increase His Difficulties	166	58
1 King 11:27-43 Rebellion Of Jeroboam;		
Death Of Solomon	167	
1 King 12:3-20 Israel Rebels Against Rehoboam	168	
1 King 14:7-9,19-20,21-31a		
Jeroboam King Of Israel; Rehoboam King Of Judah	169	
1 King 17:5-24		
Elijah Is Fed By Ravens; A Widow Has Flour And Oil	170	59
1 King 18:1-20 Elijah And Obadiah, Men Of God	171	
1 King 18:30-46		
Elijah Sacrifices To God And Ends The Drought	172	60
1 King 19:7-21 Elijah Flees And Calls Elisha	173	61
1 King 21:5-23 Jezebel Gets A Vineyard For Ahab	174	
1 King 22:7-9,17-28,34a,37		
Micaiah, A Prophet Of God; Ahab Dies	175	
2 King 2:1-15 Elijah Is Taken To Heaven	176	
2 King 4:14-21,27-37		
Elisha Raises A Boy From The Dead	177	
2 King 5:1-16 Naaman Is Healed	178	
2 King 17:6-20 Israel Is Taken In Exile To Assyria	179	
2 King 18:13-25		
Sennacherib Of Assyria Threatens Judah	180	
2 King 19:5-19,35-36		
Isaiah Foresees The Withdrawal Of Sennecharib	181	
2 King 20:1-17		
Isaiah Foresees Judah's Captivity In Babylon	182	
2 King 25:5-21		
Nebuchadnezzar Of Babylon Captures Jerusalem	183	
1 Chronicles 13:7-14;15:1-3,25-16:1a		
The Ark Brought Back To Jerusalem		62
1 Chron 16:17-29,34-36 David's Song Of Praise		63
1 Chron 17:1-19 God Promises Blessings To David		64
1 Chron 21:5-18,26-27		
God Is Angry Because David Counts His Troops		65
1 Chron 22:1-17 David Prepares To Build The Temple		66

	Vol. 1	Vol. 2

1 Chron 29:6-20
The People Bring Gifts For the Temple — 67
1 Chron 29:21-30   Solomon The New King; David Dies — 68

2 Chron 1:1-17   God Gives Wisdom To Solomon — 69
2 Chron 3:1-17   Solomon Builds The Temple — 70
2 Chron 6:12-21;7:1-5   Solomon Dedicates The Temple — 71
2 Chron 8:1-16 Solomon Consolidates His Kingdom — 72
2 Chron 9:1-14 The Queen Of Sheba Comes To Jerusalem — 73
2 Chron 28:1-11,22-25
King Ahaz Does Not Honor The Lord — 74
2 Chron 29:1-11,25-30
Ahaz' Son Hezekiah Honors The Lord — 75
2 Chron 31:3-12a,20-21
Hezekiah Encourages Gifts To The Lord — 76
2 Chron 34:1-3,16b-28a   Josiah Seeks The Ways Of God — 77

Ezra 1:1-8;2:64-70;3:1   Exiles Return To Jerusalem — 184
Ezra 3:7-4:5   The Jews Start To Rebuild The Temple — 185
Ezra 5:3-17   The Jews Appeal To Cyrus' Earlier Decree — 186
Ezra 6:2-16   Cyrus' Decree Is Confirmed By Darius;
The Temple Is Rebuilt — 187
Ezra 7:8-23a   Ezra Returns To Jerusalem — 188 — 78
Ezra 9:1-12   Ezra Disturbed About Mixed Marriages — 189 — 79

Nehemiah 1:1-2:3 Nehemiah Weeps For Jerusalem — — 80
Neh 2:6-20   Nehemiah Goes To Jerusalem — 190
Neh 4:1-18a   Jews Rebuild The Wall While Under Attack — 191
Neh 5:1-15   Nehemiah Helps The Poor — 192
Neh 6:1-16   The Wall Of Jerusalem Is Rebuilt — 193
Neh 8:1b-3,15-18
Ezra, Nehemiah, and the Levites Instruct the People — 194
Neh 13:1-13,15   Nehemiah's Final Instructions — 195

Esther 1:9-22   Queen Vashti Is Banished — 196
Esther 2:5-18   Esther Becomes Queen — 197
Esther 3:2-15   Mordecai Discovers Haman's Plot — 198
Esther 4:7-5:6   Esther Prepares A Banquet — 199
Esther 5:9-6:10   Mordecai Is Honored By The King — 200
Esther 7:3-8:8a
Haman Is Hanged, And The Jews Protected — 201

		Vol. 1	Vol. 2
Esther 9:18-32	The Jews Observe Purim	202	
Job 1:1-12,18-22	Job's Children Are Killed		81
Job 2:1-3:2;3:23-26	Job Becomes Ill And Complains		82
Job 4:1-5;5:8-11,17-27	Eliphaz Gives Counsel		83
Job 6:8-10,24-26;7:11-21	Job Replies To Eliphaz		84
Job 8:1-10,20-22;9:1-4;10:1-9	Bildad Gives Counsel And Job Replies		85
Job 11:1-5,13-18;13:1-3;14:1-2,14-16	Zaphar Gives Counsel And Job Replies		86
Job 32:1-6;33:8-15,19,26-28	Elihu Gives Counsel		87
Job 35:1-12;36:1-12,15-16	Elihu Continues His Counsel		88
Job 38:4-8,12-13,19-22,31-35; 39:26-27;40:1-5	God Replies		89
Job 42:1-17	Job Restored To Health And Wealth		90
Psalms 1 and 2			91
Psalms 4 and 5:1-8		203	92
Psalm 8			93
Psalms 14 and 16:5-11			94
Psalm 18:1-19			95
Psalm 19			96
Psalm 22:1-8,22-31			97
Psalms 23 and 24			98
Psalm 27			99
Psalm 32			100
Psalm 33			101
Psalm 34			102
Psalm 37:1-20			103
Psalm 37:21-40		204	104
Psalm 38			105
Psalm 40			106
Psalm 41			107
Psalm 42			108
Psalms 46 and 47:1-6			109
Psalm 49			110
Psalm 51			111
Psalms 53 and 54		205	112
Psalm 56			113
Psalm 66			114
Psalms 67 and 68:1-10			115

	Vol. 1	Vol. 2
Psalm 71:1-18		116
Psalm 84		117
Psalm 90	206	
Psalm 91		118
Psalms 95 and 96		119
Psalms 100 and 101		120
Psalm 103		121
Psalm 107:1-22		122
Psalms 112 and 113		123
Psalm 115		124
Psalm 116		125
Psalms 117 and 118:1-14		126
Psalm 118:15-29		127
Psalm 119:1-24		128
Psalm 119:33-40,57-64,73-80		129
Psalms 121 and 124		130
Psalms 127 and 128		131
Psalms 133 and 134 and 135:1-9		132
Psalms 137 and 138		133
Psalm 139:1-19		134
Psalms 141 and 142		135
Psalm 145		136
Psalm 147		137
Psalms 149 and 150		138
Proverbs 1:7-19;2:1-6		139
Prov 3:1-14,27-29	207	
Prov 5:1-23		140
Prov 6:1-19		141
Prov 10:1-5,12-22		142
Prov 11:1-8,16-28		143
Prov 15:1-18		144
Prov 16:3-21		145
Prov 17:1,5-6,9-10,12-16	208	146
Prov 21:1-21		147
Prov 22:1-19		148
Prov 23:4-25		149
Prov 24:3-7,23b-34		150
Prov 27:1-2,17-21;28:5-9		151
Prov 30:7-8,15b-16,18-19;31:1-9		152
Prov 31:10-31		153

	Vol. 1	Vol. 2
Ecclesiastes 2:1-18		
The Things I Toiled For I Must Leave Behind		154
Eccles 3:1-22 Every Activity Has Its Time		155
Eccles 5:4-20		
Let Man Labor And Enjoy God's Blessings		156
Eccles 11:1-2,6,9;12:1-7,13-14		
Cast Your Bread Upon The Waters		157
Song of Solomon 4:1-7;7:10-13;8:6-7		
How Beautiful Is My Beloved		158
Isaiah 1:1-4,13-20 If You Rebel You Will Be Destroyed		159
Isa 3:8-26 Judgment Pronounced On The Wicked		160
Isa 6:1-12;8:5-8 God Commissions Isaiah	209	
Isa 8:18-9:7 The Promise Of The Savior	210	
Isa 10:5-19 Woe To Assyria	211	
Isa 10:20-25;11:1-11		
A Remnant Of Israel Will Trust In God	212	161
Isa 14:3-15 Babylon Too Will Be Destroyed	213	
Isa 25:1-12 A Song Of Praise To God		162
Isa 30:15-26;31:6-9 A Call For Repentance		163
Isa 36:1-10;37:14-20		
Sennecharib, King Of Assyria, Threatens To Attack	214	
Isa 38:1-19 Hezekiah's Life Prolonged	215	
Isa 40:1-15a Good Tidings For God's People		164
Isa 49:8-18,22-23 God Promises To Remember Israel		165
Isa 53:1-12 The Messiah Will Come In Sacrifice	216	
Isa 55:1-13 God's Ways Are Above Man's Ways		166
Isa 58:5-14 True Fasting Is To Help The Poor		167
Isa 61:1-11 The Year Of The Lord		168
Isa 62:1-12 The Nations Will See Your Righteousness		169
Isa 65:16-25 A New Creation		170
Isa 66:1-2,5-6,12-14 A Blessed Hope For God's People		171
Jeremiah 1:1-19 Jeremiah Is Called To Prophesy	217	
Jer 2:13-26a Israel Has Turned Away From God	218	
Jer 3:6-20		
Both Israel And Judah Have Been Unfaithful	219	
Jer 5:14-29 God Will Punish His Unfaithful Children		172
Jer 7:8-26 God Will Help If Israel Changes Its Ways	220	

		Vol. 1	Vol. 2
Jer 10:11-25			
	God Is The Maker Of All And Will Judge All		173
Jer 11:1-17a	Judah Has Broken The Covenant	221	
Jer 18:1-20	The Potter's Clay		174
Jer 21:1-14	Zedekiah Seeks God's Help And Is Rejected	222	
Jer 23:1-8;24:1-7	God Will Gather A Remnant		175
Jer 26:5-19	Priests Want Jeremiah Killed	223	
Jer 27:8-22	Nebuchadnezzar Will Carry Away Judah	224	
Jer 28:1-17			
	But Nebuchadnezzar's Yoke Will Be Broken	225	
Jer 29:3-19	Jeremiah's Letter To The Elders In Exile	226	
Jer 30:1-3;31:1-10			
	Israel And Judah Will Return In Joy		176
Jer 31:23-33,38-40			
	God Will Bring Them Back To Rebuild The City		177
Jer 33:1-11,14-17	Call Upon Me And I Will Show		
	You Great And Mighty Things		178
Jer 34:2b-17	Freedom To The Slaves		179
Jer 36:8,16-31a	Jehoiakim Burns Jeremiah's Scroll	227	
Jer 38:2-4,14-23			
	Jeremiah Foresees The Fall Of Jerusalem	228	
Jer 39:1-17a	Jersualem Is Taken By Babylon	229	
Jer 42:5-22			
A Remnant Goes To Egypt In Spite Of God's Warning		230	
Jer 44:14-27a			
	The Remnant In Egypt To Be Destroyed	231	
Jer 51:49-64	And Babylon Will Also Be Destroyed	232	
Jer 52:4-16,27b-30	Jerusalem Is Destroyed	233	
Lamentations 1:1-8	How Deserted Lies The City		180
Lament 2:11-19a	My Eyes Fail From Weeping		181
Lament 3:19-42	Yet, We Have Hope		182
Lament 4:22-5:22	Restore Us Lord To Yourself		183
Ezekiel 1:1-3,19-28	God's Glory Appears To Ezekiel	234	
Ezek 3:3-19	Ezekiel Is Asked To Eat The Scroll		
	And Warn Israel	235	
Ezek 4:16-5:14	Siege Of Jerusalem Is Foretold	236	
Ezek 8:17-9:8	There Is Sin In The Temple	237	
Ezek 11:14-12:7a	God Will Again Gather His People		184
Ezek 16:43-59	The Sin Of Israel		185

		Vol. 1	Vol. 2
Ezek 17:1-19	Parable Of The Eagles And A Vine		186
Ezek 18:4-20	Each Generation Will Have Its Own Reward		187
Ezek 20:28-42	Israel Will Be Punished, Then Restored	238	
Ezek 33:1-16	Ezekiel Is The Watchman To Warn Israel	239	
Ezek 34:2b-17	Shepherds Care For Their Flocks		188
Ezek 37:1b-19	Valley Of Dry Bones		189
Ezek 39:1-8,17-25	Gog, From The North, Will Be Destroyed		190
Ezek 45:18-25;46:11-15	Offerings To The Lord		191
Daniel 1:1-19	Daniel And Friends Go On Vegetable Diet	240	
Dan 2:3-19a	Nebuchadnezzar Had A Dream, But Wouldn't Say What He Dreamt	241	
Dan 2:24-40	Daniel Recounts The Dream And Interprets It	242	
Dan 3:3-19	Nebuchadnezzar Casts Daniel's Friends Into The Fiery Furnace	243	
Dan 4:1-18a	Nebuchadnezzar Dreams Of A Tree	244	
Dan 4:19b-33	The King's Dream Comes True	245	
Dan 5:1-16a	A New King, Belshazzar, Sees Writing On The Wall	246	
Dan 5:17-31	Daniel Interprets The Writing	247	
Dan 6:7b-23a	A New King, Darius, Throws David To The Lions	248	
Dan 7:1-14b	Daniel Also Dreams - Of Four Beasts		192
Dan 7:15-28	Daniel Is Offered An Interpretation Of His Dream		193
Dan 8:1-17	Daniel Has A Vision Of A Ram And A Goat		194
Dan 9:1-17a	Daniel Prays For The Restoration of Israel		195
Dan 9:20-27	Gabriel Speaks Of Seventy Sevens		196
Dan 11:40-12:10	At The Time Of The End		197
Hosea 1:1-2:5a	Hosea's Adulterous Wife	249	198
Hosea 2:14-3:5	But God Will Love Even An Adulterous Wife		199
Hosea 11:1-11;14:9	God Will Heal Israel		200
Joel 1:1-3;2:12-19,26-27	Repent And God Will Hear		201

	Vol. 1	Vol. 2
Joel 3:1-2,9-12,16-21		
Judah Will Be Restored, And The Nations Judged	250	202
Amos 2:4-16		
Judgment Pronounced On Judah And Israel	251	
Amos 3:1-8;4:10-13		
God's Chosen People Will Be Punished	252	203
Amos 5:4-15,21-24		
Israel Will Live When It Seeks God	253	204
Amos 7:1-17		
Amos The Shepherd Rebukes Amaziah The Priest	254	
Amos 8:1-12		
The Lord Will Tremble Because Of Israel's Sin	255	
Amos 9:8-15 Yet, God Will Not Totally Destroy Israel	256	
Obadiah 1:10-21 Punishment Promised To Those Nations Who Do Not Defend Israel		205
Jonah 1:1-17 Jonah Tries To Run Away From God		206
Jonah 2:1-10		
Jonah, Inside The Giant Fish, Prays To God		207
Jonah 3:3-4:11 Jonah Obeys God		208
Micah 1:1-5;2:1-5,12-13		
Punishment Promised To Israel, But Also Deliverance	257	209
Micah 4:1-8;5:2-5a God's Temple Will Be Restored And Bethlehem Will Be Proud	258	
Micah 6:1-15 God's Accusation Against Israel	259	
Micah 7:8-13,15-20 But Israel Will Be Restored	260	
Nahum 1:1-15		
Condemnation of Nineveh; Judah To Be Rescued	261	
Habakkuk 1:1-6,12-13;2:2-3,20;3:1-2		
Why, Oh Lord, Do You Tolerate The Wicked?	262	210
Zephaniah 1:14-2:3		
Repent, The Day Of The Lord Is Near		211
Zeph 3:8b-20 Jerusalem Will Be Restored		212
Haggai 1:1-15 God's Call To Rebuild The Temple	263	

		Vol. 1	Vol. 2
Haggai 2:6-23	God Will Again Bless His People		213
Zechariah 1:1-17	God Promises Restoration		214
Zech 2:1-13;3:1-7	Measurements For Jerusalem; Garments For The Priests	264	
Zech 4:1-9;5:1-11	Not By Might, Nor By Power, But By My Spirit		215
Zech 7:4-14;8:1-8	Blessings Promised To Jerusalem		216
Zech 11:7-17;12:1-5	Thirty Pieces Of Silver	265	
Zech 14:1-16	God Will Gather Nations Against Jerusalem	266	
Malachi 1:1-14	Sacrifices Defiled	267	
Mal 2:7-3:4	He Will Be Like A Refiner's Fire	268	
Mal 3:7-4:6a	Bring All The Tithe		217
Matthew 1:18-2:12	Birth Of Jesus		218
Mat 3:1-17	John Presents Jesus		219
Mat 4:1-22	Jesus Is Tempted, Calls His Disciples		220
Mat 5:1-12,38-48	The Beatitudes; Love Your Enemies		221
Mat 6:5-15,25-34	The Lord's Prayer; Trust Him For Your Needs		222
Mat 7:1-6,15-29	Do Not Judge Others; Watch For False Prophets; Build On Rock		223
Mat 8:1-22	Jesus Begins Healing Ministry		224
Mat 9:1-17	Jesus Heals; Calls Matthew; Comments On Fasting		225
Mat 10:1-25a	Jesus Sends Out His Disciples		226
Mat 12:1-14,22-27,33-34	Jesus Heals On Sabbath		227
Mat 13:2-23a	Parable Of The Sower		228
Mat 13:31-50	Parables Of Mustard Seed, Yeast, Weeds, And Hidden Treasure		229
Mat 14:13-36	Jesus Feeds Five Thousand, Walks On Water		230
Mat 16:1-20	Pharisees Want Proof; Peter's Witness		231
Mat 17:1-13;18:1-9a	Transfiguration; Lesson On Greatness		232
Mat 18:10-14,21-35	Parables Of Lost Sheep And The Unmerciful Servant		233

		Vol. 1	Vol. 2
Mat 19:1-21	Jesus Teaches On Divorce, Receives Little Children, Talks To Rich Young Man		234
Mat 20:1-16,23-28	Parable Of Workers In Vineyard; Mrs. Zebedee Wants A Favor		235
Mat 21:1-17	Jesus' Triumphal Entry Into Jerusalem		236
Mat 21:23-41a	Jesus' Authority Questioned; Parables Of Two Sons, And Of Landowner		237
Mat 22:1-14,34-46	Parable Of A Wedding; The Great Commandment		238
Mat 23:2-25	Woes To False Teachers		239
Mat 24:2-27	Signs Of The End		240
Mat 25:1-13,16-26a	Parables Of Virgins, And Of Talents		241
Mat 26:6-30	Perfume For Jesus; The Last Supper		242
Mat 26:33-54	Jesus Predicts Peter's Denial And Jesus' Arrest		243
Mat 26:59-27:5	Jesus Before The Sanhedrin; Peter Denies Jesus; Judas Hangs Himself		244
Mat 27:15-37	Pilate Interrogates Jesus; Soldiers Mock Him And Crucify Him		245
Mat 27:45-66	Jesus' Death And Burial		246
Mat 28:1-20	Jesus' Resurrection; The Great Commission		247
Mark 1:1-20	Jesus Is Baptized, Calls His First Disciples	269	
Mark 1:21-45	Jesus Heals The Sick, Prays Alone	270	
Mark 2:18-27;3:8-19	Jesus Comments On Fasting, Calls Twelve Diciples	271	
Mark 4:1-20	Parable Of The Sower And The Seed	272	
Mark 5:1-20	Jesus Heals Demon-Possessed	273	
Mark 6:7-28	Jesus Sends Out His Disciples John The Baptist Is Beheaded	274	
Mark 6:30-51	Jesus Feeds Five Thousand, Walks On Water	275	
Mark 7:7-30	The Pharisees' Laws Condemned; Exemplary Faith Of The Phoenician Woman	276	
Mark 8:14-36	The Pharisees' Leaven; Jesus Heals A Blind Man; Peter's Witness	277	
Mark 9:2-9	Jesus' Transfiguration		
9:17-27	Jesus Heals Boy With Evil Spirit	278	

	Vol. 1	Vol. 2
Mark 10:1-25 Jesus Comments On Divorce, And Little Children; And Has Conversation With Rich Young Man	279	
Mark 10:32-52 Jesus Predicts His Death; John And James Want Privileges; Bartimaeus Is Healed	280	
Mark 11:1-19 Jesus Enters Jerusalem In Triumph, And Clears The Temple	281	
Mark 11:28b-12:11;12:13-17 Chief Priests Question Jesus' Authority; Parable Of Tenants; On Paying Taxes	282	
Mark 12:28-44 The Great Commandment; The Widow's Offering	283	
Mark 13:4-27 The End Days	284	
Mark 14:3-24 Jesus Anointed; The Last Supper	285	
Mark 14:29-51 Peter's Denial Predicted; Gethsemane; Jesus Arrested	286	
Mark 15:22-46 Crucifixion And Burial Of Jesus	287	
Mark 16:1-20 Resurrection Of Jesus	288	
Luke 1:5-25 The Birth Of John Foretold		248
Luke 1:26-38,46-55 Birth Of Jesus Foretold; Mary's Praise		249
Luke 2:1-24 Jesus Is Born, And Presented In The Temple		250
Luke 2:41-3:6,15-16 Young Jesus In The Temple; John The Baptist's Announcement		251
Luke 4:1-24 Temptation Of Jesus; Jesus Rejected in Nazareth		252
Luke 5:1-20 Jesus Calls His First Disciples; And Heals Leper And Paralytic		253
Luke 6:1-22 Jesus' Teaching About The Sabbath; Chooses Twelve; Teaches About Blessings And Woes		254
Luke 6:27-48 Love Your Enemies; Do Not Judge; Build On Rock		255
Luke 7:1-17,20-23 Faith Of The Centurion; Widow's Son Revived; John The Baptist Has Doubts		256
Luke 8:1-18 Parable Of The Sower; A Lamp On A Stand		257
Luke 8:22-39 Jesus Calms The Storm, Heals A Demon-Possessed		258
Luke 9:1-21 Jesus Sends Out Twelve, Feeds Five Thousand; Peter's Witness		259

		Vol. 1	Vol. 2

Luke 9:28-48   Transfiguration; Jesus Heals A Boy;
A Question Of Greatness   260
Luke 9:57b-10:20   The Cost Of Discipleship   261
Luke 10:25-42
The Good Samaritan; Mary And Martha   262
Luke 11:1-10,33-36
Jesus Comments On Prayer; A Lamp On A Stand   263
Luke 11:37-12:2   Warnings On Hypocrisy   264
Luke 12:13-35
The Foolish Rich Man; Cast Your Cares On God   265
Luke 13: 1-8,18-29   Repent!
Of Mustard Seed, Yeast, And The Narrow Door   266
Luke 14:13-35a
Parable Of The Banquet; On The Cost Of Discipleship   267
Luke 15:11-32   The Lost Son   268
Luke 16:1-8a,19-31
Parable of the Good Manager; The Rich Man and Lazarus   269
Luke 17:11-19;18:1-14   Ten Lepers Healed;
Parable Of The Persistent Widow; The Tax Collector   270
Luke 19:1-23
Zacchaeus The Tax Collector; Parable On Stewardship   271
Luke 19:32-20:8   Jesus' Triumphal Entry Into Jerusalem;
Jesus' Authority Is Questioned   272
Luke 20:9-26   Parable Of Tenants; On Paying Taxes   273
Luke 21:8-31   Signs Of The End   274
Luke 22:13b-38   The Last Supper   275
Luke 22:39-62
Jesus On The Mount Of Olives; Betrayal By Peter   276
Luke 22:70-23:25   Jesus Before Pilate   277
Luke 23:32-56   Jesus' Crucifixion, Death And Burial   278
Luke 24:1-16,30-32,48-53   Jesus' Resurrection;
Appears To His Disciples; His Ascension   279

John 1:1-27
The Word Became Flesh; Ministry Of John The Baptist   289
John 1:35-51   Jesus' First Disciples   290
John 2:1-23
Jesus At A Wedding; And Clears Out The Temple   291
John 3:1-22   Jesus And Nicodemus   292
John 4:5-26   Jesus Talks To Samaritan Woman   293

		Vol. 1	Vol. 2
John 4:45-5:14	Jesus Heals Official's Son, And Heals An Invalid On The Sabbath	294	
John 5:17-39	Eternal Life Through Jesus	295	
John 6:2-24	Jesus Feeds Five Thousand, Walks On Water	296	
John 6:32b-58	Jesus The Bread Of Life	297	
John 7:1-24	Jesus At Feast Of The Tabernacle	298	
John 7:31-52	"Is This The Christ?"	299	
John 8:13-36	Jesus' Testimony Is True	300	
John 9:2-25	Man Born Blind Is Healed	301	
John 10:1b-27	Jesus, Shepherd Of His Flock	302	
John 11:1-27,43-44a	Death And Raising Of Lazarus	303	
John 12:1-19	Jesus' Anointing At Bethany; Jesus' Triumphal Entry Into Jerusalem	304	
John 13:5-28	Jesus Washes Disciples Feet, Foresees His Betrayal	305	
John 14:4-27a	Jesus Promises The Comforter, The Holy Spirit	306	
John 15:1-24	Vine And Branches	307	
John 16:15-33	Sorrow Will Turn To Joy	308	
John 17:1b-24	Jesus Prays For His Own	309	
John 18:1-11,17-27	Jesus Arrested, Denied By Peter	310	
John 18:35b-19:14	Jesus Before Pilate	311	
John 19:23-40	Crucifixion, Death And Burial Of Jesus	312	
John 20:1-22	Resurrection Of Jesus; He Appears To Mary Magdalene And To Disciples	313	
John 20:24-21:12	Jesus Talks To Thomas, And Helps Peter Cook Fish	314	
John 21:15-25	Fellowship Of Jesus And Peter Restored	315	
Acts 1:1-11;2:1-11	Jesus Is Taken To Heaven; The Holy Spirit Comes	316	
Acts 2:14-24,36-41	Peter's Sermon In Jerusalem	317	
Acts 2:44-3:19a	The Works And Preaching Of The New Believers	318	
Acts 4:7-23	Peter And John Testify Before The Sanhedrin	319	
Acts 4:32-5:15	The Believers Share Everything	320	
Acts 5:22-41	Apostles Arrested Again	321	
Acts 6:1-15	Stephen And Other Deacons Chosen	322	
Acts 7:1-18,51	Stephen Preaches to Sanhedrin	323	

		Vol. 1	Vol. 2
Acts 8:4-8,26-40	Ministry Of Philip	324	
Acts 9:3-26	Saul Becomes A Christian	325	
Acts 10:1-23a	Cornelius Sends for Peter	326	
Acts 10:28-48a	Peter Baptizes Cornelius	327	
Acts 11:1-24	Peter Defends His Actions	328	
Acts 12:1-19a	Peter Escapes From Prison	329	
Acts 13:7b-25	Barnabas And Paul Go West And Preach	330	
Acts 13:32-52	Paul Continues Sermon In Antioch	331	
Acts 14:2-22a	Paul And Barnabas Visit Other Towns In Asia Minor	332	
Acts 15:1-20	Jerusalem Council Accepts Gentile Believers	333	
Acts 15:22-35	Letter From Jerusalem Council To Gentile Believers	334	
Acts 15:36-41	Disagreement Between Paul And Barnabas;		
16:1-10	Paul Has Vision To Go To Macedonia	335	
Acts 16:14-33a	Lydia Becomes A Believer In Philippi; Paul And Silas In Prison	336	
Acts 16:35-17:12	Paul And Silas Released From Prison, And Go To Thessalonica And Berea	337	
Acts 17:15-32	Paul Preaches In Athens	338	
Acts 18:1-22	Paul Stays With Priscilla And Aquila In Corinth	339	
Acts 19:1-21	Paul At Ephesus	340	
Acts 19:23-41	Demetrius, The Silversmith, Stirs Up A Riot	341	
Acts 20:17-38	Paul Says Farewell To Ephesian Believers	342	
Acts 21:3-24a	Paul Goes To Jerusalem	343	
Acts 21:27-22:2a	Angry Crowd Incites Paul's Arrest In Jerusalem	344	
Acts 22:2-22	Paul Tells Of His Conversion	345	
Acts 22:30-23:11	Paul Before The Sanhedrin	346	
Acts 23:12-32	Jews Plot To Kill Paul	347	
Acts 24:1-22	Paul Before Governor Felix	348	
Acts 25:4-22	Paul Is Tried Before Festus Who Consults Agrippa	349	
Acts 25:23-26:11	Paul Begins Testimony Before King Agrippa	350	

		Vol. 1	Vol. 2
Acts 26:12-31			
	Paul Ends Testimony Before King Agrippa	351	
Acts 27:3-22	Paul Sails For Rome	352	
Acts 27:29-28:5	Paul Shipwrecked On Malta	353	
Acts 28:13-31	Paul Preaches In Rome	354	
Romans 1:1-20			
	Paul Called To Preach To Jews And Gentiles	355	280
Rom 1:21-2:8	All Men Have A Knowledge Of God		281
Rom 3:9-31	Believers Are Justified By Faith		282
Rom 4:3-22	Abraham Was Justified By Faith		283
Rom 5:1-19			
	As By One Man Came Death, So By Christ Came Life		284
Rom 7:7b-8:3a	The Christian's Struggle With Sin		285
Rom 8:18,22-39	Christians Will Overcome		286
Rom 9:1-21	God Has Mercy On His Chosen people		287
Rom 9:22-33			
	Gentile Believers Are Also Heirs Of God's Promise		288
Rom 10:1-21	Christ Is The End Of The Law		289
Rom 11:1-21	Gentiles Are Blessed Through Israel		290
Rom 11:22-36	Both Gentiles And Israel Are Blessed		
	By A Sovereign God		291
Rom 12:1-21	Paul Calls For Living Sacrifices		292
Rom 13:1-14:1,13	Submit To Authorities; Do Not Judge		293
1 Corinthians 1:10-31			
	Let There Be No Divisions Among Christians		294
1 Cor 3:16-23	Christians Are Temples Of God's Spirit		
5:9-6:9a	Do Not Take A Brother To Court		295
1 Cor 6:12-7:13	On Sex And Marriage		296
1 Cor 7:15-35	On Marriage		297
1 Cor 10:9-33a			
	Lessons From Israel; The Earth Is The Lord's		298
1 Cor 11:17-34	On The Lord's Supper		299
1 Cor 12:1-24	Different Gifts		300
1 Cor 13:1-13	Love, The Perfect Way		301
1 Cor 14:2-22	Speaking In Tongues		302
1 Cor 15:3-27a	Christ Is Risen		303
1 Cor 15:35-58	The Dead Will Be Raised		304
2 Cor 4:1-5:10	A Treasure In Earthen Vessels		305

		Vol. 1	Vol. 2
2 Cor 5:11-6:2	A Ministry Of Reconciliation		
6:14-18	Be Not Yoked With Unbelievers		306
2 Cor 8:1-15;9:6-10	Believers To Be Generous		307
2 Cor 11:1-13,23-28	Warning About False Teachers		308
2 Cor 12:15-13:11			
	Paul's Concern For Corinthian Believers		309
Galatians 1:11-2:2,15-21	Paul's Message From God		310
Gal 3:6-25	Of Faith And The Law		311
Gal 3:26-4:7,21-31	Heirs Of God		312
Gal 5:1-25	Freedom In Christ		313
Ephesians 1:3-23	Blessings In Christ		314
Eph 2:1-22	Christ Is Our Peace		315
Eph 4:4-28a	One Body And One Spirit		316
Eph 5:22-6:9	Of Wives, Husbands And Children,		
	Servants And Masters		317
Eph 6:10-18	Put On The Armour Of God		318
Philippians 2:1-18			
	Consider Others Better Than Yourselves		319
Phil 3:2-4:1	Press On Toward The Goal In Christ Jesus		320
Phil 4:4-20			
	Rejoice In The Lord, And Share With Others		321
Col 1:19-23;2:6-18	All The Fulness Of God		
	Is In Christ; Live In The Freedom Of Christ		322
Col 3:1-24	Set Your Affection On Things Above;		
	Wives Submit, Husbands Love, Children Obey		323
1 Thessalonians 1:2-10;4:1-12	Living To God's Glory		324
1 Thess 4:15-5:24	Work, For The Lord Is Coming		325
2 Thess 1:5b-2:12	Work And Keep The Faith		326
2 Thess 2:13-3:16	Keep The Faith And Work		327
1 Timothy 2:2b-3:13	How To Select Church Leaders		328
1 Tim 5:1-20	Of Widows and Elders		329
1 Tim 6:3-21	Godliness With Contentment		330
2 Tim 1:3-2:6	Be Strong In God's Grace		331

		Vol. 1	Vol. 2
2 Tim 2:15-26;3:10-17	A Workman Approved Of God		332
Titus 2:1-3:7	Conduct Of The Believers		333
Philemon 1:1-25	Paul's Plea For His Friend		334
Hebrews 2:1-18	Jesus Is Like A Brother	356	
Heb 3:1-6;4:14-5:10	Jesus, The Apostle And High Priest	357	
Heb 6:1-20	Go On To Maturity	358	
Heb 7:1-22	Jesus Is Like Melchizedek	359	
Heb 8:1-13	Jesus, The High Priest Of A New Covenant	360	
Heb 9:12-28	Christ, The Mediator Of A New Covenant	361	
Heb 11:1-19a	Heroes Of The Faith	362	
Heb 11:20-40	More Heroes Of The Faith	363	
Heb 12:4-25a	Live At Peace With All Men	364	
Heb 13:1-21	Keep On Loving Each Other	365	
James 1:5-27	Christians Should Act On What They Know		335
James 2:1-24	Deeds Must Be Consistent With Confession Of Faith		336
James 3:1-18	The Tongue Can Be Both Curse And Praise		337
James 4:1-17	No One Knows About Tomorrow		338
James 5:1-20	Warning To The Rich; Pray For One Another		339
1 Peter 1:6-25	Be Holy In All You Do		340
1 Peter 2:6-25	You Are A Chosen People		341
1 Peter 3:1-18	Wives Submit, Husbands Be Considerate; Repay Evil With Blessing		342
1 Peter 4:1-19	Live For God's Glory		343
1 Peter 5:1-12	Elders, Eager To Serve; Young Men, Submissive		344
2 Peter 1:3-21	Make Your Salvation Sure; Prophets Speak God's Word		345
2 Peter 2:3-19	False Teachers Will Be Destroyed		346
2 Peter 3:1-18	Scoffers Will Come In The Last Days		347

		Vol. 1	Vol. 2
1 John 1:1-2:12	The Word Of Life Was From The Beginning; Those In The Light Have Fellowship		348
1 John 2:15-3:7a	Be Not Led Astray		349
1 John 3:11-24;4:7-16	Love One Another		350
1 John 5:1-21	To Love God Is To Obey Him		351
2 John	Walk In Love		352
3 John	Imitate The Good		353
Jude 1:8-25	Godless Men Are Condemned; God Can Keep Us From Falling		354
Revelation 1:1-16	I Heard A Loud Voice Like A Trumpet		355
Rev 1:17-2:11	Messages To Ephesus And Smyrna		356
Rev 2:12-29	Messages To Pergamum And Thyatira		357
Rev 3:1-17	Messages To Sardis, Philadelphia and Laodicea		358
Rev 4:6-5:10	I Will Tell You What Will Happen		359
Rev 7:1-4,9-17	A Great Multitude In White Robes		360
Rev 11:15-19;12:7-12	The Seventh Angel Sounds The Trumpet		361
Rev 19:6-21	Our Lord God Almighty Reigns		362
Rev 20:1-15	The Righteous Will Reign With Christ For A Thousand Years; Satan Is Doomed; The Books Are Opened		363
Rev 21:6-25	Then I Saw A New Heaven And A New Earth		364
Rev 22:3-21	The Spirit And The Bride Say, "Come"		365

AND GOD MADE MAN

Gen 1:24-2:3

And God said, "Let the land produce living creatures according to their kinds: livestock, creatures that move along the ground, and wild animals, each according to its kind." And it was so. {25} God made the wild animals according to their kinds, the livestock according to their kinds, and all the creatures that move along the ground according to their kinds. And God saw that it was good. {26} Then God said, "Let us make man in our image, in our likeness, and let them rule over the fish of the sea and the birds of the air, over the livestock, over all the earth, and over all the creatures that move along the ground." {27} So God created man in his own image, in the image of God he created him; male and female he created them. {28} God blessed them and said to them, "Be fruitful and increase in number; fill the earth and subdue it. Rule over the fish of the sea and the birds of the air and over every living creature that moves on the ground." {29} Then God said, "I give you every seed-bearing plant on the face of the whole earth and every tree that has fruit with seed in it. They will be yours for food. {30} And to all the beasts of the earth and all the birds of the air and all the creatures that move on the ground–everything that has the breath of life in it–I give every green plant for food." And it was so. {31} God saw all that he had made, and it was very good. And there was evening, and there was morning–the sixth day.

{2:1} Thus the heavens and the earth were completed in all their vast array. {2} By the seventh day God had finished the work he had been doing; so on the seventh day he rested from all his work. {3} And God blessed the seventh day and made it holy, because on it he rested from all the work of creating that he had done.

CAIN KILLS ABEL

Gen 4:1-15

Adam lay with his wife Eve, and she became pregnant and gave birth to Cain. She said, "With the help of the LORD I have brought forth a man." {2} Later she gave birth to his brother Abel. Now Abel kept flocks, and Cain worked the soil. {3} In the course of time Cain brought some of the fruits of the soil as an offering to the LORD. {4} But Abel brought fat portions from some of the firstborn of his flock. The LORD looked with favor on Abel and his offering, {5} but on Cain and his offering he did not look with favor. So Cain was very angry, and his face was downcast. {6} Then the LORD said to Cain, "Why are you angry? Why is your face downcast? {7} If you do what is right, will you not be accepted? But if you do not do what is right, sin is crouching at your door; it desires to have you, but you must master it." {8} Now Cain said to his brother Abel, "Let's go out to the field." And while they were in the field, Cain attacked his brother Abel and killed him. {9} Then the LORD said to Cain, "Where is your brother Abel?" "I don't know," he replied. "Am I my brother's keeper?" {10} The LORD said, "What have you done? Listen! Your brother's blood cries out to me from the ground. {11} Now you are under a curse and driven from the ground, which opened its mouth to receive your brother's blood from your hand. {12} When you work the ground, it will no longer yield its crops for you. You will be a restless wanderer on the earth." {13} Cain said to the LORD, "My punishment is more than I can bear. {14} Today you are driving me from the land, and I will be hidden from your presence; I will be a restless wanderer on the earth, and whoever finds me will kill me." {15} But the LORD said to him, "Not so ; if anyone kills Cain, he will suffer vengeance seven times over." Then the LORD put a mark on Cain so that no one who found him would kill him.

Gen 5:3-5

When Adam had lived 130 years, he had a son in his own likeness, in his own image; and he named him Seth. {4} After Seth was born, Adam lived 800 years and had other sons and daughters. {5} Altogether, Adam lived 930 years, and then he died.

NOAH WAS A RIGHTEOUS MAN

Gen 6:9-7:6

This is the account of Noah. Noah was a righteous man, blameless among the people of his time, and he walked with God. {10} Noah had three sons: Shem, Ham and Japheth. {11} Now the earth was corrupt in God's sight and was full of violence. {12} God saw how corrupt the earth had become, for all the people on earth had corrupted their ways. {13} So God said to Noah, "I am going to put an end to all people, for the earth is filled with violence because of them. I am surely going to destroy both them and the earth. {14} So make yourself an ark of cypress wood; make rooms in it and coat it with pitch inside and out. {15} This is how you are to build it: The ark is to be 450 feet long, 75 feet wide and 45 feet high. {16} Make a roof for it and finish the ark to within 18 inches of the top. Put a door in the side of the ark and make lower, middle and upper decks. {17} I am going to bring floodwaters on the earth to destroy all life under the heavens, every creature that has the breath of life in it. Everything on earth will perish. {18} But I will establish my covenant with you, and you will enter the ark–you and your sons and your wife and your sons' wives with you. {19} You are to bring into the ark two of all living creatures, male and female, to keep them alive with you. {20} Two of every kind of bird, of every kind of animal and of every kind of creature that moves along the ground will come to you to be kept alive. {21} You are to take every kind of food that is to be eaten and store it away as food for you and for them." {22} Noah did everything just as God commanded him.

{7:1} The LORD then said to Noah, "Go into the ark, you and your whole family, because I have found you righteous in this generation. {2} Take with you seven of every kind of clean animal, a male and its mate, and two of every kind of unclean animal, a male and its mate, {3} and also seven of every kind of bird, male and female, to keep their various kinds alive throughout the earth. {4} Seven days from now I will send rain on the earth for forty days and forty nights, and I will wipe from the face of the earth every living creature I have made." {5} And Noah did all that the LORD commanded him. {6} Noah was six hundred years old when the floodwaters came on the earth.

THE FLOODS COVERED THE EARTH

Gen 7:7-8:4

And Noah and his sons and his wife and his sons' wives entered the ark to escape the waters of the flood. {8} Pairs of clean and unclean animals, of birds and of all creatures that move along the ground, {9} male and female, came to Noah and entered the ark, as God had commanded Noah. {10} And after the seven days the floodwaters came on the earth. {11} In the six hundredth year of Noah's life, on the seventeenth day of the second month—on that day all the springs of the great deep burst forth, and the floodgates of the heavens were opened. {12} And rain fell on the earth forty days and forty nights. {13} On that very day Noah and his sons, Shem, Ham and Japheth, together with his wife and the wives of his three sons, entered the ark. {14} They had with them every wild animal according to its kind, all livestock according to their kinds, every creature that moves along the ground according to its kind and every bird according to its kind, everything with wings. {15} Pairs of all creatures that have the breath of life in them came to Noah and entered the ark. {16} The animals going in were male and female of every living thing, as God had commanded Noah. Then the LORD shut him in. {17} For forty days the flood kept coming on the earth, and as the waters increased they lifted the ark high above the earth. {18} The waters rose and increased greatly on the earth, and the ark floated on the surface of the water. {19} They rose greatly on the earth, and all the high mountains under the entire heavens were covered. {20} The waters rose and covered the mountains to a depth of more than twenty feet. {21} Every living thing that moved on the earth perished—birds, livestock, wild animals, all the creatures that swarm over the earth, and all mankind. {22} Everything on dry land that had the breath of life in its nostrils died. {23} Every living thing on the face of the earth was wiped out; men and animals and the creatures that move along the ground and the birds of the air were wiped from the earth. Only Noah was left, and those with him in the ark. {24} The waters flooded the earth for a hundred and fifty days. {8:1} But God remembered Noah and all the wild animals and the livestock that were with him in the ark, and he sent a wind over the earth, and the waters receded. {2} Now the springs of the deep and the floodgates of the heavens had been closed, and the rain had stopped falling from the sky. {3} The water receded steadily from the earth. At the end of the hundred and fifty days the water had gone down, {4} and on the seventeenth day of the seventh month the ark came to rest on the mountains of Ararat.

GOD GIVES THE RAINBOW

Gen 8:21-9:17

The LORD smelled the pleasing aroma and said in his heart: "Never again will I curse the ground because of man, even though every inclination of his heart is evil from childhood. And never again will I destroy all living creatures, as I have done. {22} "As long as the earth endures, seedtime and harvest, cold and heat, summer and winter, day and night will never cease." {9:1} Then God blessed Noah and his sons, saying to them, "Be fruitful and increase in number and fill the earth. {2} The fear and dread of you will fall upon all the beasts of the earth and all the birds of the air, upon every creature that moves along the ground, and upon all the fish of the sea; they are given into your hands. {3} Everything that lives and moves will be food for you. Just as I gave you the green plants, I now give you everything. {4} "But you must not eat meat that has its lifeblood still in it. {5} And for your lifeblood I will surely demand an accounting. I will demand an accounting from every animal. And from each man, too, I will demand an accounting for the life of his fellow man. {6} "Whoever sheds the blood of man, by man shall his blood be shed; for in the image of God has God made man. {7} As for you, be fruitful and increase in number; multiply on the earth and increase upon it." {8} Then God said to Noah and to his sons with him: {9} "I now establish my covenant with you and with your descendants after you {10} and with every living creature that was with you–the birds, the livestock and all the wild animals, all those that came out of the ark with you–every living creature on earth. {11} I establish my covenant with you: Never again will all life be cut off by the waters of a flood; never again will there be a flood to destroy the earth."

{12} And God said, "This is the sign of the covenant I am making between me and you and every living creature with you, a covenant for all generations to come: {13} I have set my rainbow in the clouds, and it will be the sign of the covenant between me and the earth. {14} Whenever I bring clouds over the earth and the rainbow appears in the clouds, {15} I will remember my covenant between me and you and all living creatures of every kind. Never again will the waters become a flood to destroy all life. {16} Whenever the rainbow appears in the clouds, I will see it and remember the everlasting covenant between God and all living creatures of every kind on the earth." {17} So God said to Noah, "This is the sign of the covenant I have established between me and all life on the earth."

ABRAM'S DESCENDANTS WILL HAVE A LAND

Gen 15:1-21

After this, the word of the LORD came to Abram in a vision: "Do not be afraid, Abram. I am your shield, your very great reward. " {2} But Abram said, "O Sovereign LORD, what can you give me since I remain childless and the one who will inherit my estate is Eliezer of Damascus?" {3} And Abram said, "You have given me no children; so a servant in my household will be my heir." {4} Then the word of the LORD came to him: "This man will not be your heir, but a son coming from your own body will be your heir." {5} He took him outside and said, "Look up at the heavens and count the stars–if indeed you can count them." Then he said to him, "So shall your offspring be." {6} Abram believed the LORD, and he credited it to him as righteousness. {7} He also said to him, "I am the LORD, who brought you out of Ur of the Chaldeans to give you this land to take possession of it." {8} But Abram said, "O Sovereign LORD, how can I know that I will gain possession of it?" {9} So the LORD said to him, "Bring me a heifer, a goat and a ram, each three years old, along with a dove and a young pigeon." {10} Abram brought all these to him, cut them in two and arranged the halves opposite each other; the birds, however, he did not cut in half. {11} Then birds of prey came down on the carcasses, but Abram drove them away. {12} As the sun was setting, Abram fell into a deep sleep, and a thick and dreadful darkness came over him. {13} Then the LORD said to him, "Know for certain that your descendants will be strangers in a country not their own, and they will be enslaved and mistreated four hundred years. {14} But I will punish the nation they serve as slaves, and afterward they will come out with great possessions. {15} You, however, will go to your fathers in peace and be buried at a good old age. {16} In the fourth generation your descendants will come back here, for the sin of the Amorites has not yet reached its full measure." {17} When the sun had set and darkness had fallen, a smoking firepot with a blazing torch appeared and passed between the pieces.

{18} On that day the LORD made a covenant with Abram and said, "To your descendants I give this land, from the river of Egypt to the great river, the Euphrates– {19} the land of the Kenites, Kenizzites, Kadmonites, {20} Hittites, Perizzites, Rephaites, {21} Amorites, Canaanites, Girgashites and Jebusites."

NO LONGER ABRAM, YOUR NAME WILL BE ABRAHAM

Gen 17:1-20a

When Abram was ninety-nine years old, the LORD appeared to him and said, "I am God Almighty; walk before me and be blameless. {2} I will confirm my covenant between me and you and will greatly increase your numbers." {3} Abram fell facedown, and God said to him, {4} "As for me, this is my covenant with you: You will be the father of many nations. {5} No longer will you be called Abram ; your name will be Abraham, for I have made you a father of many nations. {6} I will make you very fruitful; I will make nations of you, and kings will come from you. {7} I will establish my covenant as an everlasting covenant between me and you and your descendants after you for the generations to come, to be your God and the God of your descendants after you. {8} The whole land of Canaan, where you are now an alien, I will give as an everlasting possession to you and your descendants after you; and I will be their God." {9} Then God said to Abraham, "As for you, you must keep my covenant, you and your descendants after you for the generations to come. {10} This is my covenant with you and your descendants after you, the covenant you are to keep: Every male among you shall be circumcised. {11} You are to undergo circumcision, and it will be the sign of the covenant between me and you. {12} For the generations to come every male among you who is eight days old must be circumcised, including those born in your household or bought with money from a foreigner–those who are not your offspring. {13} Whether born in your household or bought with your money, they must be circumcised. My covenant in your flesh is to be an everlasting covenant. {14} Any uncircumcised male, who has not been circumcised in the flesh, will be cut off from his people; he has broken my covenant." {15} God also said to Abraham, "As for Sarai your wife, you are no longer to call her Sarai; her name will be Sarah. {16} I will bless her and will surely give you a son by her. I will bless her so that she will be the mother of nations; kings of peoples will come from her." {17} Abraham fell facedown; he laughed and said to himself, "Will a son be born to a man a hundred years old? Will Sarah bear a child at the age of ninety?" {18} And Abraham said to God, "If only Ishmael might live under your blessing!" {19} Then God said, "Yes, but your wife Sarah will bear you a son, and you will call him Isaac. I will establish my covenant with him as an everlasting covenant for his descendants after him. {20} And as for Ishmael, I have heard you: I will surely bless him; I will make him fruitful and will greatly increase his numbers.

SARAH IS PROMISED A SON

Gen 18:1-19

The LORD appeared to Abraham near the great trees of Mamre while he was sitting at the entrance to his tent in the heat of the day. {2} Abraham looked up and saw three men standing nearby. When he saw them, he hurried from the entrance of his tent to meet them and bowed low to the ground. {3} He said, "If I have found favor in your eyes, my lord, do not pass your servant by. {4} Let a little water be brought, and then you may all wash your feet and rest under this tree. {5} Let me get you something to eat, so you can be refreshed and then go on your way—now that you have come to your servant." "Very well," they answered, "do as you say." {6} So Abraham hurried into the tent to Sarah. "Quick," he said, "get three seahs of fine flour and knead it and bake some bread." {7} Then he ran to the herd and selected a choice, tender calf and gave it to a servant, who hurried to prepare it. {8} He then brought some curds and milk and the calf that had been prepared, and set these before them. While they ate, he stood near them under a tree.

{9} "Where is your wife Sarah?" they asked him. "There, in the tent," he said. {10} Then the LORD said, "I will surely return to you about this time next year, and Sarah your wife will have a son." Now Sarah was listening at the entrance to the tent, which was behind him. {11} Abraham and Sarah were already old and well advanced in years, and Sarah was past the age of childbearing. {12} So Sarah laughed to herself as she thought, "After I am worn out and my master is old, will I now have this pleasure?" {13} Then the LORD said to Abraham, "Why did Sarah laugh and say, 'Will I really have a child, now that I am old?' {14} Is anything too hard for the LORD? I will return to you at the appointed time next year and Sarah will have a son." {15} Sarah was afraid, so she lied and said, "I did not laugh." But he said, "Yes, you did laugh." {16} When the men got up to leave, they looked down toward Sodom, and Abraham walked along with them to see them on their way. {17} Then the LORD said, "Shall I hide from Abraham what I am about to do? {18} Abraham will surely become a great and powerful nation, and all nations on earth will be blessed through him. {19} For I have chosen him, so that he will direct his children and his household after him to keep the way of the LORD by doing what is right and just, so that the LORD will bring about for Abraham what he has promised him."

ISAAC IS BORN, ISHMAEL SENT AWAY

Gen 21:1-21

Now the LORD was gracious to Sarah as he had said, and the LORD did for Sarah what he had promised. {2} Sarah became pregnant and bore a son to Abraham in his old age, at the very time God had promised him. {3} Abraham gave the name Isaac to the son Sarah bore him. {4} When his son Isaac was eight days old, Abraham circumcised him, as God commanded him. {5} Abraham was a hundred years old when his son Isaac was born to him. {6} Sarah said, "God has brought me laughter, and everyone who hears about this will laugh with me." {7} And she added, "Who would have said to Abraham that Sarah would nurse children? Yet I have borne him a son in his old age." {8} The child grew and was weaned, and on the day Isaac was weaned Abraham held a great feast.

{9} But Sarah saw that the son whom Hagar the Egyptian had borne to Abraham was mocking, {10} and she said to Abraham, "Get rid of that slave woman and her son, for that slave woman's son will never share in the inheritance with my son Isaac." {11} The matter distressed Abraham greatly because it concerned his son. {12} But God said to him, "Do not be so distressed about the boy and your maidservant. Listen to whatever Sarah tells you, because it is through Isaac that your offspring will be reckoned.

{13} I will make the son of the maidservant into a nation also, because he is your offspring." {14} Early the next morning Abraham took some food and a skin of water and gave them to Hagar. He set them on her shoulders and then sent her off with the boy. She went on her way and wandered in the desert of Beersheba. {15} When the water in the skin was gone, she put the boy under one of the bushes. {16} Then she went off and sat down nearby, about a bowshot away, for she thought, "I cannot watch the boy die." And as she sat there nearby, she began to sob. {17} God heard the boy crying, and the angel of God called to Hagar from heaven and said to her, "What is the matter, Hagar? Do not be afraid; God has heard the boy crying as he lies there. {18} Lift the boy up and take him by the hand, for I will make him into a great nation." {19} Then God opened her eyes and she saw a well of water. So she went and filled the skin with water and gave the boy a drink. {20} God was with the boy as he grew up. He lived in the desert and became an archer. {21} While he was living in the Desert of Paran, his mother got a wife for him from Egypt.

ABRAHAM DIES AND IS BURIED BY ISAAC AND ISHMAEL

Gen 25:1-18a

Abraham took another wife, whose name was Keturah. {2} She bore him Zimran, Jokshan, Medan, Midian, Ishbak and Shuah. {3} Jokshan was the father of Sheba and Dedan; the descendants of Dedan were the Asshurites, the Letushites and the Leummites. {4} The sons of Midian were Ephah, Epher, Hanoch, Abida and Eldaah. All these were descendants of Keturah. {5} Abraham left everything he owned to Isaac. {6} But while he was still living, he gave gifts to the sons of his concubines and sent them away from his son Isaac to the land of the east.

{7} Altogether, Abraham lived a hundred and seventy-five years. {8} Then Abraham breathed his last and died at a good old age, an old man and full of years; and he was gathered to his people. {9} His sons Isaac and Ishmael buried him in the cave of Machpelah near Mamre, in the field of Ephron son of Zohar the Hittite, {10} the field Abraham had bought from the Hittites. There Abraham was buried with his wife Sarah.

{11} After Abraham's death, God blessed his son Isaac, who then lived near Beer Lahai Roi.

{12} This is the account of Abraham's son Ishmael, whom Sarah's maidservant, Hagar the Egyptian, bore to Abraham. {13} These are the names of the sons of Ishmael, listed in the order of their birth: Nebaioth the firstborn of Ishmael, Kedar, Adbeel, Mibsam, {14} Mishma, Dumah, Massa, {15} Hadad, Tema, Jetur, Naphish and Kedemah. {16} These were the sons of Ishmael, and these are the names of the twelve tribal rulers according to their settlements and camps. {17} Altogether, Ishmael lived a hundred and thirty-seven years. He breathed his last and died, and he was gathered to his people. {18} His descendants settled in the area from Havilah to Shur, near the border of Egypt, as you go toward Asshur.

JACOB AND ESAU

Gen 25:19-34

This is the account of Abraham's son Isaac. Abraham became the father of Isaac, {20} and Isaac was forty years old when he married Rebekah daughter of Bethuel the Aramean from Paddan Aram and sister of Laban the Aramean. {21} Isaac prayed to the LORD on behalf of his wife, because she was barren. The LORD answered his prayer, and his wife Rebekah became pregnant. {22} The babies jostled each other within her, and she said, "Why is this happening to me?" So she went to inquire of the LORD. {23} The LORD said to her, "Two nations are in your womb, and two peoples from within you will be separated; one people will be stronger than the other, and the older will serve the younger." {24} When the time came for her to give birth, there were twin boys in her womb. {25} The first to come out was red, and his whole body was like a hairy garment; so they named him Esau. {26} After this, his brother came out, with his hand grasping Esau's heel; so he was named Jacob. Isaac was sixty years old when Rebekah gave birth to them.

{27} The boys grew up, and Esau became a skillful hunter, a man of the open country, while Jacob was a quiet man, staying among the tents. {28} Isaac, who had a taste for wild game, loved Esau, but Rebekah loved Jacob.

{29} Once when Jacob was cooking some stew, Esau came in from the open country, famished. {30} He said to Jacob, "Quick, let me have some of that red stew! I'm famished!" (That is why he was also called Edom.) {31} Jacob replied, "First sell me your birthright." {32} "Look, I am about to die," Esau said. "What good is the birthright to me?" {33} But Jacob said, "Swear to me first." So he swore an oath to him, selling his birthright to Jacob. {34} Then Jacob gave Esau some bread and some lentil stew. He ate and drank, and then got up and left. So Esau despised his birthright.

Gen 26:34-35

When Esau was forty years old, he married Judith daughter of Beeri the Hittite, and also Basemath daughter of Elon the Hittite. {35} They were a source of grief to Isaac and Rebekah.

ISAAC BLESSES JACOB

Gen 27:25-40

Then he said, "My son, bring me some of your game to eat, so that I may give you my blessing." Jacob brought it to him and he ate; and he brought some wine and he drank. {26} Then his father Isaac said to him, "Come here, my son, and kiss me." {27} So he went to him and kissed him. When Isaac caught the smell of his clothes, he blessed him and said, "Ah, the smell of my son is like the smell of a field that the LORD has blessed. {28} May God give you of heaven's dew and of earth's richness– an abundance of grain and new wine. {29} May nations serve you and peoples bow down to you. Be lord over your brothers, and may the sons of your mother bow down to you. May those who curse you be cursed and those who bless you be blessed."

{30} After Isaac finished blessing him and Jacob had scarcely left his father's presence, his brother Esau came in from hunting. {31} He too prepared some tasty food and brought it to his father. Then he said to him, "My father, sit up and eat some of my game, so that you may give me your blessing." {32} His father Isaac asked him, "Who are you?" "I am your son," he answered, "your firstborn, Esau." {33} Isaac trembled violently and said, "Who was it, then, that hunted game and brought it to me? I ate it just before you came and I blessed him–and indeed he will be blessed!" {34} When Esau heard his father's words, he burst out with a loud and bitter cry and said to his father, "Bless me–me too, my father!" {35} But he said, "Your brother came deceitfully and took your blessing." {36} Esau said, "Isn't he rightly named Jacob ? He has deceived me these two times: He took my birthright, and now he's taken my blessing!" Then he asked, "Haven't you reserved any blessing for me?" {37} Isaac answered Esau, "I have made him lord over you and have made all his relatives his servants, and I have sustained him with grain and new wine. So what can I possibly do for you, my son?" {38} Esau said to his father, "Do you have only one blessing, my father? Bless me too, my father!" Then Esau wept aloud. {39} His father Isaac answered him, "Your dwelling will be away from the earth's richness, away from the dew of heaven above. {40} You will live by the sword and you will serve your brother. But when you grow restless, you will throw his yoke from off your neck."

JACOB LEAVES FOR CANAAN

Gen 31:17-36

Then Jacob put his children and his wives on camels, {18} and he drove all his livestock ahead of him, along with all the goods he had accumulated in Paddan Aram, to go to his father Isaac in the land of Canaan. {19} When Laban had gone to shear his sheep, Rachel stole her father's household gods. {20} Moreover, Jacob deceived Laban the Aramean by not telling him he was running away. {21} So he fled with all he had, and crossing the River, he headed for the hill country of Gilead. {22} On the third day Laban was told that Jacob had fled. {23} Taking his relatives with him, he pursued Jacob for seven days and caught up with him in the hill country of Gilead. {24} Then God came to Laban the Aramean in a dream at night and said to him, "Be careful not to say anything to Jacob, either good or bad."

{25} Jacob had pitched his tent in the hill country of Gilead when Laban overtook him, and Laban and his relatives camped there too. {26} Then Laban said to Jacob, "What have you done? You've deceived me, and you've carried off my daughters like captives in war. {27} Why did you run off secretly and deceive me? Why didn't you tell me, so I could send you away with joy and singing to the music of tambourines and harps? {28} You didn't even let me kiss my grandchildren and my daughters good-by. You have done a foolish thing. {29} I have the power to harm you; but last night the God of your father said to me, 'Be careful not to say anything to Jacob, either good or bad.' {30} Now you have gone off because you longed to return to your father's house. But why did you steal my gods?" {31} Jacob answered Laban, "I was afraid, because I thought you would take your daughters away from me by force. {32} But if you find anyone who has your gods, he shall not live. In the presence of our relatives, see for yourself whether there is anything of yours here with me; and if so, take it." Now Jacob did not know that Rachel had stolen the gods. {33} So Laban went into Jacob's tent and into Leah's tent and into the tent of the two maidservants, but he found nothing. After he came out of Leah's tent, he entered Rachel's tent. {34} Now Rachel had taken the household gods and put them inside her camel's saddle and was sitting on them. Laban searched through everything in the tent but found nothing. {35} Rachel said to her father, "Don't be angry, my lord, that I cannot stand up in your presence; I'm having my period." So he searched but could not find the household gods. {36} Jacob was angry and took Laban to task. "What is my crime?" he asked Laban. "What sin have I committed that you hunt me down?

JACOB AND ESAU MEET IN PEACE

Gen 33:1-18

Jacob looked up and there was Esau, coming with his four hundred men; so he divided the children among Leah, Rachel and the two maidservants. {2} He put the maidservants and their children in front, Leah and her children next, and Rachel and Joseph in the rear. {3} He himself went on ahead and bowed down to the ground seven times as he approached his brother. {4} But Esau ran to meet Jacob and embraced him; he threw his arms around his neck and kissed him. And they wept. {5} Then Esau looked up and saw the women and children. "Who are these with you?" he asked. Jacob answered, "They are the children God has graciously given your servant." {6} Then the maidservants and their children approached and bowed down. {7} Next, Leah and her children came and bowed down. Last of all came Joseph and Rachel, and they too bowed down. {8} Esau asked, "What do you mean by all these droves I met?" "To find favor in your eyes, my lord," he said.

{9} But Esau said, "I already have plenty, my brother. Keep what you have for yourself." {10} "No, please!" said Jacob. "If I have found favor in your eyes, accept this gift from me. For to see your face is like seeing the face of God, now that you have received me favorably. {11} Please accept the present that was brought to you, for God has been gracious to me and I have all I need." And because Jacob insisted, Esau accepted it. {12} Then Esau said, "Let us be on our way; I'll accompany you." {13} But Jacob said to him, "My lord knows that the children are tender and that I must care for the ewes and cows that are nursing their young. If they are driven hard just one day, all the animals will die. {14} So let my lord go on ahead of his servant, while I move along slowly at the pace of the droves before me and that of the children, until I come to my lord in Seir." {15} Esau said, "Then let me leave some of my men with you." "But why do that?" Jacob asked. "Just let me find favor in the eyes of my lord." {16} So that day Esau started on his way back to Seir.

{17} Jacob, however, went to Succoth, where he built a place for himself and made shelters for his livestock. That is why the place is called Succoth. {18} After Jacob came from Paddan Aram, he arrived safely at the city of Shechem in Canaan and camped within sight of the city.

RACHEL DIES

Gen 35:9-20

After Jacob returned from Paddan Aram, God appeared to him again and blessed him. {10} God said to him, "Your name is Jacob, but you will no longer be called Jacob; your name will be Israel." So he named him Israel. {11} And God said to him, "I am God Almighty; be fruitful and increase in number. A nation and a community of nations will come from you, and kings will come from your body. {12} The land I gave to Abraham and Isaac I also give to you, and I will give this land to your descendants after you." {13} Then God went up from him at the place where he had talked with him. {14} Jacob set up a stone pillar at the place where God had talked with him, and he poured out a drink offering on it; he also poured oil on it. {15} Jacob called the place where God had talked with him Bethel. {16} Then they moved on from Bethel.

While they were still some distance from Ephrath, Rachel began to give birth and had great difficulty. {17} And as she was having great difficulty in childbirth, the midwife said to her, "Don't be afraid, for you have another son." {18} As she breathed her last—for she was dying—she named her son Ben-Oni. But his father named him Benjamin. {19} So Rachel died and was buried on the way to Ephrath (that is, Bethlehem). {20} Over her tomb Jacob set up a pillar, and to this day that pillar marks Rachel's tomb.

ISAAC DIES AND IS BURIED BY ESAU AND JACOB

Gen 35:22c-29

Jacob had twelve sons: {23} The sons of Leah: Reuben the firstborn of Jacob, Simeon, Levi, Judah, Issachar and Zebulun. {24} The sons of Rachel: Joseph and Benjamin. {25} The sons of Rachel's maidservant Bilhah: Dan and Naphtali. {26} The sons of Leah's maidservant Zilpah: Gad and Asher. These were the sons of Jacob, who were born to him in Paddan Aram. {27} Jacob came home to his father Isaac in Mamre, near Kiriath Arba (that is, Hebron), where Abraham and Isaac had stayed. {28} Isaac lived a hundred and eighty years. {29} Then he breathed his last and died and was gathered to his people, old and full of years. And his sons Esau and Jacob buried him.

YOUNG JOSEPH HAS DREAMS

Gen 37:2b-18

Joseph, a young man of seventeen, was tending the flocks with his brothers, the sons of Bilhah and the sons of Zilpah, his father's wives, and he brought their father a bad report about them. {3} Now Israel loved Joseph more than any of his other sons, because he had been born to him in his old age; and he made a richly ornamented robe for him. {4} When his brothers saw that their father loved him more than any of them, they hated him and could not speak a kind word to him.

{5} Joseph had a dream, and when he told it to his brothers, they hated him all the more. {6} He said to them, "Listen to this dream I had: {7} We were binding sheaves of grain out in the field when suddenly my sheaf rose and stood upright, while your sheaves gathered around mine and bowed down to it." {8} His brothers said to him, "Do you intend to reign over us? Will you actually rule us?" And they hated him all the more because of his dream and what he had said.

{9} Then he had another dream, and he told it to his brothers. "Listen," he said, "I had another dream, and this time the sun and moon and eleven stars were bowing down to me." {10} When he told his father as well as his brothers, his father rebuked him and said, "What is this dream you had? Will your mother and I and your brothers actually come and bow down to the ground before you?" {11} His brothers were jealous of him, but his father kept the matter in mind. {12} Now his brothers had gone to graze their father's flocks near Shechem,

{13} and Israel said to Joseph, "As you know, your brothers are grazing the flocks near Shechem. Come, I am going to send you to them." "Very well," he replied. {14} So he said to him, "Go and see if all is well with your brothers and with the flocks, and bring word back to me." Then he sent him off from the Valley of Hebron. When Joseph arrived at Shechem, {15} a man found him wandering around in the fields and asked him, "What are you looking for?" {16} He replied, "I'm looking for my brothers. Can you tell me where they are grazing their flocks?" {17} "They have moved on from here," the man answered. "I heard them say, 'Let's go to Dothan.'" So Joseph went after his brothers and found them near Dothan. {18} But they saw him in the distance, and before he reached them, they plotted to kill him.

JOSEPH IS SOLD TO TRADERS

Gen 37:19-36

"Here comes that dreamer!" they said to each other. {20} "Come now, let's kill him and throw him into one of these cisterns and say that a ferocious animal devoured him. Then we'll see what comes of his dreams." {21} When Reuben heard this, he tried to rescue him from their hands. "Let's not take his life," he said. {22} "Don't shed any blood. Throw him into this cistern here in the desert, but don't lay a hand on him." Reuben said this to rescue him from them and take him back to his father.

{23} So when Joseph came to his brothers, they stripped him of his robe—the richly ornamented robe he was wearing– {24} and they took him and threw him into the cistern. Now the cistern was empty; there was no water in it. {25} As they sat down to eat their meal, they looked up and saw a caravan of Ishmaelites coming from Gilead. Their camels were loaded with spices, balm and myrrh, and they were on their way to take them down to Egypt. {26} Judah said to his brothers, "What will we gain if we kill our brother and cover up his blood? {27} Come, let's sell him to the Ishmaelites and not lay our hands on him; after all, he is our brother, our own flesh and blood." His brothers agreed.

{28} So when the Midianite merchants came by, his brothers pulled Joseph up out of the cistern and sold him for twenty shekels of silver to the Ishmaelites, who took him to Egypt. {29} When Reuben returned to the cistern and saw that Joseph was not there, he tore his clothes. {30} He went back to his brothers and said, "The boy isn't there! Where can I turn now?" {31} Then they got Joseph's robe, slaughtered a goat and dipped the robe in the blood. {32} They took the ornamented robe back to their father and said, "We found this. Examine it to see whether it is your son's robe." {33} He recognized it and said, "It is my son's robe! Some ferocious animal has devoured him. Joseph has surely been torn to pieces." {34} Then Jacob tore his clothes, put on sackcloth and mourned for his son many days. {35} All his sons and daughters came to comfort him, but he refused to be comforted. "No," he said, "in mourning will I go down to the grave to my son." So his father wept for him. {36} Meanwhile, the Midianites sold Joseph in Egypt to Potiphar, one of Pharaoh's officials, the captain of the guard.

JOSEPH BECOMES PRIME MINISTER

Gen 41:26-46

The seven good cows are seven years, and the seven good heads of grain are seven years; it is one and the same dream. {27} The seven lean, ugly cows that came up afterward are seven years, and so are the seven worthless heads of grain scorched by the east wind: They are seven years of famine. {28} "It is just as I said to Pharaoh: God has shown Pharaoh what he is about to do. {29} Seven years of great abundance are coming throughout the land of Egypt, {30} but seven years of famine will follow them. Then all the abundance in Egypt will be forgotten, and the famine will ravage the land. {31} The abundance in the land will not be remembered, because the famine that follows it will be so severe. {32} The reason the dream was given to Pharaoh in two forms is that the matter has been firmly decided by God, and God will do it soon. {33} "And now let Pharaoh look for a discerning and wise man and put him in charge of the land of Egypt. {34} Let Pharaoh appoint commissioners over the land to take a fifth of the harvest of Egypt during the seven years of abundance. {35} They should collect all the food of these good years that are coming and store up the grain under the authority of Pharaoh, to be kept in the cities for food. {36} This food should be held in reserve for the country, to be used during the seven years of famine that will come upon Egypt, so that the country may not be ruined by the famine." {37} The plan seemed good to Pharaoh and to all his officials. {38} So Pharaoh asked them, "Can we find anyone like this man, one in whom is the spirit of God?" {39} Then Pharaoh said to Joseph, "Since God has made all this known to you, there is no one so discerning and wise as you. {40} You shall be in charge of my palace, and all my people are to submit to your orders. Only with respect to the throne will I be greater than you." {41} So Pharaoh said to Joseph, "I hereby put you in charge of the whole land of Egypt." {42} Then Pharaoh took his signet ring from his finger and put it on Joseph's finger. He dressed him in robes of fine linen and put a gold chain around his neck. {43} He had him ride in a chariot as his second-in-command, and men shouted before him, "Make way !" Thus he put him in charge of the whole land of Egypt. {44} Then Pharaoh said to Joseph, "I am Pharaoh, but without your word no one will lift hand or foot in all Egypt." {45} Pharaoh gave Joseph the name Zaphenath-Paneah and gave him Asenath daughter of Potiphera, priest of On, to be his wife. And Joseph went throughout the land of Egypt. {46} Joseph was thirty years old when he entered the service of Pharaoh king of Egypt. And Joseph went out from Pharaoh's presence and traveled throughout Egypt.

JACOB AND HIS DESCENDANTS MOVE TO EGYPT

Gen 46:1-6

So Israel set out with all that was his, and when he reached Beersheba, he offered sacrifices to the God of his father Isaac. {2} And God spoke to Israel in a vision at night and said, "Jacob! Jacob!" "Here I am," he replied. {3} "I am God, the God of your father," he said. "Do not be afraid to go down to Egypt, for I will make you into a great nation there. {4} I will go down to Egypt with you, and I will surely bring you back again. And Joseph's own hand will close your eyes." {5} Then Jacob left Beersheba, and Israel's sons took their father Jacob and their children and their wives in the carts that Pharaoh had sent to transport him. {6} They also took with them their livestock and the possessions they had acquired in Canaan, and Jacob and all his offspring went to Egypt.

Gen 46:26-47:3

All those who went to Egypt with Jacob–those who were his direct descendants, not counting his sons' wives–numbered sixty-six persons. {27} With the two sons who had been born to Joseph in Egypt, the members of Jacob's family, which went to Egypt, were seventy in all. {28} Now Jacob sent Judah ahead of him to Joseph to get directions to Goshen. When they arrived in the region of Goshen, {29} Joseph had his chariot made ready and went to Goshen to meet his father Israel. As soon as Joseph appeared before him, he threw his arms around his father and wept for a long time. {30} Israel said to Joseph, "Now I am ready to die, since I have seen for myself that you are still alive." {31} Then Joseph said to his brothers and to his father's household, "I will go up and speak to Pharaoh and will say to him, 'My brothers and my father's household, who were living in the land of Canaan, have come to me. {32} The men are shepherds; they tend livestock, and they have brought along their flocks and herds and everything they own.' {33} When Pharaoh calls you in and asks, 'What is your occupation?' {34} you should answer, 'Your servants have tended livestock from our boyhood on, just as our fathers did.' Then you will be allowed to settle in the region of Goshen, for all shepherds are detestable to the Egyptians." {47:1} Joseph went and told Pharaoh, "My father and brothers, with their flocks and herds and everything they own, have come from the land of Canaan and are now in Goshen." {2} He chose five of his brothers and presented them before Pharaoh. {3} Pharaoh asked the brothers, "What is your occupation?" "Your servants are shepherds," they replied to Pharaoh, "just as our fathers were."

JACOB DIES

Gen 47:28-48:9

Jacob lived in Egypt seventeen years, and the years of his life were a hundred and forty-seven. {29} When the time drew near for Israel to die, he called for his son Joseph and said to him, "If I have found favor in your eyes, put your hand under my thigh and promise that you will show me kindness and faithfulness. Do not bury me in Egypt, {30} but when I rest with my fathers, carry me out of Egypt and bury me where they are buried." "I will do as you say," he said. {31} "Swear to me," he said. Then Joseph swore to him, and Israel worshiped as he leaned on the top of his staff.

{48:1} Some time later Joseph was told, "Your father is ill." So he took his two sons Manasseh and Ephraim along with him. {2} When Jacob was told, "Your son Joseph has come to you," Israel rallied his strength and sat up on the bed. {3} Jacob said to Joseph, "God Almighty appeared to me at Luz in the land of Canaan, and there he blessed me {4} and said to me, 'I am going to make you fruitful and will increase your numbers. I will make you a community of peoples, and I will give this land as an everlasting possession to your descendants after you.' {5} "Now then, your two sons born to you in Egypt before I came to you here will be reckoned as mine; Ephraim and Manasseh will be mine, just as Reuben and Simeon are mine. {6} Any children born to you after them will be yours; in the territory they inherit they will be reckoned under the names of their brothers. {7} As I was returning from Paddan, to my sorrow Rachel died in the land of Canaan while we were still on the way, a little distance from Ephrath. So I buried her there beside the road to Ephrath" (that is, Bethlehem). {8} When Israel saw the sons of Joseph, he asked, "Who are these?" {9} "They are the sons God has given me here," Joseph said to his father. Then Israel said, "Bring them to me so I may bless them."

Gen 46:29-33

Then he gave them these instructions: "I am about to be gathered to my people. Bury me with my fathers in the cave in the field of Ephron the Hittite, {30} the cave in the field of Machpelah, near Mamre in Canaan, which Abraham bought as a burial place from Ephron the Hittite, along with the field. {31} There Abraham and his wife Sarah were buried, there Isaac and his wife Rebekah were buried, and there I buried Leah. {32} The field and the cave in it were bought from the Hittites." {33} When Jacob had finished giving instructions to his sons, he drew his feet up into the bed, breathed his last and was gathered to his people.

JOSEPH AND HIS BROTHERS BURY JACOB

Gen 50:2-20

Then Joseph directed the physicians in his service to embalm his father Israel. So the physicians embalmed him, {3} taking a full forty days, for that was the time required for embalming. And the Egyptians mourned for him seventy days. {4} When the days of mourning had passed, Joseph said to Pharaoh's court, "If I have found favor in your eyes, speak to Pharaoh for me. Tell him, {5} 'My father made me swear an oath and said, "I am about to die; bury me in the tomb I dug for myself in the land of Canaan." Now let me go up and bury my father; then I will return.'" {6} Pharaoh said, "Go up and bury your father, as he made you swear to do." {7} So Joseph went up to bury his father. All Pharaoh's officials accompanied him—the dignitaries of his court and all the dignitaries of Egypt– {8} besides all the members of Joseph's household and his brothers and those belonging to his father's household. Only their children and their flocks and herds were left in Goshen. {9} Chariots and horsemen also went up with him. It was a very large company. {10} When they reached the threshing floor of Atad, near the Jordan, they lamented loudly and bitterly; and there Joseph observed a seven-day period of mourning for his father. {11} When the Canaanites who lived there saw the mourning at the threshing floor of Atad, they said, "The Egyptians are holding a solemn ceremony of mourning." That is why that place near the Jordan is called Abel Mizraim. {12} So Jacob's sons did as he had commanded them: {13} They carried him to the land of Canaan and buried him in the cave in the field of Machpelah, near Mamre, which Abraham had bought as a burial place from Ephron the Hittite, along with the field. {14} After burying his father, Joseph returned to Egypt, together with his brothers and all the others who had gone with him to bury his father. {15} When Joseph's brothers saw that their father was dead, they said, "What if Joseph holds a grudge against us and pays us back for all the wrongs we did to him?" {16} So they sent word to Joseph, saying, "Your father left these instructions before he died: {17} 'This is what you are to say to Joseph: I ask you to forgive your brothers the sins and the wrongs they committed in treating you so badly.' Now please forgive the sins of the servants of the God of your father." When their message came to him, Joseph wept. {18} His brothers then came and threw themselves down before him. "We are your slaves," they said. {19} But Joseph said to them, "Don't be afraid. Am I in the place of God? {20} You intended to harm me, but God intended it for good to accomplish what is now being done, the saving of many lives.

A NEW KING OPPRESSES THE ISRAELITES

Exo 1:6-22

Now Joseph and all his brothers and all that generation died, {7} but the Israelites were fruitful and multiplied greatly and became exceedingly numerous, so that the land was filled with them. {8} Then a new king, who did not know about Joseph, came to power in Egypt. {9} "Look," he said to his people, "the Israelites have become much too numerous for us. {10} Come, we must deal shrewdly with them or they will become even more numerous and, if war breaks out, will join our enemies, fight against us and leave the country." {11} So they put slave masters over them to oppress them with forced labor, and they built Pithom and Rameses as store cities for Pharaoh. {12} But the more they were oppressed, the more they multiplied and spread; so the Egyptians came to dread the Israelites {13} and worked them ruthlessly. {14} They made their lives bitter with hard labor in brick and mortar and with all kinds of work in the fields; in all their hard labor the Egyptians used them ruthlessly.

{15} The king of Egypt said to the Hebrew midwives, whose names were Shiphrah and Puah, {16} "When you help the Hebrew women in childbirth and observe them on the delivery stool, if it is a boy, kill him; but if it is a girl, let her live." {17} The midwives, however, feared God and did not do what the king of Egypt had told them to do; they let the boys live. {18} Then the king of Egypt summoned the midwives and asked them, "Why have you done this? Why have you let the boys live?" {19} The midwives answered Pharaoh, "Hebrew women are not like Egyptian women; they are vigorous and give birth before the midwives arrive." {20} So God was kind to the midwives and the people increased and became even more numerous. {21} And because the midwives feared God, he gave them families of their own. {22} Then Pharaoh gave this order to all his people: "Every boy that is born you must throw into the Nile, but let every girl live."

MOSES IS CALLED TO LEAD ISRAEL OUT OF EGYPT

Exo 3:1-17a

Now Moses was tending the flock of Jethro his father-in-law, the priest of Midian, and he led the flock to the far side of the desert and came to Horeb, the mountain of God. {2} There the angel of the LORD appeared to him in flames of fire from within a bush. Moses saw that though the bush was on fire it did not burn up. {3} So Moses thought, "I will go over and see this strange sight—why the bush does not burn up." {4} When the LORD saw that he had gone over to look, God called to him from within the bush, "Moses! Moses!" And Moses said, "Here I am." {5} "Do not come any closer," God said. "Take off your sandals, for the place where you are standing is holy ground." {6} Then he said, "I am the God of your father, the God of Abraham, the God of Isaac and the God of Jacob." At this, Moses hid his face, because he was afraid to look at God. {7} The LORD said, "I have indeed seen the misery of my people in Egypt. I have heard them crying out because of their slave drivers, and I am concerned about their suffering. {8} So I have come down to rescue them from the hand of the Egyptians and to bring them up out of that land into a good and spacious land, a land flowing with milk and honey— the home of the Canaanites, Hittites, Amorites, Perizzites, Hivites and Jebusites. {9} And now the cry of the Israelites has reached me, and I have seen the way the Egyptians are oppressing them.

{10} So now, go. I am sending you to Pharaoh to bring my people the Israelites out of Egypt." {11} But Moses said to God, "Who am I, that I should go to Pharaoh and bring the Israelites out of Egypt?" {12} And God said, "I will be with you. And this will be the sign to you that it is I who have sent you: When you have brought the people out of Egypt, you will worship God on this mountain."

{13} Moses said to God, "Suppose I go to the Israelites and say to them, 'The God of your fathers has sent me to you,' and they ask me, 'What is his name?' Then what shall I tell them?" {14} God said to Moses, "I AM WHO I AM. This is what you are to say to the Israelites: 'I AM has sent me to you.'" {15} God also said to Moses, "Say to the Israelites, 'The LORD, the God of your fathers—the God of Abraham, the God of Isaac and the God of Jacob—has sent me to you.' This is my name forever, the name by which I am to be remembered from generation to generation. {16} "Go, assemble the elders of Israel and say to them, 'The LORD, the God of your fathers—the God of Abraham, Isaac and Jacob— appeared to me and said: I have watched over you and have seen what has been done to you in Egypt. {17} And I have promised to bring you up out of your misery....

MOSES' APPEAL REJECTED BY PHARAOH

Exo 5:1-21a

Afterward Moses and Aaron went to Pharaoh and said, "This is what the LORD, the God of Israel, says: 'Let my people go, so that they may hold a festival to me in the desert.'" {2} Pharaoh said, "Who is the LORD, that I should obey him and let Israel go? I do not know the LORD and I will not let Israel go." {3} Then they said, "The God of the Hebrews has met with us. Now let us take a three-day journey into the desert to offer sacrifices to the LORD our God, or he may strike us with plagues or with the sword."

{4} But the king of Egypt said, "Moses and Aaron, why are you taking the people away from their labor? Get back to your work!" {5} Then Pharaoh said, "Look, the people of the land are now numerous, and you are stopping them from working." {6} That same day Pharaoh gave this order to the slave drivers and foremen in charge of the people: {7} "You are no longer to supply the people with straw for making bricks; let them go and gather their own straw. {8} But require them to make the same number of bricks as before; don't reduce the quota. They are lazy; that is why they are crying out, 'Let us go and sacrifice to our God.' {9} Make the work harder for the men so that they keep working and pay no attention to lies." {10} Then the slave drivers and the foremen went out and said to the people, "This is what Pharaoh says: 'I will not give you any more straw. {11} Go and get your own straw wherever you can find it, but your work will not be reduced at all.'" {12} So the people scattered all over Egypt to gather stubble to use for straw.

{13} The slave drivers kept pressing them, saying, "Complete the work required of you for each day, just as when you had straw." {14} The Israelite foremen appointed by Pharaoh's slave drivers were beaten and were asked, "Why didn't you meet your quota of bricks yesterday or today, as before?" {15} Then the Israelite foremen went and appealed to Pharaoh: "Why have you treated your servants this way? {16} Your servants are given no straw, yet we are told, 'Make bricks!' Your servants are being beaten, but the fault is with your own people." {17} Pharaoh said, "Lazy, that's what you are–lazy! That is why you keep saying, 'Let us go and sacrifice to the LORD.' {18} Now get to work. You will not be given any straw, yet you must produce your full quota of bricks." {19} The Israelite foremen realized they were in trouble when they were told, "You are not to reduce the number of bricks required of you for each day." {20} When they left Pharaoh, they found Moses and Aaron waiting to meet them, {21} and they said, "May the LORD look upon you and judge you! You have made us a stench to Pharaoh....

AARON HELPS MOSES

Exo 6:28-7:13

Now when the LORD spoke to Moses in Egypt, {29} he said to him, "I am the LORD. Tell Pharaoh king of Egypt everything I tell you." {30} But Moses said to the LORD, "Since I speak with faltering lips, why would Pharaoh listen to me?" {7:1} Then the LORD said to Moses, "See, I have made you like God to Pharaoh, and your brother Aaron will be your prophet. {2} You are to say everything I command you, and your brother Aaron is to tell Pharaoh to let the Israelites go out of his country. {3} But I will harden Pharaoh's heart, and though I multiply my miraculous signs and wonders in Egypt, {4} he will not listen to you. Then I will lay my hand on Egypt and with mighty acts of judgment I will bring out my divisions, my people the Israelites. {5} And the Egyptians will know that I am the LORD when I stretch out my hand against Egypt and bring the Israelites out of it."

{6} Moses and Aaron did just as the LORD commanded them. {7} Moses was eighty years old and Aaron eighty-three when they spoke to Pharaoh. {8} The LORD said to Moses and Aaron, {9} "When Pharaoh says to you, 'Perform a miracle,' then say to Aaron, 'Take your staff and throw it down before Pharaoh,' and it will become a snake." {10} So Moses and Aaron went to Pharaoh and did just as the LORD commanded. Aaron threw his staff down in front of Pharaoh and his officials, and it became a snake. {11} Pharaoh then summoned wise men and sorcerers, and the Egyptian magicians also did the same things by their secret arts: {12} Each one threw down his staff and it became a snake. But Aaron's staff swallowed up their staffs. {13} Yet Pharaoh's heart became hard and he would not listen to them, just as the LORD had said.

Exo 11:1-3

Now the LORD had said to Moses, "I will bring one more plague on Pharaoh and on Egypt. After that, he will let you go from here, and when he does, he will drive you out completely. {2} Tell the people that men and women alike are to ask their neighbors for articles of silver and gold." {3} (The LORD made the Egyptians favorably disposed toward the people, and Moses himself was highly regarded in Egypt by Pharaoh's officials and by the people.)

PASSOVER AND EXODUS

Exo 12:21-36

Then Moses summoned all the elders of Israel and said to them, "Go at once and select the animals for your families and slaughter the Passover lamb. {22} Take a bunch of hyssop, dip it into the blood in the basin and put some of the blood on the top and on both sides of the doorframe. Not one of you shall go out the door of his house until morning. {23} When the LORD goes through the land to strike down the Egyptians, he will see the blood on the top and sides of the doorframe and will pass over that doorway, and he will not permit the destroyer to enter your houses and strike you down. {24} "Obey these instructions as a lasting ordinance for you and your descendants. {25} When you enter the land that the LORD will give you as he promised, observe this ceremony. {26} And when your children ask you, 'What does this ceremony mean to you?' {27} then tell them, 'It is the Passover sacrifice to the LORD, who passed over the houses of the Israelites in Egypt and spared our homes when he struck down the Egyptians.'" Then the people bowed down and worshiped. {28} The Israelites did just what the LORD commanded Moses and Aaron.

{29} At midnight the LORD struck down all the firstborn in Egypt, from the firstborn of Pharaoh, who sat on the throne, to the firstborn of the prisoner, who was in the dungeon, and the firstborn of all the livestock as well. {30} Pharaoh and all his officials and all the Egyptians got up during the night, and there was loud wailing in Egypt, for there was not a house without someone dead.

{31} During the night Pharaoh summoned Moses and Aaron and said, "Up! Leave my people, you and the Israelites! Go, worship the LORD as you have requested. {32} Take your flocks and herds, as you have said, and go. And also bless me." {33} The Egyptians urged the people to hurry and leave the country. "For otherwise," they said, "we will all die!" {34} So the people took their dough before the yeast was added, and carried it on their shoulders in kneading troughs wrapped in clothing. {35} The Israelites did as Moses instructed and asked the Egyptians for articles of silver and gold and for clothing. {36} The LORD had made the Egyptians favorably disposed toward the people, and they gave them what they asked for; so they plundered the Egyptians.

Exo 12:50-51

All the Israelites did just what the LORD had commanded Moses and Aaron. {51} And on that very day the LORD brought the Israelites out of Egypt by their divisions.

MOSES MEETS GOD ON MT. SINAI

Exo 19:3-19

Then Moses went up to God, and the LORD called to him from the mountain and said, "This is what you are to say to the house of Jacob and what you are to tell the people of Israel: {4} 'You yourselves have seen what I did to Egypt, and how I carried you on eagles' wings and brought you to myself. {5} Now if you obey me fully and keep my covenant, then out of all nations you will be my treasured possession. Although the whole earth is mine, {6} you will be for me a kingdom of priests and a holy nation.' These are the words you are to speak to the Israelites."

{7} So Moses went back and summoned the elders of the people and set before them all the words the LORD had commanded him to speak. {8} The people all responded together, "We will do everything the LORD has said." So Moses brought their answer back to the LORD. {9} The LORD said to Moses, "I am going to come to you in a dense cloud, so that the people will hear me speaking with you and will always put their trust in you." Then Moses told the LORD what the people had said. {10} And the LORD said to Moses, "Go to the people and consecrate them today and tomorrow. Have them wash their clothes {11} and be ready by the third day, because on that day the LORD will come down on Mount Sinai in the sight of all the people. {12} Put limits for the people around the mountain and tell them, 'Be careful that you do not go up the mountain or touch the foot of it. Whoever touches the mountain shall surely be put to death. {13} He shall surely be stoned or shot with arrows; not a hand is to be laid on him. Whether man or animal, he shall not be permitted to live.' Only when the ram's horn sounds a long blast may they go up to the mountain."

{14} After Moses had gone down the mountain to the people, he consecrated them, and they washed their clothes. {15} Then he said to the people, "Prepare yourselves for the third day. Abstain from sexual relations." {16} On the morning of the third day there was thunder and lightning, with a thick cloud over the mountain, and a very loud trumpet blast. Everyone in the camp trembled. {17} Then Moses led the people out of the camp to meet with God, and they stood at the foot of the mountain. {18} Mount Sinai was covered with smoke, because the LORD descended on it in fire. The smoke billowed up from it like smoke from a furnace, the whole mountain trembled violently, {19} and the sound of the trumpet grew louder and louder. Then Moses spoke and the voice of God answered him.

THE TEN COMMANDMENTS

Exo 20:1-19

And God spoke all these words: {2} "I am the LORD your God, who brought you out of Egypt, out of the land of slavery.

{3} "You shall have no other gods before me.

{4} "You shall not make for yourself an idol in the form of anything in heaven above or on the earth beneath or in the waters below. {5} You shall not bow down to them or worship them; for I, the LORD your God, am a jealous God, punishing the children for the sin of the fathers to the third and fourth generation of those who hate me, {6} but showing love to a thousand <generations> of those who love me and keep my commandments.

{7} "You shall not misuse the name of the LORD your God, for the LORD will not hold anyone guiltless who misuses his name.

{8} "Remember the Sabbath day by keeping it holy. {9} Six days you shall labor and do all your work, {10} but the seventh day is a Sabbath to the LORD your God. On it you shall not do any work, neither you, nor your son or daughter, nor your manservant or maidservant, nor your animals, nor the alien within your gates. {11} For in six days the LORD made the heavens and the earth, the sea, and all that is in them, but he rested on the seventh day. Therefore the LORD blessed the Sabbath day and made it holy.

{12} "Honor your father and your mother, so that you may live long in the land the LORD your God is giving you.

{13} "You shall not murder.

{14} "You shall not commit adultery.

{15} "You shall not steal.

{16} "You shall not give false testimony against your neighbor.

{17} "You shall not covet your neighbor's house. You shall not covet your neighbor's wife, or his manservant or maidservant, his ox or donkey, or anything that belongs to your neighbor."

{18} When the people saw the thunder and lightning and heard the trumpet and saw the mountain in smoke, they trembled with fear. They stayed at a distance {19} and said to Moses, "Speak to us yourself and we will listen. But do not have God speak to us or we will die."

MOSES CHISELS TWO STONE TABLETS

Exo 34:1-16

The LORD said to Moses, "Chisel out two stone tablets like the first ones, and I will write on them the words that were on the first tablets, which you broke. {2} Be ready in the morning, and then come up on Mount Sinai. Present yourself to me there on top of the mountain. {3} No one is to come with you or be seen anywhere on the mountain; not even the flocks and herds may graze in front of the mountain." {4} So Moses chiseled out two stone tablets like the first ones and went up Mount Sinai early in the morning, as the LORD had commanded him; and he carried the two stone tablets in his hands. {5} Then the LORD came down in the cloud and stood there with him and proclaimed his name, the LORD. {6} And he passed in front of Moses, proclaiming, "The LORD, the LORD, the compassionate and gracious God, slow to anger, abounding in love and faithfulness, {7} maintaining love to thousands, and forgiving wickedness, rebellion and sin. Yet he does not leave the guilty unpunished; he punishes the children and their children for the sin of the fathers to the third and fourth generation." {8} Moses bowed to the ground at once and worshiped. {9} "O Lord, if I have found favor in your eyes," he said, "then let the Lord go with us. Although this is a stiff-necked people, forgive our wickedness and our sin, and take us as your inheritance."

{10} Then the LORD said: "I am making a covenant with you. Before all your people I will do wonders never before done in any nation in all the world. The people you live among will see how awesome is the work that I, the LORD, will do for you. {11} Obey what I command you today. I will drive out before you the Amorites, Canaanites, Hittites, Perizzites, Hivites and Jebusites. {12} Be careful not to make a treaty with those who live in the land where you are going, or they will be a snare among you. {13} Break down their altars, smash their sacred stones and cut down their Asherah poles. {14} Do not worship any other god, for the LORD, whose name is Jealous, is a jealous God. {15} "Be careful not to make a treaty with those who live in the land; for when they prostitute themselves to their gods and sacrifice to them, they will invite you and you will eat their sacrifices. {16} And when you choose some of their daughters as wives for your sons and those daughters prostitute themselves to their gods, they will lead your sons to do the same.

THE SIN OFFERING

Lev 4:5-21

Then the anointed priest shall take some of the bull's blood and carry it into the Tent of Meeting. {6} He is to dip his finger into the blood and sprinkle some of it seven times before the LORD, in front of the curtain of the sanctuary. {7} The priest shall then put some of the blood on the horns of the altar of fragrant incense that is before the LORD in the Tent of Meeting. The rest of the bull's blood he shall pour out at the base of the altar of burnt offering at the entrance to the Tent of Meeting. {8} He shall remove all the fat from the bull of the sin offering–the fat that covers the inner parts or is connected to them, {9} both kidneys with the fat on them near the loins, and the covering of the liver, which he will remove with the kidneys– {10} just as the fat is removed from the ox sacrificed as a fellowship offering. Then the priest shall burn them on the altar of burnt offering. {11} But the hide of the bull and all its flesh, as well as the head and legs, the inner parts and offal– {12} that is, all the rest of the bull–he must take outside the camp to a place ceremonially clean, where the ashes are thrown, and burn it in a wood fire on the ash heap. {13} "'If the whole Israelite community sins unintentionally and does what is forbidden in any of the Lord's commands, even though the community is unaware of the matter, they are guilty.

{14} When they become aware of the sin they committed, the assembly must bring a young bull as a sin offering and present it before the Tent of Meeting. {15} The elders of the community are to lay their hands on the bull's head before the LORD, and the bull shall be slaughtered before the LORD. {16} Then the anointed priest is to take some of the bull's blood into the Tent of Meeting. {17} He shall dip his finger into the blood and sprinkle it before the LORD seven times in front of the curtain. {18} He is to put some of the blood on the horns of the altar that is before the LORD in the Tent of Meeting. The rest of the blood he shall pour out at the base of the altar of burnt offering at the entrance to the Tent of Meeting. {19} He shall remove all the fat from it and burn it on the altar, {20} and do with this bull just as he did with the bull for the sin offering. In this way the priest will make atonement for them, and they will be forgiven. {21} Then he shall take the bull outside the camp and burn it as he burned the first bull. This is the sin offering for the community.

THE PRIESTS BEGIN THEIR MINISTRY

Lev 9:5-23

They took the things Moses commanded to the front of the Tent of Meeting, and the entire assembly came near and stood before the LORD. {6} Then Moses said, "This is what the LORD has commanded you to do, so that the glory of the LORD may appear to you." {7} Moses said to Aaron, "Come to the altar and sacrifice your sin offering and your burnt offering and make atonement for yourself and the people; sacrifice the offering that is for the people and make atonement for them, as the LORD has commanded." {8} So Aaron came to the altar and slaughtered the calf as a sin offering for himself. {9} His sons brought the blood to him, and he dipped his finger into the blood and put it on the horns of the altar; the rest of the blood he poured out at the base of the altar. {10} On the altar he burned the fat, the kidneys and the covering of the liver from the sin offering, as the LORD commanded Moses; {11} the flesh and the hide he burned up outside the camp. {12} Then he slaughtered the burnt offering. His sons handed him the blood, and he sprinkled it against the altar on all sides. {13} They handed him the burnt offering piece by piece, including the head, and he burned them on the altar. {14} He washed the inner parts and the legs and burned them on top of the burnt offering on the altar. {15} Aaron then brought the offering that was for the people. He took the goat for the people's sin offering and slaughtered it and offered it for a sin offering as he did with the first one. {16} He brought the burnt offering and offered it in the prescribed way. {17} He also brought the grain offering, took a handful of it and burned it on the altar in addition to the morning's burnt offering. {18} He slaughtered the ox and the ram as the fellowship offering for the people. His sons handed him the blood, and he sprinkled it against the altar on all sides. {19} But the fat portions of the ox and the ram–the fat tail, the layer of fat, the kidneys and the covering of the liver– {20} these they laid on the breasts, and then Aaron burned the fat on the altar. {21} Aaron waved the breasts and the right thigh before the LORD as a wave offering, as Moses commanded.

{22} Then Aaron lifted his hands toward the people and blessed them. And having sacrificed the sin offering, the burnt offering and the fellowship offering, he stepped down. {23} Moses and Aaron then went into the Tent of Meeting. When they came out, they blessed the people; and the glory of the LORD appeared to all the people.

RULES FOR DAILY LIVING

Lev 19:1-4

The LORD said to Moses, {2} "Speak to the entire assembly of Israel and say to them: 'Be holy because I, the LORD your God, am holy. {3} "Each of you must respect his mother and father, and you must observe my Sabbaths. I am the LORD your God. {4} "Do not turn to idols or make gods of cast metal for yourselves. I am the LORD your God.

Lev 19:9-18

"'When you reap the harvest of your land, do not reap to the very edges of your field or gather the gleanings of your harvest. {10} Do not go over your vineyard a second time or pick up the grapes that have fallen. Leave them for the poor and the alien. I am the LORD your God. {11} "Do not steal. "Do not lie. "Do not deceive one another. {12} "Do not swear falsely by my name and so profane the name of your God. I am the LORD. {13} "Do not defraud your neighbor or rob him. "Do not hold back the wages of a hired man overnight. {14} "Do not curse the deaf or put a stumbling block in front of the blind, but fear your God. I am the LORD. {15} "Do not pervert justice; do not show partiality to the poor or favoritism to the great, but judge your neighbor fairly. {16} "Do not go about spreading slander among your people. "Do not do anything that endangers your neighbor's life. I am the LORD. {17} "Do not hate your brother in your heart. Rebuke your neighbor frankly so you will not share in his guilt. {18} "Do not seek revenge or bear a grudge against one of your people, but love your neighbor as yourself. I am the LORD.

Lev 19:30-37

"'Observe my Sabbaths and have reverence for my sanctuary. I am the LORD. {31} "Do not turn to mediums or seek out spiritists, for you will be defiled by them. I am the LORD your God. {32} "Rise in the presence of the aged, show respect for the elderly and revere your God. I am the LORD. {33} "When an alien lives with you in your land, do not mistreat him. {34} The alien living with you must be treated as one of your native-born. Love him as yourself, for you were aliens in Egypt. I am the LORD your God. {35} "Do not use dishonest standards when measuring length, weight or quantity. {36} Use honest scales and honest weights, an honest ephah and an honest hin. I am the LORD your God, who brought you out of Egypt. {37} "Keep all my decrees and all my laws and follow them. I am the LORD.'"

THE SABBATICAL YEAR; THE YEAR OF JUBILEE

Lev 25:3-23

For six years sow your fields, and for six years prune your vineyards and gather their crops. {4} But in the seventh year the land is to have a sabbath of rest, a sabbath to the LORD. Do not sow your fields or prune your vineyards. {5} Do not reap what grows of itself or harvest the grapes of your untended vines. The land is to have a year of rest. {6} Whatever the land yields during the sabbath year will be food for you–for yourself, your manservant and maidservant, and the hired worker and temporary resident who live among you, {7} as well as for your livestock and the wild animals in your land. Whatever the land produces may be eaten.

{8} "'Count off seven sabbaths of years–seven times seven years– so that the seven sabbaths of years amount to a period of forty-nine years. {9} Then have the trumpet sounded everywhere on the tenth day of the seventh month; on the Day of Atonement sound the trumpet throughout your land. {10} Consecrate the fiftieth year and proclaim liberty throughout the land to all its inhabitants. It shall be a jubilee for you; each one of you is to return to his family property and each to his own clan. {11} The fiftieth year shall be a jubilee for you; do not sow and do not reap what grows of itself or harvest the untended vines. {12} For it is a jubilee and is to be holy for you; eat only what is taken directly from the fields. {13} "'In this Year of Jubilee everyone is to return to his own property. {14} "'If you sell land to one of your countrymen or buy any from him, do not take advantage of each other. {15} You are to buy from your countryman on the basis of the number of years since the Jubilee. And he is to sell to you on the basis of the number of years left for harvesting crops. {16} When the years are many, you are to increase the price, and when the years are few, you are to decrease the price, because what he is really selling you is the number of crops. {17} Do not take advantage of each other, but fear your God. I am the LORD your God. {18} "'Follow my decrees and be careful to obey my laws, and you will live safely in the land. {19} Then the land will yield its fruit, and you will eat your fill and live there in safety. {20} You may ask, "What will we eat in the seventh year if we do not plant or harvest our crops?" {21} I will send you such a blessing in the sixth year that the land will yield enough for three years. {22} While you plant during the eighth year, you will eat from the old crop and will continue to eat from it until the harvest of the ninth year comes in. {23} "'The land must not be sold permanently, because the land is mine and you are but aliens and my tenants.

THE REWARDS OF OBEDIENCE,
AND THE PUNISHMENTS FOR DISOBEDIENCE

Lev 26:3-21

"'If you follow my decrees and are careful to obey my commands, {4} I will send you rain in its season, and the ground will yield its crops and the trees of the field their fruit. {5} Your threshing will continue until grape harvest and the grape harvest will continue until planting, and you will eat all the food you want and live in safety in your land. {6} "'I will grant peace in the land, and you will lie down and no one will make you afraid. I will remove savage beasts from the land, and the sword will not pass through your country. {7} You will pursue your enemies, and they will fall by the sword before you. {8} Five of you will chase a hundred, and a hundred of you will chase ten thousand, and your enemies will fall by the sword before you. {9} "'I will look on you with favor and make you fruitful and increase your numbers, and I will keep my covenant with you. {10} You will still be eating last year's harvest when you will have to move it out to make room for the new. {11} I will put my dwelling place among you, and I will not abhor you. {12} I will walk among you and be your God, and you will be my people. {13} I am the LORD your God, who brought you out of Egypt so that you would no longer be slaves to the Egyptians; I broke the bars of your yoke and enabled you to walk with heads held high.

{14} "'But if you will not listen to me and carry out all these commands, {15} and if you reject my decrees and abhor my laws and fail to carry out all my commands and so violate my covenant, {16} then I will do this to you: I will bring upon you sudden terror, wasting diseases and fever that will destroy your sight and drain away your life. You will plant seed in vain, because your enemies will eat it. {17} I will set my face against you so that you will be defeated by your enemies; those who hate you will rule over you, and you will flee even when no one is pursuing you. {18} "'If after all this you will not listen to me, I will punish you for your sins seven times over. {19} I will break down your stubborn pride and make the sky above you like iron and the ground beneath you like bronze. {20} Your strength will be spent in vain, because your soil will not yield its crops, nor will the trees of the land yield their fruit. {21} "'If you remain hostile toward me and refuse to listen to me, I will multiply your afflictions seven times over, as your sins deserve.

A TITHE BELONGS TO THE LORD

Lev 27:16-28

"If a man dedicates to the LORD part of his family land, its value is to be set according to the amount of seed required for it–fifty shekels of silver to a homer of barley seed. {17} If he dedicates his field during the Year of Jubilee, the value that has been set remains. {18} But if he dedicates his field after the Jubilee, the priest will determine the value according to the number of years that remain until the next Year of Jubilee, and its set value will be reduced. {19} If the man who dedicates the field wishes to redeem it, he must add a fifth to its value, and the field will again become his. {20} If, however, he does not redeem the field, or if he has sold it to someone else, it can never be redeemed. {21} When the field is released in the Jubilee, it will become holy, like a field devoted to the LORD; it will become the property of the priests. {22} "If a man dedicates to the LORD a field he has bought, which is not part of his family land, {23} the priest will determine its value up to the Year of Jubilee, and the man must pay its value on that day as something holy to the LORD. {24} In the Year of Jubilee the field will revert to the person from whom he bought it, the one whose land it was. {25} Every value is to be set according to the sanctuary shekel, twenty gerahs to the shekel. {26} "'No one, however, may dedicate the firstborn of an animal, since the firstborn already belongs to the LORD; whether an ox or a sheep, it is the Lord's. {27} If it is one of the unclean animals, he may buy it back at its set value, adding a fifth of the value to it. If he does not redeem it, it is to be sold at its set value. {28} "'But nothing that a man owns and devotes to the LORD–whether man or animal or family land–may be sold or redeemed; everything so devoted is most holy to the LORD.

Lev 27:30-34

"'A tithe of everything from the land, whether grain from the soil or fruit from the trees, belongs to the LORD; it is holy to the LORD. {31} If a man redeems any of his tithe, he must add a fifth of the value to it. {32} The entire tithe of the herd and flock–every tenth animal that passes under the shepherd's rod–will be holy to the LORD. {33} He must not pick out the good from the bad or make any substitution. If he does make a substitution, both the animal and its substitute become holy and cannot be redeemed.'" {34} These are the commands the LORD gave Moses on Mount Sinai for the Israelites.

SEVENTY ELDERS APPOINTED

Num 11:11-17

He asked the LORD, "Why have you brought this trouble on your servant? What have I done to displease you that you put the burden of all these people on me? {12} Did I conceive all these people? Did I give them birth? Why do you tell me to carry them in my arms, as a nurse carries an infant, to the land you promised on oath to their forefathers? {13} Where can I get meat for all these people? They keep wailing to me, 'Give us meat to eat!' {14} I cannot carry all these people by myself; the burden is too heavy for me. {15} If this is how you are going to treat me, put me to death right now–if I have found favor in your eyes–and do not let me face my own ruin." {16} The LORD said to Moses: "Bring me seventy of Israel's elders who are known to you as leaders and officials among the people. Have them come to the Tent of Meeting, that they may stand there with you. {17} I will come down and speak with you there, and I will take of the Spirit that is on you and put the Spirit on them. They will help you carry the burden of the people so that you will not have to carry it alone.

THE PEOPLE COMPLAIN AND GET QUAIL

Num 11:31-34

Now a wind went out from the LORD and drove quail in from the sea. It brought them down all around the camp to about three feet above the ground, as far as a day's walk in any direction. {32} All that day and night and all the next day the people went out and gathered quail. No one gathered less than ten homers. Then they spread them out all around the camp. {33} But while the meat was still between their teeth and before it could be consumed, the anger of the LORD burned against the people, and he struck them with a severe plague. {34} Therefore the place was named Kibroth Hattaavah, because there they buried the people who had craved other food.

AGAIN THE PEOPLE GRUMBLE

Num 14:7-24

"The land we passed through and explored is exceedingly good. {8} If the LORD is pleased with us, he will lead us into that land, a land flowing with milk and honey, and will give it to us. {9} Only do not rebel against the LORD. And do not be afraid of the people of the land, because we will swallow them up. Their protection is gone, but the LORD is with us. Do not be afraid of them." {10} But the whole assembly talked about stoning them. Then the glory of the LORD appeared at the Tent of Meeting to all the Israelites.

{11} The LORD said to Moses, "How long will these people treat me with contempt? How long will they refuse to believe in me, in spite of all the miraculous signs I have performed among them? {12} I will strike them down with a plague and destroy them, but I will make you into a nation greater and stronger than they."

{13} Moses said to the LORD, "Then the Egyptians will hear about it! By your power you brought these people up from among them. {14} And they will tell the inhabitants of this land about it. They have already heard that you, O LORD, are with these people and that you, O LORD, have been seen face to face, that your cloud stays over them, and that you go before them in a pillar of cloud by day and a pillar of fire by night. {15} If you put these people to death all at one time, the nations who have heard this report about you will say, {16} 'The LORD was not able to bring these people into the land he promised them on oath; so he slaughtered them in the desert.' {17} "Now may the Lord's strength be displayed, just as you have declared: {18} 'The LORD is slow to anger, abounding in love and forgiving sin and rebellion. Yet he does not leave the guilty unpunished; he punishes the children for the sin of the fathers to the third and fourth generation.' {19} In accordance with your great love, forgive the sin of these people, just as you have pardoned them from the time they left Egypt until now."

{20} The LORD replied, "I have forgiven them, as you asked. {21} Nevertheless, as surely as I live and as surely as the glory of the LORD fills the whole earth, {22} not one of the men who saw my glory and the miraculous signs I performed in Egypt and in the desert but who disobeyed me and tested me ten times– {23} not one of them will ever see the land I promised on oath to their forefathers. No one who has treated me with contempt will ever see it. {24} But because my servant Caleb has a different spirit and follows me wholeheartedly, I will bring him into the land he went to, and his descendants will inherit it.

INSTRUCTIONS ON HOW TO TAKE CANAAN

Num 33:51b-56

"When you cross the Jordan into Canaan, {52} drive out all the inhabitants of the land before you. Destroy all their carved images and their cast idols, and demolish all their high places. {53} Take possession of the land and settle in it, for I have given you the land to possess. {54} Distribute the land by lot, according to your clans. To a larger group give a larger inheritance, and to a smaller group a smaller one. Whatever falls to them by lot will be theirs. Distribute it according to your ancestral tribes. {55} "But if you do not drive out the inhabitants of the land, those you allow to remain will become barbs in your eyes and thorns in your sides. They will give you trouble in the land where you will live. {56} And then I will do to you what I plan to do to them.'"

TOWNS FOR LEVITES AND CITIES OF REFUGE

Num 35:2-14

"Command the Israelites to give the Levites towns to live in from the inheritance the Israelites will possess. And give them pasturelands around the towns. {3} Then they will have towns to live in and pasturelands for their cattle, flocks and all their other livestock. {4} "The pasturelands around the towns that you give the Levites will extend out fifteen hundred feet from the town wall. {5} Outside the town, measure three thousand feet on the east side, three thousand on the south side, three thousand on the west and three thousand on the north, with the town in the center. They will have this area as pastureland for the towns. {6} "Six of the towns you give the Levites will be cities of refuge, to which a person who has killed someone may flee. In addition, give them forty-two other towns. {7} In all you must give the Levites forty-eight towns, together with their pasturelands. {8} The towns you give the Levites from the land the Israelites possess are to be given in proportion to the inheritance of each tribe: Take many towns from a tribe that has many, but few from one that has few." {9} Then the LORD said to Moses: {10} "Speak to the Israelites and say to them: 'When you cross the Jordan into Canaan, {11} select some towns to be your cities of refuge, to which a person who has killed someone accidentally may flee. {12} They will be places of refuge from the avenger, so that a person accused of murder may not die before he stands trial before the assembly. {13} These six towns you give will be your cities of refuge. {14} Give three on this side of the Jordan and three in Canaan as cities of refuge.

FEAR THE LORD AND SERVE HIM ONLY

Deu 6:3-25

Hear, O Israel, and be careful to obey so that it may go well with you and that you may increase greatly in a land flowing with milk and honey, just as the LORD, the God of your fathers, promised you. {4} Hear, O Israel: The LORD our God, the LORD is one. {5} Love the LORD your God with all your heart and with all your soul and with all your strength. {6} These commandments that I give you today are to be upon your hearts. {7} Impress them on your children. Talk about them when you sit at home and when you walk along the road, when you lie down and when you get up. {8} Tie them as symbols on your hands and bind them on your foreheads. {9} Write them on the doorframes of your houses and on your gates. {10} When the LORD your God brings you into the land he swore to your fathers, to Abraham, Isaac and Jacob, to give you–a land with large, flourishing cities you did not build, {11} houses filled with all kinds of good things you did not provide, wells you did not dig, and vineyards and olive groves you did not plant–then when you eat and are satisfied, {12} be careful that you do not forget the LORD, who brought you out of Egypt, out of the land of slavery. {13} Fear the LORD your God, serve him only and take your oaths in his name. {14} Do not follow other gods, the gods of the peoples around you; {15} for the LORD your God, who is among you, is a jealous God and his anger will burn against you, and he will destroy you from the face of the land. {16} Do not test the LORD your God as you did at Massah. {17} Be sure to keep the commands of the LORD your God and the stipulations and decrees he has given you. {18} Do what is right and good in the Lord's sight, so that it may go well with you and you may go in and take over the good land that the LORD promised on oath to your forefathers, {19} thrusting out all your enemies before you, as the LORD said.

{20} In the future, when your son asks you, "What is the meaning of the stipulations, decrees and laws the LORD our God has commanded you?" {21} tell him: "We were slaves of Pharaoh in Egypt, but the LORD brought us out of Egypt with a mighty hand. {22} Before our eyes the LORD sent miraculous signs and wonders–great and terrible–upon Egypt and Pharaoh and his whole household. {23} But he brought us out from there to bring us in and give us the land that he promised on oath to our forefathers. {24} The LORD commanded us to obey all these decrees and to fear the LORD our God, so that we might always prosper and be kept alive, as is the case today. {25} And if we are careful to obey all this law before the LORD our God, as he has commanded us, that will be our righteousness."

GIVE A TITHE; HELP THE POOR

Deu 14:22-23

Be sure to set aside a tenth of all that your fields produce each year. {23} Eat the tithe of your grain, new wine and oil, and the firstborn of your herds and flocks in the presence of the LORD your God at the place he will choose as a dwelling for his Name, so that you may learn to revere the LORD your God always.

Deu 14:27-29

And do not neglect the Levites living in your towns, for they have no allotment or inheritance of their own. {28} At the end of every three years, bring all the tithes of that year's produce and store it in your towns, {29} so that the Levites (who have no allotment or inheritance of their own) and the aliens, the fatherless and the widows who live in your towns may come and eat and be satisfied, and so that the LORD your God may bless you in all the work of your hands.

Deu 15:1-11

At the end of every seven years you must cancel debts. {2} This is how it is to be done: Every creditor shall cancel the loan he has made to his fellow Israelite. He shall not require payment from his fellow Israelite or brother, because the Lord's time for canceling debts has been proclaimed. {3} You may require payment from a foreigner, but you must cancel any debt your brother owes you. {4} However, there should be no poor among you, for in the land the LORD your God is giving you to possess as your inheritance, he will richly bless you, {5} if only you fully obey the LORD your God and are careful to follow all these commands I am giving you today. {6} For the LORD your God will bless you as he has promised, and you will lend to many nations but will borrow from none. You will rule over many nations but none will rule over you. {7} If there is a poor man among your brothers in any of the towns of the land that the LORD your God is giving you, do not be hardhearted or tightfisted toward your poor brother. {8} Rather be openhanded and freely lend him whatever he needs. {9} Be careful not to harbor this wicked thought: "The seventh year, the year for canceling debts, is near," so that you do not show ill will toward your needy brother and give him nothing. He may then appeal to the LORD against you, and you will be found guilty of sin. {10} Give generously to him and do so without a grudging heart; then because of this the LORD your God will bless you in all your work and in everything you put your hand to. {11} There will always be poor people in the land. Therefore I command you to be openhanded toward your brothers and toward the poor and needy in your land.

RESPECT EDOMITES ANS EGYPTIANS

Deu 23:7-8

Do not abhor an Edomite, for he is your brother. Do not abhor an Egyptian, because you lived as an alien in his country. {8} The third generation of children born to them may enter the assembly of the LORD.

NEWLY-MARRIEDS SHOULD STAY AT HOME

Deu 24:5

If a man has recently married, he must not be sent to war or have any other duty laid on him. For one year he is to be free to stay at home and bring happiness to the wife he has married.

LOANS, WEIGHTS, MEASURES

Deu 24:10-15

When you make a loan of any kind to your neighbor, do not go into his house to get what he is offering as a pledge. {11} Stay outside and let the man to whom you are making the loan bring the pledge out to you. {12} If the man is poor, do not go to sleep with his pledge in your possession. {13} Return his cloak to him by sunset so that he may sleep in it. Then he will thank you, and it will be regarded as a righteous act in the sight of the LORD your God. {14} Do not take advantage of a hired man who is poor and needy, whether he is a brother Israelite or an alien living in one of your towns. {15} Pay him his wages each day before sunset, because he is poor and is counting on it. Otherwise he may cry to the LORD against you, and you will be guilty of sin.

Deu 24:19-22

When you are harvesting in your field and you overlook a sheaf, do not go back to get it. Leave it for the alien, the fatherless and the widow, so that the LORD your God may bless you in all the work of your hands. {20} When you beat the olives from your trees, do not go over the branches a second time. Leave what remains for the alien, the fatherless and the widow. {21} When you harvest the grapes in your vineyard, do not go over the vines again. Leave what remains for the alien, the fatherless and the widow. {22} Remember that you were slaves in Egypt. That is why I command you to do this.

Deu 25:13-16

Do not have two differing weights in your bag—one heavy, one light. {14} Do not have two differing measures in your house—one large, one small. {15} You must have accurate and honest weights and measures, so that you may live long in the land the LORD your God is giving you. {16} For the LORD your God detests anyone who does these things, anyone who deals dishonestly.

BLESSINGS AND CURSES

Deu 28:1-14

If you fully obey the LORD your God and carefully follow all his commands I give you today, the LORD your God will set you high above all the nations on earth. {2} All these blessings will come upon you and accompany you if you obey the LORD your God: {3} You will be blessed in the city and blessed in the country. {4} The fruit of your womb will be blessed, and the crops of your land and the young of your livestock–the calves of your herds and the lambs of your flocks. {5} Your basket and your kneading trough will be blessed. {6} You will be blessed when you come in and blessed when you go out. {7} The LORD will grant that the enemies who rise up against you will be defeated before you. They will come at you from one direction but flee from you in seven. {8} The LORD will send a blessing on your barns and on everything you put your hand to. The LORD your God will bless you in the land he is giving you. {9} The LORD will establish you as his holy people, as he promised you on oath, if you keep the commands of the LORD your God and walk in his ways. {10} Then all the peoples on earth will see that you are called by the name of the LORD, and they will fear you. {11} The LORD will grant you abundant prosperity–in the fruit of your womb, the young of your livestock and the crops of your ground–in the land he swore to your forefathers to give you. {12} The LORD will open the heavens, the storehouse of his bounty, to send rain on your land in season and to bless all the work of your hands. You will lend to many nations but will borrow from none. {13} The LORD will make you the head, not the tail. If you pay attention to the commands of the LORD your God that I give you this day and carefully follow them, you will always be at the top, never at the bottom. {14} Do not turn aside from any of the commands I give you today, to the right or to the left....

Deu 28:20-24

The LORD will send on you curses, confusion and rebuke in everything you put your hand to, until you are destroyed and come to sudden ruin because of the evil you have done in forsaking him. {21} The LORD will plague you with diseases until he has destroyed you from the land you are entering to possess. {22} The LORD will strike you with wasting disease, with fever and inflammation, with scorching heat and drought, with blight and mildew, which will plague you until you perish. {23} The sky over your head will be bronze, the ground beneath you iron. {24} The LORD will turn the rain of your country into dust and powder; it will come down from the skies until you are destroyed.

PROSPERITY WHEN YOU OBEY THE LORD

Deu 30:1-18a

When all these blessings and curses I have set before you come upon you and you take them to heart wherever the LORD your God disperses you among the nations, {2} and when you and your children return to the LORD your God and obey him with all your heart and with all your soul according to everything I command you today, {3} then the LORD your God will restore your fortunes and have compassion on you and gather you again from all the nations where he scattered you. {4} Even if you have been banished to the most distant land under the heavens, from there the LORD your God will gather you and bring you back. {5} He will bring you to the land that belonged to your fathers, and you will take possession of it. He will make you more prosperous and numerous than your fathers. {6} The LORD your God will circumcise your hearts and the hearts of your descendants, so that you may love him with all your heart and with all your soul, and live. {7} The LORD your God will put all these curses on your enemies who hate and persecute you. {8} You will again obey the LORD and follow all his commands I am giving you today. {9} Then the LORD your God will make you most prosperous in all the work of your hands and in the fruit of your womb, the young of your livestock and the crops of your land. The LORD will again delight in you and make you prosperous, just as he delighted in your fathers, {10} if you obey the LORD your God and keep his commands and decrees that are written in this Book of the Law and turn to the LORD your God with all your heart and with all your soul. {11} Now what I am commanding you today is not too difficult for you or beyond your reach. {12} It is not up in heaven, so that you have to ask, "Who will ascend into heaven to get it and proclaim it to us so we may obey it?" {13} Nor is it beyond the sea, so that you have to ask, "Who will cross the sea to get it and proclaim it to us so we may obey it?" {14} No, the word is very near you; it is in your mouth and in your heart so you may obey it. {15} See, I set before you today life and prosperity, death and destruction. {16} For I command you today to love the LORD your God, to walk in his ways, and to keep his commands, decrees and laws; then you will live and increase, and the LORD your God will bless you in the land you are entering to possess. {17} But if your heart turns away and you are not obedient, and if you are drawn away to bow down to other gods and worship them, {18} I declare to you this day that you will certainly be destroyed.

GIDEON PUTS OUT A FLEECE

Judg 6:14-23

The LORD turned to him and said, "Go in the strength you have and save Israel out of Midian's hand. Am I not sending you?" {15} "But Lord," Gideon asked, "how can I save Israel? My clan is the weakest in Manasseh, and I am the least in my family." {16} The LORD answered, "I will be with you, and you will strike down all the Midianites together." {17} Gideon replied, "If now I have found favor in your eyes, give me a sign that it is really you talking to me. {18} Please do not go away until I come back and bring my offering and set it before you." And the LORD said, "I will wait until you return." {19} Gideon went in, prepared a young goat, and from an ephah of flour he made bread without yeast. Putting the meat in a basket and its broth in a pot, he brought them out and offered them to him under the oak. {20} The angel of God said to him, "Take the meat and the unleavened bread, place them on this rock, and pour out the broth." And Gideon did so. {21} With the tip of the staff that was in his hand, the angel of the LORD touched the meat and the unleavened bread. Fire flared from the rock, consuming the meat and the bread. And the angel of the LORD disappeared. {22} When Gideon realized that it was the angel of the LORD, he exclaimed, "Ah, Sovereign LORD! I have seen the angel of the LORD face to face!" {23} But the LORD said to him, "Peace! Do not be afraid. You are not going to die."

Judg 6:33-40

Now all the Midianites, Amalekites and other eastern peoples joined forces and crossed over the Jordan and camped in the Valley of Jezreel. {34} Then the Spirit of the LORD came upon Gideon, and he blew a trumpet, summoning the Abiezrites to follow him. {35} He sent messengers throughout Manasseh, calling them to arms, and also into Asher, Zebulun and Naphtali, so that they too went up to meet them. {36} Gideon said to God, "If you will save Israel by my hand as you have promised– {37} look, I will place a wool fleece on the threshing floor. If there is dew only on the fleece and all the ground is dry, then I will know that you will save Israel by my hand, as you said." {38} And that is what happened. Gideon rose early the next day; he squeezed the fleece and wrung out the dew–a bowlful of water. {39} Then Gideon said to God, "Do not be angry with me. Let me make just one more request. Allow me one more test with the fleece. This time make the fleece dry and the ground covered with dew." {40} That night God did so. Only the fleece was dry; all the ground was covered with dew.

GIDEON'S THREE HUNDRED FIGHT MIDIAN

Judg 7:5b-20

There the LORD told him, "Separate those who lap the water with their tongues like a dog from those who kneel down to drink." {6} Three hundred men lapped with their hands to their mouths. All the rest got down on their knees to drink. {7} The LORD said to Gideon, "With the three hundred men that lapped I will save you and give the Midianites into your hands. Let all the other men go, each to his own place." {8} So Gideon sent the rest of the Israelites to their tents but kept the three hundred, who took over the provisions and trumpets of the others. Now the camp of Midian lay below him in the valley. {9} During that night the LORD said to Gideon, "Get up, go down against the camp, because I am going to give it into your hands. {10} If you are afraid to attack, go down to the camp with your servant Purah {11} and listen to what they are saying. Afterward, you will be encouraged to attack the camp." So he and Purah his servant went down to the outposts of the camp. {12} The Midianites, the Amalekites and all the other eastern peoples had settled in the valley, thick as locusts. Their camels could no more be counted than the sand on the seashore. {13} Gideon arrived just as a man was telling a friend his dream. "I had a dream," he was saying. "A round loaf of barley bread came tumbling into the Midianite camp. It struck the tent with such force that the tent overturned and collapsed." {14} His friend responded, "This can be nothing other than the sword of Gideon son of Joash, the Israelite. God has given the Midianites and the whole camp into his hands." {15} When Gideon heard the dream and its interpretation, he worshiped God. He returned to the camp of Israel and called out, "Get up! The LORD has given the Midianite camp into your hands." {16} Dividing the three hundred men into three companies, he placed trumpets and empty jars in the hands of all of them, with torches inside. {17} "Watch me," he told them. "Follow my lead. When I get to the edge of the camp, do exactly as I do. {18} When I and all who are with me blow our trumpets, then from all around the camp blow yours and shout, 'For the LORD and for Gideon.'" {19} Gideon and the hundred men with him reached the edge of the camp at the beginning of the middle watch, just after they had changed the guard. They blew their trumpets and broke the jars that were in their hands. {20} The three companies blew the trumpets and smashed the jars. Grasping the torches in their left hands and holding in their right hands the trumpets they were to blow, they shouted, "A sword for the LORD and for Gideon!"

RUTH MIGRATES WITH NAOMI

Ruth 1:1-19

In the days when the judges ruled, there was a famine in the land, and a man from Bethlehem in Judah, together with his wife and two sons, went to live for a while in the country of Moab. {2} The man's name was Elimelech, his wife's name Naomi, and the names of his two sons were Mahlon and Kilion. They were Ephrathites from Bethlehem, Judah. And they went to Moab and lived there. {3} Now Elimelech, Naomi's husband, died, and she was left with her two sons. {4} They married Moabite women, one named Orpah and the other Ruth. After they had lived there about ten years, {5} both Mahlon and Kilion also died, and Naomi was left without her two sons and her husband. {6} When she heard in Moab that the LORD had come to the aid of his people by providing food for them, Naomi and her daughters-in-law prepared to return home from there. {7} With her two daughters-in-law she left the place where she had been living and set out on the road that would take them back to the land of Judah. {8} Then Naomi said to her two daughters-in-law, "Go back, each of you, to your mother's home. May the LORD show kindness to you, as you have shown to your dead and to me. {9} May the LORD grant that each of you will find rest in the home of another husband." Then she kissed them and they wept aloud {10} and said to her, "We will go back with you to your people." {11} But Naomi said, "Return home, my daughters. Why would you come with me? Am I going to have any more sons, who could become your husbands? {12} Return home, my daughters; I am too old to have another husband. Even if I thought there was still hope for me–even if I had a husband tonight and then gave birth to sons– {13} would you wait until they grew up? Would you remain unmarried for them? No, my daughters. It is more bitter for me than for you, because the Lord's hand has gone out against me!" {14} At this they wept again. Then Orpah kissed her mother-in-law good-by, but Ruth clung to her. {15} "Look," said Naomi, "your sister-in-law is going back to her people and her gods. Go back with her." {16} But Ruth replied, "Don't urge me to leave you or to turn back from you. Where you go I will go, and where you stay I will stay. Your people will be my people and your God my God. {17} Where you die I will die, and there I will be buried. May the LORD deal with me, be it ever so severely, if anything but death separates you and me." {18} When Naomi realized that Ruth was determined to go with her, she stopped urging her. {19} So the two women went on until they came to Bethlehem. When they arrived in Bethlehem, the whole town was stirred because of them, and the women exclaimed, "Can this be Naomi?"

SAMUEL IS DEDICATED TO THE LORD

1 Sam 1:21-28

When the man Elkanah went up with all his family to offer the annual sacrifice to the LORD and to fulfill his vow, {22} Hannah did not go. She said to her husband, "After the boy is weaned, I will take him and present him before the LORD, and he will live there always." {23} "Do what seems best to you," Elkanah her husband told her. "Stay here until you have weaned him; only may the LORD make good his word." So the woman stayed at home and nursed her son until she had weaned him. {24} After he was weaned, she took the boy with her, young as he was, along with a three-year-old bull, an ephah of flour and a skin of wine, and brought him to the house of the LORD at Shiloh. {25} When they had slaughtered the bull, they brought the boy to Eli, {26} and she said to him, "As surely as you live, my lord, I am the woman who stood here beside you praying to the LORD. {27} I prayed for this child, and the LORD has granted me what I asked of him. {28} So now I give him to the LORD. For his whole life he will be given over to the LORD." And he worshiped the LORD there.

1 Sam 2:19-21

Each year his mother made him a little robe and took it to him when she went up with her husband to offer the annual sacrifice. {20} Eli would bless Elkanah and his wife, saying, "May the LORD give you children by this woman to take the place of the one she prayed for and gave to the LORD." Then they would go home. {21} And the LORD was gracious to Hannah; she conceived and gave birth to three sons and two daughters. Meanwhile, the boy Samuel grew up in the presence of the LORD.

1 Sam 2:26

And the boy Samuel continued to grow in stature and in favor with the LORD and with men.

THE LORD CALLS SAMUEL

1 Sam 3:1-21

The boy Samuel ministered before the LORD under Eli. In those days the word of the LORD was rare; there were not many visions. {2} One night Eli, whose eyes were becoming so weak that he could barely see, was lying down in his usual place. {3} The lamp of God had not yet gone out, and Samuel was lying down in the temple of the LORD, where the ark of God was. {4} Then the LORD called Samuel. Samuel answered, "Here I am." {5} And he ran to Eli and said, "Here I am; you called me." But Eli said, "I did not call; go back and lie down." So he went and lay down. {6} Again the LORD called, "Samuel!" And Samuel got up and went to Eli and said, "Here I am; you called me." "My son," Eli said, "I did not call; go back and lie down." {7} Now Samuel did not yet know the LORD: The word of the LORD had not yet been revealed to him. {8} The LORD called Samuel a third time, and Samuel got up and went to Eli and said, "Here I am; you called me." Then Eli realized that the LORD was calling the boy. {9} So Eli told Samuel, "Go and lie down, and if he calls you, say, 'Speak, LORD, for your servant is listening.'" So Samuel went and lay down in his place. {10} The LORD came and stood there, calling as at the other times, "Samuel! Samuel!" Then Samuel said, "Speak, for your servant is listening." {11} And the LORD said to Samuel: "See, I am about to do something in Israel that will make the ears of everyone who hears of it tingle. {12} At that time I will carry out against Eli everything I spoke against his family—from beginning to end. {13} For I told him that I would judge his family forever because of the sin he knew about; his sons made themselves contemptible, and he failed to restrain them. {14} Therefore, I swore to the house of Eli, 'The guilt of Eli's house will never be atoned for by sacrifice or offering.'" {15} Samuel lay down until morning and then opened the doors of the house of the LORD. He was afraid to tell Eli the vision, {16} but Eli called him and said, "Samuel, my son." Samuel answered, "Here I am." {17} "What was it he said to you?" Eli asked. "Do not hide it from me. May God deal with you, be it ever so severely, if you hide from me anything he told you." {18} So Samuel told him everything, hiding nothing from him. Then Eli said, "He is the LORD; let him do what is good in his eyes." {19} The LORD was with Samuel as he grew up, and he let none of his words fall to the ground. {20} And all Israel from Dan to Beersheba recognized that Samuel was attested as a prophet of the LORD. {21} The LORD continued to appear at Shiloh, and there he revealed himself to Samuel through his word.

PEACE IN ISRAEL WHILE SAMUEL IS JUDGE

1 Sam 7:2-17

It was a long time, twenty years in all, that the ark remained at Kiriath Jearim, and all the people of Israel mourned and sought after the LORD. {3} And Samuel said to the whole house of Israel, "If you are returning to the LORD with all your hearts, then rid yourselves of the foreign gods and the Ashtoreths and commit yourselves to the LORD and serve him only, and he will deliver you out of the hand of the Philistines." {4} So the Israelites put away their Baals and Ashtoreths, and served the LORD only. {5} Then Samuel said, "Assemble all Israel at Mizpah and I will intercede with the LORD for you." {6} When they had assembled at Mizpah, they drew water and poured it out before the LORD. On that day they fasted and there they confessed, "We have sinned against the LORD." And Samuel was leader of Israel at Mizpah. {7} When the Philistines heard that Israel had assembled at Mizpah, the rulers of the Philistines came up to attack them. And when the Israelites heard of it, they were afraid because of the Philistines. {8} They said to Samuel, "Do not stop crying out to the LORD our God for us, that he may rescue us from the hand of the Philistines." {9} Then Samuel took a suckling lamb and offered it up as a whole burnt offering to the LORD. He cried out to the LORD on Israel's behalf, and the LORD answered him. {10} While Samuel was sacrificing the burnt offering, the Philistines drew near to engage Israel in battle. But that day the LORD thundered with loud thunder against the Philistines and threw them into such a panic that they were routed before the Israelites. {11} The men of Israel rushed out of Mizpah and pursued the Philistines, slaughtering them along the way to a point below Beth Car. {12} Then Samuel took a stone and set it up between Mizpah and Shen. He named it Ebenezer, saying, "Thus far has the LORD helped us." {13} So the Philistines were subdued and did not invade Israelite territory again. Throughout Samuel's lifetime, the hand of the LORD was against the Philistines. {14} The towns from Ekron to Gath that the Philistines had captured from Israel were restored to her, and Israel delivered the neighboring territory from the power of the Philistines. And there was peace between Israel and the Amorites. {15} Samuel continued as judge over Israel all the days of his life. {16} From year to year he went on a circuit from Bethel to Gilgal to Mizpah, judging Israel in all those places. {17} But he always went back to Ramah, where his home was, and there he also judged Israel. And he built an altar there to the LORD.

50

SAMUEL ANOINTS DAVID AS THE NEW KING
YET DAVID SERVES SAUL

1 Sam 16:5b-23

Then he consecrated Jesse and his sons and invited them to the sacrifice. {6} When they arrived, Samuel saw Eliab and thought, "Surely the Lord's anointed stands here before the LORD." {7} But the LORD said to Samuel, "Do not consider his appearance or his height, for I have rejected him. The LORD does not look at the things man looks at. Man looks at the outward appearance, but the LORD looks at the heart." {8} Then Jesse called Abinadab and had him pass in front of Samuel. But Samuel said, "The LORD has not chosen this one either." {9} Jesse then had Shammah pass by, but Samuel said, "Nor has the LORD chosen this one." {10} Jesse had seven of his sons pass before Samuel, but Samuel said to him, "The LORD has not chosen these." {11} So he asked Jesse, "Are these all the sons you have?" "There is still the youngest," Jesse answered, "but he is tending the sheep." Samuel said, "Send for him; we will not sit down until he arrives." {12} So he sent and had him brought in. He was ruddy, with a fine appearance and handsome features. Then the LORD said, "Rise and anoint him; he is the one." {13} So Samuel took the horn of oil and anointed him in the presence of his brothers, and from that day on the Spirit of the LORD came upon David in power. Samuel then went to Ramah. {14} Now the Spirit of the LORD had departed from Saul, and an evil spirit from the LORD tormented him. {15} Saul's attendants said to him, "See, an evil spirit from God is tormenting you. {16} Let our lord command his servants here to search for someone who can play the harp. He will play when the evil spirit from God comes upon you, and you will feel better." {17} So Saul said to his attendants, "Find someone who plays well and bring him to me." {18} One of the servants answered, "I have seen a son of Jesse of Bethlehem who knows how to play the harp. He is a brave man and a warrior. He speaks well and is a fine-looking man. And the LORD is with him." {19} Then Saul sent messengers to Jesse and said, "Send me your son David, who is with the sheep." {20} So Jesse took a donkey loaded with bread, a skin of wine and a young goat and sent them with his son David to Saul. {21} David came to Saul and entered his service. Saul liked him very much, and David became one of his armor-bearers. {22} Then Saul sent word to Jesse, saying, "Allow David to remain in my service, for I am pleased with him." {23} Whenever the spirit from God came upon Saul, David would take his harp and play. Then relief would come to Saul; he would feel better, and the evil spirit would leave him.

DAVID AND JONATHAN

1 Sam 20:24-42a

So David hid in the field, and when the New Moon festival came, the king sat down to eat. {25} He sat in his customary place by the wall, opposite Jonathan, and Abner sat next to Saul, but David's place was empty. {26} Saul said nothing that day, for he thought, "Something must have happened to David to make him ceremonially unclean–surely he is unclean." {27} But the next day, the second day of the month, David's place was empty again. Then Saul said to his son Jonathan, "Why hasn't the son of Jesse come to the meal, either yesterday or today?" {28} Jonathan answered, "David earnestly asked me for permission to go to Bethlehem. {29} He said, 'Let me go, because our family is observing a sacrifice in the town and my brother has ordered me to be there. If I have found favor in your eyes, let me get away to see my brothers.' That is why he has not come to the king's table." {30} Saul's anger flared up at Jonathan and he said to him, "You son of a perverse and rebellious woman! Don't I know that you have sided with the son of Jesse to your own shame and to the shame of the mother who bore you? {31} As long as the son of Jesse lives on this earth, neither you nor your kingdom will be established. Now send and bring him to me, for he must die!" {32} "Why should he be put to death? What has he done?" Jonathan asked his father. {33} But Saul hurled his spear at him to kill him. Then Jonathan knew that his father intended to kill David. {34} Jonathan got up from the table in fierce anger; on that second day of the month he did not eat, because he was grieved at his father's shameful treatment of David. {35} In the morning Jonathan went out to the field for his meeting with David. He had a small boy with him, {36} and he said to the boy, "Run and find the arrows I shoot." As the boy ran, he shot an arrow beyond him. {37} When the boy came to the place where Jonathan's arrow had fallen, Jonathan called out after him, "Isn't the arrow beyond you?" {38} Then he shouted, "Hurry! Go quickly! Don't stop!" The boy picked up the arrow and returned to his master. {39} (The boy knew nothing of all this; only Jonathan and David knew.) {40} Then Jonathan gave his weapons to the boy and said, "Go, carry them back to town." {41} After the boy had gone, David got up from the south side <of the stone> and bowed down before Jonathan three times, with his face to the ground. Then they kissed each other and wept together–but David wept the most. {42} Jonathan said to David, "Go in peace, for we have sworn friendship with each other in the name of the LORD, saying, 'The LORD is witness between you and me, and between your descendants and my descendants forever.'"

DAVID BECOMES KING OF ISRAEL

2 Sam 4:5-5:5

Now Recab and Baanah, the sons of Rimmon the Beerothite, set out for the house of Ish-Bosheth, and they arrived there in the heat of the day while he was taking his noonday rest. {6} They went into the inner part of the house as if to get some wheat, and they stabbed him in the stomach. Then Recab and his brother Baanah slipped away. {7} They had gone into the house while he was lying on the bed in his bedroom. After they stabbed and killed him, they cut off his head. Taking it with them, they traveled all night by way of the Arabah. {8} They brought the head of Ish-Bosheth to David at Hebron and said to the king, "Here is the head of Ish-Bosheth son of Saul, your enemy, who tried to take your life. This day the LORD has avenged my lord the king against Saul and his offspring." {9} David answered Recab and his brother Baanah, the sons of Rimmon the Beerothite, "As surely as the LORD lives, who has delivered me out of all trouble, {10} when a man told me, 'Saul is dead,' and thought he was bringing good news, I seized him and put him to death in Ziklag. That was the reward I gave him for his news! {11} How much more—when wicked men have killed an innocent man in his own house and on his own bed—should I not now demand his blood from your hand and rid the earth of you!" {12} So David gave an order to his men, and they killed them. They cut off their hands and feet and hung the bodies by the pool in Hebron. But they took the head of Ish-Bosheth and buried it in Abner's tomb at Hebron. {5:1} All the tribes of Israel came to David at Hebron and said, "We are your own flesh and blood. {2} In the past, while Saul was king over us, you were the one who led Israel on their military campaigns. And the LORD said to you, 'You will shepherd my people Israel, and you will become their ruler.'" {3} When all the elders of Israel had come to King David at Hebron, the king made a compact with them at Hebron before the LORD, and they anointed David king over Israel. {4} David was thirty years old when he became king, and he reigned forty years. {5} In Hebron he reigned over Judah seven years and six months, and in Jerusalem he reigned over all Israel and Judah thirty-three years.

DAVID SHOWS KINDNESS TO JONATHAN'S SON

2 Sam 9:1-13

David asked, "Is there anyone still left of the house of Saul to whom I can show kindness for Jonathan's sake?" {2} Now there was a servant of Saul's household named Ziba. They called him to appear before David, and the king said to him, "Are you Ziba?" "Your servant," he replied. {3} The king asked, "Is there no one still left of the house of Saul to whom I can show God's kindness?" Ziba answered the king, "There is still a son of Jonathan; he is crippled in both feet." {4} "Where is he?" the king asked. Ziba answered, "He is at the house of Makir son of Ammiel in Lo Debar." {5} So King David had him brought from Lo Debar, from the house of Makir son of Ammiel. {6} When Mephibosheth son of Jonathan, the son of Saul, came to David, he bowed down to pay him honor. David said, "Mephibosheth!" "Your servant," he replied. {7} "Don't be afraid," David said to him, "for I will surely show you kindness for the sake of your father Jonathan. I will restore to you all the land that belonged to your grandfather Saul, and you will always eat at my table." {8} Mephibosheth bowed down and said, "What is your servant, that you should notice a dead dog like me?" {9} Then the king summoned Ziba, Saul's servant, and said to him, "I have given your master's grandson everything that belonged to Saul and his family. {10} You and your sons and your servants are to farm the land for him and bring in the crops, so that your master's grandson may be provided for. And Mephibosheth, grandson of your master, will always eat at my table." (Now Ziba had fifteen sons and twenty servants.) {11} Then Ziba said to the king, "Your servant will do whatever my lord the king commands his servant to do." So Mephibosheth ate at David's table like one of the king's sons. {12} Mephibosheth had a young son named Mica, and all the members of Ziba's household were servants of Mephibosheth. {13} And Mephibosheth lived in Jerusalem, because he always ate at the king's table, and he was crippled in both feet.

DAVID REPENTS

2 Sam 12:1-18a

The LORD sent Nathan to David. When he came to him, he said, "There were two men in a certain town, one rich and the other poor. {2} The rich man had a very large number of sheep and cattle, {3} but the poor man had nothing except one little ewe lamb he had bought. He raised it, and it grew up with him and his children. It shared his food, drank from his cup and even slept in his arms. It was like a daughter to him. {4} "Now a traveler came to the rich man, but the rich man refrained from taking one of his own sheep or cattle to prepare a meal for the traveler who had come to him. Instead, he took the ewe lamb that belonged to the poor man and prepared it for the one who had come to him." {5} David burned with anger against the man and said to Nathan, "As surely as the LORD lives, the man who did this deserves to die! {6} He must pay for that lamb four times over, because he did such a thing and had no pity." {7} Then Nathan said to David, "You are the man! This is what the LORD, the God of Israel, says: 'I anointed you king over Israel, and I delivered you from the hand of Saul. {8} I gave your master's house to you, and your master's wives into your arms. I gave you the house of Israel and Judah. And if all this had been too little, I would have given you even more. {9} Why did you despise the word of the LORD by doing what is evil in his eyes? You struck down Uriah the Hittite with the sword and took his wife to be your own. You killed him with the sword of the Ammonites. {10} Now, therefore, the sword will never depart from your house, because you despised me and took the wife of Uriah the Hittite to be your own.' {11} "This is what the LORD says: 'Out of your own household I am going to bring calamity upon you. Before your very eyes I will take your wives and give them to one who is close to you, and he will lie with your wives in broad daylight. {12} You did it in secret, but I will do this thing in broad daylight before all Israel.'" {13} Then David said to Nathan, "I have sinned against the LORD." Nathan replied, "The LORD has taken away your sin. You are not going to die. {14} But because by doing this you have made the enemies of the LORD show utter contempt, the son born to you will die." {15} After Nathan had gone home, the LORD struck the child that Uriah's wife had borne to David, and he became ill. {16} David pleaded with God for the child. He fasted and went into his house and spent the nights lying on the ground. {17} The elders of his household stood beside him to get him up from the ground, but he refused, and he would not eat any food with them. {18} On the seventh day the child died.

DAVID'S FINAL INSTRUCTIONS TO SOLOMON

1 Ki 2:1-11

When the time drew near for David to die, he gave a charge to Solomon his son. {2} "I am about to go the way of all the earth," he said. "So be strong, show yourself a man, {3} and observe what the LORD your God requires: Walk in his ways, and keep his decrees and commands, his laws and requirements, as written in the Law of Moses, so that you may prosper in all you do and wherever you go, {4} and that the LORD may keep his promise to me: 'If your descendants watch how they live, and if they walk faithfully before me with all their heart and soul, you will never fail to have a man on the throne of Israel.' {5} "Now you yourself know what Joab son of Zeruiah did to me—what he did to the two commanders of Israel's armies, Abner son of Ner and Amasa son of Jether. He killed them, shedding their blood in peacetime as if in battle, and with that blood stained the belt around his waist and the sandals on his feet. {6} Deal with him according to your wisdom, but do not let his gray head go down to the grave in peace. {7} "But show kindness to the sons of Barzillai of Gilead and let them be among those who eat at your table. They stood by me when I fled from your brother Absalom. {8} "And remember, you have with you Shimei son of Gera, the Benjamite from Bahurim, who called down bitter curses on me the day I went to Mahanaim. When he came down to meet me at the Jordan, I swore to him by the LORD: 'I will not put you to death by the sword.' {9} But now, do not consider him innocent. You are a man of wisdom; you will know what to do to him. Bring his gray head down to the grave in blood." {10} Then David rested with his fathers and was buried in the City of David. {11} He had reigned forty years over Israel—seven years in Hebron and thirty-three in Jerusalem.

SOLOMON THE WISE

1 Ki 3:11-28

So God said to him, "Since you have asked for this and not for long life or wealth for yourself, nor have asked for the death of your enemies but for discernment in administering justice, {12} I will do what you have asked. I will give you a wise and discerning heart, so that there will never have been anyone like you, nor will there ever be. {13} Moreover, I will give you what you have not asked for–both riches and honor–so that in your lifetime you will have no equal among kings. {14} And if you walk in my ways and obey my statutes and commands as David your father did, I will give you a long life." {15} Then Solomon awoke–and he realized it had been a dream. He returned to Jerusalem, stood before the ark of the Lord's covenant and sacrificed burnt offerings and fellowship offerings. Then he gave a feast for all his court. {16} Now two prostitutes came to the king and stood before him. {17} One of them said, "My lord, this woman and I live in the same house. I had a baby while she was there with me. {18} The third day after my child was born, this woman also had a baby. We were alone; there was no one in the house but the two of us. {19} "During the night this woman's son died because she lay on him. {20} So she got up in the middle of the night and took my son from my side while I your servant was asleep. She put him by her breast and put her dead son by my breast. {21} The next morning, I got up to nurse my son–and he was dead! But when I looked at him closely in the morning light, I saw that it wasn't the son I had borne." {22} The other woman said, "No! The living one is my son; the dead one is yours." But the first one insisted, "No! The dead one is yours; the living one is mine." And so they argued before the king. {23} The king said, "This one says, 'My son is alive and your son is dead,' while that one says, 'No! Your son is dead and mine is alive.'" {24} Then the king said, "Bring me a sword." So they brought a sword for the king. {25} He then gave an order: "Cut the living child in two and give half to one and half to the other." {26} The woman whose son was alive was filled with compassion for her son and said to the king, "Please, my lord, give her the living baby! Don't kill him!" But the other said, "Neither I nor you shall have him. Cut him in two!" {27} Then the king gave his ruling: "Give the living baby to the first woman. Do not kill him; she is his mother." {28} When all Israel heard the verdict the king had given, they held the king in awe, because they saw that he had wisdom from God to administer justice.

GOD'S PROMISE TO SOLOMON

1 Ki 9:1-14

When Solomon had finished building the temple of the LORD and the royal palace, and had achieved all he had desired to do, {2} the LORD appeared to him a second time, as he had appeared to him at Gibeon. {3} The LORD said to him: "I have heard the prayer and plea you have made before me; I have consecrated this temple, which you have built, by putting my Name there forever. My eyes and my heart will always be there. {4} "As for you, if you walk before me in integrity of heart and uprightness, as David your father did, and do all I command and observe my decrees and laws, {5} I will establish your royal throne over Israel forever, as I promised David your father when I said, 'You shall never fail to have a man on the throne of Israel.' {6} "But if you or your sons turn away from me and do not observe the commands and decrees I have given you and go off to serve other gods and worship them, {7} then I will cut off Israel from the land I have given them and will reject this temple I have consecrated for my Name. Israel will then become a byword and an object of ridicule among all peoples. {8} And though this temple is now imposing, all who pass by will be appalled and will scoff and say, 'Why has the LORD done such a thing to this land and to this temple?' {9} People will answer, 'Because they have forsaken the LORD their God, who brought their fathers out of Egypt, and have embraced other gods, worshiping and serving them–that is why the LORD brought all this disaster on them.'" {10} At the end of twenty years, during which Solomon built these two buildings–the temple of the LORD and the royal palace– {11} King Solomon gave twenty towns in Galilee to Hiram king of Tyre, because Hiram had supplied him with all the cedar and pine and gold he wanted. {12} But when Hiram went from Tyre to see the towns that Solomon had given him, he was not pleased with them. {13} "What kind of towns are these you have given me, my brother?" he asked. And he called them the Land of Cabul, a name they have to this day. {14} Now Hiram had sent to the king 120 talents of gold.

1 Ki 9:24-25

After Pharaoh's daughter had come up from the City of David to the palace Solomon had built for her, he constructed the supporting terraces. {25} Three times a year Solomon sacrificed burnt offerings and fellowship offerings on the altar he had built for the LORD, burning incense before the LORD along with them, and so fulfilled the temple obligations.

SOLOMON'S MANY WIVES INCREASE HIS DIFFICULTIES

1 Ki 11:1-18

King Solomon, however, loved many foreign women besides Pharaoh's daughter—Moabites, Ammonites, Edomites, Sidonians and Hittites. {2} They were from nations about which the LORD had told the Israelites, "You must not intermarry with them, because they will surely turn your hearts after their gods." Nevertheless, Solomon held fast to them in love. {3} He had seven hundred wives of royal birth and three hundred concubines, and his wives led him astray. {4} As Solomon grew old, his wives turned his heart after other gods, and his heart was not fully devoted to the LORD his God, as the heart of David his father had been. {5} He followed Ashtoreth the goddess of the Sidonians, and Molech the detestable god of the Ammonites. {6} So Solomon did evil in the eyes of the LORD; he did not follow the LORD completely, as David his father had done. {7} On a hill east of Jerusalem, Solomon built a high place for Chemosh the detestable god of Moab, and for Molech the detestable god of the Ammonites. {8} He did the same for all his foreign wives, who burned incense and offered sacrifices to their gods. {9} The LORD became angry with Solomon because his heart had turned away from the LORD, the God of Israel, who had appeared to him twice. {10} Although he had forbidden Solomon to follow other gods, Solomon did not keep the Lord's command. {11} So the LORD said to Solomon, "Since this is your attitude and you have not kept my covenant and my decrees, which I commanded you, I will most certainly tear the kingdom away from you and give it to one of your subordinates. {12} Nevertheless, for the sake of David your father, I will not do it during your lifetime. I will tear it out of the hand of your son. {13} Yet I will not tear the whole kingdom from him, but will give him one tribe for the sake of David my servant and for the sake of Jerusalem, which I have chosen." {14} Then the LORD raised up against Solomon an adversary, Hadad the Edomite, from the royal line of Edom. {15} Earlier when David was fighting with Edom, Joab the commander of the army, who had gone up to bury the dead, had struck down all the men in Edom. {16} Joab and all the Israelites stayed there for six months, until they had destroyed all the men in Edom. {17} But Hadad, still only a boy, fled to Egypt with some Edomite officials who had served his father. {18} They set out from Midian and went to Paran. Then taking men from Paran with them, they went to Egypt, to Pharaoh king of Egypt, who gave Hadad a house and land and provided him with food.

ELIJAH IS FED BY RAVENS; A WIDOW HAS FLOUR AND OIL

1 Ki 17:5-24

So he did what the LORD had told him. He went to the Kerith Ravine, east of the Jordan, and stayed there. {6} The ravens brought him bread and meat in the morning and bread and meat in the evening, and he drank from the brook. {7} Some time later the brook dried up because there had been no rain in the land. {8} Then the word of the LORD came to him: {9} "Go at once to Zarephath of Sidon and stay there. I have commanded a widow in that place to supply you with food." {10} So he went to Zarephath. When he came to the town gate, a widow was there gathering sticks. He called to her and asked, "Would you bring me a little water in a jar so I may have a drink?" {11} As she was going to get it, he called, "And bring me, please, a piece of bread." {12} "As surely as the LORD your God lives," she replied, "I don't have any bread—only a handful of flour in a jar and a little oil in a jug. I am gathering a few sticks to take home and make a meal for myself and my son, that we may eat it—and die." {13} Elijah said to her, "Don't be afraid. Go home and do as you have said. But first make a small cake of bread for me from what you have and bring it to me, and then make something for yourself and your son. {14} For this is what the LORD, the God of Israel, says: 'The jar of flour will not be used up and the jug of oil will not run dry until the day the LORD gives rain on the land.'" {15} She went away and did as Elijah had told her. So there was food every day for Elijah and for the woman and her family. {16} For the jar of flour was not used up and the jug of oil did not run dry, in keeping with the word of the LORD spoken by Elijah. {17} Some time later the son of the woman who owned the house became ill. He grew worse and worse, and finally stopped breathing. {18} She said to Elijah, "What do you have against me, man of God? Did you come to remind me of my sin and kill my son?" {19} "Give me your son," Elijah replied. He took him from her arms, carried him to the upper room where he was staying, and laid him on his bed. {20} Then he cried out to the LORD, "O LORD my God, have you brought tragedy also upon this widow I am staying with, by causing her son to die?" {21} Then he stretched himself out on the boy three times and cried to the LORD, "O LORD my God, let this boy's life return to him!" {22} The LORD heard Elijah's cry, and the boy's life returned to him, and he lived. {23} Elijah picked up the child and carried him down from the room into the house. He gave him to his mother and said, "Look, your son is alive!" {24} Then the woman said to Elijah, "Now I know that you are a man of God and that the word of the LORD from your mouth is the truth."

ELIJAH SACRIFICES TO GOD AND ENDS THE DROUGHT

1 Ki 18:30-46

Then Elijah said to all the people, "Come here to me." They came to him, and he repaired the altar of the LORD, which was in ruins. {31} Elijah took twelve stones, one for each of the tribes descended from Jacob, to whom the word of the LORD had come, saying, "Your name shall be Israel." {32} With the stones he built an altar in the name of the LORD, and he dug a trench around it large enough to hold two seahs of seed. {33} He arranged the wood, cut the bull into pieces and laid it on the wood. Then he said to them, "Fill four large jars with water and pour it on the offering and on the wood." {34} "Do it again," he said, and they did it again. "Do it a third time," he ordered, and they did it the third time. {35} The water ran down around the altar and even filled the trench. {36} At the time of sacrifice, the prophet Elijah stepped forward and prayed: "O LORD, God of Abraham, Isaac and Israel, let it be known today that you are God in Israel and that I am your servant and have done all these things at your command. {37} Answer me, O LORD, answer me, so these people will know that you, O LORD, are God, and that you are turning their hearts back again." {38} Then the fire of the LORD fell and burned up the sacrifice, the wood, the stones and the soil, and also licked up the water in the trench. {39} When all the people saw this, they fell prostrate and cried, "The LORD–he is God! The LORD–he is God!" {40} Then Elijah commanded them, "Seize the prophets of Baal. Don't let anyone get away!" They seized them, and Elijah had them brought down to the Kishon Valley and slaughtered there. {41} And Elijah said to Ahab, "Go, eat and drink, for there is the sound of a heavy rain." {42} So Ahab went off to eat and drink, but Elijah climbed to the top of Carmel, bent down to the ground and put his face between his knees. {43} "Go and look toward the sea," he told his servant. And he went up and looked. "There is nothing there," he said. Seven times Elijah said, "Go back." {44} The seventh time the servant reported, "A cloud as small as a man's hand is rising from the sea." So Elijah said, "Go and tell Ahab, 'Hitch up your chariot and go down before the rain stops you.'" {45} Meanwhile, the sky grew black with clouds, the wind rose, a heavy rain came on and Ahab rode off to Jezreel. {46} The power of the LORD came upon Elijah and, tucking his cloak into his belt, he ran ahead of Ahab all the way to Jezreel.

ELIJAH FLEES AND CALLS ELISHA

1 Ki 19:7-21

The angel of the LORD came back a second time and touched him and said, "Get up and eat, for the journey is too much for you." {8} So he got up and ate and drank. Strengthened by that food, he traveled forty days and forty nights until he reached Horeb, the mountain of God. {9} There he went into a cave and spent the night. And the word of the LORD came to him: "What are you doing here, Elijah?" {10} He replied, "I have been very zealous for the LORD God Almighty. The Israelites have rejected your covenant, broken down your altars, and put your prophets to death with the sword. I am the only one left, and now they are trying to kill me too." {11} The LORD said, "Go out and stand on the mountain in the presence of the LORD, for the LORD is about to pass by." Then a great and powerful wind tore the mountains apart and shattered the rocks before the LORD, but the LORD was not in the wind. After the wind there was an earthquake, but the LORD was not in the earthquake. {12} After the earthquake came a fire, but the LORD was not in the fire. And after the fire came a gentle whisper. {13} When Elijah heard it, he pulled his cloak over his face and went out and stood at the mouth of the cave. Then a voice said to him, "What are you doing here, Elijah?" {14} He replied, "I have been very zealous for the LORD God Almighty. The Israelites have rejected your covenant, broken down your altars, and put your prophets to death with the sword. I am the only one left, and now they are trying to kill me too." {15} The LORD said to him, "Go back the way you came, and go to the Desert of Damascus. When you get there, anoint Hazael king over Aram. {16} Also, anoint Jehu son of Nimshi king over Israel, and anoint Elisha son of Shaphat from Abel Meholah to succeed you as prophet. {17} Jehu will put to death any who escape the sword of Hazael, and Elisha will put to death any who escape the sword of Jehu. {18} Yet I reserve seven thousand in Israel—all whose knees have not bowed down to Baal and all whose mouths have not kissed him." {19} So Elijah went from there and found Elisha son of Shaphat. He was plowing with twelve yoke of oxen, and he himself was driving the twelfth pair. Elijah went up to him and threw his cloak around him. {20} Elisha then left his oxen and ran after Elijah. "Let me kiss my father and mother good-by," he said, "and then I will come with you." "Go back," Elijah replied. "What have I done to you?" {21} So Elisha left him and went back. He took his yoke of oxen and slaughtered them. He burned the plowing equipment to cook the meat and gave it to the people, and they ate. Then he set out to follow Elijah and became his attendant.

THE ARK BROUGHT BACK TO JERUSALEM

1 Chr 13:7-14

They moved the ark of God from Abinadab's house on a new cart, with Uzzah and Ahio guiding it. {8} David and all the Israelites were celebrating with all their might before God, with songs and with harps, lyres, tambourines, cymbals and trumpets. {9} When they came to the threshing floor of Kidon, Uzzah reached out his hand to steady the ark, because the oxen stumbled. {10} The Lord's anger burned against Uzzah, and he struck him down because he had put his hand on the ark. So he died there before God. {11} Then David was angry because the Lord's wrath had broken out against Uzzah, and to this day that place is called Perez Uzzah. {12} David was afraid of God that day and asked, "How can I ever bring the ark of God to me?" {13} He did not take the ark to be with him in the City of David. Instead, he took it aside to the house of Obed-Edom the Gittite. {14} The ark of God remained with the family of Obed-Edom in his house for three months, and the LORD blessed his household and everything he had.

1 Chr 15:1-3

After David had constructed buildings for himself in the City of David, he prepared a place for the ark of God and pitched a tent for it. {2} Then David said, "No one but the Levites may carry the ark of God, because the LORD chose them to carry the ark of the LORD and to minister before him forever." {3} David assembled all Israel in Jerusalem to bring up the ark of the LORD to the place he had prepared for it.

1 Chr 15:25-16:1a

So David and the elders of Israel and the commanders of units of a thousand went to bring up the ark of the covenant of the LORD from the house of Obed-Edom, with rejoicing. {26} Because God had helped the Levites who were carrying the ark of the covenant of the LORD, seven bulls and seven rams were sacrificed. {27} Now David was clothed in a robe of fine linen, as were all the Levites who were carrying the ark, and as were the singers, and Kenaniah, who was in charge of the singing of the choirs. David also wore a linen ephod. {28} So all Israel brought up the ark of the covenant of the LORD with shouts, with the sounding of rams' horns and trumpets, and of cymbals, and the playing of lyres and harps. {29} As the ark of the covenant of the LORD was entering the City of David, Michal daughter of Saul watched from a window. And when she saw King David dancing and celebrating, she despised him in her heart. {16:1} They brought the ark of God and set it inside the tent that David had pitched for it....

DAVID'S SONG OF PRAISE

1 Chr 16:17-29

He confirmed it to Jacob as a decree, to Israel as an everlasting covenant: {18} "To you I will give the land of Canaan as the portion you will inherit." {19} When they were but few in number, few indeed, and strangers in it, {20} they wandered from nation to nation, from one kingdom to another. {21} He allowed no man to oppress them; for their sake he rebuked kings: {22} "Do not touch my anointed ones; do my prophets no harm." {23} Sing to the LORD, all the earth; proclaim his salvation day after day. {24} Declare his glory among the nations, his marvelous deeds among all peoples. {25} For great is the LORD and most worthy of praise; he is to be feared above all gods. {26} For all the gods of the nations are idols, but the LORD made the heavens. {27} Splendor and majesty are before him; strength and joy in his dwelling place. {28} Ascribe to the LORD, O families of nations, ascribe to the LORD glory and strength, {29} ascribe to the LORD the glory due his name. Bring an offering and come before him; worship the LORD in the splendor of his holiness.

1 Chr 16:34-36

Give thanks to the LORD, for he is good; his love endures forever. {35} Cry out, "Save us, O God our Savior; gather us and deliver us from the nations, that we may give thanks to your holy name, that we may glory in your praise." {36} Praise be to the LORD, the God of Israel, from everlasting to everlasting. Then all the people said "Amen" and "Praise the LORD."

GOD PROMISES BLESSINGS TO DAVID

1 Chr 17:1-19

After David was settled in his palace, he said to Nathan the prophet, "Here I am, living in a palace of cedar, while the ark of the covenant of the LORD is under a tent." {2} Nathan replied to David, "Whatever you have in mind, do it, for God is with you." {3} That night the word of God came to Nathan, saying: {4} "Go and tell my servant David, 'This is what the LORD says: You are not the one to build me a house to dwell in. {5} I have not dwelt in a house from the day I brought Israel up out of Egypt to this day. I have moved from one tent site to another, from one dwelling place to another. {6} Wherever I have moved with all the Israelites, did I ever say to any of their leaders whom I commanded to shepherd my people, "Why have you not built me a house of cedar?" ' {7} "Now then, tell my servant David, 'This is what the LORD Almighty says: I took you from the pasture and from following the flock, to be ruler over my people Israel. {8} I have been with you wherever you have gone, and I have cut off all your enemies from before you. Now I will make your name like the names of the greatest men of the earth. {9} And I will provide a place for my people Israel and will plant them so that they can have a home of their own and no longer be disturbed. Wicked people will not oppress them anymore, as they did at the beginning {10} and have done ever since the time I appointed leaders over my people Israel. I will also subdue all your enemies. "'I declare to you that the LORD will build a house for you: {11} When your days are over and you go to be with your fathers, I will raise up your offspring to succeed you, one of your own sons, and I will establish his kingdom. {12} He is the one who will build a house for me, and I will establish his throne forever. {13} I will be his father, and he will be my son. I will never take my love away from him, as I took it away from your predecessor. {14} I will set him over my house and my kingdom forever; his throne will be established forever.'" {15} Nathan reported to David all the words of this entire revelation. {16} Then King David went in and sat before the LORD, and he said: "Who am I, O LORD God, and what is my family, that you have brought me this far? {17} And as if this were not enough in your sight, O God, you have spoken about the future of the house of your servant. You have looked on me as though I were the most exalted of men, O LORD God. {18} "What more can David say to you for honoring your servant? For you know your servant, {19} O LORD. For the sake of your servant and according to your will, you have done this great thing and made known all these great promises.

GOD IS ANGRY BECAUSE DAVID COUNTS HIS TROOPS

1 Chr 21:5-18

Joab reported the number of the fighting men to David: In all Israel there were one million one hundred thousand men who could handle a sword, including four hundred and seventy thousand in Judah. {6} But Joab did not include Levi and Benjamin in the numbering, because the king's command was repulsive to him. {7} This command was also evil in the sight of God; so he punished Israel. {8} Then David said to God, "I have sinned greatly by doing this. Now, I beg you, take away the guilt of your servant. I have done a very foolish thing." {9} The LORD said to Gad, David's seer, {10} "Go and tell David, 'This is what the LORD says: I am giving you three options. Choose one of them for me to carry out against you.'" {11} So Gad went to David and said to him, "This is what the LORD says: 'Take your choice: {12} three years of famine, three months of being swept away before your enemies, with their swords overtaking you, or three days of the sword of the LORD–days of plague in the land, with the angel of the LORD ravaging every part of Israel.' Now then, decide how I should answer the one who sent me." {13} David said to Gad, "I am in deep distress. Let me fall into the hands of the LORD, for his mercy is very great; but do not let me fall into the hands of men." {14} So the LORD sent a plague on Israel, and seventy thousand men of Israel fell dead. {15} And God sent an angel to destroy Jerusalem. But as the angel was doing so, the LORD saw it and was grieved because of the calamity and said to the angel who was destroying the people, "Enough! Withdraw your hand." The angel of the LORD was then standing at the threshing floor of Araunah the Jebusite. {16} David looked up and saw the angel of the LORD standing between heaven and earth, with a drawn sword in his hand extended over Jerusalem. Then David and the elders, clothed in sackcloth, fell facedown. {17} David said to God, "Was it not I who ordered the fighting men to be counted? I am the one who has sinned and done wrong. These are but sheep. What have they done? O LORD my God, let your hand fall upon me and my family, but do not let this plague remain on your people." {18} Then the angel of the LORD ordered Gad to tell David to go up and build an altar to the LORD on the threshing floor of Araunah the Jebusite.

1 Chr 21:26-27

David built an altar to the LORD there and sacrificed burnt offerings and fellowship offerings. He called on the LORD, and the LORD answered him with fire from heaven on the altar of burnt offering. {27} Then the LORD spoke to the angel, and he put his sword back into its sheath.

DAVID PREPARES TO BUILD THE TEMPLE

1 Chr 22:1-17

Then David said, "The house of the LORD God is to be here, and also the altar of burnt offering for Israel." {2} So David gave orders to assemble the aliens living in Israel, and from among them he appointed stonecutters to prepare dressed stone for building the house of God. {3} He provided a large amount of iron to make nails for the doors of the gateways and for the fittings, and more bronze than could be weighed. {4} He also provided more cedar logs than could be counted, for the Sidonians and Tyrians had brought large numbers of them to David. {5} David said, "My son Solomon is young and inexperienced, and the house to be built for the LORD should be of great magnificence and fame and splendor in the sight of all the nations. Therefore I will make preparations for it." So David made extensive preparations before his death. {6} Then he called for his son Solomon and charged him to build a house for the LORD, the God of Israel. {7} David said to Solomon: "My son, I had it in my heart to build a house for the Name of the LORD my God. {8} But this word of the LORD came to me: 'You have shed much blood and have fought many wars. You are not to build a house for my Name, because you have shed much blood on the earth in my sight. {9} But you will have a son who will be a man of peace and rest, and I will give him rest from all his enemies on every side. His name will be Solomon, and I will grant Israel peace and quiet during his reign. {10} He is the one who will build a house for my Name. He will be my son, and I will be his father. And I will establish the throne of his kingdom over Israel forever.' {11} "Now, my son, the LORD be with you, and may you have success and build the house of the LORD your God, as he said you would. {12} May the LORD give you discretion and understanding when he puts you in command over Israel, so that you may keep the law of the LORD your God. {13} Then you will have success if you are careful to observe the decrees and laws that the LORD gave Moses for Israel. Be strong and courageous. Do not be afraid or discouraged. {14} "I have taken great pains to provide for the temple of the LORD a hundred thousand talents of gold, a million talents of silver, quantities of bronze and iron too great to be weighed, and wood and stone. And you may add to them. {15} You have many workmen: stonecutters, masons and carpenters, as well as men skilled in every kind of work {16} in gold and silver, bronze and iron—craftsmen beyond number. Now begin the work, and the LORD be with you." {17} Then David ordered all the leaders of Israel to help his son Solomon.

THE PEOPLE BRING GIFTS FOR THE TEMPLE

1 Chr 29:6-20

Then the leaders of families, the officers of the tribes of Israel, the commanders of thousands and commanders of hundreds, and the officials in charge of the king's work gave willingly. {7} They gave toward the work on the temple of God five thousand talents and ten thousand darics of gold, ten thousand talents of silver, eighteen thousand talents of bronze and a hundred thousand talents of iron. {8} Any who had precious stones gave them to the treasury of the temple of the LORD in the custody of Jehiel the Gershonite. {9} The people rejoiced at the willing response of their leaders, for they had given freely and wholeheartedly to the LORD. David the king also rejoiced greatly. {10} David praised the LORD in the presence of the whole assembly, saying, "Praise be to you, O LORD, God of our father Israel, from everlasting to everlasting. {11} Yours, O LORD, is the greatness and the power and the glory and the majesty and the splendor, for everything in heaven and earth is yours. Yours, O LORD, is the kingdom; you are exalted as head over all. {12} Wealth and honor come from you; you are the ruler of all things. In your hands are strength and power to exalt and give strength to all. {13} Now, our God, we give you thanks, and praise your glorious name. {14} "But who am I, and who are my people, that we should be able to give as generously as this? Everything comes from you, and we have given you only what comes from your hand. {15} We are aliens and strangers in your sight, as were all our forefathers. Our days on earth are like a shadow, without hope. {16} O LORD our God, as for all this abundance that we have provided for building you a temple for your Holy Name, it comes from your hand, and all of it belongs to you. {17} I know, my God, that you test the heart and are pleased with integrity. All these things have I given willingly and with honest intent. And now I have seen with joy how willingly your people who are here have given to you. {18} O LORD, God of our fathers Abraham, Isaac and Israel, keep this desire in the hearts of your people forever, and keep their hearts loyal to you. {19} And give my son Solomon the wholehearted devotion to keep your commands, requirements and decrees and to do everything to build the palatial structure for which I have provided." {20} Then David said to the whole assembly, "Praise the LORD your God." So they all praised the LORD, the God of their fathers; they bowed low and fell prostrate before the LORD and the king.

SOLOMON THE NEW KING; DAVID DIES

1 Chr 29:21-30

The next day they made sacrifices to the LORD and presented burnt offerings to him: a thousand bulls, a thousand rams and a thousand male lambs, together with their drink offerings, and other sacrifices in abundance for all Israel. {22} They ate and drank with great joy in the presence of the LORD that day. Then they acknowledged Solomon son of David as king a second time, anointing him before the LORD to be ruler and Zadok to be priest. {23} So Solomon sat on the throne of the LORD as king in place of his father David. He prospered and all Israel obeyed him. {24} All the officers and mighty men, as well as all of King David's sons, pledged their submission to King Solomon. {25} The LORD highly exalted Solomon in the sight of all Israel and bestowed on him royal splendor such as no king over Israel ever had before.

{26} David son of Jesse was king over all Israel. {27} He ruled over Israel forty years–seven in Hebron and thirty-three in Jerusalem. {28} He died at a good old age, having enjoyed long life, wealth and honor. His son Solomon succeeded him as king. {29} As for the events of King David's reign, from beginning to end, they are written in the records of Samuel the seer, the records of Nathan the prophet and the records of Gad the seer, {30} together with the details of his reign and power, and the circumstances that surrounded him and Israel and the kingdoms of all the other lands.

GOD GIVES WISDOM TO SOLOMON

2 Chr 1:1-17

Solomon son of David established himself firmly over his kingdom, for the LORD his God was with him and made him exceedingly great. {2} Then Solomon spoke to all Israel–to the commanders of thousands and commanders of hundreds, to the judges and to all the leaders in Israel, the heads of families– {3} and Solomon and the whole assembly went to the high place at Gibeon, for God's Tent of Meeting was there, which Moses the Lord's servant had made in the desert. {4} Now David had brought up the ark of God from Kiriath Jearim to the place he had prepared for it, because he had pitched a tent for it in Jerusalem. {5} But the bronze altar that Bezalel son of Uri, the son of Hur, had made was in Gibeon in front of the tabernacle of the LORD; so Solomon and the assembly inquired of him there. {6} Solomon went up to the bronze altar before the LORD in the Tent of Meeting and offered a thousand burnt offerings on it. {7} That night God appeared to Solomon and said to him, "Ask for whatever you want me to give you." {8} Solomon answered God, "You have shown great kindness to David my father and have made me king in his place. {9} Now, LORD God, let your promise to my father David be confirmed, for you have made me king over a people who are as numerous as the dust of the earth. {10} Give me wisdom and knowledge, that I may lead this people, for who is able to govern this great people of yours?" {11} God said to Solomon, "Since this is your heart's desire and you have not asked for wealth, riches or honor, nor for the death of your enemies, and since you have not asked for a long life but for wisdom and knowledge to govern my people over whom I have made you king, {12} therefore wisdom and knowledge will be given you. And I will also give you wealth, riches and honor, such as no king who was before you ever had and none after you will have." {13} Then Solomon went to Jerusalem from the high place at Gibeon, from before the Tent of Meeting. And he reigned over Israel. {14} Solomon accumulated chariots and horses; he had fourteen hundred chariots and twelve thousand horses, which he kept in the chariot cities and also with him in Jerusalem. {15} The king made silver and gold as common in Jerusalem as stones, and cedar as plentiful as sycamore-fig trees in the foothills. {16} Solomon's horses were imported from Egypt and from Kue –the royal merchants purchased them from Kue. {17} They imported a chariot from Egypt for six hundred shekels of silver, and a horse for a hundred and fifty. They also exported them to all the kings of the Hittites and of the Arameans.

SOLOMON BUILDS THE TEMPLE

2 Chr 3:1-17

Then Solomon began to build the temple of the LORD in Jerusalem on Mount Moriah, where the LORD had appeared to his father David. It was on the threshing floor of Araunah the Jebusite, the place provided by David. {2} He began building on the second day of the second month in the fourth year of his reign. {3} The foundation Solomon laid for building the temple of God was sixty cubits long and twenty cubits wide (using the cubit of the old standard). {4} The portico at the front of the temple was twenty cubits long across the width of the building and twenty cubits high. He overlaid the inside with pure gold. {5} He paneled the main hall with pine and covered it with fine gold and decorated it with palm tree and chain designs. {6} He adorned the temple with precious stones. And the gold he used was gold of Parvaim. {7} He overlaid the ceiling beams, doorframes, walls and doors of the temple with gold, and he carved cherubim on the walls. {8} He built the Most Holy Place, its length corresponding to the width of the temple— twenty cubits long and twenty cubits wide. He overlaid the inside with six hundred talents of fine gold. {9} The gold nails weighed fifty shekels. He also overlaid the upper parts with gold. {10} In the Most Holy Place he made a pair of sculptured cherubim and overlaid them with gold. {11} The total wingspan of the cherubim was twenty cubits. One wing of the first cherub was five cubits long and touched the temple wall, while its other wing, also five cubits long, touched the wing of the other cherub. {12} Similarly one wing of the second cherub was five cubits long and touched the other temple wall, and its other wing, also five cubits long, touched the wing of the first cherub. {13} The wings of these cherubim extended twenty cubits. They stood on their feet, facing the main hall. {14} He made the curtain of blue, purple and crimson yarn and fine linen, with cherubim worked into it. {15} In the front of the temple he made two pillars, which <together> were thirty-five cubits long, each with a capital on top measuring five cubits. {16} He made interwoven chains and put them on top of the pillars. He also made a hundred pomegranates and attached them to the chains. {17} He erected the pillars in the front of the temple, one to the south and one to the north. The one to the south he named Jakin and the one to the north Boaz.

SOLOMON DEDICATES THE TEMPLE

2 Chr 6:12-21

Then Solomon stood before the altar of the LORD in front of the whole assembly of Israel and spread out his hands. {13} Now he had made a bronze platform, five cubits long, five cubits wide and three cubits high, and had placed it in the center of the outer court. He stood on the platform and then knelt down before the whole assembly of Israel and spread out his hands toward heaven. {14} He said: "O LORD, God of Israel, there is no God like you in heaven or on earth–you who keep your covenant of love with your servants who continue wholeheartedly in your way. {15} You have kept your promise to your servant David my father; with your mouth you have promised and with your hand you have fulfilled it–as it is today. {16} "Now LORD, God of Israel, keep for your servant David my father the promises you made to him when you said, 'You shall never fail to have a man to sit before me on the throne of Israel, if only your sons are careful in all they do to walk before me according to my law, as you have done.' {17} And now, O LORD, God of Israel, let your word that you promised your servant David come true. {18} "But will God really dwell on earth with men? The heavens, even the highest heavens, cannot contain you. How much less this temple I have built! {19} Yet give attention to your servant's prayer and his plea for mercy, O LORD my God. Hear the cry and the prayer that your servant is praying in your presence. {20} May your eyes be open toward this temple day and night, this place of which you said you would put your Name there. May you hear the prayer your servant prays toward this place. {21} Hear the supplications of your servant and of your people Israel when they pray toward this place. Hear from heaven, your dwelling place; and when you hear, forgive.

2 Chr 7:1-5

When Solomon finished praying, fire came down from heaven and consumed the burnt offering and the sacrifices, and the glory of the LORD filled the temple. {2} The priests could not enter the temple of the LORD because the glory of the LORD filled it. {3} When all the Israelites saw the fire coming down and the glory of the LORD above the temple, they knelt on the pavement with their faces to the ground, and they worshiped and gave thanks to the LORD, saying, "He is good; his love endures forever." {4} Then the king and all the people offered sacrifices before the LORD. {5} And King Solomon offered a sacrifice of twenty-two thousand head of cattle and a hundred and twenty thousand sheep and goats. So the king and all the people dedicated the temple of God.

SOLOMON CONSOLIDATES HIS KINGDOM

2 Chr 8:1-16

At the end of twenty years, during which Solomon built the temple of the LORD and his own palace, {2} Solomon rebuilt the villages that Hiram had given him, and settled Israelites in them. {3} Solomon then went to Hamath Zobah and captured it. {4} He also built up Tadmor in the desert and all the store cities he had built in Hamath. {5} He rebuilt Upper Beth Horon and Lower Beth Horon as fortified cities, with walls and with gates and bars, {6} as well as Baalath and all his store cities, and all the cities for his chariots and for his horses –whatever he desired to build in Jerusalem, in Lebanon and throughout all the territory he ruled. {7} All the people left from the Hittites, Amorites, Perizzites, Hivites and Jebusites (these peoples were not Israelites), {8} that is, their descendants remaining in the land, whom the Israelites had not destroyed–these Solomon conscripted for his slave labor force, as it is to this day. {9} But Solomon did not make slaves of the Israelites for his work; they were his fighting men, commanders of his captains, and commanders of his chariots and charioteers. {10} They were also King Solomon's chief officials–two hundred and fifty officials supervising the men. {11} Solomon brought Pharaoh's daughter up from the City of David to the palace he had built for her, for he said, "My wife must not live in the palace of David king of Israel, because the places the ark of the LORD has entered are holy." {12} On the altar of the LORD that he had built in front of the portico, Solomon sacrificed burnt offerings to the LORD, {13} according to the daily requirement for offerings commanded by Moses for Sabbaths, New Moons and the three annual feasts–the Feast of Unleavened Bread, the Feast of Weeks and the Feast of Tabernacles. {14} In keeping with the ordinance of his father David, he appointed the divisions of the priests for their duties, and the Levites to lead the praise and to assist the priests according to each day's requirement. He also appointed the gatekeepers by divisions for the various gates, because this was what David the man of God had ordered. {15} They did not deviate from the king's commands to the priests or to the Levites in any matter, including that of the treasuries. {16} All Solomon's work was carried out, from the day the foundation of the temple of the LORD was laid until its completion. So the temple of the LORD was finished.

THE QUEEN OF SHEBA COMES TO JERUSALEM

2 Chr 9:1-14

When the queen of Sheba heard of Solomon's fame, she came to Jerusalem to test him with hard questions. Arriving with a very great caravan–with camels carrying spices, large quantities of gold, and precious stones–she came to Solomon and talked with him about all she had on her mind. {2} Solomon answered all her questions; nothing was too hard for him to explain to her. {3} When the queen of Sheba saw the wisdom of Solomon, as well as the palace he had built, {4} the food on his table, the seating of his officials, the attending servants in their robes, the cupbearers in their robes and the burnt offerings he made at the temple of the LORD, she was overwhelmed. {5} She said to the king, "The report I heard in my own country about your achievements and your wisdom is true. {6} But I did not believe what they said until I came and saw with my own eyes. Indeed, not even half the greatness of your wisdom was told me; you have far exceeded the report I heard. {7} How happy your men must be! How happy your officials, who continually stand before you and hear your wisdom! {8} Praise be to the LORD your God, who has delighted in you and placed you on his throne as king to rule for the LORD your God. Because of the love of your God for Israel and his desire to uphold them forever, he has made you king over them, to maintain justice and righteousness." {9} Then she gave the king 120 talents of gold, large quantities of spices, and precious stones. There had never been such spices as those the queen of Sheba gave to King Solomon.

{10} (The men of Hiram and the men of Solomon brought gold from Ophir; they also brought algumwood and precious stones. {11} The king used the algumwood to make steps for the temple of the LORD and for the royal palace, and to make harps and lyres for the musicians. Nothing like them had ever been seen in Judah.) {12} King Solomon gave the queen of Sheba all she desired and asked for; he gave her more than she had brought to him. Then she left and returned with her retinue to her own country. {13} The weight of the gold that Solomon received yearly was 666 talents, {14} not including the revenues brought in by merchants and traders. Also all the kings of Arabia and the governors of the land brought gold and silver to Solomon.

KING AHAZ DOES NOT HONOR THE LORD

2 Chr 28:1-11

Ahaz was twenty years old when he became king, and he reigned in Jerusalem sixteen years. Unlike David his father, he did not do what was right in the eyes of the LORD. {2} He walked in the ways of the kings of Israel and also made cast idols for worshiping the Baals. {3} He burned sacrifices in the Valley of Ben Hinnom and sacrificed his sons in the fire, following the detestable ways of the nations the LORD had driven out before the Israelites. {4} He offered sacrifices and burned incense at the high places, on the hilltops and under every spreading tree. {5} Therefore the LORD his God handed him over to the king of Aram. The Arameans defeated him and took many of his people as prisoners and brought them to Damascus. He was also given into the hands of the king of Israel, who inflicted heavy casualties on him. {6} In one day Pekah son of Remaliah killed a hundred and twenty thousand soldiers in Judah–because Judah had forsaken the LORD, the God of their fathers. {7} Zicri, an Ephraimite warrior, killed Maaseiah the king's son, Azrikam the officer in charge of the palace, and Elkanah, second to the king. {8} The Israelites took captive from their kinsmen two hundred thousand wives, sons and daughters. They also took a great deal of plunder, which they carried back to Samaria. {9} But a prophet of the LORD named Oded was there, and he went out to meet the army when it returned to Samaria. He said to them, "Because the LORD, the God of your fathers, was angry with Judah, he gave them into your hand. But you have slaughtered them in a rage that reaches to heaven. {10} And now you intend to make the men and women of Judah and Jerusalem your slaves. But aren't you also guilty of sins against the LORD your God? {11} Now listen to me! Send back your fellow countrymen you have taken as prisoners, for the Lord's fierce anger rests on you."

2 Chr 28:22-25

In his time of trouble King Ahaz became even more unfaithful to the LORD. {23} He offered sacrifices to the gods of Damascus, who had defeated him; for he thought, "Since the gods of the kings of Aram have helped them, I will sacrifice to them so they will help me." But they were his downfall and the downfall of all Israel. {24} Ahaz gathered together the furnishings from the temple of God and took them away. He shut the doors of the Lord's temple and set up altars at every street corner in Jerusalem. {25} In every town in Judah he built high places to burn sacrifices to other gods and provoked the LORD, the God of his fathers, to anger.

AHAZ' SON HEZEKIAH HONORS THE LORD

2 Chr 29:1-11

Hezekiah was twenty-five years old when he became king, and he reigned in Jerusalem twenty-nine years. His mother's name was Abijah daughter of Zechariah. {2} He did what was right in the eyes of the LORD, just as his father David had done. {3} In the first month of the first year of his reign, he opened the doors of the temple of the LORD and repaired them. {4} He brought in the priests and the Levites, assembled them in the square on the east side {5} and said: "Listen to me, Levites! Consecrate yourselves now and consecrate the temple of the LORD, the God of your fathers. Remove all defilement from the sanctuary. {6} Our fathers were unfaithful; they did evil in the eyes of the LORD our God and forsook him. They turned their faces away from the Lord's dwelling place and turned their backs on him. {7} They also shut the doors of the portico and put out the lamps. They did not burn incense or present any burnt offerings at the sanctuary to the God of Israel. {8} Therefore, the anger of the LORD has fallen on Judah and Jerusalem; he has made them an object of dread and horror and scorn, as you can see with your own eyes. {9} This is why our fathers have fallen by the sword and why our sons and daughters and our wives are in captivity. {10} Now I intend to make a covenant with the LORD, the God of Israel, so that his fierce anger will turn away from us. {11} My sons, do not be negligent now, for the LORD has chosen you to stand before him and serve him, to minister before him and to burn incense."

2 Chr 29:25-30

He stationed the Levites in the temple of the LORD with cymbals, harps and lyres in the way prescribed by David and Gad the king's seer and Nathan the prophet; this was commanded by the LORD through his prophets. {26} So the Levites stood ready with David's instruments, and the priests with their trumpets. {27} Hezekiah gave the order to sacrifice the burnt offering on the altar. As the offering began, singing to the LORD began also, accompanied by trumpets and the instruments of David king of Israel. {28} The whole assembly bowed in worship, while the singers sang and the trumpeters played. All this continued until the sacrifice of the burnt offering was completed. {29} When the offerings were finished, the king and everyone present with him knelt down and worshiped. {30} King Hezekiah and his officials ordered the Levites to praise the LORD with the words of David and of Asaph the seer. So they sang praises with gladness and bowed their heads and worshiped.

HEZEHIAH ENCOURAGES GIFTS TO THE LORD

2 Chr 31:3-12a

The king contributed from his own possessions for the morning and evening burnt offerings and for the burnt offerings on the Sabbaths, New Moons and appointed feasts as written in the Law of the LORD. {4} He ordered the people living in Jerusalem to give the portion due the priests and Levites so they could devote themselves to the Law of the LORD. {5} As soon as the order went out, the Israelites generously gave the firstfruits of their grain, new wine, oil and honey and all that the fields produced. They brought a great amount, a tithe of everything. {6} The men of Israel and Judah who lived in the towns of Judah also brought a tithe of their herds and flocks and a tithe of the holy things dedicated to the LORD their God, and they piled them in heaps. {7} They began doing this in the third month and finished in the seventh month. {8} When Hezekiah and his officials came and saw the heaps, they praised the LORD and blessed his people Israel. {9} Hezekiah asked the priests and Levites about the heaps; {10} and Azariah the chief priest, from the family of Zadok, answered, "Since the people began to bring their contributions to the temple of the LORD, we have had enough to eat and plenty to spare, because the LORD has blessed his people, and this great amount is left over." {11} Hezekiah gave orders to prepare storerooms in the temple of the LORD, and this was done. {12} Then they faithfully brought in the contributions, tithes and dedicated gifts.

2 Chron 31:20-21

This is what Hezekiah did throughout Judah, doing what was good and right and faithful before the LORD his God. {21} In everything that he undertook in the service of God's temple and in obedience to the law and the commands, he sought his God and worked wholeheartedly. And so he prospered.

JOSIAH SEEKS THE WAYS OF GOD

2 Chr 34:1-3

Josiah was eight years old when he became king, and he reigned in Jerusalem thirty-one years. {2} He did what was right in the eyes of the LORD and walked in the ways of his father David, not turning aside to the right or to the left. {3} In the eighth year of his reign, while he was still young, he began to seek the God of his father David. In his twelfth year he began to purge Judah and Jerusalem of high places, Asherah poles, carved idols and cast images.

2 Chr 34:16b-28a

"Your officials are doing everything that has been committed to them. {17} They have paid out the money that was in the temple of the LORD and have entrusted it to the supervisors and workers." {18} Then Shaphan the secretary informed the king, "Hilkiah the priest has given me a book." And Shaphan read from it in the presence of the king. {19} When the king heard the words of the Law, he tore his robes. {20} He gave these orders to Hilkiah, Ahikam son of Shaphan, Abdon son of Micah, Shaphan the secretary and Asaiah the king's attendant: {21} "Go and inquire of the LORD for me and for the remnant in Israel and Judah about what is written in this book that has been found. Great is the Lord's anger that is poured out on us because our fathers have not kept the word of the LORD; they have not acted in accordance with all that is written in this book." {22} Hilkiah and those the king had sent with him went to speak to the prophetess Huldah, who was the wife of Shallum son of Tokhath, the son of Hasrah, keeper of the wardrobe. She lived in Jerusalem, in the Second District. {23} She said to them, "This is what the LORD, the God of Israel, says: Tell the man who sent you to me, {24} 'This is what the LORD says: I am going to bring disaster on this place and its people—all the curses written in the book that has been read in the presence of the king of Judah. {25} Because they have forsaken me and burned incense to other gods and provoked me to anger by all that their hands have made, my anger will be poured out on this place and will not be quenched.' {26} Tell the king of Judah, who sent you to inquire of the LORD, 'This is what the LORD, the God of Israel, says concerning the words you heard: {27} Because your heart was responsive and you humbled yourself before God when you heard what he spoke against this place and its people, and because you humbled yourself before me and tore your robes and wept in my presence, I have heard you, declares the LORD. {28} Now I will gather you to your fathers, and you will be buried in peace.

EZRA RETURNS TO JERUSALEM

Ezra 7:8-23a

Ezra arrived in Jerusalem in the fifth month of the seventh year of the king. {9} He had begun his journey from Babylon on the first day of the first month, and he arrived in Jerusalem on the first day of the fifth month, for the gracious hand of his God was on him. {10} For Ezra had devoted himself to the study and observance of the Law of the LORD, and to teaching its decrees and laws in Israel. {11} This is a copy of the letter King Artaxerxes had given to Ezra the priest and teacher, a man learned in matters concerning the commands and decrees of the LORD for Israel: {12} Artaxerxes, king of kings, To Ezra the priest, a teacher of the Law of the God of heaven: Greetings. {13} Now I decree that any of the Israelites in my kingdom, including priests and Levites, who wish to go to Jerusalem with you, may go. {14} You are sent by the king and his seven advisers to inquire about Judah and Jerusalem with regard to the Law of your God, which is in your hand. {15} Moreover, you are to take with you the silver and gold that the king and his advisers have freely given to the God of Israel, whose dwelling is in Jerusalem, {16} together with all the silver and gold you may obtain from the province of Babylon, as well as the freewill offerings of the people and priests for the temple of their God in Jerusalem. {17} With this money be sure to buy bulls, rams and male lambs, together with their grain offerings and drink offerings, and sacrifice them on the altar of the temple of your God in Jerusalem. {18} You and your brother Jews may then do whatever seems best with the rest of the silver and gold, in accordance with the will of your God. {19} Deliver to the God of Jerusalem all the articles entrusted to you for worship in the temple of your God. {20} And anything else needed for the temple of your God that you may have occasion to supply, you may provide from the royal treasury. {21} Now I, King Artaxerxes, order all the treasurers of Trans-Euphrates to provide with diligence whatever Ezra the priest, a teacher of the Law of the God of heaven, may ask of you– {22} up to a hundred talents of silver, a hundred cors of wheat, a hundred baths of wine, a hundred baths of olive oil, and salt without limit. {23} Whatever the God of heaven has prescribed, let it be done with diligence for the temple of the God of heaven.

EZRA DISTURBED ABOUT MIXED MARRIAGES

Ezra 9:1-12

After these things had been done, the leaders came to me and said, "The people of Israel, including the priests and the Levites, have not kept themselves separate from the neighboring peoples with their detestable practices, like those of the Canaanites, Hittites, Perizzites, Jebusites, Ammonites, Moabites, Egyptians and Amorites. {2} They have taken some of their daughters as wives for themselves and their sons, and have mingled the holy race with the peoples around them. And the leaders and officials have led the way in this unfaithfulness." {3} When I heard this, I tore my tunic and cloak, pulled hair from my head and beard and sat down appalled. {4} Then everyone who trembled at the words of the God of Israel gathered around me because of this unfaithfulness of the exiles. And I sat there appalled until the evening sacrifice. {5} Then, at the evening sacrifice, I rose from my self-abasement, with my tunic and cloak torn, and fell on my knees with my hands spread out to the LORD my God {6} and prayed: "O my God, I am too ashamed and disgraced to lift up my face to you, my God, because our sins are higher than our heads and our guilt has reached to the heavens. {7} From the days of our forefathers until now, our guilt has been great. Because of our sins, we and our kings and our priests have been subjected to the sword and captivity, to pillage and humiliation at the hand of foreign kings, as it is today. {8} "But now, for a brief moment, the LORD our God has been gracious in leaving us a remnant and giving us a firm place in his sanctuary, and so our God gives light to our eyes and a little relief in our bondage. {9} Though we are slaves, our God has not deserted us in our bondage. He has shown us kindness in the sight of the kings of Persia: He has granted us new life to rebuild the house of our God and repair its ruins, and he has given us a wall of protection in Judah and Jerusalem. {10} "But now, O our God, what can we say after this? For we have disregarded the commands {11} you gave through your servants the prophets when you said: 'The land you are entering to possess is a land polluted by the corruption of its peoples. By their detestable practices they have filled it with their impurity from one end to the other. {12} Therefore, do not give your daughters in marriage to their sons or take their daughters for your sons. Do not seek a treaty of friendship with them at any time, that you may be strong and eat the good things of the land and leave it to your children as an everlasting inheritance.'

NEHEMIAH WEEPS FOR JERUSALEM

Neh 1:1-2:3

The words of Nehemiah son of Hacaliah: In the month of Kislev in the twentieth year, while I was in the citadel of Susa, {2} Hanani, one of my brothers, came from Judah with some other men, and I questioned them about the Jewish remnant that survived the exile, and also about Jerusalem. {3} They said to me, "Those who survived the exile and are back in the province are in great trouble and disgrace. The wall of Jerusalem is broken down, and its gates have been burned with fire." {4} When I heard these things, I sat down and wept. For some days I mourned and fasted and prayed before the God of heaven. {5} Then I said: "O LORD, God of heaven, the great and awesome God, who keeps his covenant of love with those who love him and obey his commands, {6} let your ear be attentive and your eyes open to hear the prayer your servant is praying before you day and night for your servants, the people of Israel. I confess the sins we Israelites, including myself and my father's house, have committed against you. {7} We have acted very wickedly toward you. We have not obeyed the commands, decrees and laws you gave your servant Moses. {8} "Remember the instruction you gave your servant Moses, saying, 'If you are unfaithful, I will scatter you among the nations, {9} but if you return to me and obey my commands, then even if your exiled people are at the farthest horizon, I will gather them from there and bring them to the place I have chosen as a dwelling for my Name.' {10} "They are your servants and your people, whom you redeemed by your great strength and your mighty hand. {11} O Lord, let your ear be attentive to the prayer of this your servant and to the prayer of your servants who delight in revering your name. Give your servant success today by granting him favor in the presence of this man." I was cupbearer to the king. {2:1} In the month of Nisan in the twentieth year of King Artaxerxes, when wine was brought for him, I took the wine and gave it to the king. I had not been sad in his presence before; {2} so the king asked me, "Why does your face look so sad when you are not ill? This can be nothing but sadness of heart." I was very much afraid, {3} but I said to the king, "May the king live forever! Why should my face not look sad when the city where my fathers are buried lies in ruins, and its gates have been destroyed by fire?"

JOB'S CHILDREN ARE KILLED

Job 1:1-12

In the land of Uz there lived a man whose name was Job. This man was blameless and upright; he feared God and shunned evil. {2} He had seven sons and three daughters, {3} and he owned seven thousand sheep, three thousand camels, five hundred yoke of oxen and five hundred donkeys, and had a large number of servants. He was the greatest man among all the people of the East. {4} His sons used to take turns holding feasts in their homes, and they would invite their three sisters to eat and drink with them. {5} When a period of feasting had run its course, Job would send and have them purified. Early in the morning he would sacrifice a burnt offering for each of them, thinking, "Perhaps my children have sinned and cursed God in their hearts." This was Job's regular custom. {6} One day the angels came to present themselves before the LORD, and Satan also came with them. {7} The LORD said to Satan, "Where have you come from?" Satan answered the LORD, "From roaming through the earth and going back and forth in it." {8} Then the LORD said to Satan, "Have you considered my servant Job? There is no one on earth like him; he is blameless and upright, a man who fears God and shuns evil." {9} "Does Job fear God for nothing?" Satan replied. {10} "Have you not put a hedge around him and his household and everything he has? You have blessed the work of his hands, so that his flocks and herds are spread throughout the land. {11} But stretch out your hand and strike everything he has, and he will surely curse you to your face." {12} The LORD said to Satan, "Very well, then, everything he has is in your hands, but on the man himself do not lay a finger." Then Satan went out from the presence of the LORD.

JOB 1:18-22

While he was still speaking, yet another messenger came and said, "Your sons and daughters were feasting and drinking wine at the oldest brother's house, {19} when suddenly a mighty wind swept in from the desert and struck the four corners of the house. It collapsed on them and they are dead, and I am the only one who has escaped to tell you!" {20} At this, Job got up and tore his robe and shaved his head. Then he fell to the ground in worship {21} and said: "Naked I came from my mother's womb, and naked I will depart. The LORD gave and the LORD has taken away; may the name of the LORD be praised." {22} In all this, Job did not sin by charging God with wrongdoing.

JOB BECOMES ILL AND COMPLAINS

Job 2:1-3:2

On another day the angels came to present themselves before the LORD, and Satan also came with them to present himself before him. {2} And the LORD said to Satan, "Where have you come from?" Satan answered the LORD, "From roaming through the earth and going back and forth in it." {3} Then the LORD said to Satan, "Have you considered my servant Job? There is no one on earth like him; he is blameless and upright, a man who fears God and shuns evil. And he still maintains his integrity, though you incited me against him to ruin him without any reason." {4} "Skin for skin!" Satan replied. "A man will give all he has for his own life. {5} But stretch out your hand and strike his flesh and bones, and he will surely curse you to your face." {6} The LORD said to Satan, "Very well, then, he is in your hands; but you must spare his life." {7} So Satan went out from the presence of the LORD and afflicted Job with painful sores from the soles of his feet to the top of his head. {8} Then Job took a piece of broken pottery and scraped himself with it as he sat among the ashes. {9} His wife said to him, "Are you still holding on to your integrity? Curse God and die!" {10} He replied, "You are talking like a foolish woman. Shall we accept good from God, and not trouble?" In all this, Job did not sin in what he said. {11} When Job's three friends, Eliphaz the Temanite, Bildad the Shuhite and Zophar the Naamathite, heard about all the troubles that had come upon him, they set out from their homes and met together by agreement to go and sympathize with him and comfort him. {12} When they saw him from a distance, they could hardly recognize him; they began to weep aloud, and they tore their robes and sprinkled dust on their heads. {13} Then they sat on the ground with him for seven days and seven nights. No one said a word to him, because they saw how great his suffering was. {3:1} After this, Job opened his mouth and cursed the day of his birth. {2} He said:

Job 3:23-26

Why is life given to a man whose way is hidden, whom God has hedged in? {24} For sighing comes to me instead of food; my groans pour out like water. {25} What I feared has come upon me; what I dreaded has happened to me. {26} I have no peace, no quietness; I have no rest, but only turmoil."

ELIPHAS GIVES COUNSEL

Job 4:1-5

Then Eliphaz the Temanite replied: {2} "If someone ventures a word with you, will you be impatient? But who can keep from speaking? {3} Think how you have instructed many, how you have strengthened feeble hands. {4} Your words have supported those who stumbled; you have strengthened faltering knees. {5} But now trouble comes to you, and you are discouraged; it strikes you, and you are dismayed.

Job 5:8-11

"But if it were I, I would appeal to God; I would lay my cause before him. {9} He performs wonders that cannot be fathomed, miracles that cannot be counted. {10} He bestows rain on the earth; he sends water upon the countryside. {11} The lowly he sets on high, and those who mourn are lifted to safety.

Job 5:17-27

"Blessed is the man whom God corrects; so do not despise the discipline of the Almighty. {18} For he wounds, but he also binds up; he injures, but his hands also heal. {19} From six calamities he will rescue you; in seven no harm will befall you. {20} In famine he will ransom you from death, and in battle from the stroke of the sword. {21} You will be protected from the lash of the tongue, and need not fear when destruction comes. {22} You will laugh at destruction and famine, and need not fear the beasts of the earth. {23} For you will have a covenant with the stones of the field, and the wild animals will be at peace with you. {24} You will know that your tent is secure; you will take stock of your property and find nothing missing. {25} You will know that your children will be many, and your descendants like the grass of the earth. {26} You will come to the grave in full vigor, like sheaves gathered in season. {27} "We have examined this, and it is true. So hear it and apply it to yourself."

JOB REPLIES TO ELIPHAS

Job 6:8-10

"Oh, that I might have my request, that God would grant what I hope for, {9} that God would be willing to crush me, to let loose his hand and cut me off! {10} Then I would still have this consolation– my joy in unrelenting pain– that I had not denied the words of the Holy One.

Job 6:24-26

"Teach me, and I will be quiet; show me where I have been wrong. {25} How painful are honest words! But what do your arguments prove? {26} Do you mean to correct what I say, and treat the words of a despairing man as wind?

Job 7:11-21

"Therefore I will not keep silent; I will speak out in the anguish of my spirit, I will complain in the bitterness of my soul. {12} Am I the sea, or the monster of the deep, that you put me under guard? {13} When I think my bed will comfort me and my couch will ease my complaint, {14} even then you frighten me with dreams and terrify me with visions, {15} so that I prefer strangling and death, rather than this body of mine. {16} I despise my life; I would not live forever. Let me alone; my days have no meaning. {17} "What is man that you make so much of him, that you give him so much attention, {18} that you examine him every morning and test him every moment? {19} Will you never look away from me, or let me alone even for an instant? {20} If I have sinned, what have I done to you, O watcher of men? Why have you made me your target? Have I become a burden to you? {21} Why do you not pardon my offenses and forgive my sins? For I will soon lie down in the dust; you will search for me, but I will be no more."

BILDAD GIVES COUNSEL AND JOB REPLIES

Job 8:1-10

Then Bildad the Shuhite replied: {2} "How long will you say such things? Your words are a blustering wind. {3} Does God pervert justice? Does the Almighty pervert what is right? {4} When your children sinned against him, he gave them over to the penalty of their sin. {5} But if you will look to God and plead with the Almighty, {6} if you are pure and upright, even now he will rouse himself on your behalf and restore you to your rightful place. {7} Your beginnings will seem humble, so prosperous will your future be. {8} "Ask the former generations and find out what their fathers learned, {9} for we were born only yesterday and know nothing, and our days on earth are but a shadow. {10} Will they not instruct you and tell you? Will they not bring forth words from their understanding?

Job 8:20-22

"Surely God does not reject a blameless man or strengthen the hands of evildoers. {21} He will yet fill your mouth with laughter and your lips with shouts of joy. {22} Your enemies will be clothed in shame, and the tents of the wicked will be no more."

Job 9:1-4

Then Job replied: {2} "Indeed, I know that this is true. But how can a mortal be righteous before God? {3} Though one wished to dispute with him, he could not answer him one time out of a thousand. {4} His wisdom is profound, his power is vast. Who has resisted him and come out unscathed?

Job 10:1-9

"I loathe my very life; therefore I will give free rein to my complaint and speak out in the bitterness of my soul. {2} I will say to God: Do not condemn me, but tell me what charges you have against me. {3} Does it please you to oppress me, to spurn the work of your hands, while you smile on the schemes of the wicked? {4} Do you have eyes of flesh? Do you see as a mortal sees? {5} Are your days like those of a mortal or your years like those of a man, {6} that you must search out my faults and probe after my sin– {7} though you know that I am not guilty and that no one can rescue me from your hand? {8} "Your hands shaped me and made me. Will you now turn and destroy me? {9} Remember that you molded me like clay. Will you now turn me to dust again?

ZAPHAR GIVES COUNSEL AND JOB REPLIES

Job 11:1-5

Then Zophar the Naamathite replied: {2} "Are all these words to go unanswered? Is this talker to be vindicated? {3} Will your idle talk reduce men to silence? Will no one rebuke you when you mock? {4} You say to God, 'My beliefs are flawless and I am pure in your sight.' {5} Oh, how I wish that God would speak, that he would open his lips against you

Job 11:13-18

"Yet if you devote your heart to him and stretch out your hands to him, {14} if you put away the sin that is in your hand and allow no evil to dwell in your tent, {15} then you will lift up your face without shame; you will stand firm and without fear. {16} You will surely forget your trouble, recalling it only as waters gone by. {17} Life will be brighter than noonday, and darkness will become like morning. {18} You will be secure, because there is hope; you will look about you and take your rest in safety.

Job 13:1-3

"My eyes have seen all this, my ears have heard and understood it. {2} What you know, I also know; I am not inferior to you. {3} But I desire to speak to the Almighty and to argue my case with God.

Job 14:1-2

"Man born of woman is of few days and full of trouble. {2} He springs up like a flower and withers away; like a fleeting shadow, he does not endure.

Job 14:14-16

If a man dies, will he live again? All the days of my hard service I will wait for my renewal to come. {15} You will call and I will answer you; you will long for the creature your hands have made. {16} Surely then you will count my steps but not keep track of my sin.

ELIHU GIVES COUNSEL

Job 32:1-6

So these three men stopped answering Job, because he was righteous in his own eyes. {2} But Elihu son of Barakel the Buzite, of the family of Ram, became very angry with Job for justifying himself rather than God. {3} He was also angry with the three friends, because they had found no way to refute Job, and yet had condemned him. {4} Now Elihu had waited before speaking to Job because they were older than he. {5} But when he saw that the three men had nothing more to say, his anger was aroused. {6} So Elihu son of Barakel the Buzite said: "I am young in years, and you are old; that is why I was fearful, not daring to tell you what I know.

Job 33:8-15

"But you have said in my hearing– I heard the very words– {9} 'I am pure and without sin; I am clean and free from guilt. {10} Yet God has found fault with me; he considers me his enemy. {11} He fastens my feet in shackles; he keeps close watch on all my paths.' {12} "But I tell you, in this you are not right, for God is greater than man. {13} Why do you complain to him that he answers none of man's words ? {14} For God does speak–now one way, now another– though man may not perceive it. {15} In a dream, in a vision of the night, when deep sleep falls on men as they slumber in their beds,

Job 33:19

Or a man may be chastened on a bed of pain with constant distress in his bones,

Job 33:26-28

He prays to God and finds favor with him, he sees God's face and shouts for joy; he is restored by God to his righteous state. {27} Then he comes to men and says, 'I sinned, and perverted what was right, but I did not get what I deserved. {28} He redeemed my soul from going down to the pit, and I will live to enjoy the light.'

ELIHU CONTINUES HIS COUNSEL

Job 35:1-12

Then Elihu said: {2} "Do you think this is just? You say, 'I will be cleared by God. ' {3} Yet you ask him, 'What profit is it to me, and what do I gain by not sinning?' {4} "I would like to reply to you and to your friends with you. {5} Look up at the heavens and see; gaze at the clouds so high above you. {6} If you sin, how does that affect him? If your sins are many, what does that do to him? {7} If you are righteous, what do you give to him, or what does he receive from your hand? {8} Your wickedness affects only a man like yourself, and your righteousness only the sons of men. {9} "Men cry out under a load of oppression; they plead for relief from the arm of the powerful. {10} But no one says, 'Where is God my Maker, who gives songs in the night, {11} who teaches more to us than to the beasts of the earth and makes us wiser than the birds of the air?' {12} He does not answer when men cry out because of the arrogance of the wicked.

Job 36:1-12

Elihu continued: {2} "Bear with me a little longer and I will show you that there is more to be said in God's behalf. {3} I get my knowledge from afar; I will ascribe justice to my Maker. {4} Be assured that my words are not false; one perfect in knowledge is with you. {5} "God is mighty, but does not despise men; he is mighty, and firm in his purpose. {6} He does not keep the wicked alive but gives the afflicted their rights. {7} He does not take his eyes off the righteous; he enthrones them with kings and exalts them forever. {8} But if men are bound in chains, held fast by cords of affliction, {9} he tells them what they have done– that they have sinned arrogantly. {10} He makes them listen to correction and commands them to repent of their evil. {11} If they obey and serve him, they will spend the rest of their days in prosperity and their years in contentment. {12} But if they do not listen, they will perish by the sword and die without knowledge.

Job 36:15-16

But those who suffer he delivers in their suffering; he speaks to them in their affliction. {16} "He is wooing you from the jaws of distress to a spacious place free from restriction, to the comfort of your table laden with choice food.

GOD REPLIES

Job 38:4-8

"Where were you when I laid the earth's foundation? Tell me, if you understand. {5} Who marked off its dimensions? Surely you know! Who stretched a measuring line across it? {6} On what were its footings set, or who laid its cornerstone– {7} while the morning stars sang together and all the angels shouted for joy? {8} "Who shut up the sea behind doors when it burst forth from the womb,

Job 38:12-13

"Have you ever given orders to the morning, or shown the dawn its place, {13} that it might take the earth by the edges and shake the wicked out of it?

Job 38:19-22

"What is the way to the abode of light? And where does darkness reside? {20} Can you take them to their places? Do you know the paths to their dwellings? {21} Surely you know, for you were already born! You have lived so many years! {22} "Have you entered the storehouses of the snow or seen the storehouses of the hail,

Job 38:31-35

"Can you bind the beautiful Pleiades? Can you loose the cords of Orion? {32} Can you bring forth the constellations in their seasons or lead out the Bear with its cubs? {33} Do you know the laws of the heavens? Can you set up <God's> dominion over the earth? {34} "Can you raise your voice to the clouds and cover yourself with a flood of water? {35} Do you send the lightning bolts on their way? Do they report to you, 'Here we are'?

Job 39:26-27

"Does the hawk take flight by your wisdom and spread his wings toward the south? {27} Does the eagle soar at your command and build his nest on high?

Job 40:1-5

The LORD said to Job: {2} "Will the one who contends with the Almighty correct him? Let him who accuses God answer him!" {3} Then Job answered the LORD: {4} "I am unworthy–how can I reply to you? I put my hand over my mouth. {5} I spoke once, but I have no answer– twice, but I will say no more."

JOB RESTORED TO HEALTH AND WEALTH

Job 42:1-17

Then Job replied to the LORD: {2} "I know that you can do all things; no plan of yours can be thwarted. {3} <You asked>, 'Who is this that obscures my counsel without knowledge?' Surely I spoke of things I did not understand, things too wonderful for me to know. {4} "<You said>, 'Listen now, and I will speak; I will question you, and you shall answer me.' {5} My ears had heard of you but now my eyes have seen you. {6} Therefore I despise myself and repent in dust and ashes." {7} After the LORD had said these things to Job, he said to Eliphaz the Temanite, "I am angry with you and your two friends, because you have not spoken of me what is right, as my servant Job has. {8} So now take seven bulls and seven rams and go to my servant Job and sacrifice a burnt offering for yourselves. My servant Job will pray for you, and I will accept his prayer and not deal with you according to your folly. You have not spoken of me what is right, as my servant Job has." {9} So Eliphaz the Temanite, Bildad the Shuhite and Zophar the Naamathite did what the LORD told them; and the LORD accepted Job's prayer. {10} After Job had prayed for his friends, the LORD made him prosperous again and gave him twice as much as he had before. {11} All his brothers and sisters and everyone who had known him before came and ate with him in his house. They comforted and consoled him over all the trouble the LORD had brought upon him, and each one gave him a piece of silver and a gold ring. {12} The LORD blessed the latter part of Job's life more than the first. He had fourteen thousand sheep, six thousand camels, a thousand yoke of oxen and a thousand donkeys. {13} And he also had seven sons and three daughters. {14} The first daughter he named Jemimah, the second Keziah and the third Keren-Happuch. {15} Nowhere in all the land were there found women as beautiful as Job's daughters, and their father granted them an inheritance along with their brothers. {16} After this, Job lived a hundred and forty years; he saw his children and their children to the fourth generation. {17} And so he died, old and full of years.

Psalm 1

Blessed is the man who does not walk in the counsel of the wicked or stand in the way of sinners or sit in the seat of mockers. {2} But his delight is in the law of the LORD, and on his law he meditates day and night. {3} He is like a tree planted by streams of water, which yields its fruit in season and whose leaf does not wither. Whatever he does prospers. {4} Not so the wicked! They are like chaff that the wind blows away. {5} Therefore the wicked will not stand in the judgment, nor sinners in the assembly of the righteous. {6} For the LORD watches over the way of the righteous, but the way of the wicked will perish.

Psalm 2

Why do the nations conspire and the peoples plot in vain? {2} The kings of the earth take their stand and the rulers gather together against the LORD and against his Anointed One. {3} "Let us break their chains," they say, "and throw off their fetters." {4} The One enthroned in heaven laughs; the Lord scoffs at them. {5} Then he rebukes them in his anger and terrifies them in his wrath, saying, {6} "I have installed my King on Zion, my holy hill." {7} I will proclaim the decree of the LORD: He said to me, "You are my Son ; today I have become your Father. {8} Ask of me, and I will make the nations your inheritance, the ends of the earth your possession. {9} You will rule them with an iron scepter ; you will dash them to pieces like pottery." {10} Therefore, you kings, be wise; be warned, you rulers of the earth. {11} Serve the LORD with fear and rejoice with trembling. {12} Kiss the Son, lest he be angry and you be destroyed in your way, for his wrath can flare up in a moment. Blessed are all who take refuge in him.

Psa 4

For the director of music. With stringed instruments. A psalm of David. Answer me when I call to you, O my righteous God. Give me relief from my distress; be merciful to me and hear my prayer. {2} How long, O men, will you turn my glory into shame ? How long will you love delusions and seek false gods ? <Selah> {3} Know that the LORD has set apart the godly for himself; the LORD will hear when I call to him. {4} In your anger do not sin; when you are on your beds, search your hearts and be silent. <Selah> {5} Offer right sacrifices and trust in the LORD. {6} Many are asking, "Who can show us any good?" Let the light of your face shine upon us, O LORD. {7} You have filled my heart with greater joy than when their grain and new wine abound. {8} I will lie down and sleep in peace, for you alone, O LORD, make me dwell in safety.

Psa 5:1-8

For the director of music. For flutes. A psalm of David. Give ear to my words, O LORD, consider my sighing. {2} Listen to my cry for help, my King and my God, for to you I pray. {3} In the morning, O LORD, you hear my voice; in the morning I lay my requests before you and wait in expectation. {4} You are not a God who takes pleasure in evil; with you the wicked cannot dwell. {5} The arrogant cannot stand in your presence; you hate all who do wrong. {6} You destroy those who tell lies; bloodthirsty and deceitful men the LORD abhors. {7} But I, by your great mercy, will come into your house; in reverence will I bow down toward your holy temple. {8} Lead me, O LORD, in your righteousness because of my enemies– make straight your way before me.

Psa 8

For the director of music. According to <gittith>.A psalm of David.
O LORD, our Lord, how majestic is your name in all the earth! You have
set your glory above the heavens. {2} From the lips of children and
infants you have ordained praise because of your enemies, to silence the
foe and the avenger. {3} When I consider your heavens, the work of your
fingers, the moon and the stars, which you have set in place, {4} what is
man that you are mindful of him, the son of man that you care for him?
{5} You made him a little lower than the heavenly beings and crowned
him with glory and honor. {6} You made him ruler over the works of
your hands; you put everything under his feet: {7} all flocks and herds,
and the beasts of the field, {8} the birds of the air, and the fish of the
sea, all that swim the paths of the seas. {9} O LORD, our Lord, how
majestic is your name in all the earth!

Psa 14

For the director of music. Of David. The fool says in his heart, "There is no God." They are corrupt, their deeds are vile; there is no one who does good. {2} The LORD looks down from heaven on the sons of men to see if there are any who understand, any who seek God. {3} All have turned aside, they have together become corrupt; there is no one who does good, not even one. {4} Will evildoers never learn– those who devour my people as men eat bread and who do not call on the LORD? {5} There they are, overwhelmed with dread, for God is present in the company of the righteous. {6} You evildoers frustrate the plans of the poor, but the LORD is their refuge. {7} Oh, that salvation for Israel would come out of Zion! When the LORD restores the fortunes of his people, let Jacob rejoice and Israel be glad!

Psa 16:5-11

LORD, you have assigned me my portion and my cup; you have made my lot secure. {6} The boundary lines have fallen for me in pleasant places; surely I have a delightful inheritance. {7} I will praise the LORD, who counsels me; even at night my heart instructs me. {8} I have set the LORD always before me. Because he is at my right hand, I will not be shaken. {9} Therefore my heart is glad and my tongue rejoices; my body also will rest secure, {10} because you will not abandon me to the grave, nor will you let your Holy One see decay. {11} You have made known to me the path of life; you will fill me with joy in your presence, with eternal pleasures at your right hand.

Psa 18:1-19

For the director of music. Of David the servant of the LORD. He sang to the LORD the words of this song when the LORD delivered him from the hand of all his enemies and from the hand of Saul. He said: I love you, O LORD, my strength. {2} The LORD is my rock, my fortress and my deliverer; my God is my rock, in whom I take refuge. He is my shield and the horn of my salvation, my stronghold. {3} I call to the LORD, who is worthy of praise, and I am saved from my enemies. {4} The cords of death entangled me; the torrents of destruction overwhelmed me. {5} The cords of the grave coiled around me; the snares of death confronted me. {6} In my distress I called to the LORD; I cried to my God for help. From his temple he heard my voice; my cry came before him, into his ears. {7} The earth trembled and quaked, and the foundations of the mountains shook; they trembled because he was angry. {8} Smoke rose from his nostrils; consuming fire came from his mouth, burning coals blazed out of it. {9} He parted the heavens and came down; dark clouds were under his feet. {10} He mounted the cherubim and flew; he soared on the wings of the wind. {11} He made darkness his covering, his canopy around him– the dark rain clouds of the sky. {12} Out of the brightness of his presence clouds advanced, with hailstones and bolts of lightning. {13} The LORD thundered from heaven; the voice of the Most High resounded. {14} He shot his arrows and scattered <the enemies>, great bolts of lightning and routed them. {15} The valleys of the sea were exposed and the foundations of the earth laid bare at your rebuke, O LORD, at the blast of breath from your nostrils. {16} He reached down from on high and took hold of me; he drew me out of deep waters. {17} He rescued me from my powerful enemy, from my foes, who were too strong for me. {18} They confronted me in the day of my disaster, but the LORD was my support. {19} He brought me out into a spacious place; he rescued me because he delighted in me.

Psa 19

    For the director of music. A psalm of David. The heavens declare the glory of God; the skies proclaim the work of his hands. {2} Day after day they pour forth speech; night after night they display knowledge. {3} There is no speech or language where their voice is not heard. {4} Their voice goes out into all the earth, their words to the ends of the world. In the heavens he has pitched a tent for the sun, {5} which is like a bridegroom coming forth from his pavilion, like a champion rejoicing to run his course. {6} It rises at one end of the heavens and makes its circuit to the other; nothing is hidden from its heat. {7} The law of the LORD is perfect, reviving the soul. The statutes of the LORD are trustworthy, making wise the simple. {8} The precepts of the LORD are right, giving joy to the heart. The commands of the LORD are radiant, giving light to the eyes. {9} The fear of the LORD is pure, enduring forever. The ordinances of the LORD are sure and altogether righteous. {10} They are more precious than gold, than much pure gold; they are sweeter than honey, than honey from the comb. {11} By them is your servant warned; in keeping them there is great reward. {12} Who can discern his errors? Forgive my hidden faults. {13} Keep your servant also from willful sins; may they not rule over me. Then will I be blameless, innocent of great transgression. {14} May the words of my mouth and the meditation of my heart be pleasing in your sight, O LORD, my Rock and my Redeemer.

Psa 22:1-8

For the director of music. To <the tune of> "The Doe of the Morning." A psalm of David. My God, my God, why have you forsaken me? Why are you so far from saving me, so far from the words of my groaning? {2} O my God, I cry out by day, but you do not answer, by night, and am not silent. {3} Yet you are enthroned as the Holy One; you are the praise of Israel. {4} In you our fathers put their trust; they trusted and you delivered them. {5} They cried to you and were saved; in you they trusted and were not disappointed. {6} But I am a worm and not a man, scorned by men and despised by the people. {7} All who see me mock me; they hurl insults, shaking their heads: {8} "He trusts in the LORD; let the LORD rescue him. Let him deliver him, since he delights in him."

Psa 22:22-31

I will declare your name to my brothers; in the congregation I will praise you. {23} You who fear the LORD, praise him! All you descendants of Jacob, honor him! Revere him, all you descendants of Israel! {24} For he has not despised or disdained the suffering of the afflicted one; he has not hidden his face from him but has listened to his cry for help. {25} From you comes the theme of my praise in the great assembly; before those who fear you will I fulfill my vows. {26} The poor will eat and be satisfied; they who seek the LORD will praise him– may your hearts live forever! {27} All the ends of the earth will remember and turn to the LORD, and all the families of the nations will bow down before him, {28} for dominion belongs to the LORD and he rules over the nations. {29} All the rich of the earth will feast and worship; all who go down to the dust will kneel before him– those who cannot keep themselves alive. {30} Posterity will serve him; future generations will be told about the Lord. {31} They will proclaim his righteousness to a people yet unborn– for he has done it.

Psa 23

A psalm of David. The LORD is my shepherd, I shall not be in want. {2} He makes me lie down in green pastures, he leads me beside quiet waters, {3} he restores my soul. He guides me in paths of righteousness for his name's sake. {4} Even though I walk through the valley of the shadow of death, I will fear no evil, for you are with me; your rod and your staff, they comfort me. {5} You prepare a table before me in the presence of my enemies. You anoint my head with oil; my cup overflows. {6} Surely goodness and love will follow me all the days of my life, and I will dwell in the house of the LORD forever.

Psa 24

Of David. A psalm. The earth is the Lord's, and everything in it, the world, and all who live in it; {2} for he founded it upon the seas and established it upon the waters. {3} Who may ascend the hill of the LORD? Who may stand in his holy place? {4} He who has clean hands and a pure heart, who does not lift up his soul to an idol or swear by what is false. {5} He will receive blessing from the LORD and vindication from God his Savior. {6} Such is the generation of those who seek him, who seek your face, O God of Jacob. <Selah> {7} Lift up your heads, O you gates; be lifted up, you ancient doors, that the King of glory may come in. {8} Who is this King of glory? The LORD strong and mighty, the LORD mighty in battle. {9} Lift up your heads, O you gates; lift them up, you ancient doors, that the King of glory may come in. {10} Who is he, this King of glory? The LORD Almighty– he is the King of glory. <Selah>

Psa 27

Of David. The LORD is my light and my salvation– whom shall I fear? The LORD is the stronghold of my life– of whom shall I be afraid? {2} When evil men advance against me to devour my flesh, when my enemies and my foes attack me, they will stumble and fall. {3} Though an army besiege me, my heart will not fear; though war break out against me, even then will I be confident. {4} One thing I ask of the LORD, this is what I seek: that I may dwell in the house of the LORD all the days of my life, to gaze upon the beauty of the LORD and to seek him in his temple. {5} For in the day of trouble he will keep me safe in his dwelling; he will hide me in the shelter of his tabernacle and set me high upon a rock. {6} Then my head will be exalted above the enemies who surround me; at his tabernacle will I sacrifice with shouts of joy; I will sing and make music to the LORD. {7} Hear my voice when I call, O LORD; be merciful to me and answer me. {8} My heart says of you, "Seek his face!" Your face, LORD, I will seek. {9} Do not hide your face from me, do not turn your servant away in anger; you have been my helper. Do not reject me or forsake me, O God my Savior. {10} Though my father and mother forsake me, the LORD will receive me. {11} Teach me your way, O LORD; lead me in a straight path because of my oppressors. {12} Do not turn me over to the desire of my foes, for false witnesses rise up against me, breathing out violence. {13} I am still confident of this: I will see the goodness of the LORD in the land of the living. {14} Wait for the LORD; be strong and take heart and wait for the LORD.

Psa 32

Of David. A <maskil>.Blessed is he whose transgressions are forgiven, whose sins are covered. {2} Blessed is the man whose sin the LORD does not count against him and in whose spirit is no deceit. {3} When I kept silent, my bones wasted away through my groaning all day long. {4} For day and night your hand was heavy upon me; my strength was sapped as in the heat of summer. <Selah> {5} Then I acknowledged my sin to you and did not cover up my iniquity. I said, "I will confess my transgressions to the LORD"– and you forgave the guilt of my sin. <Selah> {6} Therefore let everyone who is godly pray to you while you may be found; surely when the mighty waters rise, they will not reach him. {7} You are my hiding place; you will protect me from trouble and surround me with songs of deliverance. <Selah> {8} I will instruct you and teach you in the way you should go; I will counsel you and watch over you. {9} Do not be like the horse or the mule, which have no understanding but must be controlled by bit and bridle or they will not come to you. {10} Many are the woes of the wicked, but the Lord's unfailing love surrounds the man who trusts in him. {11} Rejoice in the LORD and be glad, you righteous; sing, all you who are upright in heart!

Psa 33

Sing joyfully to the LORD, you righteous; it is fitting for the upright to praise him. {2} Praise the LORD with the harp; make music to him on the ten-stringed lyre. {3} Sing to him a new song; play skillfully, and shout for joy. {4} For the word of the LORD is right and true; he is faithful in all he does. {5} The LORD loves righteousness and justice; the earth is full of his unfailing love. {6} By the word of the LORD were the heavens made, their starry host by the breath of his mouth. {7} He gathers the waters of the sea into jars ; he puts the deep into storehouses. {8} Let all the earth fear the LORD; let all the people of the world revere him. {9} For he spoke, and it came to be; he commanded, and it stood firm. {10} The LORD foils the plans of the nations; he thwarts the purposes of the peoples. {11} But the plans of the LORD stand firm forever, the purposes of his heart through all generations. {12} Blessed is the nation whose God is the LORD, the people he chose for his inheritance. {13} From heaven the LORD looks down and sees all mankind; {14} from his dwelling place he watches all who live on earth– {15} he who forms the hearts of all, who considers everything they do. {16} No king is saved by the size of his army; no warrior escapes by his great strength. {17} A horse is a vain hope for deliverance; despite all its great strength it cannot save. {18} But the eyes of the LORD are on those who fear him, on those whose hope is in his unfailing love, {19} to deliver them from death and keep them alive in famine. {20} We wait in hope for the LORD; he is our help and our shield. {21} In him our hearts rejoice, for we trust in his holy name. {22} May your unfailing love rest upon us, O LORD, even as we put our hope in you.

Psa 34

Of David. When he pretended to be insane before Abimelech, who drove him away, and he left. I will extol the LORD at all times; his praise will always be on my lips. {2} My soul will boast in the LORD; let the afflicted hear and rejoice. {3} Glorify the LORD with me; let us exalt his name together. {4} I sought the LORD, and he answered me; he delivered me from all my fears. {5} Those who look to him are radiant; their faces are never covered with shame. {6} This poor man called, and the LORD heard him; he saved him out of all his troubles. {7} The angel of the LORD encamps around those who fear him, and he delivers them. {8} Taste and see that the LORD is good; blessed is the man who takes refuge in him. {9} Fear the LORD, you his saints, for those who fear him lack nothing. {10} The lions may grow weak and hungry, but those who seek the LORD lack no good thing. {11} Come, my children, listen to me; I will teach you the fear of the LORD. {12} Whoever of you loves life and desires to see many good days, {13} keep your tongue from evil and your lips from speaking lies. {14} Turn from evil and do good; seek peace and pursue it. {15} The eyes of the LORD are on the righteous and his ears are attentive to their cry; {16} the face of the LORD is against those who do evil, to cut off the memory of them from the earth. {17} The righteous cry out, and the LORD hears them; he delivers them from all their troubles. {18} The LORD is close to the brokenhearted and saves those who are crushed in spirit. {19} A righteous man may have many troubles, but the LORD delivers him from them all; {20} he protects all his bones, not one of them will be broken. {21} Evil will slay the wicked; the foes of the righteous will be condemned. {22} The LORD redeems his servants; no one will be condemned who takes refuge in him.

Psa 37:1-20

Of David. Do not fret because of evil men or be envious of those who do wrong; {2} for like the grass they will soon wither, like green plants they will soon die away. {3} Trust in the LORD and do good; dwell in the land and enjoy safe pasture. {4} Delight yourself in the LORD and he will give you the desires of your heart. {5} Commit your way to the LORD; trust in him and he will do this: {6} He will make your righteousness shine like the dawn, the justice of your cause like the noonday sun. {7} Be still before the LORD and wait patiently for him; do not fret when men succeed in their ways, when they carry out their wicked schemes. {8} Refrain from anger and turn from wrath; do not fret—it leads only to evil. {9} For evil men will be cut off, but those who hope in the LORD will inherit the land. {10} A little while, and the wicked will be no more; though you look for them, they will not be found. {11} But the meek will inherit the land and enjoy great peace. {12} The wicked plot against the righteous and gnash their teeth at them; {13} but the Lord laughs at the wicked, for he knows their day is coming. {14} The wicked draw the sword and bend the bow to bring down the poor and needy, to slay those whose ways are upright. {15} But their swords will pierce their own hearts, and their bows will be broken. {16} Better the little that the righteous have than the wealth of many wicked; {17} for the power of the wicked will be broken, but the LORD upholds the righteous. {18} The days of the blameless are known to the LORD, and their inheritance will endure forever. {19} In times of disaster they will not wither; in days of famine they will enjoy plenty. {20} But the wicked will perish: The Lord's enemies will be like the beauty of the fields, they will vanish—vanish like smoke.

Psa 37:21-40

The wicked borrow and do not repay, but the righteous give generously; {22} those the LORD blesses will inherit the land, but those he curses will be cut off. {23} If the LORD delights in a man's way, he makes his steps firm; {24} though he stumble, he will not fall, for the LORD upholds him with his hand. {25} I was young and now I am old, yet I have never seen the righteous forsaken or their children begging bread. {26} They are always generous and lend freely; their children will be blessed. {27} Turn from evil and do good; then you will dwell in the land forever. {28} For the LORD loves the just and will not forsake his faithful ones. They will be protected forever, but the offspring of the wicked will be cut off; {29} the righteous will inherit the land and dwell in it forever. {30} The mouth of the righteous man utters wisdom, and his tongue speaks what is just. {31} The law of his God is in his heart; his feet do not slip. {32} The wicked lie in wait for the righteous, seeking their very lives; {33} but the LORD will not leave them in their power or let them be condemned when brought to trial. {34} Wait for the LORD and keep his way. He will exalt you to inherit the land; when the wicked are cut off, you will see it. {35} I have seen a wicked and ruthless man flourishing like a green tree in its native soil, {36} but he soon passed away and was no more; though I looked for him, he could not be found. {37} Consider the blameless, observe the upright; there is a future for the man of peace. {38} But all sinners will be destroyed; the future of the wicked will be cut off. {39} The salvation of the righteous comes from the LORD; he is their stronghold in time of trouble. {40} The LORD helps them and delivers them; he delivers them from the wicked and saves them, because they take refuge in him.

Psa 38

A psalm of David. A petition. O LORD, do not rebuke me in your anger or discipline me in your wrath. {2} For your arrows have pierced me, and your hand has come down upon me. {3} Because of your wrath there is no health in my body; my bones have no soundness because of my sin. {4} My guilt has overwhelmed me like a burden too heavy to bear. {5} My wounds fester and are loathsome because of my sinful folly. {6} I am bowed down and brought very low; all day long I go about mourning. {7} My back is filled with searing pain; there is no health in my body. {8} I am feeble and utterly crushed; I groan in anguish of heart. {9} All my longings lie open before you, O Lord; my sighing is not hidden from you. {10} My heart pounds, my strength fails me; even the light has gone from my eyes. {11} My friends and companions avoid me because of my wounds; my neighbors stay far away. {12} Those who seek my life set their traps, those who would harm me talk of my ruin; all day long they plot deception. {13} I am like a deaf man, who cannot hear, like a mute, who cannot open his mouth; {14} I have become like a man who does not hear, whose mouth can offer no reply. {15} I wait for you, O LORD; you will answer, O Lord my God. {16} For I said, "Do not let them gloat or exalt themselves over me when my foot slips." {17} For I am about to fall, and my pain is ever with me. {18} I confess my iniquity; I am troubled by my sin. {19} Many are those who are my vigorous enemies; those who hate me without reason are numerous. {20} Those who repay my good with evil slander me when I pursue what is good. {21} O LORD, do not forsake me; be not far from me, O my God. {22} Come quickly to help me, O Lord my Savior.

Psa 40

For the director of music. Of David. A psalm. I waited patiently for the LORD; he turned to me and heard my cry. {2} He lifted me out of the slimy pit, out of the mud and mire; he set my feet on a rock and gave me a firm place to stand. {3} He put a new song in my mouth, a hymn of praise to our God. Many will see and fear and put their trust in the LORD. {4} Blessed is the man who makes the LORD his trust, who does not look to the proud, to those who turn aside to false gods. {5} Many, O LORD my God, are the wonders you have done. The things you planned for us no one can recount to you; were I to speak and tell of them, they would be too many to declare. {6} Sacrifice and offering you did not desire, but my ears you have pierced; burnt offerings and sin offerings you did not require. {7} Then I said, "Here I am, I have come– it is written about me in the scroll. {8} I desire to do your will, O my God; your law is within my heart." {9} I proclaim righteousness in the great assembly; I do not seal my lips, as you know, O LORD. {10} I do not hide your righteousness in my heart; I speak of your faithfulness and salvation. I do not conceal your love and your truth from the great assembly. {11} Do not withhold your mercy from me, O LORD; may your love and your truth always protect me. {12} For troubles without number surround me; my sins have overtaken me, and I cannot see. They are more than the hairs of my head, and my heart fails within me. {13} Be pleased, O LORD, to save me; O LORD, come quickly to help me. {14} May all who seek to take my life be put to shame and confusion; may all who desire my ruin be turned back in disgrace. {15} May those who say to me, "Aha! Aha!" be appalled at their own shame. {16} But may all who seek you rejoice and be glad in you; may those who love your salvation always say, "The LORD be exalted!" {17} Yet I am poor and needy; may the Lord think of me. You are my help and my deliverer; O my God, do not delay.

Psa 41

For the director of music. A psalm of David. Blessed is he who has regard for the weak; the LORD delivers him in times of trouble. {2} The LORD will protect him and preserve his life; he will bless him in the land and not surrender him to the desire of his foes. {3} The LORD will sustain him on his sickbed and restore him from his bed of illness. {4} I said, "O LORD, have mercy on me; heal me, for I have sinned against you." {5} My enemies say of me in malice, "When will he die and his name perish?" {6} Whenever one comes to see me, he speaks falsely, while his heart gathers slander; then he goes out and spreads it abroad. {7} All my enemies whisper together against me; they imagine the worst for me, saying, {8} "A vile disease has beset him; he will never get up from the place where he lies." {9} Even my close friend, whom I trusted, he who shared my bread, has lifted up his heel against me. {10} But you, O LORD, have mercy on me; raise me up, that I may repay them. {11} I know that you are pleased with me, for my enemy does not triumph over me. {12} In my integrity you uphold me and set me in your presence forever. {13} Praise be to the LORD, the God of Israel, from everlasting to everlasting. Amen and Amen.

Psa 42

For the director of music. A <maskil> of the Sons of Korah. As the deer pants for streams of water, so my soul pants for you, O God. {2} My soul thirsts for God, for the living God. When can I go and meet with God? {3} My tears have been my food day and night, while men say to me all day long, "Where is your God?" {4} These things I remember as I pour out my soul: how I used to go with the multitude, leading the procession to the house of God, with shouts of joy and thanksgiving among the festive throng. {5} Why are you downcast, O my soul? Why so disturbed within me? Put your hope in God, for I will yet praise him, my Savior and {6} my God. My soul is downcast within me; therefore I will remember you from the land of the Jordan, the heights of Hermon—from Mount Mizar. {7} Deep calls to deep in the roar of your waterfalls; all your waves and breakers have swept over me. {8} By day the LORD directs his love, at night his song is with me— a prayer to the God of my life. {9} I say to God my Rock, "Why have you forgotten me? Why must I go about mourning, oppressed by the enemy?" {10} My bones suffer mortal agony as my foes taunt me, saying to me all day long, "Where is your God?" {11} Why are you downcast, O my soul? Why so disturbed within me? Put your hope in God, for I will yet praise him, my Savior and my God.

Psa 46

For the director of music. Of the Sons of Korah. According to
<alamoth>.A song. God is our refuge and strength, an ever-present help in
trouble. {2} Therefore we will not fear, though the earth give way and
the mountains fall into the heart of the sea, {3} though its waters roar
and foam and the mountains quake with their surging. <Selah> {4} There
is a river whose streams make glad the city of God, the holy place where
the Most High dwells. {5} God is within her, she will not fall; God will help
her at break of day. {6} Nations are in uproar, kingdoms fall; he lifts his
voice, the earth melts. {7} The LORD Almighty is with us; the God of
Jacob is our fortress. <Selah> {8} Come and see the works of the LORD,
the desolations he has brought on the earth. {9} He makes wars cease
to the ends of the earth; he breaks the bow and shatters the spear, he
burns the shields with fire. {10} "Be still, and know that I am God; I will
be exalted among the nations, I will be exalted in the earth." {11} The
LORD Almighty is with us; the God of Jacob is our fortress. <Selah>

Psa 47:1-6

For the director of music. Of the Sons of Korah. A psalm. Clap your
hands, all you nations; shout to God with cries of joy. {2} How awesome
is the LORD Most High, the great King over all the earth! {3} He subdued
nations under us, peoples under our feet. {4} He chose our inheritance
for us, the pride of Jacob, whom he loved. <Selah> {5} God has ascended
amid shouts of joy, the LORD amid the sounding of trumpets. {6} Sing
praises to God, sing praises; sing praises to our King, sing praises.

Psa 49

For the director of music. Of the Sons of Korah. A psalm. Hear this, all you peoples; listen, all who live in this world, {2} both low and high, rich and poor alike: {3} My mouth will speak words of wisdom; the utterance from my heart will give understanding. {4} I will turn my ear to a proverb; with the harp I will expound my riddle: {5} Why should I fear when evil days come, when wicked deceivers surround me– {6} those who trust in their wealth and boast of their great riches? {7} No man can redeem the life of another or give to God a ransom for him– {8} the ransom for a life is costly, no payment is ever enough– {9} that he should live on forever and not see decay. {10} For all can see that wise men die; the foolish and the senseless alike perish and leave their wealth to others. {11} Their tombs will remain their houses forever, their dwellings for endless generations, though they had named lands after themselves. {12} But man, despite his riches, does not endure; he is like the beasts that perish. {13} This is the fate of those who trust in themselves, and of their followers, who approve their sayings. <Selah> {14} Like sheep they are destined for the grave, and death will feed on them. The upright will rule over them in the morning; their forms will decay in the grave, far from their princely mansions. {15} But God will redeem my life from the grave; he will surely take me to himself. <Selah> {16} Do not be overawed when a man grows rich, when the splendor of his house increases; {17} for he will take nothing with him when he dies, his splendor will not descend with him. {18} Though while he lived he counted himself blessed– and men praise you when you prosper– {19} he will join the generation of his fathers, who will never see the light <of life>. {20} A man who has riches without understanding is like the beasts that perish.

Psa 51

For the director of music. A psalm of David. When the prophet Nathan came to him after David had committed adultery with Bathsheba. Have mercy on me, O God, according to your unfailing love; according to your great compassion blot out my transgressions. {2} Wash away all my iniquity and cleanse me from my sin. {3} For I know my transgressions, and my sin is always before me. {4} Against you, you only, have I sinned and done what is evil in your sight, so that you are proved right when you speak and justified when you judge. {5} Surely I was sinful at birth, sinful from the time my mother conceived me. {6} Surely you desire truth in the inner parts ; you teach me wisdom in the inmost place. {7} Cleanse me with hyssop, and I will be clean; wash me, and I will be whiter than snow. {8} Let me hear joy and gladness; let the bones you have crushed rejoice. {9} Hide your face from my sins and blot out all my iniquity. {10} Create in me a pure heart, O God, and renew a steadfast spirit within me. {11} Do not cast me from your presence or take your Holy Spirit from me. {12} Restore to me the joy of your salvation and grant me a willing spirit, to sustain me. {13} Then I will teach transgressors your ways, and sinners will turn back to you. {14} Save me from bloodguilt, O God, the God who saves me, and my tongue will sing of your righteousness. {15} O Lord, open my lips, and my mouth will declare your praise. {16} You do not delight in sacrifice, or I would bring it; you do not take pleasure in burnt offerings. {17} The sacrifices of God are a broken spirit; a broken and contrite heart, O God, you will not despise. {18} In your good pleasure make Zion prosper; build up the walls of Jerusalem. {19} Then there will be righteous sacrifices, whole burnt offerings to delight you; then bulls will be offered on your altar.

Psa 53

For the director of music. According to <mahalath>.A <maskil> of David. The fool says in his heart, "There is no God." They are corrupt, and their ways are vile; there is no one who does good. {2} God looks down from heaven on the sons of men to see if there are any who understand, any who seek God. {3} Everyone has turned away, they have together become corrupt; there is no one who does good, not even one. {4} Will the evildoers never learn– those who devour my people as men eat bread and who do not call on God? {5} There they were, overwhelmed with dread, where there was nothing to dread. God scattered the bones of those who attacked you; you put them to shame, for God despised them. {6} Oh, that salvation for Israel would come out of Zion! When God restores the fortunes of his people, let Jacob rejoice and Israel be glad!

Psa 54

For the director of music. With stringed instruments. A <maskil> of David. When the Ziphites had gone to Saul and said, "Is not David hiding among us?" Save me, O God, by your name; vindicate me by your might. {2} Hear my prayer, O God; listen to the words of my mouth. {3} Strangers are attacking me; ruthless men seek my life– men without regard for God. <Selah> {4} Surely God is my help; the Lord is the one who sustains me. {5} Let evil recoil on those who slander me; in your faithfulness destroy them. {6} I will sacrifice a freewill offering to you; I will praise your name, O LORD, for it is good. {7} For he has delivered me from all my troubles, and my eyes have looked in triumph on my foes.

Psa 56

For the director of music. To <the tune of> "A Dove on Distant Oaks." Of David. A <miktam>.When the Philistines had seized him in Gath. Be merciful to me, O God, for men hotly pursue me; all day long they press their attack. {2} My slanderers pursue me all day long; many are attacking me in their pride. {3} When I am afraid, I will trust in you. {4} In God, whose word I praise, in God I trust; I will not be afraid. What can mortal man do to me? {5} All day long they twist my words; they are always plotting to harm me. {6} They conspire, they lurk, they watch my steps, eager to take my life. {7} On no account let them escape; in your anger, O God, bring down the nations. {8} Record my lament; list my tears on your scroll – are they not in your record? {9} Then my enemies will turn back when I call for help. By this I will know that God is for me. {10} In God, whose word I praise, in the LORD, whose word I praise– {11} in God I trust; I will not be afraid. What can man do to me? {12} I am under vows to you, O God; I will present my thank offerings to you. {13} For you have delivered me from death and my feet from stumbling, that I may walk before God in the light of life.

Psa 66

For the director of music. A song. A psalm. Shout with joy to God, all the earth! {2} Sing the glory of his name; make his praise glorious! {3} Say to God, "How awesome are your deeds! So great is your power that your enemies cringe before you. {4} All the earth bows down to you; they sing praise to you, they sing praise to your name." <Selah> {5} Come and see what God has done, how awesome his works in man's behalf! {6} He turned the sea into dry land, they passed through the waters on foot– come, let us rejoice in him. {7} He rules forever by his power, his eyes watch the nations– let not the rebellious rise up against him. <Selah> {8} Praise our God, O peoples, let the sound of his praise be heard; {9} he has preserved our lives and kept our feet from slipping. {10} For you, O God, tested us; you refined us like silver. {11} You brought us into prison and laid burdens on our backs. {12} You let men ride over our heads; we went through fire and water, but you brought us to a place of abundance. {13} I will come to your temple with burnt offerings and fulfill my vows to you– {14} vows my lips promised and my mouth spoke when I was in trouble. {15} I will sacrifice fat animals to you and an offering of rams; I will offer bulls and goats. <Selah> {16} Come and listen, all you who fear God; let me tell you what he has done for me. {17} I cried out to him with my mouth; his praise was on my tongue. {18} If I had cherished sin in my heart, the Lord would not have listened; {19} but God has surely listened and heard my voice in prayer. {20} Praise be to God, who has not rejected my prayer or withheld his love from me!

Psa 67

For the director of music. With stringed instruments. A psalm. A song. May God be gracious to us and bless us and make his face shine upon us, <Selah> {2} that your ways may be known on earth, your salvation among all nations. {3} May the peoples praise you, O God; may all the peoples praise you. {4} May the nations be glad and sing for joy, for you rule the peoples justly and guide the nations of the earth. <Selah> {5} May the peoples praise you, O God; may all the peoples praise you. {6} Then the land will yield its harvest, and God, our God, will bless us. {7} God will bless us, and all the ends of the earth will fear him.

Psa 68:1-10

For the director of music. Of David. A psalm. A song. May God arise, may his enemies be scattered; may his foes flee before him. {2} As smoke is blown away by the wind, may you blow them away; as wax melts before the fire, may the wicked perish before God. {3} But may the righteous be glad and rejoice before God; may they be happy and joyful. {4} Sing to God, sing praise to his name, extol him who rides on the clouds – his name is the LORD– and rejoice before him. {5} A father to the fatherless, a defender of widows, is God in his holy dwelling. {6} God sets the lonely in families, he leads forth the prisoners with singing; but the rebellious live in a sun-scorched land. {7} When you went out before your people, O God, when you marched through the wasteland, <Selah> {8} the earth shook, the heavens poured down rain, before God, the One of Sinai, before God, the God of Israel. {9} You gave abundant showers, O God; you refreshed your weary inheritance. {10} Your people settled in it, and from your bounty, O God, you provided for the poor.

Psa 71:1-18

In you, O LORD, I have taken refuge; let me never be put to shame. {2} Rescue me and deliver me in your righteousness; turn your ear to me and save me. {3} Be my rock of refuge, to which I can always go; give the command to save me, for you are my rock and my fortress. {4} Deliver me, O my God, from the hand of the wicked, from the grasp of evil and cruel men. {5} For you have been my hope, O Sovereign LORD, my confidence since my youth. {6} From birth I have relied on you; you brought me forth from my mother's womb. I will ever praise you. {7} I have become like a portent to many, but you are my strong refuge. {8} My mouth is filled with your praise, declaring your splendor all day long. {9} Do not cast me away when I am old; do not forsake me when my strength is gone. {10} For my enemies speak against me; those who wait to kill me conspire together. {11} They say, "God has forsaken him; pursue him and seize him, for no one will rescue him." {12} Be not far from me, O God; come quickly, O my God, to help me. {13} May my accusers perish in shame; may those who want to harm me be covered with scorn and disgrace. {14} But as for me, I will always have hope; I will praise you more and more. {15} My mouth will tell of your righteousness, of your salvation all day long, though I know not its measure. {16} I will come and proclaim your mighty acts, O Sovereign LORD; I will proclaim your righteousness, yours alone. {17} Since my youth, O God, you have taught me, and to this day I declare your marvelous deeds. {18} Even when I am old and gray, do not forsake me, O God, till I declare your power to the next generation, your might to all who are to come.

Psa 84

For the director of music. According to <gittith>.Of the Sons of Korah. A psalm. How lovely is your dwelling place, O LORD Almighty! {2} My soul yearns, even faints, for the courts of the LORD; my heart and my flesh cry out for the living God. {3} Even the sparrow has found a home, and the swallow a nest for herself, where she may have her young– a place near your altar, O LORD Almighty, my King and my God. {4} Blessed are those who dwell in your house; they are ever praising you. <Selah> {5} Blessed are those whose strength is in you, who have set their hearts on pilgrimage. {6} As they pass through the Valley of Baca, they make it a place of springs; the autumn rains also cover it with pools. {7} They go from strength to strength, till each appears before God in Zion. {8} Hear my prayer, O LORD God Almighty; listen to me, O God of Jacob. <Selah> {9} Look upon our shield, O God; look with favor on your anointed one. {10} Better is one day in your courts than a thousand elsewhere; I would rather be a doorkeeper in the house of my God than dwell in the tents of the wicked. {11} For the LORD God is a sun and shield; the LORD bestows favor and honor; no good thing does he withhold from those whose walk is blameless. {12} O LORD Almighty, blessed is the man who trusts in you.

Psa 91

He who dwells in the shelter of the Most High will rest in the shadow of the Almighty. {2} I will say of the LORD, "He is my refuge and my fortress, my God, in whom I trust." {3} Surely he will save you from the fowler's snare and from the deadly pestilence. {4} He will cover you with his feathers, and under his wings you will find refuge; his faithfulness will be your shield and rampart. {5} You will not fear the terror of night, nor the arrow that flies by day, {6} nor the pestilence that stalks in the darkness, nor the plague that destroys at midday. {7} A thousand may fall at your side, ten thousand at your right hand, but it will not come near you. {8} You will only observe with your eyes and see the punishment of the wicked. {9} If you make the Most High your dwelling– even the LORD, who is my refuge– {10} then no harm will befall you, no disaster will come near your tent. {11} For he will command his angels concerning you to guard you in all your ways; {12} they will lift you up in their hands, so that you will not strike your foot against a stone. {13} You will tread upon the lion and the cobra; you will trample the great lion and the serpent. {14} "Because he loves me," says the LORD, "I will rescue him; I will protect him, for he acknowledges my name. {15} He will call upon me, and I will answer him; I will be with him in trouble, I will deliver him and honor him. {16} With long life will I satisfy him and show him my salvation."

Psa 95

Come, let us sing for joy to the LORD; let us shout aloud to the Rock of our salvation. {2} Let us come before him with thanksgiving and extol him with music and song. {3} For the LORD is the great God, the great King above all gods. {4} In his hand are the depths of the earth, and the mountain peaks belong to him. {5} The sea is his, for he made it, and his hands formed the dry land. {6} Come, let us bow down in worship, let us kneel before the LORD our Maker; {7} for he is our God and we are the people of his pasture, the flock under his care. Today, if you hear his voice, {8} do not harden your hearts as you did at Meribah, as you did that day at Massah in the desert, {9} where your fathers tested and tried me, though they had seen what I did. {10} For forty years I was angry with that generation; I said, "They are a people whose hearts go astray, and they have not known my ways." {11} So I declared on oath in my anger, "They shall never enter my rest."

Psa 96

Sing to the LORD a new song; sing to the LORD, all the earth. {2} Sing to the LORD, praise his name; proclaim his salvation day after day. {3} Declare his glory among the nations, his marvelous deeds among all peoples. {4} For great is the LORD and most worthy of praise; he is to be feared above all gods. {5} For all the gods of the nations are idols, but the LORD made the heavens. {6} Splendor and majesty are before him; strength and glory are in his sanctuary. {7} Ascribe to the LORD, O families of nations, ascribe to the LORD glory and strength. {8} Ascribe to the LORD the glory due his name; bring an offering and come into his courts. {9} Worship the LORD in the splendor of his holiness; tremble before him, all the earth. {10} Say among the nations, "The LORD reigns." The world is firmly established, it cannot be moved; he will judge the peoples with equity. {11} Let the heavens rejoice, let the earth be glad; let the sea resound, and all that is in it; {12} let the fields be jubilant, and everything in them. Then all the trees of the forest will sing for joy; {13} they will sing before the LORD, for he comes, he comes to judge the earth. He will judge the world in righteousness and the peoples in his truth.

Psa 100

A psalm. For giving thanks. Shout for joy to the LORD, all the earth. {2} Worship the LORD with gladness; come before him with joyful songs. {3} Know that the LORD is God. It is he who made us, and we are his ; we are his people, the sheep of his pasture. {4} Enter his gates with thanksgiving and his courts with praise; give thanks to him and praise his name. {5} For the LORD is good and his love endures forever; his faithfulness continues through all generations.

Psa 101

Of David. A psalm. I will sing of your love and justice; to you, O LORD, I will sing praise. {2} I will be careful to lead a blameless life— when will you come to me? I will walk in my house with blameless heart. {3} I will set before my eyes no vile thing. The deeds of faithless men I hate; they will not cling to me. {4} Men of perverse heart shall be far from me; I will have nothing to do with evil. {5} Whoever slanders his neighbor in secret, him will I put to silence; whoever has haughty eyes and a proud heart, him will I not endure. {6} My eyes will be on the faithful in the land, that they may dwell with me; he whose walk is blameless will minister to me. {7} No one who practices deceit will dwell in my house; no one who speaks falsely will stand in my presence. {8} Every morning I will put to silence all the wicked in the land; I will cut off every evildoer from the city of the LORD.

Psa 103

Of David. Praise the LORD, O my soul; all my inmost being, praise his holy name. {2} Praise the LORD, O my soul, and forget not all his benefits– {3} who forgives all your sins and heals all your diseases, {4} who redeems your life from the pit and crowns you with love and compassion, {5} who satisfies your desires with good things so that your youth is renewed like the eagle's. {6} The LORD works righteousness and justice for all the oppressed. {7} He made known his ways to Moses, his deeds to the people of Israel: {8} The LORD is compassionate and gracious, slow to anger, abounding in love. {9} He will not always accuse, nor will he harbor his anger forever; {10} he does not treat us as our sins deserve or repay us according to our iniquities. {11} For as high as the heavens are above the earth, so great is his love for those who fear him; {12} as far as the east is from the west, so far has he removed our transgressions from us. {13} As a father has compassion on his children, so the LORD has compassion on those who fear him; {14} for he knows how we are formed, he remembers that we are dust. {15} As for man, his days are like grass, he flourishes like a flower of the field; {16} the wind blows over it and it is gone, and its place remembers it no more. {17} But from everlasting to everlasting the Lord's love is with those who fear him, and his righteousness with their children's children– {18} with those who keep his covenant and remember to obey his precepts. {19} The LORD has established his throne in heaven, and his kingdom rules over all. {20} Praise the LORD, you his angels, you mighty ones who do his bidding, who obey his word. {21} Praise the LORD, all his heavenly hosts, you his servants who do his will. {22} Praise the LORD, all his works everywhere in his dominion. Praise the LORD, O my soul.

Psa 107:1-22

Give thanks to the LORD, for he is good; his love endures forever. {2} Let the redeemed of the LORD say this– those he redeemed from the hand of the foe, {3} those he gathered from the lands, from east and west, from north and south. {4} Some wandered in desert wastelands, finding no way to a city where they could settle. {5} They were hungry and thirsty, and their lives ebbed away. {6} Then they cried out to the LORD in their trouble, and he delivered them from their distress. {7} He led them by a straight way to a city where they could settle. {8} Let them give thanks to the LORD for his unfailing love and his wonderful deeds for men, {9} for he satisfies the thirsty and fills the hungry with good things. {10} Some sat in darkness and the deepest gloom, prisoners suffering in iron chains, {11} for they had rebelled against the words of God and despised the counsel of the Most High. {12} So he subjected them to bitter labor; they stumbled, and there was no one to help. {13} Then they cried to the LORD in their trouble, and he saved them from their distress. {14} He brought them out of darkness and the deepest gloom and broke away their chains. {15} Let them give thanks to the LORD for his unfailing love and his wonderful deeds for men, {16} for he breaks down gates of bronze and cuts through bars of iron. {17} Some became fools through their rebellious ways and suffered affliction because of their iniquities. {18} They loathed all food and drew near the gates of death. {19} Then they cried to the LORD in their trouble, and he saved them from their distress. {20} He sent forth his word and healed them; he rescued them from the grave. {21} Let them give thanks to the LORD for his unfailing love and his wonderful deeds for men. {22} Let them sacrifice thank offerings and tell of his works with songs of joy.

Psa 112

Praise the LORD. Blessed is the man who fears the LORD, who finds great delight in his commands. {2} His children will be mighty in the land; the generation of the upright will be blessed. {3} Wealth and riches are in his house, and his righteousness endures forever. {4} Even in darkness light dawns for the upright, for the gracious and compassionate and righteous man. {5} Good will come to him who is generous and lends freely, who conducts his affairs with justice. {6} Surely he will never be shaken; a righteous man will be remembered forever. {7} He will have no fear of bad news; his heart is steadfast, trusting in the LORD. {8} His heart is secure, he will have no fear; in the end he will look in triumph on his foes. {9} He has scattered abroad his gifts to the poor, his righteousness endures forever; his horn will be lifted high in honor. {10} The wicked man will see and be vexed, he will gnash his teeth and waste away; the longings of the wicked will come to nothing.

Psa 113

Praise the LORD. Praise, O servants of the LORD, praise the name of the LORD. {2} Let the name of the LORD be praised, both now and forevermore. {3} From the rising of the sun to the place where it sets, the name of the LORD is to be praised. {4} The LORD is exalted over all the nations, his glory above the heavens. {5} Who is like the LORD our God, the One who sits enthroned on high, {6} who stoops down to look on the heavens and the earth? {7} He raises the poor from the dust and lifts the needy from the ash heap; {8} he seats them with princes, with the princes of their people. {9} He settles the barren woman in her home as a happy mother of children. Praise the LORD.

Psa 115

Not to us, O LORD, not to us but to your name be the glory, because of your love and faithfulness. {2} Why do the nations say, "Where is their God?" {3} Our God is in heaven; he does whatever pleases him. {4} But their idols are silver and gold, made by the hands of men. {5} They have mouths, but cannot speak, eyes, but they cannot see; {6} they have ears, but cannot hear, noses, but they cannot smell; {7} they have hands, but cannot feel, feet, but they cannot walk; nor can they utter a sound with their throats. {8} Those who make them will be like them, and so will all who trust in them. {9} O house of Israel, trust in the LORD– he is their help and shield. {10} O house of Aaron, trust in the LORD– he is their help and shield. {11} You who fear him, trust in the LORD– he is their help and shield. {12} The LORD remembers us and will bless us: He will bless the house of Israel, he will bless the house of Aaron, {13} he will bless those who fear the LORD– small and great alike. {14} May the LORD make you increase, both you and your children. {15} May you be blessed by the LORD, the Maker of heaven and earth. {16} The highest heavens belong to the LORD, but the earth he has given to man. {17} It is not the dead who praise the LORD, those who go down to silence; {18} it is we who extol the LORD, both now and forevermore. Praise the LORD.

Psa 116

I love the LORD, for he heard my voice; he heard my cry for mercy. {2} Because he turned his ear to me, I will call on him as long as I live. {3} The cords of death entangled me, the anguish of the grave came upon me; I was overcome by trouble and sorrow. {4} Then I called on the name of the LORD: "O LORD, save me!" {5} The LORD is gracious and righteous; our God is full of compassion. {6} The LORD protects the simplehearted; when I was in great need, he saved me. {7} Be at rest once more, O my soul, for the LORD has been good to you. {8} For you, O LORD, have delivered my soul from death, my eyes from tears, my feet from stumbling, {9} that I may walk before the LORD in the land of the living. {10} I believed; therefore I said, "I am greatly afflicted." {11} And in my dismay I said, "All men are liars." {12} How can I repay the LORD for all his goodness to me? {13} I will lift up the cup of salvation and call on the name of the LORD. {14} I will fulfill my vows to the LORD in the presence of all his people. {15} Precious in the sight of the LORD is the death of his saints. {16} O LORD, truly I am your servant; I am your servant, the son of your maidservant ; you have freed me from my chains. {17} I will sacrifice a thank offering to you and call on the name of the LORD. {18} I will fulfill my vows to the LORD in the presence of all his people, {19} in the courts of the house of the LORD– in your midst, O Jerusalem. Praise the LORD.

Psa 117

Praise the LORD, all you nations; extol him, all you peoples. {2} For great is his love toward us, and the faithfulness of the LORD endures forever. Praise the LORD.

Psa 118:1-14

Give thanks to the LORD, for he is good; his love endures forever. {2} Let Israel say: "His love endures forever." {3} Let the house of Aaron say: "His love endures forever." {4} Let those who fear the LORD say: "His love endures forever." {5} In my anguish I cried to the LORD, and he answered by setting me free. {6} The LORD is with me; I will not be afraid. What can man do to me? {7} The LORD is with me; he is my helper. I will look in triumph on my enemies. {8} It is better to take refuge in the LORD than to trust in man. {9} It is better to take refuge in the LORD than to trust in princes. {10} All the nations surrounded me, but in the name of the LORD I cut them off. {11} They surrounded me on every side, but in the name of the LORD I cut them off. {12} They swarmed around me like bees, but they died out as quickly as burning thorns; in the name of the LORD I cut them off. {13} I was pushed back and about to fall, but the LORD helped me. {14} The LORD is my strength and my song; he has become my salvation.

Psa 118:15-29

Shouts of joy and victory resound in the tents of the righteous: "The Lord's right hand has done mighty things! {16} The Lord's right hand is lifted high; the Lord's right hand has done mighty things!" {17} I will not die but live, and will proclaim what the LORD has done. {18} The LORD has chastened me severely, but he has not given me over to death. {19} Open for me the gates of righteousness; I will enter and give thanks to the LORD. {20} This is the gate of the LORD through which the righteous may enter. {21} I will give you thanks, for you answered me; you have become my salvation. {22} The stone the builders rejected has become the capstone; {23} the LORD has done this, and it is marvelous in our eyes. {24} This is the day the LORD has made; let us rejoice and be glad in it. {25} O LORD, save us; O LORD, grant us success. {26} Blessed is he who comes in the name of the LORD. From the house of the LORD we bless you. {27} The LORD is God, and he has made his light shine upon us. With boughs in hand, join in the festal procession up to the horns of the altar. {28} You are my God, and I will give you thanks; you are my God, and I will exalt you. {29} Give thanks to the LORD, for he is good; his love endures forever.

Psa 119:1-24

Blessed are they whose ways are blameless, who walk according to the law of the LORD. {2} Blessed are they who keep his statutes and seek him with all their heart. {3} They do nothing wrong; they walk in his ways. {4} You have laid down precepts that are to be fully obeyed. {5} Oh, that my ways were steadfast in obeying your decrees! {6} Then I would not be put to shame when I consider all your commands. {7} I will praise you with an upright heart as I learn your righteous laws. {8} I will obey your decrees; do not utterly forsake me. {9} How can a young man keep his way pure? By living according to your word. {10} I seek you with all my heart; do not let me stray from your commands. {11} I have hidden your word in my heart that I might not sin against you. {12} Praise be to you, O LORD; teach me your decrees. {13} With my lips I recount all the laws that come from your mouth. {14} I rejoice in following your statutes as one rejoices in great riches. {15} I meditate on your precepts and consider your ways. {16} I delight in your decrees; I will not neglect your word. {17} Do good to your servant, and I will live; I will obey your word. {18} Open my eyes that I may see wonderful things in your law. {19} I am a stranger on earth; do not hide your commands from me. {20} My soul is consumed with longing for your laws at all times. {21} You rebuke the arrogant, who are cursed and who stray from your commands. {22} Remove from me scorn and contempt, for I keep your statutes. {23} Though rulers sit together and slander me, your servant will meditate on your decrees. {24} Your statutes are my delight; they are my counselors.

Psa 119:33-40

Teach me, O LORD, to follow your decrees; then I will keep them to the end. {34} Give me understanding, and I will keep your law and obey it with all my heart. {35} Direct me in the path of your commands, for there I find delight. {36} Turn my heart toward your statutes and not toward selfish gain. {37} Turn my eyes away from worthless things; preserve my life according to your word. {38} Fulfill your promise to your servant, so that you may be feared. {39} Take away the disgrace I dread, for your laws are good. {40} How I long for your precepts! Preserve my life in your righteousness.

Psa 119:57-64

You are my portion, O LORD; I have promised to obey your words. {58} I have sought your face with all my heart; be gracious to me according to your promise. {59} I have considered my ways and have turned my steps to your statutes. {60} I will hasten and not delay to obey your commands. {61} Though the wicked bind me with ropes, I will not forget your law. {62} At midnight I rise to give you thanks for your righteous laws. {63} I am a friend to all who fear you, to all who follow your precepts. {64} The earth is filled with your love, O LORD; teach me your decrees.

Psa 119:73-80

Your hands made me and formed me; give me understanding to learn your commands. {74} May those who fear you rejoice when they see me, for I have put my hope in your word. {75} I know, O LORD, that your laws are righteous, and in faithfulness you have afflicted me. {76} May your unfailing love be my comfort, according to your promise to your servant. {77} Let your compassion come to me that I may live, for your law is my delight. {78} May the arrogant be put to shame for wronging me without cause; but I will meditate on your precepts. {79} May those who fear you turn to me, those who understand your statutes. {80} May my heart be blameless toward your decrees, that I may not be put to shame.

Psa 121

A song of ascents. I lift up my eyes to the hills– where does my help come from? {2} My help comes from the LORD, the Maker of heaven and earth. {3} He will not let your foot slip– he who watches over you will not slumber; {4} indeed, he who watches over Israel will neither slumber nor sleep. {5} The LORD watches over you– the LORD is your shade at your right hand; {6} the sun will not harm you by day, nor the moon by night. {7} The LORD will keep you from all harm– he will watch over your life; {8} the LORD will watch over your coming and going both now and forevermore.

Psa 124

A song of ascents. Of David. If the LORD had not been on our side– let Israel say– {2} if the LORD had not been on our side when men attacked us, {3} when their anger flared against us, they would have swallowed us alive; {4} the flood would have engulfed us, the torrent would have swept over us, {5} the raging waters would have swept us away. {6} Praise be to the LORD, who has not let us be torn by their teeth. {7} We have escaped like a bird out of the fowler's snare; the snare has been broken, and we have escaped. {8} Our help is in the name of the LORD, the Maker of heaven and earth.

Psa 127

A song of ascents. Of Solomon. Unless the LORD builds the house, its builders labor in vain. Unless the LORD watches over the city, the watchmen stand guard in vain. {2} In vain you rise early and stay up late, toiling for food to eat– for he grants sleep to those he loves. {3} Sons are a heritage from the LORD, children a reward from him. {4} Like arrows in the hands of a warrior are sons born in one's youth. {5} Blessed is the man whose quiver is full of them. They will not be put to shame when they contend with their enemies in the gate.

Psa 128

A song of ascents. Blessed are all who fear the LORD, who walk in his ways. {2} You will eat the fruit of your labor; blessings and prosperity will be yours. {3} Your wife will be like a fruitful vine within your house; your sons will be like olive shoots around your table. {4} Thus is the man blessed who fears the LORD. {5} May the LORD bless you from Zion all the days of your life; may you see the prosperity of Jerusalem, {6} and may you live to see your children's children. Peace be upon Israel.

Psa 133

A song of ascents. Of David. How good and pleasant it is when brothers live together in unity! {2} It is like precious oil poured on the head, running down on the beard, running down on Aaron's beard, down upon the collar of his robes. {3} It is as if the dew of Hermon were falling on Mount Zion. For there the LORD bestows his blessing, even life forevermore.

Psa 134

A song of ascents. Praise the LORD, all you servants of the LORD who minister by night in the house of the LORD. {2} Lift up your hands in the sanctuary and praise the LORD. {3} May the LORD, the Maker of heaven and earth, bless you from Zion.

Psa 135:1-9

Praise the LORD. Praise the name of the LORD; praise him, you servants of the LORD, {2} you who minister in the house of the LORD, in the courts of the house of our God. {3} Praise the LORD, for the LORD is good; sing praise to his name, for that is pleasant. {4} For the LORD has chosen Jacob to be his own, Israel to be his treasured possession. {5} I know that the LORD is great, that our Lord is greater than all gods. {6} The LORD does whatever pleases him, in the heavens and on the earth, in the seas and all their depths. {7} He makes clouds rise from the ends of the earth; he sends lightning with the rain and brings out the wind from his storehouses. {8} He struck down the firstborn of Egypt, the firstborn of men and animals. {9} He sent his signs and wonders into your midst, O Egypt, against Pharaoh and all his servants.

Psa 137

By the rivers of Babylon we sat and wept when we remembered Zion. {2} There on the poplars we hung our harps, {3} for there our captors asked us for songs, our tormentors demanded songs of joy; they said, "Sing us one of the songs of Zion!" {4} How can we sing the songs of the LORD while in a foreign land? {5} If I forget you, O Jerusalem, may my right hand forget <its skill>. {6} May my tongue cling to the roof of my mouth if I do not remember you, if I do not consider Jerusalem my highest joy. {7} Remember, O LORD, what the Edomites did on the day Jerusalem fell. "Tear it down," they cried, "tear it down to its foundations!" {8} O Daughter of Babylon, doomed to destruction, happy is he who repays you for what you have done to us– {9} he who seizes your infants and dashes them against the rocks.

Psa 138

Of David. I will praise you, O LORD, with all my heart; before the "gods" I will sing your praise. {2} I will bow down toward your holy temple and will praise your name for your love and your faithfulness, for you have exalted above all things your name and your word. {3} When I called, you answered me; you made me bold and stouthearted. {4} May all the kings of the earth praise you, O LORD, when they hear the words of your mouth. {5} May they sing of the ways of the LORD, for the glory of the LORD is great. {6} Though the LORD is on high, he looks upon the lowly, but the proud he knows from afar. {7} Though I walk in the midst of trouble, you preserve my life; you stretch out your hand against the anger of my foes, with your right hand you save me. {8} The LORD will fulfill <his purpose> for me; your love, O LORD, endures forever– do not abandon the works of your hands.

Psa 139:1-19

For the director of music. Of David. A psalm. O LORD, you have searched me and you know me. {2} You know when I sit and when I rise; you perceive my thoughts from afar. {3} You discern my going out and my lying down; you are familiar with all my ways. {4} Before a word is on my tongue you know it completely, O LORD. {5} You hem me in— behind and before; you have laid your hand upon me. {6} Such knowledge is too wonderful for me, too lofty for me to attain. {7} Where can I go from your Spirit? Where can I flee from your presence? {8} If I go up to the heavens, you are there; if I make my bed in the depths, you are there. {9} If I rise on the wings of the dawn, if I settle on the far side of the sea, {10} even there your hand will guide me, your right hand will hold me fast. {11} If I say, "Surely the darkness will hide me and the light become night around me," {12} even the darkness will not be dark to you; the night will shine like the day, for darkness is as light to you. {13} For you created my inmost being; you knit me together in my mother's womb. {14} I praise you because I am fearfully and wonderfully made; your works are wonderful, I know that full well. {15} My frame was not hidden from you when I was made in the secret place. When I was woven together in the depths of the earth, {16} your eyes saw my unformed body. All the days ordained for me were written in your book before one of them came to be. {17} How precious to me are your thoughts, O God! How vast is the sum of them! {18} Were I to count them, they would outnumber the grains of sand. When I awake, I am still with you. {19} If only you would slay the wicked, O God! Away from me, you bloodthirsty men!

Psa 141

A psalm of David. O LORD, I call to you; come quickly to me. Hear my voice when I call to you. {2} May my prayer be set before you like incense; may the lifting up of my hands be like the evening sacrifice. {3} Set a guard over my mouth, O LORD; keep watch over the door of my lips. {4} Let not my heart be drawn to what is evil, to take part in wicked deeds with men who are evildoers; let me not eat of their delicacies. {5} Let a righteous man strike me–it is a kindness; let him rebuke me–it is oil on my head. My head will not refuse it. Yet my prayer is ever against the deeds of evildoers; {6} their rulers will be thrown down from the cliffs, and the wicked will learn that my words were well spoken. {7} <They will say>, "As one plows and breaks up the earth, so our bones have been scattered at the mouth of the grave." {8} But my eyes are fixed on you, O Sovereign LORD; in you I take refuge–do not give me over to death. {9} Keep me from the snares they have laid for me, from the traps set by evildoers. {10} Let the wicked fall into their own nets, while I pass by in safety.

Psa 142

A <maskil> of David. When he was in the cave. A prayer. I cry aloud to the LORD; I lift up my voice to the LORD for mercy. {2} I pour out my complaint before him; before him I tell my trouble. {3} When my spirit grows faint within me, it is you who know my way. In the path where I walk men have hidden a snare for me. {4} Look to my right and see; no one is concerned for me. I have no refuge; no one cares for my life. {5} I cry to you, O LORD; I say, "You are my refuge, my portion in the land of the living." {6} Listen to my cry, for I am in desperate need; rescue me from those who pursue me, for they are too strong for me. {7} Set me free from my prison, that I may praise your name. Then the righteous will gather about me because of your goodness to me.

Psa 145

A psalm of praise. Of David. I will exalt you, my God the King; I will praise your name for ever and ever. {2} Every day I will praise you and extol your name for ever and ever. {3} Great is the LORD and most worthy of praise; his greatness no one can fathom. {4} One generation will commend your works to another; they will tell of your mighty acts. {5} They will speak of the glorious splendor of your majesty, and I will meditate on your wonderful works. {6} They will tell of the power of your awesome works, and I will proclaim your great deeds. {7} They will celebrate your abundant goodness and joyfully sing of your righteousness. {8} The LORD is gracious and compassionate, slow to anger and rich in love. {9} The LORD is good to all; he has compassion on all he has made. {10} All you have made will praise you, O LORD; your saints will extol you. {11} They will tell of the glory of your kingdom and speak of your might, {12} so that all men may know of your mighty acts and the glorious splendor of your kingdom. {13} Your kingdom is an everlasting kingdom, and your dominion endures through all generations. The LORD is faithful to all his promises and loving toward all he has made. {14} The LORD upholds all those who fall and lifts up all who are bowed down. {15} The eyes of all look to you, and you give them their food at the proper time. {16} You open your hand and satisfy the desires of every living thing. {17} The LORD is righteous in all his ways and loving toward all he has made. {18} The LORD is near to all who call on him, to all who call on him in truth. {19} He fulfills the desires of those who fear him; he hears their cry and saves them. {20} The LORD watches over all who love him, but all the wicked he will destroy. {21} My mouth will speak in praise of the LORD. Let every creature praise his holy name for ever and ever.

Psa 147

Praise the LORD. How good it is to sing praises to our God, how pleasant and fitting to praise him! {2} The LORD builds up Jerusalem; he gathers the exiles of Israel. {3} He heals the brokenhearted and binds up their wounds. {4} He determines the number of the stars and calls them each by name. {5} Great is our Lord and mighty in power; his understanding has no limit. {6} The LORD sustains the humble but casts the wicked to the ground. {7} Sing to the LORD with thanksgiving; make music to our God on the harp. {8} He covers the sky with clouds; he supplies the earth with rain and makes grass grow on the hills. {9} He provides food for the cattle and for the young ravens when they call. {10} His pleasure is not in the strength of the horse, nor his delight in the legs of a man; {11} the LORD delights in those who fear him, who put their hope in his unfailing love. {12} Extol the LORD, O Jerusalem; praise your God, O Zion, {13} for he strengthens the bars of your gates and blesses your people within you. {14} He grants peace to your borders and satisfies you with the finest of wheat. {15} He sends his command to the earth; his word runs swiftly. {16} He spreads the snow like wool and scatters the frost like ashes. {17} He hurls down his hail like pebbles. Who can withstand his icy blast? {18} He sends his word and melts them; he stirs up his breezes, and the waters flow. {19} He has revealed his word to Jacob, his laws and decrees to Israel. {20} He has done this for no other nation; they do not know his laws. Praise the LORD.

Psa 149

Praise the LORD. Sing to the LORD a new song, his praise in the assembly of the saints. {2} Let Israel rejoice in their Maker; let the people of Zion be glad in their King. {3} Let them praise his name with dancing and make music to him with tambourine and harp. {4} For the LORD takes delight in his people; he crowns the humble with salvation. {5} Let the saints rejoice in this honor and sing for joy on their beds. {6} May the praise of God be in their mouths and a double-edged sword in their hands, {7} to inflict vengeance on the nations and punishment on the peoples, {8} to bind their kings with fetters, their nobles with shackles of iron, {9} to carry out the sentence written against them. This is the glory of all his saints. Praise the LORD.

Psa 150

Praise the LORD. Praise God in his sanctuary; praise him in his mighty heavens. {2} Praise him for his acts of power; praise him for his surpassing greatness. {3} Praise him with the sounding of the trumpet, praise him with the harp and lyre, {4} praise him with tambourine and dancing, praise him with the strings and flute, {5} praise him with the clash of cymbals, praise him with resounding cymbals. {6} Let everything that has breath praise the LORD. Praise the LORD.

Prov 1:7-19

The fear of the LORD is the beginning of knowledge, but fools despise wisdom and discipline. {8} Listen, my son, to your father's instruction and do not forsake your mother's teaching. {9} They will be a garland to grace your head and a chain to adorn your neck. {10} My son, if sinners entice you, do not give in to them. {11} If they say, "Come along with us; let's lie in wait for someone's blood, let's waylay some harmless soul; {12} let's swallow them alive, like the grave, and whole, like those who go down to the pit; {13} we will get all sorts of valuable things and fill our houses with plunder; {14} throw in your lot with us, and we will share a common purse"– {15} my son, do not go along with them, do not set foot on their paths; {16} for their feet rush into sin, they are swift to shed blood. {17} How useless to spread a net in full view of all the birds! {18} These men lie in wait for their own blood; they waylay only themselves! {19} Such is the end of all who go after ill-gotten gain; it takes away the lives of those who get it.

Prov 2:1-6

My son, if you accept my words and store up my commands within you, {2} turning your ear to wisdom and applying your heart to understanding, {3} and if you call out for insight and cry aloud for understanding, {4} and if you look for it as for silver and search for it as for hidden treasure, {5} then you will understand the fear of the LORD and find the knowledge of God. {6} For the LORD gives wisdom, and from his mouth come knowledge and understanding.

Prov 5:1-23

My son, pay attention to my wisdom, listen well to my words of insight, {2} that you may maintain discretion and your lips may preserve knowledge. {3} For the lips of an adulteress drip honey, and her speech is smoother than oil; {4} but in the end she is bitter as gall, sharp as a double-edged sword. {5} Her feet go down to death; her steps lead straight to the grave. {6} She gives no thought to the way of life; her paths are crooked, but she knows it not. {7} Now then, my sons, listen to me; do not turn aside from what I say. {8} Keep to a path far from her, do not go near the door of her house, {9} lest you give your best strength to others and your years to one who is cruel, {10} lest strangers feast on your wealth and your toil enrich another man's house. {11} At the end of your life you will groan, when your flesh and body are spent. {12} You will say, "How I hated discipline! How my heart spurned correction! {13} I would not obey my teachers or listen to my instructors. {14} I have come to the brink of utter ruin in the midst of the whole assembly." {15} Drink water from your own cistern, running water from your own well. {16} Should your springs overflow in the streets, your streams of water in the public squares? {17} Let them be yours alone, never to be shared with strangers. {18} May your fountain be blessed, and may you rejoice in the wife of your youth. {19} A loving doe, a graceful deer– may her breasts satisfy you always, may you ever be captivated by her love. {20} Why be captivated, my son, by an adulteress? Why embrace the bosom of another man's wife? {21} For a man's ways are in full view of the LORD, and he examines all his paths. {22} The evil deeds of a wicked man ensnare him; the cords of his sin hold him fast. {23} He will die for lack of discipline, led astray by his own great folly.

Prov 6:1-19

My son, if you have put up security for your neighbor, if you have struck hands in pledge for another, {2} if you have been trapped by what you said, ensnared by the words of your mouth, {3} then do this, my son, to free yourself, since you have fallen into your neighbor's hands: Go and humble yourself; press your plea with your neighbor! {4} Allow no sleep to your eyes, no slumber to your eyelids. {5} Free yourself, like a gazelle from the hand of the hunter, like a bird from the snare of the fowler. {6} Go to the ant, you sluggard; consider its ways and be wise! {7} It has no commander, no overseer or ruler, {8} yet it stores its provisions in summer and gathers its food at harvest. {9} How long will you lie there, you sluggard? When will you get up from your sleep? {10} A little sleep, a little slumber, a little folding of the hands to rest– {11} and poverty will come on you like a bandit and scarcity like an armed man. {12} A scoundrel and villain, who goes about with a corrupt mouth, {13} who winks with his eye, signals with his feet and motions with his fingers, {14} who plots evil with deceit in his heart– he always stirs up dissension. {15} Therefore disaster will overtake him in an instant; he will suddenly be destroyed–without remedy. {16} There are six things the LORD hates, seven that are detestable to him: {17} haughty eyes, a lying tongue, hands that shed innocent blood, {18} a heart that devises wicked schemes, feet that are quick to rush into evil, {19} a false witness who pours out lies and a man who stirs up dissension among brothers.

Prov 10:1-5

The proverbs of Solomon: A wise son brings joy to his father, but a foolish son grief to his mother. {2} Ill-gotten treasures are of no value, but righteousness delivers from death. {3} The LORD does not let the righteous go hungry but he thwarts the craving of the wicked. {4} Lazy hands make a man poor, but diligent hands bring wealth. {5} He who gathers crops in summer is a wise son, but he who sleeps during harvest is a disgraceful son.

Prov 10:12-22

Hatred stirs up dissension, but love covers over all wrongs. {13} Wisdom is found on the lips of the discerning, but a rod is for the back of him who lacks judgment. {14} Wise men store up knowledge, but the mouth of a fool invites ruin. {15} The wealth of the rich is their fortified city, but poverty is the ruin of the poor. {16} The wages of the righteous bring them life, but the income of the wicked brings them punishment. {17} He who heeds discipline shows the way to life, but whoever ignores correction leads others astray. {18} He who conceals his hatred has lying lips, and whoever spreads slander is a fool. {19} When words are many, sin is not absent, but he who holds his tongue is wise. {20} The tongue of the righteous is choice silver, but the heart of the wicked is of little value. {21} The lips of the righteous nourish many, but fools die for lack of judgment. {22} The blessing of the LORD brings wealth, and he adds no trouble to it.

Prov 11:1-8

The LORD abhors dishonest scales, but accurate weights are his delight. {2} When pride comes, then comes disgrace, but with humility comes wisdom. {3} The integrity of the upright guides them, but the unfaithful are destroyed by their duplicity. {4} Wealth is worthless in the day of wrath, but righteousness delivers from death. {5} The righteousness of the blameless makes a straight way for them, but the wicked are brought down by their own wickedness. {6} The righteousness of the upright delivers them, but the unfaithful are trapped by evil desires. {7} When a wicked man dies, his hope perishes; all he expected from his power comes to nothing. {8} The righteous man is rescued from trouble, and it comes on the wicked instead.

Prov 11:16-28

A kindhearted woman gains respect, but ruthless men gain only wealth. {17} A kind man benefits himself, but a cruel man brings trouble on himself. {18} The wicked man earns deceptive wages, but he who sows righteousness reaps a sure reward. {19} The truly righteous man attains life, but he who pursues evil goes to his death. {20} The LORD detests men of perverse heart but he delights in those whose ways are blameless. {21} Be sure of this: The wicked will not go unpunished, but those who are righteous will go free. {22} Like a gold ring in a pig's snout is a beautiful woman who shows no discretion. {23} The desire of the righteous ends only in good, but the hope of the wicked only in wrath. {24} One man gives freely, yet gains even more; another withholds unduly, but comes to poverty. {25} A generous man will prosper; he who refreshes others will himself be refreshed. {26} People curse the man who hoards grain, but blessing crowns him who is willing to sell. {27} He who seeks good finds goodwill, but evil comes to him who searches for it. {28} Whoever trusts in his riches will fall, but the righteous will thrive like a green leaf.

Prov 15:1-18

A gentle answer turns away wrath, but a harsh word stirs up anger. {2} The tongue of the wise commends knowledge, but the mouth of the fool gushes folly. {3} The eyes of the LORD are everywhere, keeping watch on the wicked and the good. {4} The tongue that brings healing is a tree of life, but a deceitful tongue crushes the spirit. {5} A fool spurns his father's discipline, but whoever heeds correction shows prudence. {6} The house of the righteous contains great treasure, but the income of the wicked brings them trouble. {7} The lips of the wise spread knowledge; not so the hearts of fools. {8} The LORD detests the sacrifice of the wicked, but the prayer of the upright pleases him. {9} The LORD detests the way of the wicked but he loves those who pursue righteousness. {10} Stern discipline awaits him who leaves the path; he who hates correction will die. {11} Death and Destruction lie open before the LORD— how much more the hearts of men! {12} A mocker resents correction; he will not consult the wise. {13} A happy heart makes the face cheerful, but heartache crushes the spirit. {14} The discerning heart seeks knowledge, but the mouth of a fool feeds on folly. {15} All the days of the oppressed are wretched, but the cheerful heart has a continual feast. {16} Better a little with the fear of the LORD than great wealth with turmoil. {17} Better a meal of vegetables where there is love than a fattened calf with hatred. {18} A hot-tempered man stirs up dissension, but a patient man calms a quarrel.

Prov 16:3-21

Commit to the LORD whatever you do, and your plans will succeed. {4} The LORD works out everything for his own ends– even the wicked for a day of disaster. {5} The LORD detests all the proud of heart. Be sure of this: They will not go unpunished. {6} Through love and faithfulness sin is atoned for; through the fear of the LORD a man avoids evil. {7} When a man's ways are pleasing to the LORD, he makes even his enemies live at peace with him. {8} Better a little with righteousness than much gain with injustice. {9} In his heart a man plans his course, but the LORD determines his steps. {10} The lips of a king speak as an oracle, and his mouth should not betray justice. {11} Honest scales and balances are from the LORD; all the weights in the bag are of his making. {12} Kings detest wrongdoing, for a throne is established through righteousness. {13} Kings take pleasure in honest lips; they value a man who speaks the truth. {14} A king's wrath is a messenger of death, but a wise man will appease it. {15} When a king's face brightens, it means life; his favor is like a rain cloud in spring. {16} How much better to get wisdom than gold, to choose understanding rather than silver! {17} The highway of the upright avoids evil; he who guards his way guards his life. {18} Pride goes before destruction, a haughty spirit before a fall. {19} Better to be lowly in spirit and among the oppressed than to share plunder with the proud. {20} Whoever gives heed to instruction prospers, and blessed is he who trusts in the LORD. {21} The wise in heart are called discerning, and pleasant words promote instruction.

Prov 17:1

Better a dry crust with peace and quiet than a house full of feasting, with strife.

Prov 17:5-6

He who mocks the poor shows contempt for their Maker; whoever gloats over disaster will not go unpunished. {6} Children's children are a crown to the aged, and parents are the pride of their children.

Prov 17:9-10

He who covers over an offense promotes love, but whoever repeats the matter separates close friends. {10} A rebuke impresses a man of discernment more than a hundred lashes a fool.

Prov 17:12-16

Better to meet a bear robbed of her cubs than a fool in his folly. {13} If a man pays back evil for good, evil will never leave his house. {14} Starting a quarrel is like breaching a dam; so drop the matter before a dispute breaks out. {15} Acquitting the guilty and condemning the innocent– the LORD detests them both. {16} Of what use is money in the hand of a fool, since he has no desire to get wisdom?

Prov 21:1-21

The king's heart is in the hand of the LORD; he directs it like a watercourse wherever he pleases. {2} All a man's ways seem right to him, but the LORD weighs the heart. {3} To do what is right and just is more acceptable to the LORD than sacrifice. {4} Haughty eyes and a proud heart, the lamp of the wicked, are sin! {5} The plans of the diligent lead to profit as surely as haste leads to poverty. {6} A fortune made by a lying tongue is a fleeting vapor and a deadly snare. {7} The violence of the wicked will drag them away, for they refuse to do what is right. {8} The way of the guilty is devious, but the conduct of the innocent is upright. {9} Better to live on a corner of the roof than share a house with a quarrelsome wife. {10} The wicked man craves evil; his neighbor gets no mercy from him. {11} When a mocker is punished, the simple gain wisdom; when a wise man is instructed, he gets knowledge. {12} The Righteous One takes note of the house of the wicked and brings the wicked to ruin. {13} If a man shuts his ears to the cry of the poor, he too will cry out and not be answered. {14} A gift given in secret soothes anger, and a bribe concealed in the cloak pacifies great wrath. {15} When justice is done, it brings joy to the righteous but terror to evildoers. {16} A man who strays from the path of understanding comes to rest in the company of the dead. {17} He who loves pleasure will become poor; whoever loves wine and oil will never be rich. {18} The wicked become a ransom for the righteous, and the unfaithful for the upright. {19} Better to live in a desert than with a quarrelsome and ill-tempered wife. {20} In the house of the wise are stores of choice food and oil, but a foolish man devours all he has. {21} He who pursues righteousness and love finds life, prosperity and honor.

Prov 22:1-19

A good name is more desirable than great riches; to be esteemed is better than silver or gold. {2} Rich and poor have this in common: The LORD is the Maker of them all. {3} A prudent man sees danger and takes refuge, but the simple keep going and suffer for it. {4} Humility and the fear of the LORD bring wealth and honor and life. {5} In the paths of the wicked lie thorns and snares, but he who guards his soul stays far from them. {6} Train a child in the way he should go, and when he is old he will not turn from it. {7} The rich rule over the poor, and the borrower is servant to the lender. {8} He who sows wickedness reaps trouble, and the rod of his fury will be destroyed. {9} A generous man will himself be blessed, for he shares his food with the poor. {10} Drive out the mocker, and out goes strife; quarrels and insults are ended. {11} He who loves a pure heart and whose speech is gracious will have the king for his friend. {12} The eyes of the LORD keep watch over knowledge, but he frustrates the words of the unfaithful. {13} The sluggard says, "There is a lion outside!" or, "I will be murdered in the streets!" {14} The mouth of an adulteress is a deep pit; he who is under the Lord's wrath will fall into it. {15} Folly is bound up in the heart of a child, but the rod of discipline will drive it far from him. {16} He who oppresses the poor to increase his wealth and he who gives gifts to the rich—both come to poverty. {17} Pay attention and listen to the sayings of the wise; apply your heart to what I teach, {18} for it is pleasing when you keep them in your heart and have all of them ready on your lips. {19} So that your trust may be in the LORD, I teach you today, even you.

Prov 23:4-25

Do not wear yourself out to get rich; have the wisdom to show restraint. {5} Cast but a glance at riches, and they are gone, for they will surely sprout wings and fly off to the sky like an eagle. {6} Do not eat the food of a stingy man, do not crave his delicacies; {7} for he is the kind of man who is always thinking about the cost. "Eat and drink," he says to you, but his heart is not with you. {8} You will vomit up the little you have eaten and will have wasted your compliments. {9} Do not speak to a fool, for he will scorn the wisdom of your words. {10} Do not move an ancient boundary stone or encroach on the fields of the fatherless, {11} for their Defender is strong; he will take up their case against you. {12} Apply your heart to instruction and your ears to words of knowledge. {13} Do not withhold discipline from a child; if you punish him with the rod, he will not die. {14} Punish him with the rod and save his soul from death. {15} My son, if your heart is wise, then my heart will be glad; {16} my inmost being will rejoice when your lips speak what is right. {17} Do not let your heart envy sinners, but always be zealous for the fear of the LORD. {18} There is surely a future hope for you, and your hope will not be cut off. {19} Listen, my son, and be wise, and keep your heart on the right path. {20} Do not join those who drink too much wine or gorge themselves on meat, {21} for drunkards and gluttons become poor, and drowsiness clothes them in rags. {22} Listen to your father, who gave you life, and do not despise your mother when she is old. {23} Buy the truth and do not sell it; get wisdom, discipline and understanding. {24} The father of a righteous man has great joy; he who has a wise son delights in him. {25} May your father and mother be glad; may she who gave you birth rejoice!

Prov 24:3-7

By wisdom a house is built, and through understanding it is established; {4} through knowledge its rooms are filled with rare and beautiful treasures. {5} A wise man has great power, and a man of knowledge increases strength; {6} for waging war you need guidance, and for victory many advisers. {7} Wisdom is too high for a fool; in the assembly at the gate he has nothing to say.

Prov 24:23b-34

To show partiality in judging is not good: {24} Whoever says to the guilty, "You are innocent"– peoples will curse him and nations denounce him. {25} But it will go well with those who convict the guilty, and rich blessing will come upon them. {26} An honest answer is like a kiss on the lips. {27} Finish your outdoor work and get your fields ready; after that, build your house. {28} Do not testify against your neighbor without cause, or use your lips to deceive. {29} Do not say, "I'll do to him as he has done to me; I'll pay that man back for what he did." {30} I went past the field of the sluggard, past the vineyard of the man who lacks judgment; {31} thorns had come up everywhere, the ground was covered with weeds, and the stone wall was in ruins. {32} I applied my heart to what I observed and learned a lesson from what I saw: {33} A little sleep, a little slumber, a little folding of the hands to rest– {34} and poverty will come on you like a bandit and scarcity like an armed man.

Prov 27:1-2

Do not boast about tomorrow, for you do not know what a day may bring forth. {2} Let another praise you, and not your own mouth; someone else, and not your own lips.

Prov 27:17-21

As iron sharpens iron, so one man sharpens another. {18} He who tends a fig tree will eat its fruit, and he who looks after his master will be honored. {19} As water reflects a face, so a man's heart reflects the man. {20} Death and Destruction are never satisfied, and neither are the eyes of man. {21} The crucible for silver and the furnace for gold, but man is tested by the praise he receives.

Prov 28:5-9

Evil men do not understand justice, but those who seek the LORD understand it fully. {6} Better a poor man whose walk is blameless than a rich man whose ways are perverse. {7} He who keeps the law is a discerning son, but a companion of gluttons disgraces his father. {8} He who increases his wealth by exorbitant interest amasses it for another, who will be kind to the poor. {9} If anyone turns a deaf ear to the law, even his prayers are detestable.

Prov 30:7-8

"Two things I ask of you, O LORD; do not refuse me before I die: {8} Keep falsehood and lies far from me; give me neither poverty nor riches, but give me only my daily bread.

Prov 30:15b-16

"There are three things that are never satisfied, four that never say, 'Enough!': {16} the grave, the barren womb, land, which is never satisfied with water, and fire, which never says, 'Enough!'

Prov 30:18-19

"There are three things that are too amazing for me, four that I do not understand: {19} the way of an eagle in the sky, the way of a snake on a rock, the way of a ship on the high seas, and the way of a man with a maiden.

Prov 31:1-9

The sayings of King Lemuel–an oracle his mother taught him: {2} "O my son, O son of my womb, O son of my vows, {3} do not spend your strength on women, your vigor on those who ruin kings. {4} "It is not for kings, O Lemuel– not for kings to drink wine, not for rulers to crave beer, {5} lest they drink and forget what the law decrees, and deprive all the oppressed of their rights. {6} Give beer to those who are perishing, wine to those who are in anguish; {7} let them drink and forget their poverty and remember their misery no more. {8} "Speak up for those who cannot speak for themselves, for the rights of all who are destitute. {9} Speak up and judge fairly; defend the rights of the poor and needy."

Prov 31:10-31

A wife of noble character who can find? She is worth far more than rubies. {11} Her husband has full confidence in her and lacks nothing of value. {12} She brings him good, not harm, all the days of her life. {13} She selects wool and flax and works with eager hands. {14} She is like the merchant ships, bringing her food from afar. {15} She gets up while it is still dark; she provides food for her family and portions for her servant girls. {16} She considers a field and buys it; out of her earnings she plants a vineyard. {17} She sets about her work vigorously; her arms are strong for her tasks. {18} She sees that her trading is profitable, and her lamp does not go out at night. {19} In her hand she holds the distaff and grasps the spindle with her fingers. {20} She opens her arms to the poor and extends her hands to the needy. {21} When it snows, she has no fear for her household; for all of them are clothed in scarlet. {22} She makes coverings for her bed; she is clothed in fine linen and purple. {23} Her husband is respected at the city gate, where he takes his seat among the elders of the land. {24} She makes linen garments and sells them, and supplies the merchants with sashes. {25} She is clothed with strength and dignity; she can laugh at the days to come. {26} She speaks with wisdom, and faithful instruction is on her tongue. {27} She watches over the affairs of her household and does not eat the bread of idleness. {28} Her children arise and call her blessed; her husband also, and he praises her: {29} "Many women do noble things, but you surpass them all." {30} Charm is deceptive, and beauty is fleeting; but a woman who fears the LORD is to be praised. {31} Give her the reward she has earned, and let her works bring her praise at the city gate.

THE THINGS I TOILED FOR I MUST LEAVE BEHIND

Eccl 2:1-18

I thought in my heart, "Come now, I will test you with pleasure to find out what is good." But that also proved to be meaningless. {2} "Laughter," I said, "is foolish. And what does pleasure accomplish?" {3} I tried cheering myself with wine, and embracing folly–my mind still guiding me with wisdom. I wanted to see what was worthwhile for men to do under heaven during the few days of their lives. {4} I undertook great projects: I built houses for myself and planted vineyards. {5} I made gardens and parks and planted all kinds of fruit trees in them. {6} I made reservoirs to water groves of flourishing trees. {7} I bought male and female slaves and had other slaves who were born in my house. I also owned more herds and flocks than anyone in Jerusalem before me. {8} I amassed silver and gold for myself, and the treasure of kings and provinces. I acquired men and women singers, and a harem as well–the delights of the heart of man. {9} I became greater by far than anyone in Jerusalem before me. In all this my wisdom stayed with me. {10} I denied myself nothing my eyes desired; I refused my heart no pleasure. My heart took delight in all my work, and this was the reward for all my labor. {11} Yet when I surveyed all that my hands had done and what I had toiled to achieve, everything was meaningless, a chasing after the wind; nothing was gained under the sun. {12} Then I turned my thoughts to consider wisdom, and also madness and folly. What more can the king's successor do than what has already been done? {13} I saw that wisdom is better than folly, just as light is better than darkness. {14} The wise man has eyes in his head, while the fool walks in the darkness; but I came to realize that the same fate overtakes them both. {15} Then I thought in my heart, "The fate of the fool will overtake me also. What then do I gain by being wise?" I said in my heart, "This too is meaningless." {16} For the wise man, like the fool, will not be long remembered; in days to come both will be forgotten. Like the fool, the wise man too must die! {17} So I hated life, because the work that is done under the sun was grievous to me. All of it is meaningless, a chasing after the wind. {18} I hated all the things I had toiled for under the sun, because I must leave them to the one who comes after me.

EVERY ACTIVITY HAS ITS TIME

Eccl 3:1-22

There is a time for everything, and a season for every activity under heaven: {2} a time to be born and a time to die, a time to plant and a time to uproot, {3} a time to kill and a time to heal, a time to tear down and a time to build, {4} a time to weep and a time to laugh, a time to mourn and a time to dance, {5} a time to scatter stones and a time to gather them, a time to embrace and a time to refrain, {6} a time to search and a time to give up, a time to keep and a time to throw away, {7} a time to tear and a time to mend, a time to be silent and a time to speak, {8} a time to love and a time to hate, a time for war and a time for peace. {9} What does the worker gain from his toil? {10} I have seen the burden God has laid on men. {11} He has made everything beautiful in its time. He has also set eternity in the hearts of men; yet they cannot fathom what God has done from beginning to end. {12} I know that there is nothing better for men than to be happy and do good while they live. {13} That everyone may eat and drink, and find satisfaction in all his toil–this is the gift of God. {14} I know that everything God does will endure forever; nothing can be added to it and nothing taken from it. God does it so that men will revere him. {15} Whatever is has already been, and what will be has been before; and God will call the past to account. {16} And I saw something else under the sun: In the place of judgment–wickedness was there, in the place of justice–wickedness was there. {17} I thought in my heart, "God will bring to judgment both the righteous and the wicked, for there will be a time for every activity, a time for every deed." {18} I also thought, "As for men, God tests them so that they may see that they are like the animals. {19} Man's fate is like that of the animals; the same fate awaits them both: As one dies, so dies the other. All have the same breath ; man has no advantage over the animal. Everything is meaningless. {20} All go to the same place; all come from dust, and to dust all return. {21} Who knows if the spirit of man rises upward and if the spirit of the animal goes down into the earth?" {22} So I saw that there is nothing better for a man than to enjoy his work, because that is his lot. For who can bring him to see what will happen after him?

LET MAN LABOR AND ENJOY GOD'S BLESSINGS

Eccl 5:4-20

When you make a vow to God, do not delay in fulfilling it. He has no pleasure in fools; fulfill your vow. {5} It is better not to vow than to make a vow and not fulfill it. {6} Do not let your mouth lead you into sin. And do not protest to the <temple> messenger, "My vow was a mistake." Why should God be angry at what you say and destroy the work of your hands? {7} Much dreaming and many words are meaningless. Therefore stand in awe of God. {8} If you see the poor oppressed in a district, and justice and rights denied, do not be surprised at such things; for one official is eyed by a higher one, and over them both are others higher still. {9} The increase from the land is taken by all; the king himself profits from the fields. {10} Whoever loves money never has money enough; whoever loves wealth is never satisfied with his income. This too is meaningless. {11} As goods increase, so do those who consume them. And what benefit are they to the owner except to feast his eyes on them? {12} The sleep of a laborer is sweet, whether he eats little or much, but the abundance of a rich man permits him no sleep. {13} I have seen a grievous evil under the sun: wealth hoarded to the harm of its owner, {14} or wealth lost through some misfortune, so that when he has a son there is nothing left for him. {15} Naked a man comes from his mother's womb, and as he comes, so he departs. He takes nothing from his labor that he can carry in his hand. {16} This too is a grievous evil: As a man comes, so he departs, and what does he gain, since he toils for the wind? {17} All his days he eats in darkness, with great frustration, affliction and anger. {18} Then I realized that it is good and proper for a man to eat and drink, and to find satisfaction in his toilsome labor under the sun during the few days of life God has given him—for this is his lot. {19} Moreover, when God gives any man wealth and possessions, and enables him to enjoy them, to accept his lot and be happy in his work—this is a gift of God. {20} He seldom reflects on the days of his life, because God keeps him occupied with gladness of heart.

CAST YOUR BREAD UPON THE WATERS

Eccl 11:1-2
Cast your bread upon the waters, for after many days you will find it again. {2} Give portions to seven, yes to eight, for you do not know what disaster may come upon the land.

Eccl 11:6
Sow your seed in the morning, and at evening let not your hands be idle, for you do not know which will succeed, whether this or that, or whether both will do equally well.

Eccl 11:9
Be happy, young man, while you are young, and let your heart give you joy in the days of your youth. Follow the ways of your heart and whatever your eyes see, but know that for all these things God will bring you to judgment.

Eccl 12:1-7
Remember your Creator in the days of your youth, before the days of trouble come and the years approach when you will say, "I find no pleasure in them"– {2} before the sun and the light and the moon and the stars grow dark, and the clouds return after the rain; {3} when the keepers of the house tremble, and the strong men stoop, when the grinders cease because they are few, and those looking through the windows grow dim; {4} when the doors to the street are closed and the sound of grinding fades; when men rise up at the sound of birds, but all their songs grow faint; {5} when men are afraid of heights and of dangers in the streets; when the almond tree blossoms and the grasshopper drags himself along and desire no longer is stirred. Then man goes to his eternal home and mourners go about the streets. {6} Remember him–before the silver cord is severed, or the golden bowl is broken; before the pitcher is shattered at the spring, or the wheel broken at the well, {7} and the dust returns to the ground it came from, and the spirit returns to God who gave it.

Eccl 12:13-14
Now all has been heard; here is the conclusion of the matter: Fear God and keep his commandments, for this is the whole <duty> of man. {14} For God will bring every deed into judgment, including every hidden thing, whether it is good or evil.

HOW BEAUTIFUL IS MY BELOVED

Song 4:1-7

How beautiful you are, my darling! Oh, how beautiful! Your eyes behind your veil are doves. Your hair is like a flock of goats descending from Mount Gilead. {2} Your teeth are like a flock of sheep just shorn, coming up from the washing. Each has its twin; not one of them is alone. {3} Your lips are like a scarlet ribbon; your mouth is lovely. Your temples behind your veil are like the halves of a pomegranate. {4} Your neck is like the tower of David, built with elegance; on it hang a thousand shields, all of them shields of warriors. {5} Your two breasts are like two fawns, like twin fawns of a gazelle that browse among the lilies. {6} Until the day breaks and the shadows flee, I will go to the mountain of myrrh and to the hill of incense. {7} All beautiful you are, my darling; there is no flaw in you.

Song 7:10-13

I belong to my lover, and his desire is for me. {11} Come, my lover, let us go to the countryside, let us spend the night in the villages. {12} Let us go early to the vineyards to see if the vines have budded, if their blossoms have opened, and if the pomegranates are in bloom– there I will give you my love. {13} The mandrakes send out their fragrance, and at our door is every delicacy, both new and old, that I have stored up for you, my lover.

Song 8:6-7

Place me like a seal over your heart, like a seal on your arm; for love is as strong as death, its jealousy unyielding as the grave. It burns like blazing fire, like a mighty flame. {7} Many waters cannot quench love; rivers cannot wash it away. If one were to give all the wealth of his house for love, it would be utterly scorned.

IF YOU REBEL YOU WILL BE DESTROYED

Isa 1:1-4

The vision concerning Judah and Jerusalem that Isaiah son of Amoz saw during the reigns of Uzziah, Jotham, Ahaz and Hezekiah, kings of Judah. {2} Hear, O heavens! Listen, O earth! For the LORD has spoken: "I reared children and brought them up, but they have rebelled against me. {3} The ox knows his master, the donkey his owner's manger, but Israel does not know, my people do not understand." {4} Ah, sinful nation, a people loaded with guilt, a brood of evildoers, children given to corruption! They have forsaken the LORD; they have spurned the Holy One of Israel and turned their backs on him.

Isa 1:13-20

Stop bringing meaningless offerings! Your incense is detestable to me. New Moons, Sabbaths and convocations– I cannot bear your evil assemblies. {14} Your New Moon festivals and your appointed feasts my soul hates. They have become a burden to me; I am weary of bearing them. {15} When you spread out your hands in prayer, I will hide my eyes from you; even if you offer many prayers, I will not listen. Your hands are full of blood; {16} wash and make yourselves clean. Take your evil deeds out of my sight! Stop doing wrong, {17} learn to do right! Seek justice, encourage the oppressed. Defend the cause of the fatherless, plead the case of the widow. {18} "Come now, let us reason together," says the LORD. "Though your sins are like scarlet, they shall be as white as snow; though they are red as crimson, they shall be like wool. {19} If you are willing and obedient, you will eat the best from the land; {20} but if you resist and rebel, you will be devoured by the sword." For the mouth of the LORD has spoken.

JUDGMENT PRONOUNCED ON THE WICKED

Isa 3:8-26

Jerusalem staggers, Judah is falling; their words and deeds are against the LORD, defying his glorious presence. {9} The look on their faces testifies against them; they parade their sin like Sodom; they do not hide it. Woe to them! They have brought disaster upon themselves. {10} Tell the righteous it will be well with them, for they will enjoy the fruit of their deeds. {11} Woe to the wicked! Disaster is upon them! They will be paid back for what their hands have done. {12} Youths oppress my people, women rule over them. O my people, your guides lead you astray; they turn you from the path. {13} The LORD takes his place in court; he rises to judge the people. {14} The LORD enters into judgment against the elders and leaders of his people: "It is you who have ruined my vineyard; the plunder from the poor is in your houses. {15} What do you mean by crushing my people and grinding the faces of the poor?" declares the Lord, the LORD Almighty. {16} The LORD says, "The women of Zion are haughty, walking along with outstretched necks, flirting with their eyes, tripping along with mincing steps, with ornaments jingling on their ankles. {17} Therefore the Lord will bring sores on the heads of the women of Zion; the LORD will make their scalps bald." {18} In that day the Lord will snatch away their finery: the bangles and headbands and crescent necklaces, {19} the earrings and bracelets and veils, {20} the headdresses and ankle chains and sashes, the perfume bottles and charms, {21} the signet rings and nose rings, {22} the fine robes and the capes and cloaks, the purses {23} and mirrors, and the linen garments and tiaras and shawls. {24} Instead of fragrance there will be a stench; instead of a sash, a rope; instead of well-dressed hair, baldness; instead of fine clothing, sackcloth; instead of beauty, branding. {25} Your men will fall by the sword, your warriors in battle. {26} The gates of Zion will lament and mourn; destitute, she will sit on the ground.

A REMNANT OF ISRAEL WILL TRUST IN GOD

Isa 10:20-25
In that day the remnant of Israel, the survivors of the house of Jacob, will no longer rely on him who struck them down but will truly rely on the LORD, the Holy One of Israel. {21} A remnant will return, a remnant of Jacob will return to the Mighty God. {22} Though your people, O Israel, be like the sand by the sea, only a remnant will return. Destruction has been decreed, overwhelming and righteous. {23} The Lord, the LORD Almighty, will carry out the destruction decreed upon the whole land. {24} Therefore, this is what the Lord, the LORD Almighty, says: "O my people who live in Zion, do not be afraid of the Assyrians, who beat you with a rod and lift up a club against you, as Egypt did. {25} Very soon my anger against you will end and my wrath will be directed to their destruction."

Isa 11:1-11
A shoot will come up from the stump of Jesse; from his roots a Branch will bear fruit. {2} The Spirit of the LORD will rest on him– the Spirit of wisdom and of understanding, the Spirit of counsel and of power, the Spirit of knowledge and of the fear of the LORD– {3} and he will delight in the fear of the LORD. He will not judge by what he sees with his eyes, or decide by what he hears with his ears; {4} but with righteousness he will judge the needy, with justice he will give decisions for the poor of the earth. He will strike the earth with the rod of his mouth; with the breath of his lips he will slay the wicked. {5} Righteousness will be his belt and faithfulness the sash around his waist. {6} The wolf will live with the lamb, the leopard will lie down with the goat, the calf and the lion and the yearling together; and a little child will lead them. {7} The cow will feed with the bear, their young will lie down together, and the lion will eat straw like the ox. {8} The infant will play near the hole of the cobra, and the young child put his hand into the viper's nest. {9} They will neither harm nor destroy on all my holy mountain, for the earth will be full of the knowledge of the LORD as the waters cover the sea. {10} In that day the Root of Jesse will stand as a banner for the peoples; the nations will rally to him, and his place of rest will be glorious. {11} In that day the Lord will reach out his hand a second time to reclaim the remnant that is left of his people from Assyria, from Lower Egypt, from Upper Egypt, from Cush, from Elam, from Babylonia, from Hamath and from the islands of the sea.

A SONG OF PRAISE TO GOD

Isa 25:1-12

O LORD, you are my God; I will exalt you and praise your name, for in perfect faithfulness you have done marvelous things, things planned long ago. {2} You have made the city a heap of rubble, the fortified town a ruin, the foreigners' stronghold a city no more; it will never be rebuilt. {3} Therefore strong peoples will honor you; cities of ruthless nations will revere you. {4} You have been a refuge for the poor, a refuge for the needy in his distress, a shelter from the storm and a shade from the heat. For the breath of the ruthless is like a storm driving against a wall {5} and like the heat of the desert. You silence the uproar of foreigners; as heat is reduced by the shadow of a cloud, so the song of the ruthless is stilled. {6} On this mountain the LORD Almighty will prepare a feast of rich food for all peoples, a banquet of aged wine– the best of meats and the finest of wines. {7} On this mountain he will destroy the shroud that enfolds all peoples, the sheet that covers all nations; {8} he will swallow up death forever. The Sovereign LORD will wipe away the tears from all faces; he will remove the disgrace of his people from all the earth. The LORD has spoken. {9} In that day they will say, "Surely this is our God; we trusted in him, and he saved us. This is the LORD, we trusted in him; let us rejoice and be glad in his salvation." {10} The hand of the LORD will rest on this mountain; but Moab will be trampled under him as straw is trampled down in the manure. {11} They will spread out their hands in it, as a swimmer spreads out his hands to swim. God will bring down their pride despite the cleverness of their hands. {12} He will bring down your high fortified walls and lay them low; he will bring them down to the ground, to the very dust.

A CALL FOR REPENTANCE

Isa 30:15-26

This is what the Sovereign LORD, the Holy One of Israel, says: "In repentance and rest is your salvation, in quietness and trust is your strength, but you would have none of it. {16} You said, 'No, we will flee on horses.' Therefore you will flee! You said, 'We will ride off on swift horses.' Therefore your pursuers will be swift! {17} A thousand will flee at the threat of one; at the threat of five you will all flee away, till you are left like a flagstaff on a mountaintop, like a banner on a hill." {18} Yet the LORD longs to be gracious to you; he rises to show you compassion. For the LORD is a God of justice. Blessed are all who wait for him! {19} O people of Zion, who live in Jerusalem, you will weep no more. How gracious he will be when you cry for help! As soon as he hears, he will answer you. {20} Although the Lord gives you the bread of adversity and the water of affliction, your teachers will be hidden no more; with your own eyes you will see them. {21} Whether you turn to the right or to the left, your ears will hear a voice behind you, saying, "This is the way; walk in it." {22} Then you will defile your idols overlaid with silver and your images covered with gold; you will throw them away like a menstrual cloth and say to them, "Away with you!" {23} He will also send you rain for the seed you sow in the ground, and the food that comes from the land will be rich and plentiful. In that day your cattle will graze in broad meadows. {24} The oxen and donkeys that work the soil will eat fodder and mash, spread out with fork and shovel. {25} In the day of great slaughter, when the towers fall, streams of water will flow on every high mountain and every lofty hill. {26} The moon will shine like the sun, and the sunlight will be seven times brighter, like the light of seven full days, when the LORD binds up the bruises of his people and heals the wounds he inflicted.

Isa 31:6-9

Return to him you have so greatly revolted against, O Israelites. {7} For in that day every one of you will reject the idols of silver and gold your sinful hands have made. {8} "Assyria will fall by a sword that is not of man; a sword, not of mortals, will devour them. They will flee before the sword and their young men will be put to forced labor. {9} Their stronghold will fall because of terror; at sight of the battle standard their commanders will panic," declares the LORD, whose fire is in Zion, whose furnace is in Jerusalem.

GOOD TIDINGS FOR GOD'S PEOPLE

Isa 40:1-15a

Comfort, comfort my people, says your God. {2} Speak tenderly to Jerusalem, and proclaim to her that her hard service has been completed, that her sin has been paid for, that she has received from the Lord's hand double for all her sins. {3} A voice of one calling: "In the desert prepare the way for the LORD; make straight in the wilderness a highway for our God. {4} Every valley shall be raised up, every mountain and hill made low; the rough ground shall become level, the rugged places a plain. {5} And the glory of the LORD will be revealed, and all mankind together will see it. For the mouth of the LORD has spoken." {6} A voice says, "Cry out." And I said, "What shall I cry?" "All men are like grass, and all their glory is like the flowers of the field. {7} The grass withers and the flowers fall, because the breath of the LORD blows on them. Surely the people are grass. {8} The grass withers and the flowers fall, but the word of our God stands forever." {9} You who bring good tidings to Zion, go up on a high mountain. You who bring good tidings to Jerusalem, lift up your voice with a shout, lift it up, do not be afraid; say to the towns of Judah, "Here is your God!" {10} See, the Sovereign LORD comes with power, and his arm rules for him. See, his reward is with him, and his recompense accompanies him. {11} He tends his flock like a shepherd: He gathers the lambs in his arms and carries them close to his heart; he gently leads those that have young. {12} Who has measured the waters in the hollow of his hand, or with the breadth of his hand marked off the heavens? Who has held the dust of the earth in a basket, or weighed the mountains on the scales and the hills in a balance? {13} Who has understood the mind of the LORD, or instructed him as his counselor? {14} Whom did the LORD consult to enlighten him, and who taught him the right way? Who was it that taught him knowledge or showed him the path of understanding? {15} Surely the nations are like a drop in a bucket; they are regarded as dust on the scales....

GOD PROMISES TO REMEMBER ISRAEL

Isa 49:8-18

This is what the LORD says: "In the time of my favor I will answer you, and in the day of salvation I will help you; I will keep you and will make you to be a covenant for the people, to restore the land and to reassign its desolate inheritances, {9} to say to the captives, 'Come out,' and to those in darkness, 'Be free!' "They will feed beside the roads and find pasture on every barren hill. {10} They will neither hunger nor thirst, nor will the desert heat or the sun beat upon them. He who has compassion on them will guide them and lead them beside springs of water. {11} I will turn all my mountains into roads, and my highways will be raised up. {12} See, they will come from afar— some from the north, some from the west, some from the region of Aswan." {13} Shout for joy, O heavens; rejoice, O earth; burst into song, O mountains! For the LORD comforts his people and will have compassion on his afflicted ones. {14} But Zion said, "The LORD has forsaken me, the Lord has forgotten me." {15} "Can a mother forget the baby at her breast and have no compassion on the child she has borne? Though she may forget, I will not forget you! {16} See, I have engraved you on the palms of my hands; your walls are ever before me. {17} Your sons hasten back, and those who laid you waste depart from you. {18} Lift up your eyes and look around; all your sons gather and come to you. As surely as I live," declares the LORD, "you will wear them all as ornaments; you will put them on, like a bride.

Isa 49:22-23

This is what the Sovereign LORD says: "See, I will beckon to the Gentiles, I will lift up my banner to the peoples; they will bring your sons in their arms and carry your daughters on their shoulders. {23} Kings will be your foster fathers, and their queens your nursing mothers. They will bow down before you with their faces to the ground; they will lick the dust at your feet. Then you will know that I am the LORD; those who hope in me will not be disappointed."

GOD'S WAYS ARE ABOVE MAN'S WAYS

Isa 55:1-13

"Come, all you who are thirsty, come to the waters; and you who have no money, come, buy and eat! Come, buy wine and milk without money and without cost. {2} Why spend money on what is not bread, and your labor on what does not satisfy? Listen, listen to me, and eat what is good, and your soul will delight in the richest of fare. {3} Give ear and come to me; hear me, that your soul may live. I will make an everlasting covenant with you, my faithful love promised to David. {4} See, I have made him a witness to the peoples, a leader and commander of the peoples. {5} Surely you will summon nations you know not, and nations that do not know you will hasten to you, because of the LORD your God, the Holy One of Israel, for he has endowed you with splendor." {6} Seek the LORD while he may be found; call on him while he is near. {7} Let the wicked forsake his way and the evil man his thoughts. Let him turn to the LORD, and he will have mercy on him, and to our God, for he will freely pardon. {8} "For my thoughts are not your thoughts, neither are your ways my ways," declares the LORD. {9} "As the heavens are higher than the earth, so are my ways higher than your ways and my thoughts than your thoughts. {10} As the rain and the snow come down from heaven, and do not return to it without watering the earth and making it bud and flourish, so that it yields seed for the sower and bread for the eater, {11} so is my word that goes out from my mouth: It will not return to me empty, but will accomplish what I desire and achieve the purpose for which I sent it. {12} You will go out in joy and be led forth in peace; the mountains and hills will burst into song before you, and all the trees of the field will clap their hands. {13} Instead of the thornbush will grow the pine tree, and instead of briers the myrtle will grow. This will be for the Lord's renown, for an everlasting sign, which will not be destroyed."

TRUE FASTING IS TO HELP THE POOR

Isa 58:5-14

Is this the kind of fast I have chosen, only a day for a man to humble himself? Is it only for bowing one's head like a reed and for lying on sackcloth and ashes? Is that what you call a fast, a day acceptable to the LORD? {6} "Is not this the kind of fasting I have chosen: to loose the chains of injustice and untie the cords of the yoke, to set the oppressed free and break every yoke? {7} Is it not to share your food with the hungry and to provide the poor wanderer with shelter– when you see the naked, to clothe him, and not to turn away from your own flesh and blood? {8} Then your light will break forth like the dawn, and your healing will quickly appear; then your righteousness will go before you, and the glory of the LORD will be your rear guard. {9} Then you will call, and the LORD will answer; you will cry for help, and he will say: Here am I. "If you do away with the yoke of oppression, with the pointing finger and malicious talk, {10} and if you spend yourselves in behalf of the hungry and satisfy the needs of the oppressed, then your light will rise in the darkness, and your night will become like the noonday. {11} The LORD will guide you always; he will satisfy your needs in a sun-scorched land and will strengthen your frame. You will be like a well-watered garden, like a spring whose waters never fail. {12} Your people will rebuild the ancient ruins and will raise up the age-old foundations; you will be called Repairer of Broken Walls, Restorer of Streets with Dwellings. {13} "If you keep your feet from breaking the Sabbath and from doing as you please on my holy day, if you call the Sabbath a delight and the Lord's holy day honorable, and if you honor it by not going your own way and not doing as you please or speaking idle words, {14} then you will find your joy in the LORD, and I will cause you to ride on the heights of the land and to feast on the inheritance of your father Jacob." The mouth of the LORD has spoken.

THE YEAR OF THE LORD

Isa 61:1-11

The Spirit of the Sovereign LORD is on me, because the LORD has anointed me to preach good news to the poor. He has sent me to bind up the brokenhearted, to proclaim freedom for the captives and release from darkness for the prisoners, {2} to proclaim the year of the Lord's favor and the day of vengeance of our God, to comfort all who mourn, {3} and provide for those who grieve in Zion– to bestow on them a crown of beauty instead of ashes, the oil of gladness instead of mourning, and a garment of praise instead of a spirit of despair. They will be called oaks of righteousness, a planting of the LORD for the display of his splendor. {4} They will rebuild the ancient ruins and restore the places long devastated; they will renew the ruined cities that have been devastated for generations. {5} Aliens will shepherd your flocks; foreigners will work your fields and vineyards. {6} And you will be called priests of the LORD, you will be named ministers of our God. You will feed on the wealth of nations, and in their riches you will boast. {7} Instead of their shame my people will receive a double portion, and instead of disgrace they will rejoice in their inheritance; and so they will inherit a double portion in their land, and everlasting joy will be theirs. {8} "For I, the LORD, love justice; I hate robbery and iniquity. In my faithfulness I will reward them and make an everlasting covenant with them. {9} Their descendants will be known among the nations and their offspring among the peoples. All who see them will acknowledge that they are a people the LORD has blessed." {10} I delight greatly in the LORD; my soul rejoices in my God. For he has clothed me with garments of salvation and arrayed me in a robe of righteousness, as a bridegroom adorns his head like a priest, and as a bride adorns herself with her jewels. {11} For as the soil makes the sprout come up and a garden causes seeds to grow, so the Sovereign LORD will make righteousness and praise spring up before all nations.

THE NATIONS WILL SEE YOUR RIGHTEOUSNESS

Isa 62:1-12

For Zion's sake I will not keep silent, for Jerusalem's sake I will not remain quiet, till her righteousness shines out like the dawn, her salvation like a blazing torch. {2} The nations will see your righteousness, and all kings your glory; you will be called by a new name that the mouth of the LORD will bestow. {3} You will be a crown of splendor in the Lord's hand, a royal diadem in the hand of your God. {4} No longer will they call you Deserted, or name your land Desolate. But you will be called Hephzibah, and your land Beulah ; for the LORD will take delight in you, and your land will be married. {5} As a young man marries a maiden, so will your sons marry you; as a bridegroom rejoices over his bride, so will your God rejoice over you. {6} I have posted watchmen on your walls, O Jerusalem; they will never be silent day or night. You who call on the LORD, give yourselves no rest, {7} and give him no rest till he establishes Jerusalem and makes her the praise of the earth. {8} The LORD has sworn by his right hand and by his mighty arm: "Never again will I give your grain as food for your enemies, and never again will foreigners drink the new wine for which you have toiled; {9} but those who harvest it will eat it and praise the LORD, and those who gather the grapes will drink it in the courts of my sanctuary." {10} Pass through, pass through the gates! Prepare the way for the people. Build up, build up the highway! Remove the stones. Raise a banner for the nations. {11} The LORD has made proclamation to the ends of the earth: "Say to the Daughter of Zion, 'See, your Savior comes! See, his reward is with him, and his recompense accompanies him.'" {12} They will be called the Holy People, the Redeemed of the LORD; and you will be called Sought After, the City No Longer Deserted.

A NEW CREATION

Isa 65:16-25

Whoever invokes a blessing in the land will do so by the God of truth; he who takes an oath in the land will swear by the God of truth. For the past troubles will be forgotten and hidden from my eyes. {17} "Behold, I will create new heavens and a new earth. The former things will not be remembered, nor will they come to mind. {18} But be glad and rejoice forever in what I will create, for I will create Jerusalem to be a delight and its people a joy. {19} I will rejoice over Jerusalem and take delight in my people; the sound of weeping and of crying will be heard in it no more. {20} "Never again will there be in it an infant who lives but a few days, or an old man who does not live out his years; he who dies at a hundred will be thought a mere youth; he who fails to reach a hundred will be considered accursed. {21} They will build houses and dwell in them; they will plant vineyards and eat their fruit. {22} No longer will they build houses and others live in them, or plant and others eat. For as the days of a tree, so will be the days of my people; my chosen ones will long enjoy the works of their hands. {23} They will not toil in vain or bear children doomed to misfortune; for they will be a people blessed by the LORD, they and their descendants with them. {24} Before they call I will answer; while they are still speaking I will hear. {25} The wolf and the lamb will feed together, and the lion will eat straw like the ox, but dust will be the serpent's food. They will neither harm nor destroy on all my holy mountain," says the LORD.

A BLESSED HOPE FOR GOD'S PEOPLE

Isa 66:1-2

This is what the LORD says: "Heaven is my throne, and the earth is my footstool. Where is the house you will build for me? Where will my resting place be? {2} Has not my hand made all these things, and so they came into being?" declares the LORD. "This is the one I esteem: he who is humble and contrite in spirit, and trembles at my word.

Isa 66:5-6

Hear the word of the LORD, you who tremble at his word: "Your brothers who hate you, and exclude you because of my name, have said, 'Let the LORD be glorified, that we may see your joy!' Yet they will be put to shame. {6} Hear that uproar from the city, hear that noise from the temple! It is the sound of the LORD repaying his enemies all they deserve.

Isa 66:12-14

For this is what the LORD says: "I will extend peace to her like a river, and the wealth of nations like a flooding stream; you will nurse and be carried on her arm and dandled on her knees. {13} As a mother comforts her child, so will I comfort you; and you will be comforted over Jerusalem." {14} When you see this, your heart will rejoice and you will flourish like grass; the hand of the LORD will be made known to his servants, but his fury will be shown to his foes.

GOD WILL PUNISH HIS UNFAITHFUL CHILDREN

Jer 5:14-29

Therefore this is what the LORD God Almighty says: "Because the people have spoken these words, I will make my words in your mouth a fire and these people the wood it consumes. {15} O house of Israel," declares the LORD, "I am bringing a distant nation against you– an ancient and enduring nation, a people whose language you do not know, whose speech you do not understand. {16} Their quivers are like an open grave; all of them are mighty warriors. {17} They will devour your harvests and food, devour your sons and daughters; they will devour your flocks and herds, devour your vines and fig trees. With the sword they will destroy the fortified cities in which you trust. {18} "Yet even in those days," declares the LORD, "I will not destroy you completely. {19} And when the people ask, 'Why has the LORD our God done all this to us?' you will tell them, 'As you have forsaken me and served foreign gods in your own land, so now you will serve foreigners in a land not your own.' {20} "Announce this to the house of Jacob and proclaim it in Judah: {21} Hear this, you foolish and senseless people, who have eyes but do not see, who have ears but do not hear: {22} Should you not fear me?" declares the LORD. "Should you not tremble in my presence? I made the sand a boundary for the sea, an everlasting barrier it cannot cross. The waves may roll, but they cannot prevail; they may roar, but they cannot cross it. {23} But these people have stubborn and rebellious hearts; they have turned aside and gone away. {24} They do not say to themselves, 'Let us fear the LORD our God, who gives autumn and spring rains in season, who assures us of the regular weeks of harvest.' {25} Your wrongdoings have kept these away; your sins have deprived you of good. {26} "Among my people are wicked men who lie in wait like men who snare birds and like those who set traps to catch men. {27} Like cages full of birds, their houses are full of deceit; they have become rich and powerful {28} and have grown fat and sleek. Their evil deeds have no limit; they do not plead the case of the fatherless to win it, they do not defend the rights of the poor. {29} Should I not punish them for this?" declares the LORD. "Should I not avenge myself on such a nation as this?

GOD IS THE MAKER OF ALL AND WILL JUDGE ALL

Jer 10:11-25
"Tell them this: 'These gods, who did not make the heavens and the earth, will perish from the earth and from under the heavens.'" {12} But God made the earth by his power; he founded the world by his wisdom and stretched out the heavens by his understanding. {13} When he thunders, the waters in the heavens roar; he makes clouds rise from the ends of the earth. He sends lightning with the rain and brings out the wind from his storehouses. {14} Everyone is senseless and without knowledge; every goldsmith is shamed by his idols. His images are a fraud; they have no breath in them. {15} They are worthless, the objects of mockery; when their judgment comes, they will perish. {16} He who is the Portion of Jacob is not like these, for he is the Maker of all things, including Israel, the tribe of his inheritance– the LORD Almighty is his name. {17} Gather up your belongings to leave the land, you who live under siege. {18} For this is what the LORD says: "At this time I will hurl out those who live in this land; I will bring distress on them so that they may be captured." {19} Woe to me because of my injury! My wound is incurable! Yet I said to myself, "This is my sickness, and I must endure it." {20} My tent is destroyed; all its ropes are snapped. My sons are gone from me and are no more; no one is left now to pitch my tent or to set up my shelter. {21} The shepherds are senseless and do not inquire of the LORD; so they do not prosper and all their flock is scattered. {22} Listen! The report is coming– a great commotion from the land of the north! It will make the towns of Judah desolate, a haunt of jackals. {23} I know, O LORD, that a man's life is not his own; it is not for man to direct his steps. {24} Correct me, LORD, but only with justice– not in your anger, lest you reduce me to nothing. {25} Pour out your wrath on the nations that do not acknowledge you, on the peoples who do not call on your name. For they have devoured Jacob; they have devoured him completely and destroyed his homeland.

THE POTTER'S CLAY

Jer 18:1-20

This is the word that came to Jeremiah from the LORD: {2} "Go down to the potter's house, and there I will give you my message." {3} So I went down to the potter's house, and I saw him working at the wheel. {4} But the pot he was shaping from the clay was marred in his hands; so the potter formed it into another pot, shaping it as seemed best to him. {5} Then the word of the LORD came to me: {6} "O house of Israel, can I not do with you as this potter does?" declares the LORD. "Like clay in the hand of the potter, so are you in my hand, O house of Israel. {7} If at any time I announce that a nation or kingdom is to be uprooted, torn down and destroyed, {8} and if that nation I warned repents of its evil, then I will relent and not inflict on it the disaster I had planned. {9} And if at another time I announce that a nation or kingdom is to be built up and planted, {10} and if it does evil in my sight and does not obey me, then I will reconsider the good I had intended to do for it. {11} "Now therefore say to the people of Judah and those living in Jerusalem, 'This is what the LORD says: Look! I am preparing a disaster for you and devising a plan against you. So turn from your evil ways, each one of you, and reform your ways and your actions.' {12} But they will reply, 'It's no use. We will continue with our own plans; each of us will follow the stubbornness of his evil heart.'" {13} Therefore this is what the LORD says: "Inquire among the nations: Who has ever heard anything like this? A most horrible thing has been done by Virgin Israel. {14} Does the snow of Lebanon ever vanish from its rocky slopes? Do its cool waters from distant sources ever cease to flow? {15} Yet my people have forgotten me; they burn incense to worthless idols, which made them stumble in their ways and in the ancient paths. They made them walk in bypaths and on roads not built up. {16} Their land will be laid waste, an object of lasting scorn; all who pass by will be appalled and will shake their heads. {17} Like a wind from the east, I will scatter them before their enemies; I will show them my back and not my face in the day of their disaster." {18} They said, "Come, let's make plans against Jeremiah; for the teaching of the law by the priest will not be lost, nor will counsel from the wise, nor the word from the prophets. So come, let's attack him with our tongues and pay no attention to anything he says." {19} Listen to me, O LORD; hear what my accusers are saying! {20} Should good be repaid with evil? Yet they have dug a pit for me. Remember that I stood before you and spoke in their behalf to turn your wrath away from them.

GOD WILL GATHER A REMNANT

Jer 23:1-8

"Woe to the shepherds who are destroying and scattering the sheep of my pasture!" declares the LORD. {2} Therefore this is what the LORD, the God of Israel, says to the shepherds who tend my people: "Because you have scattered my flock and driven them away and have not bestowed care on them, I will bestow punishment on you for the evil you have done," declares the LORD. {3} "I myself will gather the remnant of my flock out of all the countries where I have driven them and will bring them back to their pasture, where they will be fruitful and increase in number. {4} I will place shepherds over them who will tend them, and they will no longer be afraid or terrified, nor will any be missing," declares the LORD. {5} "The days are coming," declares the LORD, "when I will raise up to David a righteous Branch, a King who will reign wisely and do what is just and right in the land. {6} In his days Judah will be saved and Israel will live in safety. This is the name by which he will be called: The LORD Our Righteousness. {7} "So then, the days are coming," declares the LORD, "when people will no longer say, 'As surely as the LORD lives, who brought the Israelites up out of Egypt,' {8} but they will say, 'As surely as the LORD lives, who brought the descendants of Israel up out of the land of the north and out of all the countries where he had banished them.' Then they will live in their own land."

Jer 24:1-7

After Jehoiachin son of Jehoiakim king of Judah and the officials, the craftsmen and the artisans of Judah were carried into exile from Jerusalem to Babylon by Nebuchadnezzar king of Babylon, the LORD showed me two baskets of figs placed in front of the temple of the LORD. {2} One basket had very good figs, like those that ripen early; the other basket had very poor figs, so bad they could not be eaten. {3} Then the LORD asked me, "What do you see, Jeremiah?" "Figs," I answered. "The good ones are very good, but the poor ones are so bad they cannot be eaten." {4} Then the word of the LORD came to me: {5} "This is what the LORD, the God of Israel, says: 'Like these good figs, I regard as good the exiles from Judah, whom I sent away from this place to the land of the Babylonians. {6} My eyes will watch over them for their good, and I will bring them back to this land. I will build them up and not tear them down; I will plant them and not uproot them. {7} I will give them a heart to know me, that I am the LORD. They will be my people, and I will be their God, for they will return to me with all their heart.

ISRAEL AND JUDAH WILL RETURN IN JOY

Jer 30:1-3

This is the word that came to Jeremiah from the LORD: {2} "This is what the LORD, the God of Israel, says: 'Write in a book all the words I have spoken to you. {3} The days are coming,' declares the LORD, 'when I will bring my people Israel and Judah back from captivity and restore them to the land I gave their forefathers to possess,' says the LORD."

Jer 31:1-10

"At that time," declares the LORD, "I will be the God of all the clans of Israel, and they will be my people." {2} This is what the LORD says: "The people who survive the sword will find favor in the desert; I will come to give rest to Israel." {3} The LORD appeared to us in the past, saying: "I have loved you with an everlasting love; I have drawn you with loving-kindness. {4} I will build you up again and you will be rebuilt, O Virgin Israel. Again you will take up your tambourines and go out to dance with the joyful. {5} Again you will plant vineyards on the hills of Samaria; the farmers will plant them and enjoy their fruit. {6} There will be a day when watchmen cry out on the hills of Ephraim, 'Come, let us go up to Zion, to the LORD our God.'" {7} This is what the LORD says: "Sing with joy for Jacob; shout for the foremost of the nations. Make your praises heard, and say, 'O LORD, save your people, the remnant of Israel.' {8} See, I will bring them from the land of the north and gather them from the ends of the earth. Among them will be the blind and the lame, expectant mothers and women in labor; a great throng will return. {9} They will come with weeping; they will pray as I bring them back. I will lead them beside streams of water on a level path where they will not stumble, because I am Israel's father, and Ephraim is my firstborn son. {10} "Hear the word of the LORD, O nations; proclaim it in distant coastlands: 'He who scattered Israel will gather them and will watch over his flock like a shepherd.'

GOD WILL BRING THEM BACK TO REBUILD THE CITY

Jer 31:23-33

This is what the LORD Almighty, the God of Israel, says: "When I bring them back from captivity, the people in the land of Judah and in its towns will once again use these words: 'The LORD bless you, O righteous dwelling, O sacred mountain.' {24} People will live together in Judah and all its towns–farmers and those who move about with their flocks. {25} I will refresh the weary and satisfy the faint." {26} At this I awoke and looked around. My sleep had been pleasant to me. {27} "The days are coming," declares the LORD, "when I will plant the house of Israel and the house of Judah with the offspring of men and of animals. {28} Just as I watched over them to uproot and tear down, and to overthrow, destroy and bring disaster, so I will watch over them to build and to plant," declares the LORD. {29} "In those days people will no longer say, 'The fathers have eaten sour grapes, and the children's teeth are set on edge.' {30} Instead, everyone will die for his own sin; whoever eats sour grapes–his own teeth will be set on edge. {31} "The time is coming," declares the LORD, "when I will make a new covenant with the house of Israel and with the house of Judah. {32} It will not be like the covenant I made with their forefathers when I took them by the hand to lead them out of Egypt, because they broke my covenant, though I was a husband to them," declares the LORD. {33} "This is the covenant I will make with the house of Israel after that time," declares the LORD. "I will put my law in their minds and write it on their hearts. I will be their God, and they will be my people.

Jer 31:38-40

"The days are coming," declares the LORD, "when this city will be rebuilt for me from the Tower of Hananel to the Corner Gate. {39} The measuring line will stretch from there straight to the hill of Gareb and then turn to Goah. {40} The whole valley where dead bodies and ashes are thrown, and all the terraces out to the Kidron Valley on the east as far as the corner of the Horse Gate, will be holy to the LORD. The city will never again be uprooted or demolished."

CALL UPON ME AND I WILL SHOW YOU
GREAT AND MIGHTY THINGS

Jer 33:1-11

While Jeremiah was still confined in the courtyard of the guard, the word of the LORD came to him a second time: {2} "This is what the LORD says, he who made the earth, the LORD who formed it and established it–the LORD is his name: {3} 'Call to me and I will answer you and tell you great and unsearchable things you do not know.' {4} For this is what the LORD, the God of Israel, says about the houses in this city and the royal palaces of Judah that have been torn down to be used against the siege ramps and the sword {5} in the fight with the Babylonians: 'They will be filled with the dead bodies of the men I will slay in my anger and wrath. I will hide my face from this city because of all its wickedness. {6} "'Nevertheless, I will bring health and healing to it; I will heal my people and will let them enjoy abundant peace and security. {7} I will bring Judah and Israel back from captivity and will rebuild them as they were before. {8} I will cleanse them from all the sin they have committed against me and will forgive all their sins of rebellion against me. {9} Then this city will bring me renown, joy, praise and honor before all nations on earth that hear of all the good things I do for it; and they will be in awe and will tremble at the abundant prosperity and peace I provide for it.' {10} "This is what the LORD says: 'You say about this place, "It is a desolate waste, without men or animals." Yet in the towns of Judah and the streets of Jerusalem that are deserted, inhabited by neither men nor animals, there will be heard once more {11} the sounds of joy and gladness, the voices of bride and bridegroom, and the voices of those who bring thank offerings to the house of the LORD, saying, "Give thanks to the LORD Almighty, for the LORD is good; his love endures forever." For I will restore the fortunes of the land as they were before,' says the LORD.

Jer 33:14-17

"'The days are coming,' declares the LORD, 'when I will fulfill the gracious promise I made to the house of Israel and to the house of Judah. {15} "'In those days and at that time I will make a righteous Branch sprout from David's line; he will do what is just and right in the land. {16} In those days Judah will be saved and Jerusalem will live in safety. This is the name by which it will be called: The LORD Our Righteousness.' {17} For this is what the LORD says: 'David will never fail to have a man to sit on the throne of the house of Israel,

FREEDOM TO THE SLAVES

Jer 34:2b-17

'This is what the LORD says: I am about to hand this city over to the king of Babylon, and he will burn it down. {3} You will not escape from his grasp but will surely be captured and handed over to him. You will see the king of Babylon with your own eyes, and he will speak with you face to face. And you will go to Babylon. {4} "'Yet hear the promise of the LORD, O Zedekiah king of Judah. This is what the LORD says concerning you: You will not die by the sword; {5} you will die peacefully. As people made a funeral fire in honor of your fathers, the former kings who preceded you, so they will make a fire in your honor and lament, "Alas, O master!" I myself make this promise, declares the LORD.'" {6} Then Jeremiah the prophet told all this to Zedekiah king of Judah, in Jerusalem, {7} while the army of the king of Babylon was fighting against Jerusalem and the other cities of Judah that were still holding out—Lachish and Azekah. These were the only fortified cities left in Judah. {8} The word came to Jeremiah from the LORD after King Zedekiah had made a covenant with all the people in Jerusalem to proclaim freedom for the slaves. {9} Everyone was to free his Hebrew slaves, both male and female; no one was to hold a fellow Jew in bondage. {10} So all the officials and people who entered into this covenant agreed that they would free their male and female slaves and no longer hold them in bondage. They agreed, and set them free. {11} But afterward they changed their minds and took back the slaves they had freed and enslaved them again. {12} Then the word of the LORD came to Jeremiah: {13} "This is what the LORD, the God of Israel, says: I made a covenant with your forefathers when I brought them out of Egypt, out of the land of slavery. I said, {14} 'Every seventh year each of you must free any fellow Hebrew who has sold himself to you. After he has served you six years, you must let him go free.' Your fathers, however, did not listen to me or pay attention to me. {15} Recently you repented and did what is right in my sight: Each of you proclaimed freedom to his countrymen. You even made a covenant before me in the house that bears my Name. {16} But now you have turned around and profaned my name; each of you has taken back the male and female slaves you had set free to go where they wished. You have forced them to become your slaves again. {17} "Therefore, this is what the LORD says: You have not obeyed me; you have not proclaimed freedom for your fellow countrymen. So I now proclaim 'freedom' for you, declares the LORD—'freedom' to fall by the sword, plague and famine. I will make you abhorrent to all the kingdoms of the earth.

HOW DESERTED LIES THE CITY

Lam 1:1-8

How deserted lies the city, once so full of people! How like a widow is she, who once was great among the nations! She who was queen among the provinces has now become a slave. {2} Bitterly she weeps at night, tears are upon her cheeks. Among all her lovers there is none to comfort her. All her friends have betrayed her; they have become her enemies. {3} After affliction and harsh labor, Judah has gone into exile. She dwells among the nations; she finds no resting place. All who pursue her have overtaken her in the midst of her distress. {4} The roads to Zion mourn, for no one comes to her appointed feasts. All her gateways are desolate, her priests groan, her maidens grieve, and she is in bitter anguish. {5} Her foes have become her masters; her enemies are at ease. The LORD has brought her grief because of her many sins. Her children have gone into exile, captive before the foe. {6} All the splendor has departed from the Daughter of Zion. Her princes are like deer that find no pasture; in weakness they have fled before the pursuer. {7} In the days of her affliction and wandering Jerusalem remembers all the treasures that were hers in days of old. When her people fell into enemy hands, there was no one to help her. Her enemies looked at her and laughed at her destruction. {8} Jerusalem has sinned greatly and so has become unclean. All who honored her despise her, for they have seen her nakedness; she herself groans and turns away.

MY EYES FAIL FROM WEEPING

Lam 2:11-19a

My eyes fail from weeping, I am in torment within, my heart is poured out on the ground because my people are destroyed, because children and infants faint in the streets of the city. {12} They say to their mothers, "Where is bread and wine?" as they faint like wounded men in the streets of the city, as their lives ebb away in their mothers' arms. {13} What can I say for you? With what can I compare you, O Daughter of Jerusalem? To what can I liken you, that I may comfort you, O Virgin Daughter of Zion? Your wound is as deep as the sea. Who can heal you? {14} The visions of your prophets were false and worthless; they did not expose your sin to ward off your captivity. The oracles they gave you were false and misleading. {15} All who pass your way clap their hands at you; they scoff and shake their heads at the Daughter of Jerusalem: "Is this the city that was called the perfection of beauty, the joy of the whole earth?" {16} All your enemies open their mouths wide against you; they scoff and gnash their teeth and say, "We have swallowed her up. This is the day we have waited for; we have lived to see it." {17} The LORD has done what he planned; he has fulfilled his word, which he decreed long ago. He has overthrown you without pity, he has let the enemy gloat over you, he has exalted the horn of your foes. {18} The hearts of the people cry out to the Lord. O wall of the Daughter of Zion, let your tears flow like a river day and night; give yourself no relief, your eyes no rest. {19} Arise, cry out in the night, as the watches of the night begin; pour out your heart like water in the presence of the Lord.

YET, WE HAVE HOPE

Lam 3:19-42

I remember my affliction and my wandering, the bitterness and the gall. {20} I well remember them, and my soul is downcast within me. {21} Yet this I call to mind and therefore I have hope: {22} Because of the Lord's great love we are not consumed, for his compassions never fail. {23} They are new every morning; great is your faithfulness. {24} I say to myself, "The LORD is my portion; therefore I will wait for him." {25} The LORD is good to those whose hope is in him, to the one who seeks him; {26} it is good to wait quietly for the salvation of the LORD. {27} It is good for a man to bear the yoke while he is young. {28} Let him sit alone in silence, for the LORD has laid it on him. {29} Let him bury his face in the dust– there may yet be hope. {30} Let him offer his cheek to one who would strike him, and let him be filled with disgrace. {31} For men are not cast off by the Lord forever. {32} Though he brings grief, he will show compassion, so great is his unfailing love. {33} For he does not willingly bring affliction or grief to the children of men. {34} To crush underfoot all prisoners in the land, {35} to deny a man his rights before the Most High, {36} to deprive a man of justice– would not the Lord see such things? {37} Who can speak and have it happen if the Lord has not decreed it? {38} Is it not from the mouth of the Most High that both calamities and good things come? {39} Why should any living man complain when punished for his sins? {40} Let us examine our ways and test them, and let us return to the LORD. {41} Let us lift up our hearts and our hands to God in heaven, and say: {42} "We have sinned and rebelled and you have not forgiven.

RESTORE US LORD TO YOURSELF

Lam 4:22-5:22

O Daughter of Zion, your punishment will end; he will not prolong your exile. But, O Daughter of Edom, he will punish your sin and expose your wickedness. {5:1} Remember, O LORD, what has happened to us; look, and see our disgrace. {2} Our inheritance has been turned over to aliens, our homes to foreigners. {3} We have become orphans and fatherless, our mothers like widows. {4} We must buy the water we drink; our wood can be had only at a price. {5} Those who pursue us are at our heels; we are weary and find no rest. {6} We submitted to Egypt and Assyria to get enough bread. {7} Our fathers sinned and are no more, and we bear their punishment. {8} Slaves rule over us, and there is none to free us from their hands. {9} We get our bread at the risk of our lives because of the sword in the desert. {10} Our skin is hot as an oven, feverish from hunger. {11} Women have been ravished in Zion, and virgins in the towns of Judah. {12} Princes have been hung up by their hands; elders are shown no respect. {13} Young men toil at the millstones; boys stagger under loads of wood. {14} The elders are gone from the city gate; the young men have stopped their music. {15} Joy is gone from our hearts; our dancing has turned to mourning. {16} The crown has fallen from our head. Woe to us, for we have sinned! {17} Because of this our hearts are faint, because of these things our eyes grow dim {18} for Mount Zion, which lies desolate, with jackals prowling over it. {19} You, O LORD, reign forever; your throne endures from generation to generation. {20} Why do you always forget us? Why do you forsake us so long? {21} Restore us to yourself, O LORD, that we may return; renew our days as of old {22} unless you have utterly rejected us and are angry with us beyond measure.

GOD WILL AGAIN GATHER HIS PEOPLE

Ezek 11:14-12:7a

The word of the LORD came to me: {15} "Son of man, your brothers–your brothers who are your blood relatives and the whole house of Israel–are those of whom the people of Jerusalem have said, 'They are far away from the LORD; this land was given to us as our possession.' {16} "Therefore say: 'This is what the Sovereign LORD says: Although I sent them far away among the nations and scattered them among the countries, yet for a little while I have been a sanctuary for them in the countries where they have gone.' {17} "Therefore say: 'This is what the Sovereign LORD says: I will gather you from the nations and bring you back from the countries where you have been scattered, and I will give you back the land of Israel again.' {18} "They will return to it and remove all its vile images and detestable idols. {19} I will give them an undivided heart and put a new spirit in them; I will remove from them their heart of stone and give them a heart of flesh. {20} Then they will follow my decrees and be careful to keep my laws. They will be my people, and I will be their God. {21} But as for those whose hearts are devoted to their vile images and detestable idols, I will bring down on their own heads what they have done, declares the Sovereign LORD." {22} Then the cherubim, with the wheels beside them, spread their wings, and the glory of the God of Israel was above them. {23} The glory of the LORD went up from within the city and stopped above the mountain east of it. {24} The Spirit lifted me up and brought me to the exiles in Babylonia in the vision given by the Spirit of God. Then the vision I had seen went up from me, {25} and I told the exiles everything the LORD had shown me. {12:1} The word of the LORD came to me: {2} "Son of man, you are living among a rebellious people. They have eyes to see but do not see and ears to hear but do not hear, for they are a rebellious people. {3} "Therefore, son of man, pack your belongings for exile and in the daytime, as they watch, set out and go from where you are to another place. Perhaps they will understand, though they are a rebellious house. {4} During the daytime, while they watch, bring out your belongings packed for exile. Then in the evening, while they are watching, go out like those who go into exile. {5} While they watch, dig through the wall and take your belongings out through it. {6} Put them on your shoulder as they are watching and carry them out at dusk. Cover your face so that you cannot see the land, for I have made you a sign to the house of Israel." {7} So I did as I was commanded. During the day I brought out my things packed for exile. Then in the evening I dug through the wall with my hands.

THE SIN OF ISRAEL

Ezek 16:43-59

"'Because you did not remember the days of your youth but enraged me with all these things, I will surely bring down on your head what you have done, declares the Sovereign LORD. Did you not add lewdness to all your other detestable practices? {44} "'Everyone who quotes proverbs will quote this proverb about you: "Like mother, like daughter." {45} You are a true daughter of your mother, who despised her husband and her children; and you are a true sister of your sisters, who despised their husbands and their children. Your mother was a Hittite and your father an Amorite. {46} Your older sister was Samaria, who lived to the north of you with her daughters; and your younger sister, who lived to the south of you with her daughters, was Sodom. {47} You not only walked in their ways and copied their detestable practices, but in all your ways you soon became more depraved than they. {48} As surely as I live, declares the Sovereign LORD, your sister Sodom and her daughters never did what you and your daughters have done. {49} "'Now this was the sin of your sister Sodom: She and her daughters were arrogant, overfed and unconcerned; they did not help the poor and needy. {50} They were haughty and did detestable things before me. Therefore I did away with them as you have seen. {51} Samaria did not commit half the sins you did. You have done more detestable things than they, and have made your sisters seem righteous by all these things you have done. {52} Bear your disgrace, for you have furnished some justification for your sisters. Because your sins were more vile than theirs, they appear more righteous than you. So then, be ashamed and bear your disgrace, for you have made your sisters appear righteous. {53} "'However, I will restore the fortunes of Sodom and her daughters and of Samaria and her daughters, and your fortunes along with them, {54} so that you may bear your disgrace and be ashamed of all you have done in giving them comfort. {55} And your sisters, Sodom with her daughters and Samaria with her daughters, will return to what they were before; and you and your daughters will return to what you were before. {56} You would not even mention your sister Sodom in the day of your pride, {57} before your wickedness was uncovered. Even so, you are now scorned by the daughters of Edom and all her neighbors and the daughters of the Philistines—all those around you who despise you. {58} You will bear the consequences of your lewdness and your detestable practices, declares the LORD. {59} "'This is what the Sovereign LORD says: I will deal with you as you deserve, because you have despised my oath by breaking the covenant.

PARABLE OF THE EAGLES AND A VINE

Ezek 17:3-19

Say to them, 'This is what the Sovereign LORD says: A great eagle with powerful wings, long feathers and full plumage of varied colors came to Lebanon. Taking hold of the top of a cedar, {4} he broke off its topmost shoot and carried it away to a land of merchants, where he planted it in a city of traders. {5} "'He took some of the seed of your land and put it in fertile soil. He planted it like a willow by abundant water, {6} and it sprouted and became a low, spreading vine. Its branches turned toward him, but its roots remained under it. So it became a vine and produced branches and put out leafy boughs. {7} "'But there was another great eagle with powerful wings and full plumage. The vine now sent out its roots toward him from the plot where it was planted and stretched out its branches to him for water. {8} It had been planted in good soil by abundant water so that it would produce branches, bear fruit and become a splendid vine.' {9} "Say to them, 'This is what the Sovereign LORD says: Will it thrive? Will it not be uprooted and stripped of its fruit so that it withers? All its new growth will wither. It will not take a strong arm or many people to pull it up by the roots. {10} Even if it is transplanted, will it thrive? Will it not wither completely when the east wind strikes it—wither away in the plot where it grew?'" {11} Then the word of the LORD came to me: {12} "Say to this rebellious house, 'Do you not know what these things mean?' Say to them: 'The king of Babylon went to Jerusalem and carried off her king and her nobles, bringing them back with him to Babylon. {13} Then he took a member of the royal family and made a treaty with him, putting him under oath. He also carried away the leading men of the land, {14} so that the kingdom would be brought low, unable to rise again, surviving only by keeping his treaty. {15} But the king rebelled against him by sending his envoys to Egypt to get horses and a large army. Will he succeed? Will he who does such things escape? Will he break the treaty and yet escape? {16} "'As surely as I live, declares the Sovereign LORD, he shall die in Babylon, in the land of the king who put him on the throne, whose oath he despised and whose treaty he broke. {17} Pharaoh with his mighty army and great horde will be of no help to him in war, when ramps are built and siege works erected to destroy many lives. {18} He despised the oath by breaking the covenant. Because he had given his hand in pledge and yet did all these things, he shall not escape. {19} "'Therefore this is what the Sovereign LORD says: As surely as I live, I will bring down on his head my oath that he despised and my covenant that he broke.

EACH GENERATION WILL HAVE ITS OWN REWARD

Ezek 18:4-20

For every living soul belongs to me, the father as well as the son–both alike belong to me. The soul who sins is the one who will die. {5} "Suppose there is a righteous man who does what is just and right. {6} He does not eat at the mountain shrines or look to the idols of the house of Israel. He does not defile his neighbor's wife or lie with a woman during her period. {7} He does not oppress anyone, but returns what he took in pledge for a loan. He does not commit robbery but gives his food to the hungry and provides clothing for the naked. {8} He does not lend at usury or take excessive interest. He withholds his hand from doing wrong and judges fairly between man and man. {9} He follows my decrees and faithfully keeps my laws. That man is righteous; he will surely live, declares the Sovereign LORD. {10} "Suppose he has a violent son, who sheds blood or does any of these other things {11} (though the father has done none of them): "He eats at the mountain shrines. He defiles his neighbor's wife. {12} He oppresses the poor and needy. He commits robbery. He does not return what he took in pledge. He looks to the idols. He does detestable things. {13} He lends at usury and takes excessive interest. Will such a man live? He will not! Because he has done all these detestable things, he will surely be put to death and his blood will be on his own head. {14} "But suppose this son has a son who sees all the sins his father commits, and though he sees them, he does not do such things: {15} "He does not eat at the mountain shrines or look to the idols of the house of Israel. He does not defile his neighbor's wife. {16} He does not oppress anyone or require a pledge for a loan. He does not commit robbery but gives his food to the hungry and provides clothing for the naked. {17} He withholds his hand from sin and takes no usury or excessive interest. He keeps my laws and follows my decrees. He will not die for his father's sin; he will surely live. {18} But his father will die for his own sin, because he practiced extortion, robbed his brother and did what was wrong among his people. {19} "Yet you ask, 'Why does the son not share the guilt of his father?' Since the son has done what is just and right and has been careful to keep all my decrees, he will surely live. {20} The soul who sins is the one who will die. The son will not share the guilt of the father, nor will the father share the guilt of the son. The righteousness of the righteous man will be credited to him, and the wickedness of the wicked will be charged against him.

SHEPHERDS CARE FOR THEIR FLOCKS

Ezek 34:2b-17

Woe to the shepherds of Israel who only take care of themselves! Should not shepherds take care of the flock? {3} You eat the curds, clothe yourselves with the wool and slaughter the choice animals, but you do not take care of the flock. {4} You have not strengthened the weak or healed the sick or bound up the injured. You have not brought back the strays or searched for the lost. You have ruled them harshly and brutally. {5} So they were scattered because there was no shepherd, and when they were scattered they became food for all the wild animals. {6} My sheep wandered over all the mountains and on every high hill. They were scattered over the whole earth, and no one searched or looked for them. {7} "Therefore, you shepherds, hear the word of the LORD: {8} As surely as I live, declares the Sovereign LORD, because my flock lacks a shepherd and so has been plundered and has become food for all the wild animals, and because my shepherds did not search for my flock but cared for themselves rather than for my flock, {9} therefore, O shepherds, hear the word of the LORD: {10} This is what the Sovereign LORD says: I am against the shepherds and will hold them accountable for my flock. I will remove them from tending the flock so that the shepherds can no longer feed themselves. I will rescue my flock from their mouths, and it will no longer be food for them. {11} "For this is what the Sovereign LORD says: I myself will search for my sheep and look after them. {12} As a shepherd looks after his scattered flock when he is with them, so will I look after my sheep. I will rescue them from all the places where they were scattered on a day of clouds and darkness. {13} I will bring them out from the nations and gather them from the countries, and I will bring them into their own land. I will pasture them on the mountains of Israel, in the ravines and in all the settlements in the land. {14} I will tend them in a good pasture, and the mountain heights of Israel will be their grazing land. There they will lie down in good grazing land, and there they will feed in a rich pasture on the mountains of Israel. {15} I myself will tend my sheep and have them lie down, declares the Sovereign LORD. {16} I will search for the lost and bring back the strays. I will bind up the injured and strengthen the weak, but the sleek and the strong I will destroy. I will shepherd the flock with justice. {17} "As for you, my flock, this is what the Sovereign LORD says: I will judge between one sheep and another, and between rams and goats.

VALLEY OF DRY BONES

Ezek 37:1b-19
          And he brought me out by the Spirit of the LORD and set me in the middle of a valley; it was full of bones. {2} He led me back and forth among them, and I saw a great many bones on the floor of the valley, bones that were very dry. {3} He asked me, "Son of man, can these bones live?" I said, "O Sovereign LORD, you alone know." {4} Then he said to me, "Prophesy to these bones and say to them, 'Dry bones, hear the word of the LORD! {5} This is what the Sovereign LORD says to these bones: I will make breath enter you, and you will come to life. {6} I will attach tendons to you and make flesh come upon you and cover you with skin; I will put breath in you, and you will come to life. Then you will know that I am the LORD.'" {7} So I prophesied as I was commanded. And as I was prophesying, there was a noise, a rattling sound, and the bones came together, bone to bone. {8} I looked, and tendons and flesh appeared on them and skin covered them, but there was no breath in them. {9} Then he said to me, "Prophesy to the breath; prophesy, son of man, and say to it, 'This is what the Sovereign LORD says: Come from the four winds, O breath, and breathe into these slain, that they may live.'" {10} So I prophesied as he commanded me, and breath entered them; they came to life and stood up on their feet–a vast army. {11} Then he said to me: "Son of man, these bones are the whole house of Israel. They say, 'Our bones are dried up and our hope is gone; we are cut off.' {12} Therefore prophesy and say to them: 'This is what the Sovereign LORD says: O my people, I am going to open your graves and bring you up from them; I will bring you back to the land of Israel. {13} Then you, my people, will know that I am the LORD, when I open your graves and bring you up from them. {14} I will put my Spirit in you and you will live, and I will settle you in your own land. Then you will know that I the LORD have spoken, and I have done it, declares the LORD.'" {15} The word of the LORD came to me: {16} "Son of man, take a stick of wood and write on it, 'Belonging to Judah and the Israelites associated with him.' Then take another stick of wood, and write on it, 'Ephraim's stick, belonging to Joseph and all the house of Israel associated with him.' {17} Join them together into one stick so that they will become one in your hand. {18} "When your countrymen ask you, 'Won't you tell us what you mean by this?' {19} say to them, 'This is what the Sovereign LORD says: I am going to take the stick of Joseph–which is in Ephraim's hand–and of the Israelite tribes associated with him, and join it to Judah's stick, making them a single stick of wood, and they will become one in my hand.'

GOG, FROM THE NORTH, WILL BE DESTROYED

Ezek 39:1-8

"Son of man, prophesy against Gog and say: 'This is what the Sovereign LORD says: I am against you, O Gog, chief prince of Meshech and Tubal. {2} I will turn you around and drag you along. I will bring you from the far north and send you against the mountains of Israel. {3} Then I will strike your bow from your left hand and make your arrows drop from your right hand. {4} On the mountains of Israel you will fall, you and all your troops and the nations with you. I will give you as food to all kinds of carrion birds and to the wild animals. {5} You will fall in the open field, for I have spoken, declares the Sovereign LORD. {6} I will send fire on Magog and on those who live in safety in the coastlands, and they will know that I am the LORD. {7} "'I will make known my holy name among my people Israel. I will no longer let my holy name be profaned, and the nations will know that I the LORD am the Holy One in Israel. {8} It is coming! It will surely take place, declares the Sovereign LORD. This is the day I have spoken of.

Ezek 39:17-25

"Son of man, this is what the Sovereign LORD says: Call out to every kind of bird and all the wild animals: 'Assemble and come together from all around to the sacrifice I am preparing for you, the great sacrifice on the mountains of Israel. There you will eat flesh and drink blood. {18} You will eat the flesh of mighty men and drink the blood of the princes of the earth as if they were rams and lambs, goats and bulls—all of them fattened animals from Bashan. {19} At the sacrifice I am preparing for you, you will eat fat till you are glutted and drink blood till you are drunk. {20} At my table you will eat your fill of horses and riders, mighty men and soldiers of every kind,' declares the Sovereign LORD. {21} "I will display my glory among the nations, and all the nations will see the punishment I inflict and the hand I lay upon them. {22} From that day forward the house of Israel will know that I am the LORD their God. {23} And the nations will know that the people of Israel went into exile for their sin, because they were unfaithful to me. So I hid my face from them and handed them over to their enemies, and they all fell by the sword. {24} I dealt with them according to their uncleanness and their offenses, and I hid my face from them. {25} "Therefore this is what the Sovereign LORD says: I will now bring Jacob back from captivity and will have compassion on all the people of Israel, and I will be zealous for my holy name.

OFFERINGS TO THE LORD

Ezek 45:18-25

"This is what the Sovereign LORD says: In the first month on the first day you are to take a young bull without defect and purify the sanctuary. {19} The priest is to take some of the blood of the sin offering and put it on the doorposts of the temple, on the four corners of the upper ledge of the altar and on the gateposts of the inner court. {20} You are to do the same on the seventh day of the month for anyone who sins unintentionally or through ignorance; so you are to make atonement for the temple. {21} "In the first month on the fourteenth day you are to observe the Passover, a feast lasting seven days, during which you shall eat bread made without yeast. {22} On that day the prince is to provide a bull as a sin offering for himself and for all the people of the land. {23} Every day during the seven days of the Feast he is to provide seven bulls and seven rams without defect as a burnt offering to the LORD, and a male goat for a sin offering. {24} He is to provide as a grain offering an ephah for each bull and an ephah for each ram, along with a hin of oil for each ephah. {25} "During the seven days of the Feast, which begins in the seventh month on the fifteenth day, he is to make the same provision for sin offerings, burnt offerings, grain offerings and oil.

Ezek 46:11-15

"'At the festivals and the appointed feasts, the grain offering is to be an ephah with a bull, an ephah with a ram, and with the lambs as much as one pleases, along with a hin of oil for each ephah. {12} When the prince provides a freewill offering to the LORD–whether a burnt offering or fellowship offerings–the gate facing east is to be opened for him. He shall offer his burnt offering or his fellowship offerings as he does on the Sabbath day. Then he shall go out, and after he has gone out, the gate will be shut. {13} "'Every day you are to provide a year-old lamb without defect for a burnt offering to the LORD; morning by morning you shall provide it. {14} You are also to provide with it morning by morning a grain offering, consisting of a sixth of an ephah with a third of a hin of oil to moisten the flour. The presenting of this grain offering to the LORD is a lasting ordinance. {15} So the lamb and the grain offering and the oil shall be provided morning by morning for a regular burnt offering.

DANIEL ALSO DREAMS - OF FOUR BEASTS

Dan 7:1-14b

In the first year of Belshazzar king of Babylon, Daniel had a dream, and visions passed through his mind as he was lying on his bed. He wrote down the substance of his dream. {2} Daniel said: "In my vision at night I looked, and there before me were the four winds of heaven churning up the great sea. {3} Four great beasts, each different from the others, came up out of the sea. {4} "The first was like a lion, and it had the wings of an eagle. I watched until its wings were torn off and it was lifted from the ground so that it stood on two feet like a man, and the heart of a man was given to it. {5} "And there before me was a second beast, which looked like a bear. It was raised up on one of its sides, and it had three ribs in its mouth between its teeth. It was told, 'Get up and eat your fill of flesh!' {6} "After that, I looked, and there before me was another beast, one that looked like a leopard. And on its back it had four wings like those of a bird. This beast had four heads, and it was given authority to rule. {7} "After that, in my vision at night I looked, and there before me was a fourth beast–terrifying and frightening and very powerful. It had large iron teeth; it crushed and devoured its victims and trampled underfoot whatever was left. It was different from all the former beasts, and it had ten horns. {8} "While I was thinking about the horns, there before me was another horn, a little one, which came up among them; and three of the first horns were uprooted before it. This horn had eyes like the eyes of a man and a mouth that spoke boastfully. {9} "As I looked, "thrones were set in place, and the Ancient of Days took his seat. His clothing was as white as snow; the hair of his head was white like wool. His throne was flaming with fire, and its wheels were all ablaze. {10} A river of fire was flowing, coming out from before him. Thousands upon thousands attended him; ten thousand times ten thousand stood before him. The court was seated, and the books were opened. {11} "Then I continued to watch because of the boastful words the horn was speaking. I kept looking until the beast was slain and its body destroyed and thrown into the blazing fire. {12} (The other beasts had been stripped of their authority, but were allowed to live for a period of time.) {13} "In my vision at night I looked, and there before me was one like a son of man, coming with the clouds of heaven. He approached the Ancient of Days and was led into his presence. {14} He was given authority, glory and sovereign power; all peoples, nations and men of every language worshiped him. His dominion is an everlasting dominion that will not pass away....

DANIEL IS OFFERED AN INTERPRETATION OF HIS DREAM

Dan 7:15-28

"I, Daniel, was troubled in spirit, and the visions that passed through my mind disturbed me. {16} I approached one of those standing there and asked him the true meaning of all this. "So he told me and gave me the interpretation of these things: {17} 'The four great beasts are four kingdoms that will rise from the earth. {18} But the saints of the Most High will receive the kingdom and will possess it forever–yes, for ever and ever.' {19} "Then I wanted to know the true meaning of the fourth beast, which was different from all the others and most terrifying, with its iron teeth and bronze claws–the beast that crushed and devoured its victims and trampled underfoot whatever was left. {20} I also wanted to know about the ten horns on its head and about the other horn that came up, before which three of them fell–the horn that looked more imposing than the others and that had eyes and a mouth that spoke boastfully. {21} As I watched, this horn was waging war against the saints and defeating them, {22} until the Ancient of Days came and pronounced judgment in favor of the saints of the Most High, and the time came when they possessed the kingdom. {23} "He gave me this explanation: 'The fourth beast is a fourth kingdom that will appear on earth. It will be different from all the other kingdoms and will devour the whole earth, trampling it down and crushing it. {24} The ten horns are ten kings who will come from this kingdom. After them another king will arise, different from the earlier ones; he will subdue three kings. {25} He will speak against the Most High and oppress his saints and try to change the set times and the laws. The saints will be handed over to him for a time, times and half a time. {26} "But the court will sit, and his power will be taken away and completely destroyed forever. {27} Then the sovereignty, power and greatness of the kingdoms under the whole heaven will be handed over to the saints, the people of the Most High. His kingdom will be an everlasting kingdom, and all rulers will worship and obey him.' {28} "This is the end of the matter. I, Daniel, was deeply troubled by my thoughts, and my face turned pale, but I kept the matter to myself."

DANIEL HAS A VISION OF A RAM AND A GOAT

Dan 8:1-17

In the third year of King Belshazzar's reign, I, Daniel, had a vision, after the one that had already appeared to me. {2} In my vision I saw myself in the citadel of Susa in the province of Elam; in the vision I was beside the Ulai Canal. {3} I looked up, and there before me was a ram with two horns, standing beside the canal, and the horns were long. One of the horns was longer than the other but grew up later. {4} I watched the ram as he charged toward the west and the north and the south. No animal could stand against him, and none could rescue from his power. He did as he pleased and became great. {5} As I was thinking about this, suddenly a goat with a prominent horn between his eyes came from the west, crossing the whole earth without touching the ground. {6} He came toward the two-horned ram I had seen standing beside the canal and charged at him in great rage. {7} I saw him attack the ram furiously, striking the ram and shattering his two horns. The ram was powerless to stand against him; the goat knocked him to the ground and trampled on him, and none could rescue the ram from his power. {8} The goat became very great, but at the height of his power his large horn was broken off, and in its place four prominent horns grew up toward the four winds of heaven. {9} Out of one of them came another horn, which started small but grew in power to the south and to the east and toward the Beautiful Land. {10} It grew until it reached the host of the heavens, and it threw some of the starry host down to the earth and trampled on them. {11} It set itself up to be as great as the Prince of the host; it took away the daily sacrifice from him, and the place of his sanctuary was brought low. {12} Because of rebellion, the host <of the saints> and the daily sacrifice were given over to it. It prospered in everything it did, and truth was thrown to the ground. {13} Then I heard a holy one speaking, and another holy one said to him, "How long will it take for the vision to be fulfilled--the vision concerning the daily sacrifice, the rebellion that causes desolation, and the surrender of the sanctuary and of the host that will be trampled underfoot?" {14} He said to me, "It will take 2,300 evenings and mornings; then the sanctuary will be reconsecrated." {15} While I, Daniel, was watching the vision and trying to understand it, there before me stood one who looked like a man. {16} And I heard a man's voice from the Ulai calling, "Gabriel, tell this man the meaning of the vision." {17} As he came near the place where I was standing, I was terrified and fell prostrate. "Son of man," he said to me, "understand that the vision concerns the time of the end."

DANIEL PRAYS FOR THE RESTORATION OF ISRAEL

Dan 9:1-17a

In the first year of Darius son of Xerxes (a Mede by descent), who was made ruler over the Babylonian kingdom– {2} in the first year of his reign, I, Daniel, understood from the Scriptures, according to the word of the LORD given to Jeremiah the prophet, that the desolation of Jerusalem would last seventy years. {3} So I turned to the Lord God and pleaded with him in prayer and petition, in fasting, and in sackcloth and ashes. {4} I prayed to the LORD my God and confessed: "O Lord, the great and awesome God, who keeps his covenant of love with all who love him and obey his commands, {5} we have sinned and done wrong. We have been wicked and have rebelled; we have turned away from your commands and laws. {6} We have not listened to your servants the prophets, who spoke in your name to our kings, our princes and our fathers, and to all the people of the land. {7} "Lord, you are righteous, but this day we are covered with shame–the men of Judah and people of Jerusalem and all Israel, both near and far, in all the countries where you have scattered us because of our unfaithfulness to you. {8} O LORD, we and our kings, our princes and our fathers are covered with shame because we have sinned against you. {9} The Lord our God is merciful and forgiving, even though we have rebelled against him; {10} we have not obeyed the LORD our God or kept the laws he gave us through his servants the prophets. {11} All Israel has transgressed your law and turned away, refusing to obey you. "Therefore the curses and sworn judgments written in the Law of Moses, the servant of God, have been poured out on us, because we have sinned against you. {12} You have fulfilled the words spoken against us and against our rulers by bringing upon us great disaster. Under the whole heaven nothing has ever been done like what has been done to Jerusalem. {13} Just as it is written in the Law of Moses, all this disaster has come upon us, yet we have not sought the favor of the LORD our God by turning from our sins and giving attention to your truth. {14} The LORD did not hesitate to bring the disaster upon us, for the LORD our God is righteous in everything he does; yet we have not obeyed him. {15} "Now, O Lord our God, who brought your people out of Egypt with a mighty hand and who made for yourself a name that endures to this day, we have sinned, we have done wrong. {16} O Lord, in keeping with all your righteous acts, turn away your anger and your wrath from Jerusalem, your city, your holy hill. Our sins and the iniquities of our fathers have made Jerusalem and your people an object of scorn to all those around us. {17} "Now, our God, hear the prayers and petitions of your servant.

GABRIEL SPEAKS OF SEVENTY SEVENS

Dan 9:20-27

While I was speaking and praying, confessing my sin and the sin of my people Israel and making my request to the LORD my God for his holy hill– {21} while I was still in prayer, Gabriel, the man I had seen in the earlier vision, came to me in swift flight about the time of the evening sacrifice. {22} He instructed me and said to me, "Daniel, I have now come to give you insight and understanding. {23} As soon as you began to pray, an answer was given, which I have come to tell you, for you are highly esteemed. Therefore, consider the message and understand the vision: {24} "Seventy 'sevens' are decreed for your people and your holy city to finish transgression, to put an end to sin, to atone for wickedness, to bring in everlasting righteousness, to seal up vision and prophecy and to anoint the most holy. {25} "Know and understand this: From the issuing of the decree to restore and rebuild Jerusalem until the Anointed One, the ruler, comes, there will be seven 'sevens,' and sixty-two 'sevens.' It will be rebuilt with streets and a trench, but in times of trouble. {26} After the sixty-two 'sevens,' the Anointed One will be cut off and will have nothing. The people of the ruler who will come will destroy the city and the sanctuary. The end will come like a flood: War will continue until the end, and desolations have been decreed. {27} He will confirm a covenant with many for one 'seven.' In the middle of the 'seven' he will put an end to sacrifice and offering. And on a wing <of the temple> he will set up an abomination that causes desolation, until the end that is decreed is poured out on him."

AT THE TIME OF THE END

Dan 11:40-12:10

"At the time of the end the king of the South will engage him in battle, and the king of the North will storm out against him with chariots and cavalry and a great fleet of ships. He will invade many countries and sweep through them like a flood. {41} He will also invade the Beautiful Land. Many countries will fall, but Edom, Moab and the leaders of Ammon will be delivered from his hand. {42} He will extend his power over many countries; Egypt will not escape. {43} He will gain control of the treasures of gold and silver and all the riches of Egypt, with the Libyans and Nubians in submission. {44} But reports from the east and the north will alarm him, and he will set out in a great rage to destroy and annihilate many. {45} He will pitch his royal tents between the seas at the beautiful holy mountain. Yet he will come to his end, and no one will help him. {12:1} "At that time Michael, the great prince who protects your people, will arise. There will be a time of distress such as has not happened from the beginning of nations until then. But at that time your people–everyone whose name is found written in the book–will be delivered. {2} Multitudes who sleep in the dust of the earth will awake: some to everlasting life, others to shame and everlasting contempt. {3} Those who are wise will shine like the brightness of the heavens, and those who lead many to righteousness, like the stars for ever and ever. {4} But you, Daniel, close up and seal the words of the scroll until the time of the end. Many will go here and there to increase knowledge." {5} Then I, Daniel, looked, and there before me stood two others, one on this bank of the river and one on the opposite bank. {6} One of them said to the man clothed in linen, who was above the waters of the river, "How long will it be before these astonishing things are fulfilled?" {7} The man clothed in linen, who was above the waters of the river, lifted his right hand and his left hand toward heaven, and I heard him swear by him who lives forever, saying, "It will be for a time, times and half a time. When the power of the holy people has been finally broken, all these things will be completed." {8} I heard, but I did not understand. So I asked, "My lord, what will the outcome of all this be?" {9} He replied, "Go your way, Daniel, because the words are closed up and sealed until the time of the end. {10} Many will be purified, made spotless and refined, but the wicked will continue to be wicked. None of the wicked will understand, but those who are wise will understand.

HOSEA'S ADULTEROUS WIFE

Hosea 1:1-2:5

The word of the LORD that came to Hosea son of Beeri during the reigns of Uzziah, Jotham, Ahaz and Hezekiah, kings of Judah, and during the reign of Jeroboam son of Jehoash king of Israel: {2} When the LORD began to speak through Hosea, the LORD said to him, "Go, take to yourself an adulterous wife and children of unfaithfulness, because the land is guilty of the vilest adultery in departing from the LORD." {3} So he married Gomer daughter of Diblaim, and she conceived and bore him a son. {4} Then the LORD said to Hosea, "Call him Jezreel, because I will soon punish the house of Jehu for the massacre at Jezreel, and I will put an end to the kingdom of Israel. {5} In that day I will break Israel's bow in the Valley of Jezreel." {6} Gomer conceived again and gave birth to a daughter. Then the LORD said to Hosea, "Call her Lo-Ruhamah, for I will no longer show love to the house of Israel, that I should at all forgive them. {7} Yet I will show love to the house of Judah; and I will save them–not by bow, sword or battle, or by horses and horsemen, but by the LORD their God." {8} After she had weaned Lo-Ruhamah, Gomer had another son. {9} Then the LORD said, "Call him Lo-Ammi, for you are not my people, and I am not your God. {10} "Yet the Israelites will be like the sand on the seashore, which cannot be measured or counted. In the place where it was said to them, 'You are not my people,' they will be called 'sons of the living God.' {11} The people of Judah and the people of Israel will be reunited, and they will appoint one leader and will come up out of the land, for great will be the day of Jezreel.

{2:1} "Say of your brothers, 'My people,' and of your sisters, 'My loved one.' {2} "Rebuke your mother, rebuke her, for she is not my wife, and I am not her husband. Let her remove the adulterous look from her face and the unfaithfulness from between her breasts. {3} Otherwise I will strip her naked and make her as bare as on the day she was born; I will make her like a desert, turn her into a parched land, and slay her with thirst. {4} I will not show my love to her children, because they are the children of adultery. {5} Their mother has been unfaithful and has conceived them in disgrace. She said, 'I will go after my lovers, who give me my food and my water, my wool and my linen, my oil and my drink.'

BUT GOD WILL LOVE EVEN AN ADULTEROUS WIFE

Hosea 2:14-3:5

"Therefore I am now going to allure her; I will lead her into the desert and speak tenderly to her. {15} There I will give her back her vineyards, and will make the Valley of Achor a door of hope. There she will sing as in the days of her youth, as in the day she came up out of Egypt. {16} "In that day," declares the LORD, "you will call me 'my husband'; you will no longer call me 'my master. ' {17} I will remove the names of the Baals from her lips; no longer will their names be invoked. {18} In that day I will make a covenant for them with the beasts of the field and the birds of the air and the creatures that move along the ground. Bow and sword and battle I will abolish from the land, so that all may lie down in safety. {19} I will betroth you to me forever; I will betroth you in righteousness and justice, in love and compassion. {20} I will betroth you in faithfulness, and you will acknowledge the LORD. {21} "In that day I will respond," declares the LORD– "I will respond to the skies, and they will respond to the earth; {22} and the earth will respond to the grain, the new wine and oil, and they will respond to Jezreel. {23} I will plant her for myself in the land; I will show my love to the one I called 'Not my loved one. ' I will say to those called 'Not my people, ' 'You are my people'; and they will say, 'You are my God.'" {3:1} The LORD said to me, "Go, show your love to your wife again, though she is loved by another and is an adulteress. Love her as the LORD loves the Israelites, though they turn to other gods and love the sacred raisin cakes." {2} So I bought her for fifteen shekels of silver and about a homer and a lethek of barley. {3} Then I told her, "You are to live with me many days; you must not be a prostitute or be intimate with any man, and I will live with you." {4} For the Israelites will live many days without king or prince, without sacrifice or sacred stones, without ephod or idol. {5} Afterward the Israelites will return and seek the LORD their God and David their king. They will come trembling to the LORD and to his blessings in the last days.

GOD WILL HEAL ISRAEL

Hosea 11:1-11

"When Israel was a child, I loved him, and out of Egypt I called my son. {2} But the more I called Israel, the further they went from me. They sacrificed to the Baals and they burned incense to images. {3} It was I who taught Ephraim to walk, taking them by the arms; but they did not realize it was I who healed them. {4} I led them with cords of human kindness, with ties of love; I lifted the yoke from their neck and bent down to feed them. {5} "Will they not return to Egypt and will not Assyria rule over them because they refuse to repent? {6} Swords will flash in their cities, will destroy the bars of their gates and put an end to their plans. {7} My people are determined to turn from me. Even if they call to the Most High, he will by no means exalt them. {8} "How can I give you up, Ephraim? How can I hand you over, Israel? How can I treat you like Admah? How can I make you like Zeboiim? My heart is changed within me; all my compassion is aroused. {9} I will not carry out my fierce anger, nor will I turn and devastate Ephraim. For I am God, and not man– the Holy One among you. I will not come in wrath. {10} They will follow the LORD; he will roar like a lion. When he roars, his children will come trembling from the west. {11} They will come trembling like birds from Egypt, like doves from Assyria. I will settle them in their homes," declares the LORD.

Hosea 14:9

Who is wise? He will realize these things. Who is discerning? He will understand them. The ways of the LORD are right; the righteous walk in them, but the rebellious stumble in them.

REPENT AND GOD WILL HEAR

Joel 1:1-3

The word of the LORD that came to Joel son of Pethuel. {2} Hear this, you elders; listen, all who live in the land. Has anything like this ever happened in your days or in the days of your forefathers? {3} Tell it to your children, and let your children tell it to their children, and their children to the next generation.

Joel 2:12-19

'Even now,' declares the LORD, 'return to me with all your heart, with fasting and weeping and mourning.' {13} Rend your heart and not your garments. Return to the LORD your God, for he is gracious and compassionate, slow to anger and abounding in love, and he relents from sending calamity. {14} Who knows? He may turn and have pity and leave behind a blessing– grain offerings and drink offerings for the LORD your God. {15} Blow the trumpet in Zion, declare a holy fast, call a sacred assembly. {16} Gather the people, consecrate the assembly; bring together the elders, gather the children, those nursing at the breast. Let the bridegroom leave his room and the bride her chamber. {17} Let the priests, who minister before the LORD, weep between the temple porch and the altar. Let them say, 'Spare your people, O LORD. Do not make your inheritance an object of scorn, a byword among the nations. Why should they say among the peoples, 'Where is their God?'" {18} Then the LORD will be jealous for his land and take pity on his people. {19} The LORD will reply to them: 'I am sending you grain, new wine and oil, enough to satisfy you fully; never again will I make you an object of scorn to the nations.

Joel 2:26-27

You will have plenty to eat, until you are full, and you will praise the name of the LORD your God, who has worked wonders for you; never again will my people be shamed. {27} Then you will know that I am in Israel, that I am the LORD your God, and that there is no other; never again will my people be shamed.

JUDAH WILL BE RESTORED, AND THE NATIONS JUDGED

Joel 3:1-2

'In those days and at that time, when I restore the fortunes of Judah and Jerusalem, {2} I will gather all nations and bring them down to the Valley of Jehoshaphat. There I will enter into judgment against them concerning my inheritance, my people Israel, for they scattered my people among the nations and divided up my land.

Joel 3:9-12

Proclaim this among the nations: Prepare for war! Rouse the warriors! Let all the fighting men draw near and attack. {10} Beat your plowshares into swords and your pruning hooks into spears. Let the weakling say, 'I am strong!' {11} Come quickly, all you nations from every side, and assemble there. Bring down your warriors, O LORD! {12} 'Let the nations be roused; let them advance into the Valley of Jehoshaphat, for there I will sit to judge all the nations on every side.

Joel 3:16-21

The LORD will roar from Zion and thunder from Jerusalem; the earth and the sky will tremble. But the LORD will be a refuge for his people, a stronghold for the people of Israel. {17} 'Then you will know that I, the LORD your God, dwell in Zion, my holy hill. Jerusalem will be holy; never again will foreigners invade her. {18} 'In that day the mountains will drip new wine, and the hills will flow with milk; all the ravines of Judah will run with water. A fountain will flow out of the Lord's house and will water the valley of acacias. {19} But Egypt will be desolate, Edom a desert waste, because of violence done to the people of Judah, in whose land they shed innocent blood. {20} Judah will be inhabited forever and Jerusalem through all generations. {21} Their bloodguilt, which I have not pardoned, I will pardon.' The LORD dwells in Zion!

GOD'S CHOSEN PEOPLE WILL BE PUNISHED

Amos 3:1-8
     Hear this word the LORD has spoken against you, O people of Israel–against the whole family I brought up out of Egypt: {2} "You only have I chosen of all the families of the earth; therefore I will punish you for all your sins." {3} Do two walk together unless they have agreed to do so? {4} Does a lion roar in the thicket when he has no prey? Does he growl in his den when he has caught nothing? {5} Does a bird fall into a trap on the ground where no snare has been set? Does a trap spring up from the earth when there is nothing to catch? {6} When a trumpet sounds in a city, do not the people tremble? When disaster comes to a city, has not the LORD caused it? {7} Surely the Sovereign LORD does nothing without revealing his plan to his servants the prophets. {8} The lion has roared– who will not fear? The Sovereign LORD has spoken– who can but prophesy?

Amos 4:10-13
     "I sent plagues among you as I did to Egypt. I killed your young men with the sword, along with your captured horses. I filled your nostrils with the stench of your camps, yet you have not returned to me," declares the LORD. {11} "I overthrew some of you as I overthrew Sodom and Gomorrah. You were like a burning stick snatched from the fire, yet you have not returned to me," declares the LORD. {12} "Therefore this is what I will do to you, Israel, and because I will do this to you, prepare to meet your God, O Israel." {13} He who forms the mountains, creates the wind, and reveals his thoughts to man, he who turns dawn to darkness, and treads the high places of the earth– the LORD God Almighty is his name.

ISRAEL WILL LIVE WHEN IT SEEKS GOD

Amos 5:4-15

This is what the LORD says to the house of Israel: "Seek me and live; {5} do not seek Bethel, do not go to Gilgal, do not journey to Beersheba. For Gilgal will surely go into exile, and Bethel will be reduced to nothing." {6} Seek the LORD and live, or he will sweep through the house of Joseph like a fire; it will devour, and Bethel will have no one to quench it. {7} You who turn justice into bitterness and cast righteousness to the ground {8} (he who made the Pleiades and Orion, who turns blackness into dawn and darkens day into night, who calls for the waters of the sea and pours them out over the face of the land– the LORD is his name– {9} he flashes destruction on the stronghold and brings the fortified city to ruin), {10} you hate the one who reproves in court and despise him who tells the truth. {11} You trample on the poor and force him to give you grain. Therefore, though you have built stone mansions, you will not live in them; though you have planted lush vineyards, you will not drink their wine. {12} For I know how many are your offenses and how great your sins. You oppress the righteous and take bribes and you deprive the poor of justice in the courts. {13} Therefore the prudent man keeps quiet in such times, for the times are evil. {14} Seek good, not evil, that you may live. Then the LORD God Almighty will be with you, just as you say he is. {15} Hate evil, love good; maintain justice in the courts. Perhaps the LORD God Almighty will have mercy on the remnant of Joseph.

Amos 5:21-24

"I hate, I despise your religious feasts; I cannot stand your assemblies. {22} Even though you bring me burnt offerings and grain offerings, I will not accept them. Though you bring choice fellowship offerings, I will have no regard for them. {23} Away with the noise of your songs! I will not listen to the music of your harps. {24} But let justice roll on like a river, righteousness like a never-failing stream!

PUNISHMENT PROMISED TO THOSE NATIONS
WHO DO NOT DEFEND ISRAEL

Oba 1:10-21

Because of the violence against your brother Jacob, you will be covered with shame; you will be destroyed forever. {11} On the day you stood aloof while strangers carried off his wealth and foreigners entered his gates and cast lots for Jerusalem, you were like one of them. {12} You should not look down on your brother in the day of his misfortune, nor rejoice over the people of Judah in the day of their destruction, nor boast so much in the day of their trouble. {13} You should not march through the gates of my people in the day of their disaster, nor look down on them in their calamity in the day of their disaster, nor seize their wealth in the day of their disaster. {14} You should not wait at the crossroads to cut down their fugitives, nor hand over their survivors in the day of their trouble. {15} "The day of the LORD is near for all nations. As you have done, it will be done to you; your deeds will return upon your own head. {16} Just as you drank on my holy hill, so all the nations will drink continually; they will drink and drink and be as if they had never been. {17} But on Mount Zion will be deliverance; it will be holy, and the house of Jacob will possess its inheritance. {18} The house of Jacob will be a fire and the house of Joseph a flame; the house of Esau will be stubble, and they will set it on fire and consume it. There will be no survivors from the house of Esau." The LORD has spoken. {19} People from the Negev will occupy the mountains of Esau, and people from the foothills will possess the land of the Philistines. They will occupy the fields of Ephraim and Samaria, and Benjamin will possess Gilead. {20} This company of Israelite exiles who are in Canaan will possess <the land> as far as Zarephath; the exiles from Jerusalem who are in Sepharad will possess the towns of the Negev. {21} Deliverers will go up on Mount Zion to govern the mountains of Esau. And the kingdom will be the Lord's.

JONAH TRIES TO RUN AWAY FROM GOD

Jonah 1:1-17

The word of the LORD came to Jonah son of Amittai: {2} "Go to the great city of Nineveh and preach against it, because its wickedness has come up before me." {3} But Jonah ran away from the LORD and headed for Tarshish. He went down to Joppa, where he found a ship bound for that port. After paying the fare, he went aboard and sailed for Tarshish to flee from the LORD. {4} Then the LORD sent a great wind on the sea, and such a violent storm arose that the ship threatened to break up. {5} All the sailors were afraid and each cried out to his own god. And they threw the cargo into the sea to lighten the ship. But Jonah had gone below deck, where he lay down and fell into a deep sleep. {6} The captain went to him and said, "How can you sleep? Get up and call on your god! Maybe he will take notice of us, and we will not perish." {7} Then the sailors said to each other, "Come, let us cast lots to find out who is responsible for this calamity." They cast lots and the lot fell on Jonah. {8} So they asked him, "Tell us, who is responsible for making all this trouble for us? What do you do? Where do you come from? What is your country? From what people are you?" {9} He answered, "I am a Hebrew and I worship the LORD, the God of heaven, who made the sea and the land." {10} This terrified them and they asked, "What have you done?" (They knew he was running away from the LORD, because he had already told them so.) {11} The sea was getting rougher and rougher. So they asked him, "What should we do to you to make the sea calm down for us?" {12} "Pick me up and throw me into the sea," he replied, "and it will become calm. I know that it is my fault that this great storm has come upon you." {13} Instead, the men did their best to row back to land. But they could not, for the sea grew even wilder than before. {14} Then they cried to the LORD, "O LORD, please do not let us die for taking this man's life. Do not hold us accountable for killing an innocent man, for you, O LORD, have done as you pleased." {15} Then they took Jonah and threw him overboard, and the raging sea grew calm. {16} At this the men greatly feared the LORD, and they offered a sacrifice to the LORD and made vows to him. {17} But the LORD provided a great fish to swallow Jonah, and Jonah was inside the fish three days and three nights.

JONAH, INSIDE THE GIANT FISH, PRAYS TO GOD

Jonah 2:1-10

From inside the fish Jonah prayed to the LORD his God. {2} He said: "In my distress I called to the LORD, and he answered me. From the depths of the grave I called for help, and you listened to my cry. {3} You hurled me into the deep, into the very heart of the seas, and the currents swirled about me; all your waves and breakers swept over me. {4} I said, 'I have been banished from your sight; yet I will look again toward your holy temple.' {5} The engulfing waters threatened me, the deep surrounded me; seaweed was wrapped around my head. {6} To the roots of the mountains I sank down; the earth beneath barred me in forever. But you brought my life up from the pit, O LORD my God. {7} "When my life was ebbing away, I remembered you, LORD, and my prayer rose to you, to your holy temple. {8} "Those who cling to worthless idols forfeit the grace that could be theirs. {9} But I, with a song of thanksgiving, will sacrifice to you. What I have vowed I will make good. Salvation comes from the LORD." {10} And the LORD commanded the fish, and it vomited Jonah onto dry land.

JONAH OBEYS GOD

Jonah 3:3-4:11

Jonah obeyed the word of the LORD and went to Nineveh. Now Nineveh was a very important city—a visit required three days. {4} On the first day, Jonah started into the city. He proclaimed: "Forty more days and Nineveh will be overturned." {5} The Ninevites believed God. They declared a fast, and all of them, from the greatest to the least, put on sackcloth. {6} When the news reached the king of Nineveh, he rose from his throne, took off his royal robes, covered himself with sackcloth and sat down in the dust. {7} Then he issued a proclamation in Nineveh: "By the decree of the king and his nobles: Do not let any man or beast, herd or flock, taste anything; do not let them eat or drink. {8} But let man and beast be covered with sackcloth. Let everyone call urgently on God. Let them give up their evil ways and their violence. {9} Who knows? God may yet relent and with compassion turn from his fierce anger so that we will not perish." {10} When God saw what they did and how they turned from their evil ways, he had compassion and did not bring upon them the destruction he had threatened. {4:1} But Jonah was greatly displeased and became angry. {2} He prayed to the LORD, "O LORD, is this not what I said when I was still at home? That is why I was so quick to flee to Tarshish. I knew that you are a gracious and compassionate God, slow to anger and abounding in love, a God who relents from sending calamity. {3} Now, O LORD, take away my life, for it is better for me to die than to live." {4} But the LORD replied, "Have you any right to be angry?" {5} Jonah went out and sat down at a place east of the city. There he made himself a shelter, sat in its shade and waited to see what would happen to the city. {6} Then the LORD God provided a vine and made it grow up over Jonah to give shade for his head to ease his discomfort, and Jonah was very happy about the vine. {7} But at dawn the next day God provided a worm, which chewed the vine so that it withered. {8} When the sun rose, God provided a scorching east wind, and the sun blazed on Jonah's head so that he grew faint. He wanted to die, and said, "It would be better for me to die than to live." {9} But God said to Jonah, "Do you have a right to be angry about the vine?" "I do," he said. "I am angry enough to die." {10} But the LORD said, "You have been concerned about this vine, though you did not tend it or make it grow. It sprang up overnight and died overnight. {11} But Nineveh has more than a hundred and twenty thousand people who cannot tell their right hand from their left, and many cattle as well. Should I not be concerned about that great city?"

PUNISHMENT PROMISED TO ISRAEL,
BUT ALSO DELIVERANCE

Micah 1:1-5

The word of the LORD that came to Micah of Moresheth during the reigns of Jotham, Ahaz and Hezekiah, kings of Judah–the vision he saw concerning Samaria and Jerusalem. {2} Hear, O peoples, all of you, listen, O earth and all who are in it, that the Sovereign LORD may witness against you, the Lord from his holy temple. {3} Look! The LORD is coming from his dwelling place; he comes down and treads the high places of the earth. {4} The mountains melt beneath him and the valleys split apart, like wax before the fire, like water rushing down a slope. {5} All this is because of Jacob's transgression, because of the sins of the house of Israel. What is Jacob's transgression? Is it not Samaria? What is Judah's high place? Is it not Jerusalem?

Micah 2:1-5

Woe to those who plan iniquity, to those who plot evil on their beds! At morning's light they carry it out because it is in their power to do it. {2} They covet fields and seize them, and houses, and take them. They defraud a man of his home, a fellowman of his inheritance. {3} Therefore, the LORD says: "I am planning disaster against this people, from which you cannot save yourselves. You will no longer walk proudly, for it will be a time of calamity. {4} In that day men will ridicule you; they will taunt you with this mournful song: 'We are utterly ruined; my people's possession is divided up. He takes it from me! He assigns our fields to traitors.'" {5} Therefore you will have no one in the assembly of the LORD to divide the land by lot.

Micah 2:12-13

"I will surely gather all of you, O Jacob; I will surely bring together the remnant of Israel. I will bring them together like sheep in a pen, like a flock in its pasture; the place will throng with people. {13} One who breaks open the way will go up before them; they will break through the gate and go out. Their king will pass through before them, the LORD at their head."

WHY, OH LORD, DO YOU TOLERATE THE WICKED?

Hab 1:1-6

The oracle that Habakkuk the prophet received. {2} How long, O LORD, must I call for help, but you do not listen? Or cry out to you, "Violence!" but you do not save? {3} Why do you make me look at injustice? Why do you tolerate wrong? Destruction and violence are before me; there is strife, and conflict abounds. {4} Therefore the law is paralyzed, and justice never prevails. The wicked hem in the righteous, so that justice is perverted. {5} "Look at the nations and watch– and be utterly amazed. For I am going to do something in your days that you would not believe, even if you were told. {6} I am raising up the Babylonians, that ruthless and impetuous people, who sweep across the whole earth to seize dwelling places not their own.

Hab 1:12-13

O LORD, are you not from everlasting? My God, my Holy One, we will not die. O LORD, you have appointed them to execute judgment; O Rock, you have ordained them to punish. {13} Your eyes are too pure to look on evil; you cannot tolerate wrong. Why then do you tolerate the treacherous? Why are you silent while the wicked swallow up those more righteous than themselves?

Hab 2:2-3

Then the LORD replied: "Write down the revelation and make it plain on tablets so that a herald may run with it. {3} For the revelation awaits an appointed time; it speaks of the end and will not prove false. Though it linger, wait for it; it will certainly come and will not delay.

Hab 2:20

But the LORD is in his holy temple; let all the earth be silent before him."

Hab 3:1-2

A prayer of Habakkuk the prophet. On <shigionoth>. {2} LORD, I have heard of your fame; I stand in awe of your deeds, O LORD. Renew them in our day, in our time make them known; in wrath remember mercy.

REPENT, THE DAY OF THE LORD IS NEAR

Zep 1:14-2:3

"The great day of the LORD is near– near and coming quickly. Listen! The cry on the day of the LORD will be bitter, the shouting of the warrior there. {15} That day will be a day of wrath, a day of distress and anguish, a day of trouble and ruin, a day of darkness and gloom, a day of clouds and blackness, {16} a day of trumpet and battle cry against the fortified cities and against the corner towers. {17} I will bring distress on the people and they will walk like blind men, because they have sinned against the LORD. Their blood will be poured out like dust and their entrails like filth. {18} Neither their silver nor their gold will be able to save them on the day of the Lord's wrath. In the fire of his jealousy the whole world will be consumed, for he will make a sudden end of all who live in the earth." {2:1} Gather together, gather together, O shameful nation, {2} before the appointed time arrives and that day sweeps on like chaff, before the fierce anger of the LORD comes upon you, before the day of the Lord's wrath comes upon you. {3} Seek the LORD, all you humble of the land, you who do what he commands. Seek righteousness, seek humility; perhaps you will be sheltered on the day of the Lord's anger.

JERUSALEM WILL BE RESTORED

Zep 3:8b-20

I have decided to assemble the nations, to gather the kingdoms and to pour out my wrath on them– all my fierce anger. The whole world will be consumed by the fire of my jealous anger. {9} "Then will I purify the lips of the peoples, that all of them may call on the name of the LORD and serve him shoulder to shoulder. {10} From beyond the rivers of Cush my worshipers, my scattered people, will bring me offerings. {11} On that day you will not be put to shame for all the wrongs you have done to me, because I will remove from this city those who rejoice in their pride. Never again will you be haughty on my holy hill. {12} But I will leave within you the meek and humble, who trust in the name of the LORD. {13} The remnant of Israel will do no wrong; they will speak no lies, nor will deceit be found in their mouths. They will eat and lie down and no one will make them afraid." {14} Sing, O Daughter of Zion; shout aloud, O Israel! Be glad and rejoice with all your heart, O Daughter of Jerusalem! {15} The LORD has taken away your punishment, he has turned back your enemy. The LORD, the King of Israel, is with you; never again will you fear any harm. {16} On that day they will say to Jerusalem, "Do not fear, O Zion; do not let your hands hang limp. {17} The LORD your God is with you, he is mighty to save. He will take great delight in you, he will quiet you with his love, he will rejoice over you with singing." {18} "The sorrows for the appointed feasts I will remove from you; they are a burden and a reproach to you. {19} At that time I will deal with all who oppressed you; I will rescue the lame and gather those who have been scattered. I will give them praise and honor in every land where they were put to shame. {20} At that time I will gather you; at that time I will bring you home. I will give you honor and praise among all the peoples of the earth when I restore your fortunes before your very eyes," says the LORD.

GOD WILL AGAIN BLESS HIS PEOPLE

Hag 2:6-23

"This is what the LORD Almighty says: 'In a little while I will once more shake the heavens and the earth, the sea and the dry land. {7} I will shake all nations, and the desired of all nations will come, and I will fill this house with glory,' says the LORD Almighty. {8} 'The silver is mine and the gold is mine,' declares the LORD Almighty. {9} 'The glory of this present house will be greater than the glory of the former house,' says the LORD Almighty. 'And in this place I will grant peace,' declares the LORD Almighty." {10} On the twenty-fourth day of the ninth month, in the second year of Darius, the word of the LORD came to the prophet Haggai: {11} "This is what the LORD Almighty says: 'Ask the priests what the law says: {12} If a person carries consecrated meat in the fold of his garment, and that fold touches some bread or stew, some wine, oil or other food, does it become consecrated?'" The priests answered, "No." {13} Then Haggai said, "If a person defiled by contact with a dead body touches one of these things, does it become defiled?" "Yes," the priests replied, "it becomes defiled." {14} Then Haggai said, "'So it is with this people and this nation in my sight,' declares the LORD. 'Whatever they do and whatever they offer there is defiled. {15} "'Now give careful thought to this from this day on —consider how things were before one stone was laid on another in the Lord's temple. {16} When anyone came to a heap of twenty measures, there were only ten. When anyone went to a wine vat to draw fifty measures, there were only twenty. {17} I struck all the work of your hands with blight, mildew and hail, yet you did not turn to me,' declares the LORD. {18} 'From this day on, from this twenty-fourth day of the ninth month, give careful thought to the day when the foundation of the Lord's temple was laid. Give careful thought: {19} Is there yet any seed left in the barn? Until now, the vine and the fig tree, the pomegranate and the olive tree have not borne fruit. "'From this day on I will bless you.'" {20} The word of the LORD came to Haggai a second time on the twenty-fourth day of the month: {21} "Tell Zerubbabel governor of Judah that I will shake the heavens and the earth. {22} I will overturn royal thrones and shatter the power of the foreign kingdoms. I will overthrow chariots and their drivers; horses and their riders will fall, each by the sword of his brother. {23} "'On that day,' declares the LORD Almighty, 'I will take you, my servant Zerubbabel son of Shealtiel,' declares the LORD, 'and I will make you like my signet ring, for I have chosen you,' declares the LORD Almighty."

GOD PROMISES RESTORATION

Zec 1:1-17

In the eighth month of the second year of Darius, the word of the LORD came to the prophet Zechariah son of Berekiah, the son of Iddo: {2} "The LORD was very angry with your forefathers. {3} Therefore tell the people: This is what the LORD Almighty says: 'Return to me,' declares the LORD Almighty, 'and I will return to you,' says the LORD Almighty. {4} Do not be like your forefathers, to whom the earlier prophets proclaimed: This is what the LORD Almighty says: 'Turn from your evil ways and your evil practices.' But they would not listen or pay attention to me, declares the LORD. {5} Where are your forefathers now? And the prophets, do they live forever? {6} But did not my words and my decrees, which I commanded my servants the prophets, overtake your forefathers? "Then they repented and said, 'The LORD Almighty has done to us what our ways and practices deserve, just as he determined to do.'" {7} On the twenty-fourth day of the eleventh month, the month of Shebat, in the second year of Darius, the word of the LORD came to the prophet Zechariah son of Berekiah, the son of Iddo. {8} During the night I had a vision—and there before me was a man riding a red horse! He was standing among the myrtle trees in a ravine. Behind him were red, brown and white horses. {9} I asked, "What are these, my lord?" The angel who was talking with me answered, "I will show you what they are." {10} Then the man standing among the myrtle trees explained, "They are the ones the LORD has sent to go throughout the earth." {11} And they reported to the angel of the LORD, who was standing among the myrtle trees, "We have gone throughout the earth and found the whole world at rest and in peace." {12} Then the angel of the LORD said, "LORD Almighty, how long will you withhold mercy from Jerusalem and from the towns of Judah, which you have been angry with these seventy years?" {13} So the LORD spoke kind and comforting words to the angel who talked with me. {14} Then the angel who was speaking to me said, "Proclaim this word: This is what the LORD Almighty says: 'I am very jealous for Jerusalem and Zion, {15} but I am very angry with the nations that feel secure. I was only a little angry, but they added to the calamity.' {16} "Therefore, this is what the LORD says: 'I will return to Jerusalem with mercy, and there my house will be rebuilt. And the measuring line will be stretched out over Jerusalem,' declares the LORD Almighty. {17} "Proclaim further: This is what the LORD Almighty says: 'My towns will again overflow with prosperity, and the LORD will again comfort Zion and choose Jerusalem.'"

NOT BY MIGHT, NOR BY POWER, BUT BY MY SPIRIT

Zec 4:1-9

Then the angel who talked with me returned and wakened me, as a man is wakened from his sleep. {2} He asked me, "What do you see?" I answered, "I see a solid gold lampstand with a bowl at the top and seven lights on it, with seven channels to the lights. {3} Also there are two olive trees by it, one on the right of the bowl and the other on its left." {4} I asked the angel who talked with me, "What are these, my lord?" {5} He answered, "Do you not know what these are?" "No, my lord," I replied. {6} So he said to me, "This is the word of the LORD to Zerubbabel: 'Not by might nor by power, but by my Spirit,' says the LORD Almighty. {7} "What are you, O mighty mountain? Before Zerubbabel you will become level ground. Then he will bring out the capstone to shouts of 'God bless it! God bless it!'" {8} Then the word of the LORD came to me: {9} "The hands of Zerubbabel have laid the foundation of this temple; his hands will also complete it. Then you will know that the LORD Almighty has sent me to you.

Zec 5:1-11

I looked again—and there before me was a flying scroll! {2} He asked me, "What do you see?" I answered, "I see a flying scroll, thirty feet long and fifteen feet wide." {3} And he said to me, "This is the curse that is going out over the whole land; for according to what it says on one side, every thief will be banished, and according to what it says on the other, everyone who swears falsely will be banished. {4} The LORD Almighty declares, 'I will send it out, and it will enter the house of the thief and the house of him who swears falsely by my name. It will remain in his house and destroy it, both its timbers and its stones.'" {5} Then the angel who was speaking to me came forward and said to me, "Look up and see what this is that is appearing." {6} I asked, "What is it?" He replied, "It is a measuring basket." And he added, "This is the iniquity of the people throughout the land." {7} Then the cover of lead was raised, and there in the basket sat a woman! {8} He said, "This is wickedness," and he pushed her back into the basket and pushed the lead cover down over its mouth. {9} Then I looked up—and there before me were two women, with the wind in their wings! They had wings like those of a stork, and they lifted up the basket between heaven and earth. {10} "Where are they taking the basket?" I asked the angel who was speaking to me. {11} He replied, "To the country of Babylonia to build a house for it. When it is ready, the basket will be set there in its place."

BLESSINGS PROMISED TO JERUSALEM

Zec 7:4-14

Then the word of the LORD Almighty came to me: {5} "Ask all the people of the land and the priests, 'When you fasted and mourned in the fifth and seventh months for the past seventy years, was it really for me that you fasted? {6} And when you were eating and drinking, were you not just feasting for yourselves? {7} Are these not the words the LORD proclaimed through the earlier prophets when Jerusalem and its surrounding towns were at rest and prosperous, and the Negev and the western foothills were settled?'" {8} And the word of the LORD came again to Zechariah: {9} "This is what the LORD Almighty says: 'Administer true justice; show mercy and compassion to one another. {10} Do not oppress the widow or the fatherless, the alien or the poor. In your hearts do not think evil of each other.' {11} "But they refused to pay attention; stubbornly they turned their backs and stopped up their ears. {12} They made their hearts as hard as flint and would not listen to the law or to the words that the LORD Almighty had sent by his Spirit through the earlier prophets. So the LORD Almighty was very angry. {13} "'When I called, they did not listen; so when they called, I would not listen,' says the LORD Almighty. {14} 'I scattered them with a whirlwind among all the nations, where they were strangers. The land was left so desolate behind them that no one could come or go. This is how they made the pleasant land desolate.'"

Zec 8:1-8

Again the word of the LORD Almighty came to me. {2} This is what the LORD Almighty says: "I am very jealous for Zion; I am burning with jealousy for her." {3} This is what the LORD says: "I will return to Zion and dwell in Jerusalem. Then Jerusalem will be called the City of Truth, and the mountain of the LORD Almighty will be called the Holy Mountain." {4} This is what the LORD Almighty says: "Once again men and women of ripe old age will sit in the streets of Jerusalem, each with cane in hand because of his age. {5} The city streets will be filled with boys and girls playing there." {6} This is what the LORD Almighty says: "It may seem marvelous to the remnant of this people at that time, but will it seem marvelous to me?" declares the LORD Almighty. {7} This is what the LORD Almighty says: "I will save my people from the countries of the east and the west. {8} I will bring them back to live in Jerusalem; they will be my people, and I will be faithful and righteous to them as their God."

BRING ALL THE TITHE

Mal 3:7-4:6a

Ever since the time of your forefathers you have turned away from my decrees and have not kept them. Return to me, and I will return to you," says the LORD Almighty. "But you ask, 'How are we to return?' {8} "Will a man rob God? Yet you rob me. "But you ask, 'How do we rob you?' "In tithes and offerings. {9} You are under a curse—the whole nation of you—because you are robbing me. {10} Bring the whole tithe into the storehouse, that there may be food in my house. Test me in this," says the LORD Almighty, "and see if I will not throw open the floodgates of heaven and pour out so much blessing that you will not have room enough for it. {11} I will prevent pests from devouring your crops, and the vines in your fields will not cast their fruit," says the LORD Almighty. {12} "Then all the nations will call you blessed, for yours will be a delightful land," says the LORD Almighty. {13} "You have said harsh things against me," says the LORD. "Yet you ask, 'What have we said against you?' {14} "You have said, 'It is futile to serve God. What did we gain by carrying out his requirements and going about like mourners before the LORD Almighty? {15} But now we call the arrogant blessed. Certainly the evildoers prosper, and even those who challenge God escape.'" {16} Then those who feared the LORD talked with each other, and the LORD listened and heard. A scroll of remembrance was written in his presence concerning those who feared the LORD and honored his name. {17} "They will be mine," says the LORD Almighty, "in the day when I make up my treasured possession. I will spare them, just as in compassion a man spares his son who serves him. {18} And you will again see the distinction between the righteous and the wicked, between those who serve God and those who do not. {4:1} "Surely the day is coming; it will burn like a furnace. All the arrogant and every evildoer will be stubble, and that day that is coming will set them on fire," says the LORD Almighty. "Not a root or a branch will be left to them. {2} But for you who revere my name, the sun of righteousness will rise with healing in its wings. And you will go out and leap like calves released from the stall. {3} Then you will trample down the wicked; they will be ashes under the soles of your feet on the day when I do these things," says the LORD Almighty. {4} "Remember the law of my servant Moses, the decrees and laws I gave him at Horeb for all Israel. {5} "See, I will send you the prophet Elijah before that great and dreadful day of the LORD comes. {6} He will turn the hearts of the fathers to their children, and the hearts of the children to their fathers....

BIRTH OF JESUS

Mat 1:18-2:12

This is how the birth of Jesus Christ came about: His mother Mary was pledged to be married to Joseph, but before they came together, she was found to be with child through the Holy Spirit. {19} Because Joseph her husband was a righteous man and did not want to expose her to public disgrace, he had in mind to divorce her quietly. {20} But after he had considered this, an angel of the Lord appeared to him in a dream and said, "Joseph son of David, do not be afraid to take Mary home as your wife, because what is conceived in her is from the Holy Spirit. {21} She will give birth to a son, and you are to give him the name Jesus, because he will save his people from their sins." {22} All this took place to fulfill what the Lord had said through the prophet: {23} "The virgin will be with child and will give birth to a son, and they will call him Immanuel" – which means, "God with us." {24} When Joseph woke up, he did what the angel of the Lord had commanded him and took Mary home as his wife. {25} But he had no union with her until she gave birth to a son. And he gave him the name Jesus. {2:1} After Jesus was born in Bethlehem in Judea, during the time of King Herod, Magi from the east came to Jerusalem {2} and asked, "Where is the one who has been born king of the Jews? We saw his star in the east and have come to worship him." {3} When King Herod heard this he was disturbed, and all Jerusalem with him. {4} When he had called together all the people's chief priests and teachers of the law, he asked them where the Christ was to be born. {5} "In Bethlehem in Judea," they replied, "for this is what the prophet has written: {6} "'But you, Bethlehem, in the land of Judah, are by no means least among the rulers of Judah; for out of you will come a ruler who will be the shepherd of my people Israel.' " {7} Then Herod called the Magi secretly and found out from them the exact time the star had appeared. {8} He sent them to Bethlehem and said, "Go and make a careful search for the child. As soon as you find him, report to me, so that I too may go and worship him." {9} After they had heard the king, they went on their way, and the star they had seen in the east went ahead of them until it stopped over the place where the child was. {10} When they saw the star, they were overjoyed. {11} On coming to the house, they saw the child with his mother Mary, and they bowed down and worshiped him. Then they opened their treasures and presented him with gifts of gold and of incense and of myrrh. {12} And having been warned in a dream not to go back to Herod, they returned to their country by another route.

JOHN PRESENTS JESUS

Mat 3:1-17

In those days John the Baptist came, preaching in the Desert of Judea {2} and saying, "Repent, for the kingdom of heaven is near." {3} This is he who was spoken of through the prophet Isaiah: "A voice of one calling in the desert, 'Prepare the way for the Lord, make straight paths for him.'" {4} John's clothes were made of camel's hair, and he had a leather belt around his waist. His food was locusts and wild honey. {5} People went out to him from Jerusalem and all Judea and the whole region of the Jordan. {6} Confessing their sins, they were baptized by him in the Jordan River. {7} But when he saw many of the Pharisees and Sadducees coming to where he was baptizing, he said to them: "You brood of vipers! Who warned you to flee from the coming wrath? {8} Produce fruit in keeping with repentance. {9} And do not think you can say to yourselves, 'We have Abraham as our father.' I tell you that out of these stones God can raise up children for Abraham. {10} The ax is already at the root of the trees, and every tree that does not produce good fruit will be cut down and thrown into the fire. {11} "I baptize you with water for repentance. But after me will come one who is more powerful than I, whose sandals I am not fit to carry. He will baptize you with the Holy Spirit and with fire. {12} His winnowing fork is in his hand, and he will clear his threshing floor, gathering his wheat into the barn and burning up the chaff with unquenchable fire." {13} Then Jesus came from Galilee to the Jordan to be baptized by John. {14} But John tried to deter him, saying, "I need to be baptized by you, and do you come to me?" {15} Jesus replied, "Let it be so now; it is proper for us to do this to fulfill all righteousness." Then John consented. {16} As soon as Jesus was baptized, he went up out of the water. At that moment heaven was opened, and he saw the Spirit of God descending like a dove and lighting on him. {17} And a voice from heaven said, "This is my Son, whom I love; with him I am well pleased."

JESUS IS TEMPTED, CALLS HIS DISCIPLES

Mat 4:1-22

Then Jesus was led by the Spirit into the desert to be tempted by the devil. {2} After fasting forty days and forty nights, he was hungry. {3} The tempter came to him and said, "If you are the Son of God, tell these stones to become bread." {4} Jesus answered, "It is written: 'Man does not live on bread alone, but on every word that comes from the mouth of God.'" {5} Then the devil took him to the holy city and had him stand on the highest point of the temple. {6} "If you are the Son of God," he said, "throw yourself down. For it is written: "'He will command his angels concerning you, and they will lift you up in their hands, so that you will not strike your foot against a stone.'" {7} Jesus answered him, "It is also written: 'Do not put the Lord your God to the test.'" {8} Again, the devil took him to a very high mountain and showed him all the kingdoms of the world and their splendor. {9} "All this I will give you," he said, "if you will bow down and worship me." {10} Jesus said to him, "Away from me, Satan! For it is written: 'Worship the Lord your God, and serve him only.'" {11} Then the devil left him, and angels came and attended him. {12} When Jesus heard that John had been put in prison, he returned to Galilee. {13} Leaving Nazareth, he went and lived in Capernaum, which was by the lake in the area of Zebulun and Naphtali– {14} to fulfill what was said through the prophet Isaiah: {15} "Land of Zebulun and land of Naphtali, the way to the sea, along the Jordan, Galilee of the Gentiles– {16} the people living in darkness have seen a great light; on those living in the land of the shadow of death a light has dawned." {17} From that time on Jesus began to preach, "Repent, for the kingdom of heaven is near." {18} As Jesus was walking beside the Sea of Galilee, he saw two brothers, Simon called Peter and his brother Andrew. They were casting a net into the lake, for they were fishermen. {19} "Come, follow me," Jesus said, "and I will make you fishers of men." {20} At once they left their nets and followed him. {21} Going on from there, he saw two other brothers, James son of Zebedee and his brother John. They were in a boat with their father Zebedee, preparing their nets. Jesus called them, {22} and immediately they left the boat and their father and followed him.

THE BEATITUDES; LOVE YOUR ENEMIES

Mat 5:1-12

Now when he saw the crowds, he went up on a mountainside and sat down. His disciples came to him, {2} and he began to teach them, saying: {3} "Blessed are the poor in spirit, for theirs is the kingdom of heaven. {4} Blessed are those who mourn, for they will be comforted. {5} Blessed are the meek, for they will inherit the earth. {6} Blessed are those who hunger and thirst for righteousness, for they will be filled. {7} Blessed are the merciful, for they will be shown mercy. {8} Blessed are the pure in heart, for they will see God. {9} Blessed are the peacemakers, for they will be called sons of God. {10} Blessed are those who are persecuted because of righteousness, for theirs is the kingdom of heaven. {11} "Blessed are you when people insult you, persecute you and falsely say all kinds of evil against you because of me. {12} Rejoice and be glad, because great is your reward in heaven, for in the same way they persecuted the prophets who were before you.

Mat 5:38-48

"You have heard that it was said, 'Eye for eye, and tooth for tooth.' {39} But I tell you, Do not resist an evil person. If someone strikes you on the right cheek, turn to him the other also. {40} And if someone wants to sue you and take your tunic, let him have your cloak as well. {41} If someone forces you to go one mile, go with him two miles. {42} Give to the one who asks you, and do not turn away from the one who wants to borrow from you. {43} "You have heard that it was said, 'Love your neighbor and hate your enemy.' {44} But I tell you: Love your enemies and pray for those who persecute you, {45} that you may be sons of your Father in heaven. He causes his sun to rise on the evil and the good, and sends rain on the righteous and the unrighteous. {46} If you love those who love you, what reward will you get? Are not even the tax collectors doing that? {47} And if you greet only your brothers, what are you doing more than others? Do not even pagans do that? {48} Be perfect, therefore, as your heavenly Father is perfect.

THE LORD'S PRAYER; TRUST HIM FOR YOUR NEEDS

Mat 6:5-15

"And when you pray, do not be like the hypocrites, for they love to pray standing in the synagogues and on the street corners to be seen by men. I tell you the truth, they have received their reward in full. {6} But when you pray, go into your room, close the door and pray to your Father, who is unseen. Then your Father, who sees what is done in secret, will reward you. {7} And when you pray, do not keep on babbling like pagans, for they think they will be heard because of their many words. {8} Do not be like them, for your Father knows what you need before you ask him. {9} "This, then, is how you should pray: "'Our Father in heaven, hallowed be your name, {10} your kingdom come, your will be done on earth as it is in heaven. {11} Give us today our daily bread. {12} Forgive us our debts, as we also have forgiven our debtors. {13} And lead us not into temptation, but deliver us from the evil one.' {14} For if you forgive men when they sin against you, your heavenly Father will also forgive you. {15} But if you do not forgive men their sins, your Father will not forgive your sins.

Mat 6:25-34

"Therefore I tell you, do not worry about your life, what you will eat or drink; or about your body, what you will wear. Is not life more important than food, and the body more important than clothes? {26} Look at the birds of the air; they do not sow or reap or store away in barns, and yet your heavenly Father feeds them. Are you not much more valuable than they? {27} Who of you by worrying can add a single hour to his life? {28} "And why do you worry about clothes? See how the lilies of the field grow. They do not labor or spin. {29} Yet I tell you that not even Solomon in all his splendor was dressed like one of these. {30} If that is how God clothes the grass of the field, which is here today and tomorrow is thrown into the fire, will he not much more clothe you, O you of little faith? {31} So do not worry, saying, 'What shall we eat?' or 'What shall we drink?' or 'What shall we wear?' {32} For the pagans run after all these things, and your heavenly Father knows that you need them. {33} But seek first his kingdom and his righteousness, and all these things will be given to you as well. {34} Therefore do not worry about tomorrow, for tomorrow will worry about itself. Each day has enough trouble of its own.

DO NOT JUDGE OTHERS;
WATCH FOR FALSE PROPHETS; BUILD ON ROCK

Mat 7:1-6

"Do not judge, or you too will be judged. {2} For in the same way you judge others, you will be judged, and with the measure you use, it will be measured to you. {3} "Why do you look at the speck of sawdust in your brother's eye and pay no attention to the plank in your own eye? {4} How can you say to your brother, 'Let me take the speck out of your eye,' when all the time there is a plank in your own eye? {5} You hypocrite, first take the plank out of your own eye, and then you will see clearly to remove the speck from your brother's eye. {6} "Do not give dogs what is sacred; do not throw your pearls to pigs. If you do, they may trample them under their feet, and then turn and tear you to pieces.

Mat 7:15-23

"Watch out for false prophets. They come to you in sheep's clothing, but inwardly they are ferocious wolves. {16} By their fruit you will recognize them. Do people pick grapes from thornbushes, or figs from thistles? {17} Likewise every good tree bears good fruit, but a bad tree bears bad fruit. {18} A good tree cannot bear bad fruit, and a bad tree cannot bear good fruit. {19} Every tree that does not bear good fruit is cut down and thrown into the fire. {20} Thus, by their fruit you will recognize them. {21} "Not everyone who says to me, 'Lord, Lord,' will enter the kingdom of heaven, but only he who does the will of my Father who is in heaven. {22} Many will say to me on that day, 'Lord, Lord, did we not prophesy in your name, and in your name drive out demons and perform many miracles?' {23} Then I will tell them plainly, 'I never knew you. Away from me, you evildoers!'

Mat 7:24-29

"Therefore everyone who hears these words of mine and puts them into practice is like a wise man who built his house on the rock. {25} The rain came down, the streams rose, and the winds blew and beat against that house; yet it did not fall, because it had its foundation on the rock. {26} But everyone who hears these words of mine and does not put them into practice is like a foolish man who built his house on sand. {27} The rain came down, the streams rose, and the winds blew and beat against that house, and it fell with a great crash." {28} When Jesus had finished saying these things, the crowds were amazed at his teaching, {29} because he taught as one who had authority, and not as their teachers of the law.

JESUS BEGINS HEALING MINISTRY

Mat 8:1-22

When he came down from the mountainside, large crowds followed him. {2} A man with leprosy came and knelt before him and said, "Lord, if you are willing, you can make me clean." {3} Jesus reached out his hand and touched the man. "I am willing," he said. "Be clean!" Immediately he was cured of his leprosy. {4} Then Jesus said to him, "See that you don't tell anyone. But go, show yourself to the priest and offer the gift Moses commanded, as a testimony to them." {5} When Jesus had entered Capernaum, a centurion came to him, asking for help. {6} "Lord," he said, "my servant lies at home paralyzed and in terrible suffering." {7} Jesus said to him, "I will go and heal him." {8} The centurion replied, "Lord, I do not deserve to have you come under my roof. But just say the word, and my servant will be healed. {9} For I myself am a man under authority, with soldiers under me. I tell this one, 'Go,' and he goes; and that one, 'Come,' and he comes. I say to my servant, 'Do this,' and he does it." {10} When Jesus heard this, he was astonished and said to those following him, "I tell you the truth, I have not found anyone in Israel with such great faith. {11} I say to you that many will come from the east and the west, and will take their places at the feast with Abraham, Isaac and Jacob in the kingdom of heaven. {12} But the subjects of the kingdom will be thrown outside, into the darkness, where there will be weeping and gnashing of teeth." {13} Then Jesus said to the centurion, "Go ! It will be done just as you believed it would." And his servant was healed at that very hour. {14} When Jesus came into Peter's house, he saw Peter's mother-in-law lying in bed with a fever. {15} He touched her hand and the fever left her, and she got up and began to wait on him. {16} When evening came, many who were demon-possessed were brought to him, and he drove out the spirits with a word and healed all the sick. {17} This was to fulfill what was spoken through the prophet Isaiah: "He took up our infirmities and carried our diseases." {18} When Jesus saw the crowd around him, he gave orders to cross to the other side of the lake. {19} Then a teacher of the law came to him and said, "Teacher, I will follow you wherever you go." {20} Jesus replied, "Foxes have holes and birds of the air have nests, but the Son of Man has no place to lay his head." {21} Another disciple said to him, "Lord, first let me go and bury my father." {22} But Jesus told him, "Follow me, and let the dead bury their own dead."

JESUS HEALS; CALLS MATTHEW; COMMENTS ON FASTING

Mat 9:1-26

Jesus stepped into a boat, crossed over and came to his own town. {2} Some men brought to him a paralytic, lying on a mat. When Jesus saw their faith, he said to the paralytic, "Take heart, son; your sins are forgiven." {3} At this, some of the teachers of the law said to themselves, "This fellow is blaspheming!" {4} Knowing their thoughts, Jesus said, "Why do you entertain evil thoughts in your hearts? {5} Which is easier: to say, 'Your sins are forgiven,' or to say, 'Get up and walk'? {6} But so that you may know that the Son of Man has authority on earth to forgive sins. . . ." Then he said to the paralytic, "Get up, take your mat and go home." {7} And the man got up and went home. {8} When the crowd saw this, they were filled with awe; and they praised God, who had given such authority to men.

{9} As Jesus went on from there, he saw a man named Matthew sitting at the tax collector's booth. "Follow me," he told him, and Matthew got up and followed him. {10} While Jesus was having dinner at Matthew's house, many tax collectors and "sinners" came and ate with him and his disciples. {11} When the Pharisees saw this, they asked his disciples, "Why does your teacher eat with tax collectors and 'sinners'?" {12} On hearing this, Jesus said, "It is not the healthy who need a doctor, but the sick. {13} But go and learn what this means: 'I desire mercy, not sacrifice.' For I have not come to call the righteous, but sinners."

{14} Then John's disciples came and asked him, "How is it that we and the Pharisees fast, but your disciples do not fast?" {15} Jesus answered, "How can the guests of the bridegroom mourn while he is with them? The time will come when the bridegroom will be taken from them; then they will fast. {16} "No one sews a patch of unshrunk cloth on an old garment, for the patch will pull away from the garment, making the tear worse. {17} Neither do men pour new wine into old wineskins. If they do, the skins will burst, the wine will run out and the wineskins will be ruined. No, they pour new wine into new wineskins, and both are preserved."

JESUS SENDS OUT HIS DISCIPLES

Mat 10:1-25a

He called his twelve disciples to him and gave them authority to drive out evil spirits and to heal every disease and sickness. {2} These are the names of the twelve apostles: first, Simon (who is called Peter) and his brother Andrew; James son of Zebedee, and his brother John; {3} Philip and Bartholomew; Thomas and Matthew the tax collector; James son of Alphaeus, and Thaddaeus; {4} Simon the Zealot and Judas Iscariot, who betrayed him. {5} These twelve Jesus sent out with the following instructions: "Do not go among the Gentiles or enter any town of the Samaritans. {6} Go rather to the lost sheep of Israel. {7} As you go, preach this message: 'The kingdom of heaven is near.' {8} Heal the sick, raise the dead, cleanse those who have leprosy, drive out demons. Freely you have received, freely give. {9} Do not take along any gold or silver or copper in your belts; {10} take no bag for the journey, or extra tunic, or sandals or a staff; for the worker is worth his keep. {11} "Whatever town or village you enter, search for some worthy person there and stay at his house until you leave. {12} As you enter the home, give it your greeting. {13} If the home is deserving, let your peace rest on it; if it is not, let your peace return to you. {14} If anyone will not welcome you or listen to your words, shake the dust off your feet when you leave that home or town. {15} I tell you the truth, it will be more bearable for Sodom and Gomorrah on the day of judgment than for that town. {16} I am sending you out like sheep among wolves. Therefore be as shrewd as snakes and as innocent as doves. {17} "Be on your guard against men; they will hand you over to the local councils and flog you in their synagogues. {18} On my account you will be brought before governors and kings as witnesses to them and to the Gentiles. {19} But when they arrest you, do not worry about what to say or how to say it. At that time you will be given what to say, {20} for it will not be you speaking, but the Spirit of your Father speaking through you. {21} "Brother will betray brother to death, and a father his child; children will rebel against their parents and have them put to death. {22} All men will hate you because of me, but he who stands firm to the end will be saved. {23} When you are persecuted in one place, flee to another. I tell you the truth, you will not finish going through the cities of Israel before the Son of Man comes. {24} "A student is not above his teacher, nor a servant above his master. {25} It is enough for the student to be like his teacher, and the servant like his master.

JESUS HEALS ON SABBATH

Mat 12:1-14

At that time Jesus went through the grainfields on the Sabbath. His disciples were hungry and began to pick some heads of grain and eat them. {2} When the Pharisees saw this, they said to him, "Look! Your disciples are doing what is unlawful on the Sabbath." {3} He answered, "Haven't you read what David did when he and his companions were hungry? {4} He entered the house of God, and he and his companions ate the consecrated bread–which was not lawful for them to do, but only for the priests. {5} Or haven't you read in the Law that on the Sabbath the priests in the temple desecrate the day and yet are innocent? {6} I tell you that one greater than the temple is here. {7} If you had known what these words mean, 'I desire mercy, not sacrifice,' you would not have condemned the innocent. {8} For the Son of Man is Lord of the Sabbath." {9} Going on from that place, he went into their synagogue, {10} and a man with a shriveled hand was there. Looking for a reason to accuse Jesus, they asked him, "Is it lawful to heal on the Sabbath?" {11} He said to them, "If any of you has a sheep and it falls into a pit on the Sabbath, will you not take hold of it and lift it out? {12} How much more valuable is a man than a sheep! Therefore it is lawful to do good on the Sabbath." {13} Then he said to the man, "Stretch out your hand." So he stretched it out and it was completely restored, just as sound as the other. {14} But the Pharisees went out and plotted how they might kill Jesus.

Mat 12:22-27

Then they brought him a demon-possessed man who was blind and mute, and Jesus healed him, so that he could both talk and see. {23} All the people were astonished and said, "Could this be the Son of David?" {24} But when the Pharisees heard this, they said, "It is only by Beelzebub, the prince of demons, that this fellow drives out demons." {25} Jesus knew their thoughts and said to them, "Every kingdom divided against itself will be ruined, and every city or household divided against itself will not stand. {26} If Satan drives out Satan, he is divided against himself. How then can his kingdom stand? {27} And if I drive out demons by Beelzebub, by whom do your people drive them out? So then, they will be your judges.

Mat 12:33-34

"Make a tree good and its fruit will be good, or make a tree bad and its fruit will be bad, for a tree is recognized by its fruit. {34} You brood of vipers, how can you who are evil say anything good?

PARABLE OF THE SOWER

Mat 13:2-23a

Such large crowds gathered around him that he got into a boat and sat in it, while all the people stood on the shore. {3} Then he told them many things in parables, saying: "A farmer went out to sow his seed. {4} As he was scattering the seed, some fell along the path, and the birds came and ate it up. {5} Some fell on rocky places, where it did not have much soil. It sprang up quickly, because the soil was shallow. {6} But when the sun came up, the plants were scorched, and they withered because they had no root. {7} Other seed fell among thorns, which grew up and choked the plants. {8} Still other seed fell on good soil, where it produced a crop—a hundred, sixty or thirty times what was sown. {9} He who has ears, let him hear." {10} The disciples came to him and asked, "Why do you speak to the people in parables?" {11} He replied, "The knowledge of the secrets of the kingdom of heaven has been given to you, but not to them. {12} Whoever has will be given more, and he will have an abundance. Whoever does not have, even what he has will be taken from him. {13} This is why I speak to them in parables: "Though seeing, they do not see; though hearing, they do not hear or understand. {14} In them is fulfilled the prophecy of Isaiah: "'You will be ever hearing but never understanding; you will be ever seeing but never perceiving. {15} For this people's heart has become calloused; they hardly hear with their ears, and they have closed their eyes. Otherwise they might see with their eyes, hear with their ears, understand with their hearts and turn, and I would heal them.' {16} But blessed are your eyes because they see, and your ears because they hear. {17} For I tell you the truth, many prophets and righteous men longed to see what you see but did not see it, and to hear what you hear but did not hear it. {18} "Listen then to what the parable of the sower means: {19} When anyone hears the message about the kingdom and does not understand it, the evil one comes and snatches away what was sown in his heart. This is the seed sown along the path. {20} The one who received the seed that fell on rocky places is the man who hears the word and at once receives it with joy. {21} But since he has no root, he lasts only a short time. When trouble or persecution comes because of the word, he quickly falls away. {22} The one who received the seed that fell among the thorns is the man who hears the word, but the worries of this life and the deceitfulness of wealth choke it, making it unfruitful. {23} But the one who received the seed that fell on good soil is the man who hears the word and understands it.

PARABLES OF MUSTARD SEED, YEAST, WEEDS, AND HIDDEN TREASURE

Mat 13:31-50

He told them another parable: "The kingdom of heaven is like a mustard seed, which a man took and planted in his field. {32} Though it is the smallest of all your seeds, yet when it grows, it is the largest of garden plants and becomes a tree, so that the birds of the air come and perch in its branches." {33} He told them still another parable: "The kingdom of heaven is like yeast that a woman took and mixed into a large amount of flour until it worked all through the dough." {34} Jesus spoke all these things to the crowd in parables; he did not say anything to them without using a parable. {35} So was fulfilled what was spoken through the prophet: "I will open my mouth in parables, I will utter things hidden since the creation of the world." {36} Then he left the crowd and went into the house. His disciples came to him and said, "Explain to us the parable of the weeds in the field." {37} He answered, "The one who sowed the good seed is the Son of Man. {38} The field is the world, and the good seed stands for the sons of the kingdom. The weeds are the sons of the evil one, {39} and the enemy who sows them is the devil. The harvest is the end of the age, and the harvesters are angels. {40} "As the weeds are pulled up and burned in the fire, so it will be at the end of the age. {41} The Son of Man will send out his angels, and they will weed out of his kingdom everything that causes sin and all who do evil. {42} They will throw them into the fiery furnace, where there will be weeping and gnashing of teeth. {43} Then the righteous will shine like the sun in the kingdom of their Father. He who has ears, let him hear.

{44} "The kingdom of heaven is like treasure hidden in a field. When a man found it, he hid it again, and then in his joy went and sold all he had and bought that field. {45} "Again , the kingdom of heaven is like a merchant looking for fine pearls. {46} When he found one of great value, he went away and sold everything he had and bought it. {47} "Once again, the kingdom of heaven is like a net that was let down into the lake and caught all kinds of fish. {48} When it was full, the fishermen pulled it up on the shore. Then they sat down and collected the good fish in baskets, but threw the bad away. {49} This is how it will be at the end of the age. The angels will come and separate the wicked from the righteous {50} and throw them into the fiery furnace, where there will be weeping and gnashing of teeth.

JESUS FEEDS FIVE THOUSAND, WALKS ON WATER

Mat 14:13-36

When Jesus heard what had happened, he withdrew by boat privately to a solitary place. Hearing of this, the crowds followed him on foot from the towns. {14} When Jesus landed and saw a large crowd, he had compassion on them and healed their sick. {15} As evening approached, the disciples came to him and said, "This is a remote place, and it's already getting late. Send the crowds away, so they can go to the villages and buy themselves some food." {16} Jesus replied, "They do not need to go away. You give them something to eat." {17} "We have here only five loaves of bread and two fish," they answered. {18} "Bring them here to me," he said. {19} And he directed the people to sit down on the grass. Taking the five loaves and the two fish and looking up to heaven, he gave thanks and broke the loaves. Then he gave them to the disciples, and the disciples gave them to the people. {20} They all ate and were satisfied, and the disciples picked up twelve basketfuls of broken pieces that were left over. {21} The number of those who ate was about five thousand men, besides women and children.

{22} Immediately Jesus made the disciples get into the boat and go on ahead of him to the other side, while he dismissed the crowd. {23} After he had dismissed them, he went up on a mountainside by himself to pray. When evening came, he was there alone, {24} but the boat was already a considerable distance from land, buffeted by the waves because the wind was against it. {25} During the fourth watch of the night Jesus went out to them, walking on the lake. {26} When the disciples saw him walking on the lake, they were terrified. "It's a ghost," they said, and cried out in fear. {27} But Jesus immediately said to them: "Take courage! It is I. Don't be afraid." {28} "Lord, if it's you," Peter replied, "tell me to come to you on the water." {29} "Come," he said. Then Peter got down out of the boat, walked on the water and came toward Jesus. {30} But when he saw the wind, he was afraid and, beginning to sink, cried out, "Lord, save me!" {31} Immediately Jesus reached out his hand and caught him. "You of little faith," he said, "why did you doubt?" {32} And when they climbed into the boat, the wind died down. {33} Then those who were in the boat worshiped him, saying, "Truly you are the Son of God." {34} When they had crossed over, they landed at Gennesaret. {35} And when the men of that place recognized Jesus, they sent word to all the surrounding country. People brought all their sick to him {36} and begged him to let the sick just touch the edge of his cloak, and all who touched him were healed.

PHARISEES WANT PROOF; PETER'S WITNESS

Mat 16:1-20

The Pharisees and Sadducees came to Jesus and tested him by asking him to show them a sign from heaven. {2} He replied, "When evening comes, you say, 'It will be fair weather, for the sky is red,' {3} and in the morning, 'Today it will be stormy, for the sky is red and overcast.' You know how to interpret the appearance of the sky, but you cannot interpret the signs of the times. {4} A wicked and adulterous generation looks for a miraculous sign, but none will be given it except the sign of Jonah." Jesus then left them and went away. {5} When they went across the lake, the disciples forgot to take bread. {6} "Be careful," Jesus said to them. "Be on your guard against the yeast of the Pharisees and Sadducees." {7} They discussed this among themselves and said, "It is because we didn't bring any bread." {8} Aware of their discussion, Jesus asked, "You of little faith, why are you talking among yourselves about having no bread? {9} Do you still not understand? Don't you remember the five loaves for the five thousand, and how many basketfuls you gathered? {10} Or the seven loaves for the four thousand, and how many basketfuls you gathered? {11} How is it you don't understand that I was not talking to you about bread? But be on your guard against the yeast of the Pharisees and Sadducees." {12} Then they understood that he was not telling them to guard against the yeast used in bread, but against the teaching of the Pharisees and Sadducees.

{13} When Jesus came to the region of Caesarea Philippi, he asked his disciples, "Who do people say the Son of Man is?" {14} They replied, "Some say John the Baptist; others say Elijah; and still others, Jeremiah or one of the prophets." {15} "But what about you?" he asked. "Who do you say I am?" {16} Simon Peter answered, "You are the Christ, the Son of the living God." {17} Jesus replied, "Blessed are you, Simon son of Jonah, for this was not revealed to you by man, but by my Father in heaven. {18} And I tell you that you are Peter, and on this rock I will build my church, and the gates of Hades will not overcome it. {19} I will give you the keys of the kingdom of heaven; whatever you bind on earth will be bound in heaven, and whatever you loose on earth will be loosed in heaven." {20} Then he warned his disciples not to tell anyone that he was the Christ.

TRANSFIGURATION; LESSON ON GREATNESS

Mat 17:1-13

After six days Jesus took with him Peter, James and John the brother of James, and led them up a high mountain by themselves. {2} There he was transfigured before them. His face shone like the sun, and his clothes became as white as the light. {3} Just then there appeared before them Moses and Elijah, talking with Jesus. {4} Peter said to Jesus, "Lord, it is good for us to be here. If you wish, I will put up three shelters—one for you, one for Moses and one for Elijah." {5} While he was still speaking, a bright cloud enveloped them, and a voice from the cloud said, "This is my Son, whom I love; with him I am well pleased. Listen to him!" {6} When the disciples heard this, they fell facedown to the ground, terrified. {7} But Jesus came and touched them. "Get up," he said. "Don't be afraid." {8} When they looked up, they saw no one except Jesus. {9} As they were coming down the mountain, Jesus instructed them, "Don't tell anyone what you have seen, until the Son of Man has been raised from the dead." {10} The disciples asked him, "Why then do the teachers of the law say that Elijah must come first?" {11} Jesus replied, "To be sure, Elijah comes and will restore all things. {12} But I tell you, Elijah has already come, and they did not recognize him, but have done to him everything they wished. In the same way the Son of Man is going to suffer at their hands." {13} Then the disciples understood that he was talking to them about John the Baptist.

Mat 18:1-9a

At that time the disciples came to Jesus and asked, "Who is the greatest in the kingdom of heaven?" {2} He called a little child and had him stand among them. {3} And he said: "I tell you the truth, unless you change and become like little children, you will never enter the kingdom of heaven. {4} Therefore , whoever humbles himself like this child is the greatest in the kingdom of heaven. {5} "And whoever welcomes a little child like this in my name welcomes me. {6} But if anyone causes one of these little ones who believe in me to sin, it would be better for him to have a large millstone hung around his neck and to be drowned in the depths of the sea. {7} "Woe to the world because of the things that cause people to sin! Such things must come, but woe to the man through whom they come! {8} If your hand or your foot causes you to sin cut it off and throw it away. It is better for you to enter life maimed or crippled than to have two hands or two feet and be thrown into eternal fire. {9} And if your eye causes you to sin, gouge it out and throw it away.

PARABLES OF LOST SHEEP AND THE UNMERCIFUL SERVANT

Mat 18:10-14

"See that you do not look down on one of these little ones. For I tell you that their angels in heaven always see the face of my Father in heaven. {11} {12} "What do you think? If a man owns a hundred sheep, and one of them wanders away, will he not leave the ninety-nine on the hills and go to look for the one that wandered off? {13} And if he finds it, I tell you the truth, he is happier about that one sheep than about the ninety-nine that did not wander off. {14} In the same way your Father in heaven is not willing that any of these little ones should be lost.

Mat 18:21-35

Then Peter came to Jesus and asked, "Lord, how many times shall I forgive my brother when he sins against me? Up to seven times?" {22} Jesus answered, "I tell you, not seven times, but seventy-seven times. {23} "Therefore, the kingdom of heaven is like a king who wanted to settle accounts with his servants. {24} As he began the settlement, a man who owed him ten thousand talents was brought to him. {25} Since he was not able to pay, the master ordered that he and his wife and his children and all that he had be sold to repay the debt. {26} "The servant fell on his knees before him. 'Be patient with me,' he begged, 'and I will pay back everything.' {27} The servant's master took pity on him, canceled the debt and let him go. {28} "But when that servant went out, he found one of his fellow servants who owed him a hundred denarii. He grabbed him and began to choke him. 'Pay back what you owe me!' he demanded. {29} "His fellow servant fell to his knees and begged him, 'Be patient with me, and I will pay you back.' {30} "But he refused. Instead, he went off and had the man thrown into prison until he could pay the debt. {31} When the other servants saw what had happened, they were greatly distressed and went and told their master everything that had happened. {32} "Then the master called the servant in. 'You wicked servant,' he said, 'I canceled all that debt of yours because you begged me to. {33} Shouldn't you have had mercy on your fellow servant just as I had on you?' {34} In anger his master turned him over to the jailers to be tortured, until he should pay back all he owed. {35} "This is how my heavenly Father will treat each of you unless you forgive your brother from your heart."

234

JESUS TEACHES ON DIVORCE, RECEIVES LITTLE CHILDREN, TALKS TO RICH YOUNG RULER

Mat 19:1-21

When Jesus had finished saying these things, he left Galilee and went into the region of Judea to the other side of the Jordan. {2} Large crowds followed him, and he healed them there. {3} Some Pharisees came to him to test him. They asked, "Is it lawful for a man to divorce his wife for any and every reason?" {4} "Haven't you read," he replied, "that at the beginning the Creator 'made them male and female,' {5} and said, 'For this reason a man will leave his father and mother and be united to his wife, and the two will become one flesh'? {6} So they are no longer two, but one. Therefore what God has joined together, let man not separate." {7} "Why then," they asked, "did Moses command that a man give his wife a certificate of divorce and send her away?" {8} Jesus replied, "Moses permitted you to divorce your wives because your hearts were hard. But it was not this way from the beginning. {9} I tell you that anyone who divorces his wife, except for marital unfaithfulness, and marries another woman commits adultery." {10} The disciples said to him, "If this is the situation between a husband and wife, it is better not to marry." {11} Jesus replied, "Not everyone can accept this word, but only those to whom it has been given. {12} For some are eunuchs because they were born that way; others were made that way by men; and others have renounced marriage because of the kingdom of heaven. The one who can accept this should accept it."

{13} Then little children were brought to Jesus for him to place his hands on them and pray for them. But the disciples rebuked those who brought them. {14} Jesus said, "Let the little children come to me, and do not hinder them, for the kingdom of heaven belongs to such as these." {15} When he had placed his hands on them, he went on from there.

{16} Now a man came up to Jesus and asked, "Teacher, what good thing must I do to get eternal life?" {17} "Why do you ask me about what is good?" Jesus replied. "There is only One who is good. If you want to enter life, obey the commandments." {18} "Which ones?" the man inquired. Jesus replied, "'Do not murder, do not commit adultery, do not steal, do not give false testimony, {19} honor your father and mother,' and 'love your neighbor as yourself.' " {20} "All these I have kept," the young man said. "What do I still lack?" {21} Jesus answered, "If you want to be perfect, go, sell your possessions and give to the poor, and you will have treasure in heaven. Then come, follow me."

PARABLE OF WORKERS IN VINEYARD;
MRS. ZEBEDEE WANTS A FAVOR

Mat 20:1-16

"For the kingdom of heaven is like a landowner who went out early in the morning to hire men to work in his vineyard. {2} He agreed to pay them a denarius for the day and sent them into his vineyard. {3} "About the third hour he went out and saw others standing in the marketplace doing nothing. {4} He told them, 'You also go and work in my vineyard, and I will pay you whatever is right.' {5} So they went. "He went out again about the sixth hour and the ninth hour and did the same thing. {6} About the eleventh hour he went out and found still others standing around. He asked them, 'Why have you been standing here all day long doing nothing?' {7} "'Because no one has hired us,' they answered. "He said to them, 'You also go and work in my vineyard.' {8} "When evening came, the owner of the vineyard said to his foreman, 'Call the workers and pay them their wages, beginning with the last ones hired and going on to the first.' {9} "The workers who were hired about the eleventh hour came and each received a denarius. {10} So when those came who were hired first, they expected to receive more. But each one of them also received a denarius. {11} When they received it, they began to grumble against the landowner. {12} 'These men who were hired last worked only one hour,' they said, 'and you have made them equal to us who have borne the burden of the work and the heat of the day.' {13} "But he answered one of them, 'Friend, I am not being unfair to you. Didn't you agree to work for a denarius? {14} Take your pay and go. I want to give the man who was hired last the same as I gave you. {15} Don't I have the right to do what I want with my own money? Or are you envious because I am generous?' {16} "So the last will be first, and the first will be last."

Mat 20:23-28

Jesus said to them, "You will indeed drink from my cup, but to sit at my right or left is not for me to grant. These places belong to those for whom they have been prepared by my Father." {24} When the ten heard about this, they were indignant with the two brothers. {25} Jesus called them together and said, "You know that the rulers of the Gentiles lord it over them, and their high officials exercise authority over them. {26} Not so with you. Instead, whoever wants to become great among you must be your servant, {27} and whoever wants to be first must be your slave— {28} just as the Son of Man did not come to be served, but to serve, and to give his life as a ransom for many."

JESUS' TRIUMPHAL ENTRY INTO JERUSALEM

Mat 21:1-17

As they approached Jerusalem and came to Bethphage on the Mount of Olives, Jesus sent two disciples, {2} saying to them, "Go to the village ahead of you, and at once you will find a donkey tied there, with her colt by her. Untie them and bring them to me. {3} If anyone says anything to you, tell him that the Lord needs them, and he will send them right away." {4} This took place to fulfill what was spoken through the prophet: {5} "Say to the Daughter of Zion, 'See, your king comes to you, gentle and riding on a donkey, on a colt, the foal of a donkey.'" {6} The disciples went and did as Jesus had instructed them. {7} They brought the donkey and the colt, placed their cloaks on them, and Jesus sat on them. {8} A very large crowd spread their cloaks on the road, while others cut branches from the trees and spread them on the road. {9} The crowds that went ahead of him and those that followed shouted, "Hosanna to the Son of David!" "Blessed is he who comes in the name of the Lord!" "Hosanna in the highest!" {10} When Jesus entered Jerusalem, the whole city was stirred and asked, "Who is this?" {11} The crowds answered, "This is Jesus, the prophet from Nazareth in Galilee." {12} Jesus entered the temple area and drove out all who were buying and selling there. He overturned the tables of the money changers and the benches of those selling doves. {13} "It is written," he said to them, "'My house will be called a house of prayer,' but you are making it a 'den of robbers.'" {14} The blind and the lame came to him at the temple, and he healed them. {15} But when the chief priests and the teachers of the law saw the wonderful things he did and the children shouting in the temple area, "Hosanna to the Son of David," they were indignant. {16} "Do you hear what these children are saying?" they asked him. "Yes," replied Jesus, "have you never read, "'From the lips of children and infants you have ordained praise'?" {17} And he left them and went out of the city to Bethany, where he spent the night.

JESUS' AUTHORITY QUESTIONED;
PARABLES OF TWO SONS, AND OF LANDOWNER

Mat 21:23-41a

Jesus entered the temple courts, and, while he was teaching, the chief priests and the elders of the people came to him. "By what authority are you doing these things?" they asked. "And who gave you this authority?" {24} Jesus replied, "I will also ask you one question. If you answer me, I will tell you by what authority I am doing these things. {25} John's baptism—where did it come from? Was it from heaven, or from men?" They discussed it among themselves and said, "If we say, 'From heaven,' he will ask, 'Then why didn't you believe him?' {26} But if we say, 'From men'—we are afraid of the people, for they all hold that John was a prophet." {27} So they answered Jesus, "We don't know." Then he said, "Neither will I tell you by what authority I am doing these things.

{28} "What do you think? There was a man who had two sons. He went to the first and said, 'Son, go and work today in the vineyard.' {29} "'I will not,' he answered, but later he changed his mind and went. {30} "Then the father went to the other son and said the same thing. He answered, 'I will, sir,' but he did not go. {31} "Which of the two did what his father wanted?" "The first," they answered. Jesus said to them, "I tell you the truth, the tax collectors and the prostitutes are entering the kingdom of God ahead of you. {32} For John came to you to show you the way of righteousness, and you did not believe him, but the tax collectors and the prostitutes did. And even after you saw this, you did not repent and believe him.

{33} "Listen to another parable: There was a landowner who planted a vineyard. He put a wall around it, dug a winepress in it and built a watchtower. Then he rented the vineyard to some farmers and went away on a journey. {34} When the harvest time approached, he sent his servants to the tenants to collect his fruit. {35} "The tenants seized his servants; they beat one, killed another, and stoned a third. {36} Then he sent other servants to them, more than the first time, and the tenants treated them the same way. {37} Last of all, he sent his son to them. 'They will respect my son,' he said. {38} "But when the tenants saw the son, they said to each other, 'This is the heir. Come, let's kill him and take his inheritance.' {39} So they took him and threw him out of the vineyard and killed him. {40} "Therefore, when the owner of the vineyard comes, what will he do to those tenants?" {41} "He will bring those wretches to a wretched end," they replied, "and he will rent the vineyard to other tenants....

PARABLE OF A WEDDING; THE GREAT COMMANDMENT

Mat 22:1-14

Jesus spoke to them again in parables, saying: {2} "The kingdom of heaven is like a king who prepared a wedding banquet for his son. {3} He sent his servants to those who had been invited to the banquet to tell them to come, but they refused to come. {4} "Then he sent some more servants and said, 'Tell those who have been invited that I have prepared my dinner: My oxen and fattened cattle have been butchered, and everything is ready. Come to the wedding banquet.' {5} "But they paid no attention and went off–one to his field, another to his business. {6} The rest seized his servants, mistreated them and killed them. {7} The king was enraged. He sent his army and destroyed those murderers and burned their city. {8} "Then he said to his servants, 'The wedding banquet is ready, but those I invited did not deserve to come. {9} Go to the street corners and invite to the banquet anyone you find.' {10} So the servants went out into the streets and gathered all the people they could find, both good and bad, and the wedding hall was filled with guests. {11} "But when the king came in to see the guests, he noticed a man there who was not wearing wedding clothes. {12} 'Friend,' he asked, 'how did you get in here without wedding clothes?' The man was speechless. {13} "Then the king told the attendants, 'Tie him hand and foot, and throw him outside, into the darkness, where there will be weeping and gnashing of teeth.' {14} "For many are invited, but few are chosen."

Mat 22:34-46

Hearing that Jesus had silenced the Sadducees, the Pharisees got together. {35} One of them, an expert in the law, tested him with this question: {36} "Teacher, which is the greatest commandment in the Law?" {37} Jesus replied: "'Love the Lord your God with all your heart and with all your soul and with all your mind.' {38} This is the first and greatest commandment. {39} And the second is like it: 'Love your neighbor as yourself.' {40} All the Law and the Prophets hang on these two commandments." {41} While the Pharisees were gathered together, Jesus asked them, {42} "What do you think about the Christ ? Whose son is he?" "The son of David," they replied. {43} He said to them, "How is it then that David, speaking by the Spirit, calls him 'Lord'? For he says, {44} "'The Lord said to my Lord: "Sit at my right hand until I put your enemies under your feet." ' {45} If then David calls him 'Lord,' how can he be his son?" {46} No one could say a word in reply, and from that day on no one dared to ask him any more questions.

WOES TO FALSE TEACHERS

Mat 23:2-25

The teachers of the law and the Pharisees sit in Moses' seat. {3} So you must obey them and do everything they tell you. But do not do what they do, for they do not practice what they preach. {4} They tie up heavy loads and put them on men's shoulders, but they themselves are not willing to lift a finger to move them. {5} "Everything they do is done for men to see: They make their phylacteries wide and the tassels on their garments long; {6} they love the place of honor at banquets and the most important seats in the synagogues; {7} they love to be greeted in the marketplaces and to have men call them 'Rabbi.' {8} "But you are not to be called 'Rabbi,' for you have only one Master and you are all brothers. {9} And do not call anyone on earth 'father,' for you have one Father, and he is in heaven. {10} Nor are you to be called 'teacher,' for you have one Teacher, the Christ. {11} The greatest among you will be your servant. {12} For whoever exalts himself will be humbled, and whoever humbles himself will be exalted. {13} "Woe to you, teachers of the law and Pharisees, you hypocrites! You shut the kingdom of heaven in men's faces. You yourselves do not enter, nor will you let those enter who are trying to. {14} {15} "Woe to you, teachers of the law and Pharisees, you hypocrites! You travel over land and sea to win a single convert, and when he becomes one, you make him twice as much a son of hell as you are. {16} "Woe to you, blind guides! You say, 'If anyone swears by the temple, it means nothing; but if anyone swears by the gold of the temple, he is bound by his oath.' {17} You blind fools! Which is greater: the gold, or the temple that makes the gold sacred? {18} You also say, 'If anyone swears by the altar, it means nothing; but if anyone swears by the gift on it, he is bound by his oath.' {19} You blind men! Which is greater: the gift, or the altar that makes the gift sacred? {20} Therefore , he who swears by the altar swears by it and by everything on it. {21} And he who swears by the temple swears by it and by the one who dwells in it. {22} And he who swears by heaven swears by God's throne and by the one who sits on it. {23} "Woe to you, teachers of the law and Pharisees, you hypocrites! You give a tenth of your spices—mint, dill and cummin. But you have neglected the more important matters of the law—justice, mercy and faithfulness. You should have practiced the latter, without neglecting the former. {24} You blind guides! You strain out a gnat but swallow a camel. {25} "Woe to you, teachers of the law and Pharisees, you hypocrites! You clean the outside of the cup and dish, but inside they are full of greed and self-indulgence.

SIGNS OF THE END

Mat 24:2-27

"Do you see all these things?" he asked. "I tell you the truth, not one stone here will be left on another; every one will be thrown down." {3} As Jesus was sitting on the Mount of Olives, the disciples came to him privately. "Tell us," they said, "when will this happen, and what will be the sign of your coming and of the end of the age?" {4} Jesus answered: "Watch out that no one deceives you. {5} For many will come in my name, claiming, 'I am the Christ, ' and will deceive many. {6} You will hear of wars and rumors of wars, but see to it that you are not alarmed. Such things must happen, but the end is still to come. {7} Nation will rise against nation, and kingdom against kingdom. There will be famines and earthquakes in various places. {8} All these are the beginning of birth pains. {9} "Then you will be handed over to be persecuted and put to death, and you will be hated by all nations because of me. {10} At that time many will turn away from the faith and will betray and hate each other, {11} and many false prophets will appear and deceive many people. {12} Because of the increase of wickedness, the love of most will grow cold, {13} but he who stands firm to the end will be saved. {14} And this gospel of the kingdom will be preached in the whole world as a testimony to all nations, and then the end will come. {15} "So when you see standing in the holy place 'the abomination that causes desolation,' spoken of through the prophet Daniel—let the reader understand— {16} then let those who are in Judea flee to the mountains. {17} Let no one on the roof of his house go down to take anything out of the house. {18} Let no one in the field go back to get his cloak. {19} How dreadful it will be in those days for pregnant women and nursing mothers! {20} Pray that your flight will not take place in winter or on the Sabbath. {21} For then there will be great distress, unequaled from the beginning of the world until now—and never to be equaled again. {22} If those days had not been cut short, no one would survive, but for the sake of the elect those days will be shortened. {23} At that time if anyone says to you, 'Look, here is the Christ!' or, 'There he is!' do not believe it. {24} For false Christs and false prophets will appear and perform great signs and miracles to deceive even the elect—if that were possible. {25} See , I have told you ahead of time. {26} "So if anyone tells you, 'There he is, out in the desert,' do not go out; or, 'Here he is, in the inner rooms,' do not believe it. {27} For as lightning that comes from the east is visible even in the west, so will be the coming of the Son of Man.

PARABLES OF VIRGINS, AND OF TALENTS

Mat 25:1-13

"At that time the kingdom of heaven will be like ten virgins who took their lamps and went out to meet the bridegroom. {2} Five of them were foolish and five were wise. {3} The foolish ones took their lamps but did not take any oil with them. {4} The wise, however, took oil in jars along with their lamps. {5} The bridegroom was a long time in coming, and they all became drowsy and fell asleep. {6} "At midnight the cry rang out: 'Here's the bridegroom! Come out to meet him!' {7} "Then all the virgins woke up and trimmed their lamps. {8} The foolish ones said to the wise, 'Give us some of your oil; our lamps are going out.' {9} "'No,' they replied, 'there may not be enough for both us and you. Instead, go to those who sell oil and buy some for yourselves.' {10} "But while they were on their way to buy the oil, the bridegroom arrived. The virgins who were ready went in with him to the wedding banquet. And the door was shut. {11} "Later the others also came. 'Sir! Sir!' they said. 'Open the door for us!' {12} "But he replied, 'I tell you the truth, I don't know you.' {13} "Therefore keep watch, because you do not know the day or the hour.

Mat 25:16-26a

The man who had received the five talents went at once and put his money to work and gained five more. {17} So also, the one with the two talents gained two more. {18} But the man who had received the one talent went off, dug a hole in the ground and hid his master's money. {19} "After a long time the master of those servants returned and settled accounts with them. {20} The man who had received the five talents brought the other five. 'Master,' he said, 'you entrusted me with five talents. See, I have gained five more.' {21} "His master replied, 'Well done, good and faithful servant! You have been faithful with a few things; I will put you in charge of many things. Come and share your master's happiness!' {22} "The man with the two talents also came. 'Master,' he said, 'you entrusted me with two talents; see, I have gained two more.' {23} "His master replied, 'Well done, good and faithful servant! You have been faithful with a few things; I will put you in charge of many things. Come and share your master's happiness!' {24} "Then the man who had received the one talent came. 'Master,' he said, 'I knew that you are a hard man, harvesting where you have not sown and gathering where you have not scattered seed. {25} So I was afraid and went out and hid your talent in the ground. See, here is what belongs to you.' {26} "His master replied, 'You wicked, lazy servant!

PERFUME FOR JESUS; THE LAST SUPPER

Mat 26:6-30

While Jesus was in Bethany in the home of a man known as Simon the Leper, {7} a woman came to him with an alabaster jar of very expensive perfume, which she poured on his head as he was reclining at the table. {8} When the disciples saw this, they were indignant. "Why this waste?" they asked. {9} "This perfume could have been sold at a high price and the money given to the poor." {10} Aware of this, Jesus said to them, "Why are you bothering this woman? She has done a beautiful thing to me. {11} The poor you will always have with you, but you will not always have me. {12} When she poured this perfume on my body, she did it to prepare me for burial. {13} I tell you the truth, wherever this gospel is preached throughout the world, what she has done will also be told, in memory of her."

{14} Then one of the Twelve—the one called Judas Iscariot—went to the chief priests {15} and asked, "What are you willing to give me if I hand him over to you?" So they counted out for him thirty silver coins. {16} From then on Judas watched for an opportunity to hand him over. {17} On the first day of the Feast of Unleavened Bread, the disciples came to Jesus and asked, "Where do you want us to make preparations for you to eat the Passover?" {18} He replied, "Go into the city to a certain man and tell him, 'The Teacher says: My appointed time is near. I am going to celebrate the Passover with my disciples at your house.'" {19} So the disciples did as Jesus had directed them and prepared the Passover. {20} When evening came, Jesus was reclining at the table with the Twelve. {21} And while they were eating, he said, "I tell you the truth, one of you will betray me." {22} They were very sad and began to say to him one after the other, "Surely not I, Lord?" {23} Jesus replied, "The one who has dipped his hand into the bowl with me will betray me. {24} The Son of Man will go just as it is written about him. But woe to that man who betrays the Son of Man! It would be better for him if he had not been born." {25} Then Judas, the one who would betray him, said, "Surely not I, Rabbi?" Jesus answered, "Yes , it is you." {26} While they were eating, Jesus took bread, gave thanks and broke it, and gave it to his disciples, saying, "Take and eat; this is my body." {27} Then he took the cup, gave thanks and offered it to them, saying, "Drink from it, all of you. {28} This is my blood of the covenant, which is poured out for many for the forgiveness of sins. {29} I tell you, I will not drink of this fruit of the vine from now on until that day when I drink it anew with you in my Father's kingdom." {30} When they had sung a hymn, they went out to the Mount of Olives.

JESUS PREDICTS PETER'S DENIAL AND JESUS' ARREST

Mat 26:33-54

Peter replied, "Even if all fall away on account of you, I never will." {34} "I tell you the truth," Jesus answered, "this very night, before the rooster crows, you will disown me three times." {35} But Peter declared, "Even if I have to die with you, I will never disown you." And all the other disciples said the same. {36} Then Jesus went with his disciples to a place called Gethsemane, and he said to them, "Sit here while I go over there and pray." {37} He took Peter and the two sons of Zebedee along with him, and he began to be sorrowful and troubled. {38} Then he said to them, "My soul is overwhelmed with sorrow to the point of death. Stay here and keep watch with me." {39} Going a little farther, he fell with his face to the ground and prayed, "My Father, if it is possible, may this cup be taken from me. Yet not as I will, but as you will." {40} Then he returned to his disciples and found them sleeping. "Could you men not keep watch with me for one hour?" he asked Peter. {41} "Watch and pray so that you will not fall into temptation. The spirit is willing, but the body is weak." {42} He went away a second time and prayed, "My Father, if it is not possible for this cup to be taken away unless I drink it, may your will be done." {43} When he came back, he again found them sleeping, because their eyes were heavy. {44} So he left them and went away once more and prayed the third time, saying the same thing. {45} Then he returned to the disciples and said to them, "Are you still sleeping and resting? Look, the hour is near, and the Son of Man is betrayed into the hands of sinners. {46} Rise , let us go! Here comes my betrayer!" {47} While he was still speaking, Judas, one of the Twelve, arrived. With him was a large crowd armed with swords and clubs, sent from the chief priests and the elders of the people. {48} Now the betrayer had arranged a signal with them: "The one I kiss is the man; arrest him." {49} Going at once to Jesus, Judas said, "Greetings, Rabbi!" and kissed him. {50} Jesus replied, "Friend , do what you came for." Then the men stepped forward, seized Jesus and arrested him. {51} With that, one of Jesus' companions reached for his sword, drew it out and struck the servant of the high priest, cutting off his ear. {52} "Put your sword back in its place," Jesus said to him, "for all who draw the sword will die by the sword. {53} Do you think I cannot call on my Father, and he will at once put at my disposal more than twelve legions of angels? {54} But how then would the Scriptures be fulfilled that say it must happen in this way?"

JESUS BEFORE THE SANHEDRIN;
PETER DENIES JESUS; JUDAS HANGS HIMSELF

Mat 26:59-27:5

The chief priests and the whole Sanhedrin were looking for false evidence against Jesus so that they could put him to death. {60} But they did not find any, though many false witnesses came forward. Finally two came forward {61} and declared, "This fellow said, 'I am able to destroy the temple of God and rebuild it in three days.'" {62} Then the high priest stood up and said to Jesus, "Are you not going to answer? What is this testimony that these men are bringing against you?" {63} But Jesus remained silent. The high priest said to him, "I charge you under oath by the living God: Tell us if you are the Christ, the Son of God." {64} "Yes , it is as you say," Jesus replied. "But I say to all of you: In the future you will see the Son of Man sitting at the right hand of the Mighty One and coming on the clouds of heaven." {65} Then the high priest tore his clothes and said, "He has spoken blasphemy! Why do we need any more witnesses? Look, now you have heard the blasphemy. {66} What do you think?" "He is worthy of death," they answered. {67} Then they spit in his face and struck him with their fists. Others slapped him {68} and said, "Prophesy to us, Christ. Who hit you?"

{69} Now Peter was sitting out in the courtyard, and a servant girl came to him. "You also were with Jesus of Galilee," she said. {70} But he denied it before them all. "I don't know what you're talking about," he said. {71} Then he went out to the gateway, where another girl saw him and said to the people there, "This fellow was with Jesus of Nazareth." {72} He denied it again, with an oath: "I don't know the man!" {73} After a little while, those standing there went up to Peter and said, "Surely you are one of them, for your accent gives you away." {74} Then he began to call down curses on himself and he swore to them, "I don't know the man!" Immediately a rooster crowed. {75} Then Peter remembered the word Jesus had spoken: "Before the rooster crows, you will disown me three times." And he went outside and wept bitterly. {27:1} Early in the morning, all the chief priests and the elders of the people came to the decision to put Jesus to death. {2} They bound him, led him away and handed him over to Pilate, the governor. {3} When Judas, who had betrayed him, saw that Jesus was condemned, he was seized with remorse and returned the thirty silver coins to the chief priests and the elders. {4} "I have sinned," he said, "for I have betrayed innocent blood." "What is that to us?" they replied. "That's your responsibility." {5} So Judas threw the money into the temple and left. Then he went away and hanged himself.

PILATE INTERROGATES JESUS;
SOLDIERS MOCK HIM AND CRUCIFY HIM

Mat 27:15-37

Now it was the governor's custom at the Feast to release a prisoner chosen by the crowd. {16} At that time they had a notorious prisoner, called Barabbas. {17} So when the crowd had gathered, Pilate asked them, "Which one do you want me to release to you: Barabbas, or Jesus who is called Christ?" {18} For he knew it was out of envy that they had handed Jesus over to him. {19} While Pilate was sitting on the judge's seat, his wife sent him this message: "Don't have anything to do with that innocent man, for I have suffered a great deal today in a dream because of him." {20} But the chief priests and the elders persuaded the crowd to ask for Barabbas and to have Jesus executed. {21} "Which of the two do you want me to release to you?" asked the governor. "Barabbas," they answered. {22} "What shall I do, then, with Jesus who is called Christ?" Pilate asked. They all answered, "Crucify him!" {23} "Why? What crime has he committed?" asked Pilate. But they shouted all the louder, "Crucify him!" {24} When Pilate saw that he was getting nowhere, but that instead an uproar was starting, he took water and washed his hands in front of the crowd. "I am innocent of this man's blood," he said. "It is your responsibility!" {25} All the people answered, "Let his blood be on us and on our children!" {26} Then he released Barabbas to them. But he had Jesus flogged, and handed him over to be crucified. {27} Then the governor's soldiers took Jesus into the Praetorium and gathered the whole company of soldiers around him. {28} They stripped him and put a scarlet robe on him, {29} and then twisted together a crown of thorns and set it on his head. They put a staff in his right hand and knelt in front of him and mocked him. "Hail, king of the Jews!" they said. {30} They spit on him, and took the staff and struck him on the head again and again. {31} After they had mocked him, they took off the robe and put his own clothes on him. Then they led him away to crucify him. {32} As they were going out, they met a man from Cyrene, named Simon, and they forced him to carry the cross. {33} They came to a place called Golgotha (which means The Place of the Skull). {34} There they offered Jesus wine to drink, mixed with gall; but after tasting it, he refused to drink it. {35} When they had crucified him, they divided up his clothes by casting lots. {36} And sitting down, they kept watch over him there. {37} Above his head they placed the written charge against him: THIS IS JESUS, THE KING OF THE JEWS.

JESUS' DEATH AND BURIAL

Mat 27:45-66

From the sixth hour until the ninth hour darkness came over all the land. {46} About the ninth hour Jesus cried out in a loud voice, <"Eloi>, <Eloi>, <lama sabachthani>?"–which means, "My God, my God, why have you forsaken me?" {47} When some of those standing there heard this, they said, "He's calling Elijah." {48} Immediately one of them ran and got a sponge. He filled it with wine vinegar, put it on a stick, and offered it to Jesus to drink. {49} The rest said, "Now leave him alone. Let's see if Elijah comes to save him." {50} And when Jesus had cried out again in a loud voice, he gave up his spirit. {51} At that moment the curtain of the temple was torn in two from top to bottom. The earth shook and the rocks split. {52} The tombs broke open and the bodies of many holy people who had died were raised to life. {53} They came out of the tombs, and after Jesus' resurrection they went into the holy city and appeared to many people. {54} When the centurion and those with him who were guarding Jesus saw the earthquake and all that had happened, they were terrified, and exclaimed, "Surely he was the Son of God!" {55} Many women were there, watching from a distance. They had followed Jesus from Galilee to care for his needs. {56} Among them were Mary Magdalene, Mary the mother of James and Joses, and the mother of Zebedee's sons. {57} As evening approached, there came a rich man from Arimathea, named Joseph, who had himself become a disciple of Jesus. {58} Going to Pilate, he asked for Jesus' body, and Pilate ordered that it be given to him. {59} Joseph took the body, wrapped it in a clean linen cloth, {60} and placed it in his own new tomb that he had cut out of the rock. He rolled a big stone in front of the entrance to the tomb and went away. {61} Mary Magdalene and the other Mary were sitting there opposite the tomb. {62} The next day, the one after Preparation Day, the chief priests and the Pharisees went to Pilate. {63} "Sir," they said, "we remember that while he was still alive that deceiver said, 'After three days I will rise again.' {64} So give the order for the tomb to be made secure until the third day. Otherwise, his disciples may come and steal the body and tell the people that he has been raised from the dead. This last deception will be worse than the first." {65} "Take a guard," Pilate answered. "Go, make the tomb as secure as you know how." {66} So they went and made the tomb secure by putting a seal on the stone and posting the guard.

JESUS' RESURRECTION; THE GREAT COMMISSION

Mat 28:1-20

After the Sabbath, at dawn on the first day of the week, Mary Magdalene and the other Mary went to look at the tomb. {2} There was a violent earthquake, for an angel of the Lord came down from heaven and, going to the tomb, rolled back the stone and sat on it. {3} His appearance was like lightning, and his clothes were white as snow. {4} The guards were so afraid of him that they shook and became like dead men. {5} The angel said to the women, "Do not be afraid, for I know that you are looking for Jesus, who was crucified. {6} He is not here; he has risen, just as he said. Come and see the place where he lay. {7} Then go quickly and tell his disciples: 'He has risen from the dead and is going ahead of you into Galilee. There you will see him.' Now I have told you." {8} So the women hurried away from the tomb, afraid yet filled with joy, and ran to tell his disciples. {9} Suddenly Jesus met them. "Greetings," he said. They came to him, clasped his feet and worshiped him. {10} Then Jesus said to them, "Do not be afraid. Go and tell my brothers to go to Galilee; there they will see me." {11} While the women were on their way, some of the guards went into the city and reported to the chief priests everything that had happened. {12} When the chief priests had met with the elders and devised a plan, they gave the soldiers a large sum of money, {13} telling them, "You are to say, 'His disciples came during the night and stole him away while we were asleep.' {14} If this report gets to the governor, we will satisfy him and keep you out of trouble." {15} So the soldiers took the money and did as they were instructed. And this story has been widely circulated among the Jews to this very day. {16} Then the eleven disciples went to Galilee, to the mountain where Jesus had told them to go. {17} When they saw him, they worshiped him; but some doubted. {18} Then Jesus came to them and said, "All authority in heaven and on earth has been given to me. {19} Therefore go and make disciples of all nations, baptizing them in the name of the Father and of the Son and of the Holy Spirit, {20} and teaching them to obey everything I have commanded you. And surely I am with you always, to the very end of the age."

THE BIRTH OF JOHN FORETOLD

Luke 1:5-25

In the time of Herod king of Judea there was a priest named Zechariah, who belonged to the priestly division of Abijah; his wife Elizabeth was also a descendant of Aaron. {6} Both of them were upright in the sight of God, observing all the Lord's commandments and regulations blamelessly. {7} But they had no children, because Elizabeth was barren; and they were both well along in years. {8} Once when Zechariah's division was on duty and he was serving as priest before God, {9} he was chosen by lot, according to the custom of the priesthood, to go into the temple of the Lord and burn incense. {10} And when the time for the burning of incense came, all the assembled worshipers were praying outside. {11} Then an angel of the Lord appeared to him, standing at the right side of the altar of incense. {12} When Zechariah saw him, he was startled and was gripped with fear. {13} But the angel said to him: "Do not be afraid, Zechariah; your prayer has been heard. Your wife Elizabeth will bear you a son, and you are to give him the name John. {14} He will be a joy and delight to you, and many will rejoice because of his birth, {15} for he will be great in the sight of the Lord. He is never to take wine or other fermented drink, and he will be filled with the Holy Spirit even from birth. {16} Many of the people of Israel will he bring back to the Lord their God. {17} And he will go on before the Lord, in the spirit and power of Elijah, to turn the hearts of the fathers to their children and the disobedient to the wisdom of the righteous–to make ready a people prepared for the Lord." {18} Zechariah asked the angel, "How can I be sure of this? I am an old man and my wife is well along in years." {19} The angel answered, "I am Gabriel. I stand in the presence of God, and I have been sent to speak to you and to tell you this good news. {20} And now you will be silent and not able to speak until the day this happens, because you did not believe my words, which will come true at their proper time." {21} Meanwhile, the people were waiting for Zechariah and wondering why he stayed so long in the temple. {22} When he came out, he could not speak to them. They realized he had seen a vision in the temple, for he kept making signs to them but remained unable to speak. {23} When his time of service was completed, he returned home. {24} After this his wife Elizabeth became pregnant and for five months remained in seclusion. {25} "The Lord has done this for me," she said. "In these days he has shown his favor and taken away my disgrace among the people."

BIRTH OF JESUS FORETOLD; MARY'S PRAISE

Luke 1:26-38

In the sixth month, God sent the angel Gabriel to Nazareth, a town in Galilee, {27} to a virgin pledged to be married to a man named Joseph, a descendant of David. The virgin's name was Mary. {28} The angel went to her and said, "Greetings, you who are highly favored! The Lord is with you." {29} Mary was greatly troubled at his words and wondered what kind of greeting this might be. {30} But the angel said to her, "Do not be afraid, Mary, you have found favor with God. {31} You will be with child and give birth to a son, and you are to give him the name Jesus. {32} He will be great and will be called the Son of the Most High. The Lord God will give him the throne of his father David, {33} and he will reign over the house of Jacob forever; his kingdom will never end." {34} "How will this be," Mary asked the angel, "since I am a virgin?" {35} The angel answered, "The Holy Spirit will come upon you, and the power of the Most High will overshadow you. So the holy one to be born will be called the Son of God. {36} Even Elizabeth your relative is going to have a child in her old age, and she who was said to be barren is in her sixth month. {37} For nothing is impossible with God." {38} "I am the Lord's servant," Mary answered. "May it be to me as you have said." Then the angel left her.

Luke 1:46-55

And Mary said: "My soul glorifies the Lord {47} and my spirit rejoices in God my Savior, {48} for he has been mindful of the humble state of his servant. From now on all generations will call me blessed, {49} for the Mighty One has done great things for me– holy is his name. {50} His mercy extends to those who fear him, from generation to generation. {51} He has performed mighty deeds with his arm; he has scattered those who are proud in their inmost thoughts. {52} He has brought down rulers from their thrones but has lifted up the humble. {53} He has filled the hungry with good things but has sent the rich away empty. {54} He has helped his servant Israel, remembering to be merciful {55} to Abraham and his descendants forever, even as he said to our fathers."

JESUS IS BORN, AND PRESENTED IN THE TEMPLE

Luke 2:1-24

In those days Caesar Augustus issued a decree that a census should be taken of the entire Roman world. {2} (This was the first census that took place while Quirinius was governor of Syria.) {3} And everyone went to his own town to register. {4} So Joseph also went up from the town of Nazareth in Galilee to Judea, to Bethlehem the town of David, because he belonged to the house and line of David. {5} He went there to register with Mary, who was pledged to be married to him and was expecting a child. {6} While they were there, the time came for the baby to be born, {7} and she gave birth to her firstborn, a son. She wrapped him in cloths and placed him in a manger, because there was no room for them in the inn. {8} And there were shepherds living out in the fields nearby, keeping watch over their flocks at night. {9} An angel of the Lord appeared to them, and the glory of the Lord shone around them, and they were terrified. {10} But the angel said to them, "Do not be afraid. I bring you good news of great joy that will be for all the people. {11} Today in the town of David a Savior has been born to you; he is Christ the Lord. {12} This will be a sign to you: You will find a baby wrapped in cloths and lying in a manger." {13} Suddenly a great company of the heavenly host appeared with the angel, praising God and saying, {14} "Glory to God in the highest, and on earth peace to men on whom his favor rests." {15} When the angels had left them and gone into heaven, the shepherds said to one another, "Let's go to Bethlehem and see this thing that has happened, which the Lord has told us about." {16} So they hurried off and found Mary and Joseph, and the baby, who was lying in the manger. {17} When they had seen him, they spread the word concerning what had been told them about this child, {18} and all who heard it were amazed at what the shepherds said to them. {19} But Mary treasured up all these things and pondered them in her heart. {20} The shepherds returned, glorifying and praising God for all the things they had heard and seen, which were just as they had been told. {21} On the eighth day, when it was time to circumcise him, he was named Jesus, the name the angel had given him before he had been conceived.

{22} When the time of their purification according to the Law of Moses had been completed, Joseph and Mary took him to Jerusalem to present him to the Lord {23} (as it is written in the Law of the Lord, "Every firstborn male is to be consecrated to the Lord"), {24} and to offer a sacrifice in keeping with what is said in the Law of the Lord: "a pair of doves or two young pigeons."

YOUNG JESUS IN THE TEMPLE;
JOHN THE BAPTIST'S ANNOUNCEMENT

Luke 2:41-3:6

Every year his parents went to Jerusalem for the Feast of the Passover. {42} When he was twelve years old, they went up to the Feast, according to the custom. {43} After the Feast was over, while his parents were returning home, the boy Jesus stayed behind in Jerusalem, but they were unaware of it. {44} Thinking he was in their company, they traveled on for a day. Then they began looking for him among their relatives and friends. {45} When they did not find him, they went back to Jerusalem to look for him. {46} After three days they found him in the temple courts, sitting among the teachers, listening to them and asking them questions. {47} Everyone who heard him was amazed at his understanding and his answers. {48} When his parents saw him, they were astonished. His mother said to him, "Son, why have you treated us like this? Your father and I have been anxiously searching for you." {49} "Why were you searching for me?" he asked. "Didn't you know I had to be in my Father's house?" {50} But they did not understand what he was saying to them. {51} Then he went down to Nazareth with them and was obedient to them. But his mother treasured all these things in her heart. {52} And Jesus grew in wisdom and stature, and in favor with God and men.

{3:1} In the fifteenth year of the reign of Tiberius Caesar–when Pontius Pilate was governor of Judea, Herod tetrarch of Galilee, his brother Philip tetrarch of Iturea and Traconitis, and Lysanias tetrarch of Abilene– {2} during the high priesthood of Annas and Caiaphas, the word of God came to John son of Zechariah in the desert. {3} He went into all the country around the Jordan, preaching a baptism of repentance for the forgiveness of sins. {4} As is written in the book of the words of Isaiah the prophet: "A voice of one calling in the desert, 'Prepare the way for the Lord, make straight paths for him. {5} Every valley shall be filled in, every mountain and hill made low. The crooked roads shall become straight, the rough ways smooth. {6} And all mankind will see God's salvation.'"

Luke 3:15-16

The people were waiting expectantly and were all wondering in their hearts if John might possibly be the Christ. {16} John answered them all, "I baptize you with water. But one more powerful than I will come, the thongs of whose sandals I am not worthy to untie. He will baptize you with the Holy Spirit and with fire.

TEMPTATION OF JESUS; JESUS REJECTED IN NAZARETH

Luke 4:1-24
 Jesus, full of the Holy Spirit, returned from the Jordan and was led by the Spirit in the desert, {2} where for forty days he was tempted by the devil. He ate nothing during those days, and at the end of them he was hungry. {3} The devil said to him, "If you are the Son of God, tell this stone to become bread." {4} Jesus answered, "It is written: 'Man does not live on bread alone.'" {5} The devil led him up to a high place and showed him in an instant all the kingdoms of the world. {6} And he said to him, "I will give you all their authority and splendor, for it has been given to me, and I can give it to anyone I want to. {7} So if you worship me, it will all be yours." {8} Jesus answered, "It is written: 'Worship the Lord your God and serve him only.'" {9} The devil led him to Jerusalem and had him stand on the highest point of the temple. "If you are the Son of God," he said, "throw yourself down from here. {10} For it is written: "'He will command his angels concerning you to guard you carefully; {11} they will lift you up in their hands, so that you will not strike your foot against a stone.'" {12} Jesus answered, "It says: 'Do not put the Lord your God to the test.'" {13} When the devil had finished all this tempting, he left him until an opportune time.

 {14} Jesus returned to Galilee in the power of the Spirit, and news about him spread through the whole countryside. {15} He taught in their synagogues, and everyone praised him. {16} He went to Nazareth, where he had been brought up, and on the Sabbath day he went into the synagogue, as was his custom. And he stood up to read. {17} The scroll of the prophet Isaiah was handed to him. Unrolling it, he found the place where it is written: {18} "The Spirit of the Lord is on me, because he has anointed me to preach good news to the poor. He has sent me to proclaim freedom for the prisoners and recovery of sight for the blind, to release the oppressed, {19} to proclaim the year of the Lord's favor." {20} Then he rolled up the scroll, gave it back to the attendant and sat down. The eyes of everyone in the synagogue were fastened on him, {21} and he began by saying to them, "Today this scripture is fulfilled in your hearing." {22} All spoke well of him and were amazed at the gracious words that came from his lips. "Isn't this Joseph's son?" they asked. {23} Jesus said to them, "Surely you will quote this proverb to me: 'Physician, heal yourself! Do here in your hometown what we have heard that you did in Capernaum.'" {24} "I tell you the truth," he continued, "no prophet is accepted in his hometown.

JESUS CALLS HIS FIRST DISCIPLES;
AND HEALS LEPER AND PARALYTIC

Luke 5:1-20

One day as Jesus was standing by the Lake of Gennesaret, with the people crowding around him and listening to the word of God, {2} he saw at the water's edge two boats, left there by the fishermen, who were washing their nets. {3} He got into one of the boats, the one belonging to Simon, and asked him to put out a little from shore. Then he sat down and taught the people from the boat. {4} When he had finished speaking, he said to Simon, "Put out into deep water, and let down the nets for a catch." {5} Simon answered, "Master, we've worked hard all night and haven't caught anything. But because you say so, I will let down the nets." {6} When they had done so, they caught such a large number of fish that their nets began to break. {7} So they signaled their partners in the other boat to come and help them, and they came and filled both boats so full that they began to sink. {8} When Simon Peter saw this, he fell at Jesus' knees and said, "Go away from me, Lord; I am a sinful man!" {9} For he and all his companions were astonished at the catch of fish they had taken, {10} and so were James and John, the sons of Zebedee, Simon's partners. Then Jesus said to Simon, "Don't be afraid; from now on you will catch men." {11} So they pulled their boats up on shore, left everything and followed him.

{12} While Jesus was in one of the towns, a man came along who was covered with leprosy. When he saw Jesus, he fell with his face to the ground and begged him, "Lord, if you are willing, you can make me clean." {13} Jesus reached out his hand and touched the man. "I am willing," he said. "Be clean!" And immediately the leprosy left him. {14} Then Jesus ordered him, "Don't tell anyone, but go, show yourself to the priest and offer the sacrifices that Moses commanded for your cleansing, as a testimony to them." {15} Yet the news about him spread all the more, so that crowds of people came to hear him and to be healed of their sicknesses. {16} But Jesus often withdrew to lonely places and prayed. {17} One day as he was teaching, Pharisees and teachers of the law, who had come from every village of Galilee and from Judea and Jerusalem, were sitting there. And the power of the Lord was present for him to heal the sick. {18} Some men came carrying a paralytic on a mat and tried to take him into the house to lay him before Jesus. {19} When they could not find a way to do this because of the crowd, they went up on the roof and lowered him on his mat through the tiles into the middle of the crowd, right in front of Jesus. {20} When Jesus saw their faith, he said, "Friend , your sins are forgiven."

JESUS' TEACHING ABOUT THE SABBATH;
CHOOSES TWELVE; TEACHES ABOUT BLESSINGS AND WOES

Luke 6:1-22

One Sabbath Jesus was going through the grainfields, and his disciples began to pick some heads of grain, rub them in their hands and eat the kernels. {2} Some of the Pharisees asked, "Why are you doing what is unlawful on the Sabbath?" {3} Jesus answered them, "Have you never read what David did when he and his companions were hungry? {4} He entered the house of God, and taking the consecrated bread, he ate what is lawful only for priests to eat. And he also gave some to his companions." {5} Then Jesus said to them, "The Son of Man is Lord of the Sabbath." {6} On another Sabbath he went into the synagogue and was teaching, and a man was there whose right hand was shriveled. {7} The Pharisees and the teachers of the law were looking for a reason to accuse Jesus, so they watched him closely to see if he would heal on the Sabbath. {8} But Jesus knew what they were thinking and said to the man with the shriveled hand, "Get up and stand in front of everyone." So he got up and stood there. {9} Then Jesus said to them, "I ask you, which is lawful on the Sabbath: to do good or to do evil, to save life or to destroy it?" {10} He looked around at them all, and then said to the man, "Stretch out your hand." He did so, and his hand was completely restored. {11} But they were furious and began to discuss with one another what they might do to Jesus.

{12} One of those days Jesus went out to a mountainside to pray, and spent the night praying to God. {13} When morning came, he called his disciples to him and chose twelve of them, whom he also designated apostles: {14} Simon (whom he named Peter), his brother Andrew, James, John, Philip, Bartholomew, {15} Matthew, Thomas, James son of Alphaeus, Simon who was called the Zealot, {16} Judas son of James, and Judas Iscariot, who became a traitor.

{17} He went down with them and stood on a level place. A large crowd of his disciples was there and a great number of people from all over Judea, from Jerusalem, and from the coast of Tyre and Sidon, {18} who had come to hear him and to be healed of their diseases. Those troubled by evil spirits were cured, {19} and the people all tried to touch him, because power was coming from him and healing them all. {20} Looking at his disciples, he said: "Blessed are you who are poor, for yours is the kingdom of God. {21} Blessed are you who hunger now, for you will be satisfied. Blessed are you who weep now, for you will laugh. {22} Blessed are you when men hate you, when they exclude you and insult you and reject your name as evil, because of the Son of Man.

LOVE YOUR ENEMIES; DO NOT JUDGE; BUILD ON ROCK

Luke 6:27-48

"But I tell you who hear me: Love your enemies, do good to those who hate you, {28} bless those who curse you, pray for those who mistreat you. {29} If someone strikes you on one cheek, turn to him the other also. If someone takes your cloak, do not stop him from taking your tunic. {30} Give to everyone who asks you, and if anyone takes what belongs to you, do not demand it back. {31} Do to others as you would have them do to you. {32} "If you love those who love you, what credit is that to you? Even 'sinners' love those who love them. {33} And if you do good to those who are good to you, what credit is that to you? Even 'sinners' do that. {34} And if you lend to those from whom you expect repayment, what credit is that to you? Even 'sinners' lend to 'sinners,' expecting to be repaid in full. {35} But love your enemies, do good to them, and lend to them without expecting to get anything back. Then your reward will be great, and you will be sons of the Most High, because he is kind to the ungrateful and wicked. {36} Be merciful, just as your Father is merciful.

{37} "Do not judge, and you will not be judged. Do not condemn, and you will not be condemned. Forgive, and you will be forgiven. {38} Give, and it will be given to you. A good measure, pressed down, shaken together and running over, will be poured into your lap. For with the measure you use, it will be measured to you." {39} He also told them this parable: "Can a blind man lead a blind man? Will they not both fall into a pit? {40} A student is not above his teacher, but everyone who is fully trained will be like his teacher. {41} "Why do you look at the speck of sawdust in your brother's eye and pay no attention to the plank in your own eye? {42} How can you say to your brother, 'Brother, let me take the speck out of your eye,' when you yourself fail to see the plank in your own eye? You hypocrite, first take the plank out of your eye, and then you will see clearly to remove the speck from your brother's eye. {43} "No good tree bears bad fruit, nor does a bad tree bear good fruit. {44} Each tree is recognized by its own fruit. People do not pick figs from thornbushes, or grapes from briers. {45} The good man brings good things out of the good stored up in his heart, and the evil man brings evil things out of the evil stored up in his heart. For out of the overflow of his heart his mouth speaks. {46} "Why do you call me, 'Lord, Lord,' and do not do what I say? {47} I will show you what he is like who comes to me and hears my words and puts them into practice. {48} He is like a man building a house, who dug down deep and laid the foundation on rock.

FAITH OF THE CENTURION; WIDOW'S SON REVIVED; JOHN THE BAPTIST HAS DOUBTS

Luke 7:1-17

When Jesus had finished saying all this in the hearing of the people, he entered Capernaum. {2} There a centurion's servant, whom his master valued highly, was sick and about to die. {3} The centurion heard of Jesus and sent some elders of the Jews to him, asking him to come and heal his servant. {4} When they came to Jesus, they pleaded earnestly with him, "This man deserves to have you do this, {5} because he loves our nation and has built our synagogue." {6} So Jesus went with them. He was not far from the house when the centurion sent friends to say to him: "Lord, don't trouble yourself, for I do not deserve to have you come under my roof. {7} That is why I did not even consider myself worthy to come to you. But say the word, and my servant will be healed. {8} For I myself am a man under authority, with soldiers under me. I tell this one, 'Go,' and he goes; and that one, 'Come,' and he comes. I say to my servant, 'Do this,' and he does it." {9} When Jesus heard this, he was amazed at him, and turning to the crowd following him, he said, "I tell you, I have not found such great faith even in Israel." {10} Then the men who had been sent returned to the house and found the servant well.

{11} Soon afterward, Jesus went to a town called Nain, and his disciples and a large crowd went along with him. {12} As he approached the town gate, a dead person was being carried out–the only son of his mother, and she was a widow. And a large crowd from the town was with her. {13} When the Lord saw her, his heart went out to her and he said, "Don't cry." {14} Then he went up and touched the coffin, and those carrying it stood still. He said, "Young man, I say to you, get up!" {15} The dead man sat up and began to talk, and Jesus gave him back to his mother. {16} They were all filled with awe and praised God. "A great prophet has appeared among us," they said. "God has come to help his people." {17} This news about Jesus spread throughout Judea and the surrounding country.

Luke 7:20-23

When the men came to Jesus, they said, "John the Baptist sent us to you to ask, 'Are you the one who was to come, or should we expect someone else?'" {21} At that very time Jesus cured many who had diseases, sicknesses and evil spirits, and gave sight to many who were blind. {22} So he replied to the messengers, "Go back and report to John what you have seen and heard: The blind receive sight, the lame walk, those who have leprosy are cured, the deaf hear, the dead are raised, and the good news is preached to the poor. {23} Blessed is the man who does not fall away on account of me."

PARABLE OF THE SOWER; A LAMP ON A STAND

Luke 8:1-18

After this, Jesus traveled about from one town and village to another, proclaiming the good news of the kingdom of God. The Twelve were with him, {2} and also some women who had been cured of evil spirits and diseases: Mary (called Magdalene) from whom seven demons had come out; {3} Joanna the wife of Cuza, the manager of Herod's household; Susanna; and many others. These women were helping to support them out of their own means. {4} While a large crowd was gathering and people were coming to Jesus from town after town, he told this parable: {5} "A farmer went out to sow his seed. As he was scattering the seed, some fell along the path; it was trampled on, and the birds of the air ate it up. {6} Some fell on rock, and when it came up, the plants withered because they had no moisture. {7} Other seed fell among thorns, which grew up with it and choked the plants. {8} Still other seed fell on good soil. It came up and yielded a crop, a hundred times more than was sown." When he said this, he called out, "He who has ears to hear, let him hear." {9} His disciples asked him what this parable meant. {10} He said, "The knowledge of the secrets of the kingdom of God has been given to you, but to others I speak in parables, so that, "'though seeing, they may not see; though hearing, they may not understand.' {11} "This is the meaning of the parable: The seed is the word of God. {12} Those along the path are the ones who hear, and then the devil comes and takes away the word from their hearts, so that they may not believe and be saved. {13} Those on the rock are the ones who receive the word with joy when they hear it, but they have no root. They believe for a while, but in the time of testing they fall away. {14} The seed that fell among thorns stands for those who hear, but as they go on their way they are choked by life's worries, riches and pleasures, and they do not mature. {15} But the seed on good soil stands for those with a noble and good heart, who hear the word, retain it, and by persevering produce a crop.

{16} "No one lights a lamp and hides it in a jar or puts it under a bed. Instead, he puts it on a stand, so that those who come in can see the light. {17} For there is nothing hidden that will not be disclosed, and nothing concealed that will not be known or brought out into the open. {18} Therefore consider carefully how you listen. Whoever has will be given more; whoever does not have, even what he thinks he has will be taken from him."

JESUS CALMS THE STORM, HEALS A DEMON-POSSESSED

Luke 8:22-39

One day Jesus said to his disciples, "Let's go over to the other side of the lake." So they got into a boat and set out. {23} As they sailed, he fell asleep. A squall came down on the lake, so that the boat was being swamped, and they were in great danger. {24} The disciples went and woke him, saying, "Master, Master, we're going to drown!" He got up and rebuked the wind and the raging waters; the storm subsided, and all was calm. {25} "Where is your faith?" he asked his disciples. In fear and amazement they asked one another, "Who is this? He commands even the winds and the water, and they obey him." {26} They sailed to the region of the Gerasenes, which is across the lake from Galilee.

{27} When Jesus stepped ashore, he was met by a demon-possessed man from the town. For a long time this man had not worn clothes or lived in a house, but had lived in the tombs. {28} When he saw Jesus, he cried out and fell at his feet, shouting at the top of his voice, "What do you want with me, Jesus, Son of the Most High God? I beg you, don't torture me!" {29} For Jesus had commanded the evil spirit to come out of the man. Many times it had seized him, and though he was chained hand and foot and kept under guard, he had broken his chains and had been driven by the demon into solitary places. {30} Jesus asked him, "What is your name?" "Legion," he replied, because many demons had gone into him. {31} And they begged him repeatedly not to order them to go into the Abyss. {32} A large herd of pigs was feeding there on the hillside. The demons begged Jesus to let them go into them, and he gave them permission. {33} When the demons came out of the man, they went into the pigs, and the herd rushed down the steep bank into the lake and was drowned. {34} When those tending the pigs saw what had happened, they ran off and reported this in the town and countryside, {35} and the people went out to see what had happened. When they came to Jesus, they found the man from whom the demons had gone out, sitting at Jesus' feet, dressed and in his right mind; and they were afraid. {36} Those who had seen it told the people how the demon-possessed man had been cured. {37} Then all the people of the region of the Gerasenes asked Jesus to leave them, because they were overcome with fear. So he got into the boat and left. {38} The man from whom the demons had gone out begged to go with him, but Jesus sent him away, saying, {39} "Return home and tell how much God has done for you." So the man went away and told all over town how much Jesus had done for him.

JESUS SENDS OUT TWELVE, FEEDS FIVE THOUSAND; PETER'S WITNESS

Luke 9:1-21

When Jesus had called the Twelve together, he gave them power and authority to drive out all demons and to cure diseases, {2} and he sent them out to preach the kingdom of God and to heal the sick. {3} He told them: "Take nothing for the journey—no staff, no bag, no bread, no money, no extra tunic. {4} Whatever house you enter, stay there until you leave that town. {5} If people do not welcome you, shake the dust off your feet when you leave their town, as a testimony against them." {6} So they set out and went from village to village, preaching the gospel and healing people everywhere. {7} Now Herod the tetrarch heard about all that was going on. And he was perplexed, because some were saying that John had been raised from the dead, {8} others that Elijah had appeared, and still others that one of the prophets of long ago had come back to life. {9} But Herod said, "I beheaded John. Who, then, is this I hear such things about?" And he tried to see him. {10} When the apostles returned, they reported to Jesus what they had done. Then he took them with him and they withdrew by themselves to a town called Bethsaida, {11} but the crowds learned about it and followed him. He welcomed them and spoke to them about the kingdom of God, and healed those who needed healing.

{12} Late in the afternoon the Twelve came to him and said, "Send the crowd away so they can go to the surrounding villages and countryside and find food and lodging, because we are in a remote place here." {13} He replied, "You give them something to eat." They answered, "We have only five loaves of bread and two fish—unless we go and buy food for all this crowd." {14} (About five thousand men were there.) But he said to his disciples, "Have them sit down in groups of about fifty each." {15} The disciples did so, and everybody sat down. {16} Taking the five loaves and the two fish and looking up to heaven, he gave thanks and broke them. Then he gave them to the disciples to set before the people. {17} They all ate and were satisfied, and the disciples picked up twelve basketfuls of broken pieces that were left over.

{18} Once when Jesus was praying in private and his disciples were with him, he asked them, "Who do the crowds say I am?" {19} They replied, "Some say John the Baptist; others say Elijah; and still others, that one of the prophets of long ago has come back to life." {20} "But what about you?" he asked. "Who do you say I am?" Peter answered, "The Christ of God." {21} Jesus strictly warned them not to tell this to anyone.

TRANSFIGURATION; JESUS HEALS A BOY; A QUESTION OF GREATNESS

Luke 9:28-48

About eight days after Jesus said this, he took Peter, John and James with him and went up onto a mountain to pray. {29} As he was praying, the appearance of his face changed, and his clothes became as bright as a flash of lightning. {30} Two men, Moses and Elijah, {31} appeared in glorious splendor, talking with Jesus. They spoke about his departure, which he was about to bring to fulfillment at Jerusalem. {32} Peter and his companions were very sleepy, but when they became fully awake, they saw his glory and the two men standing with him. {33} As the men were leaving Jesus, Peter said to him, "Master, it is good for us to be here. Let us put up three shelters—one for you, one for Moses and one for Elijah." (He did not know what he was saying.) {34} While he was speaking, a cloud appeared and enveloped them, and they were afraid as they entered the cloud. {35} A voice came from the cloud, saying, "This is my Son, whom I have chosen; listen to him." {36} When the voice had spoken, they found that Jesus was alone. The disciples kept this to themselves, and told no one at that time what they had seen.

{37} The next day, when they came down from the mountain, a large crowd met him. {38} A man in the crowd called out, "Teacher, I beg you to look at my son, for he is my only child. {39} A spirit seizes him and he suddenly screams; it throws him into convulsions so that he foams at the mouth. It scarcely ever leaves him and is destroying him. {40} I begged your disciples to drive it out, but they could not." {41} "O unbelieving and perverse generation," Jesus replied, "how long shall I stay with you and put up with you? Bring your son here." {42} Even while the boy was coming, the demon threw him to the ground in a convulsion. But Jesus rebuked the evil spirit, healed the boy and gave him back to his father. {43} And they were all amazed at the greatness of God. While everyone was marveling at all that Jesus did, he said to his disciples, {44} "Listen carefully to what I am about to tell you: The Son of Man is going to be betrayed into the hands of men." {45} But they did not understand what this meant. It was hidden from them, so that they did not grasp it, and they were afraid to ask him about it.

{46} An argument started among the disciples as to which of them would be the greatest. {47} Jesus, knowing their thoughts, took a little child and had him stand beside him. {48} Then he said to them, "Whoever welcomes this little child in my name welcomes me; and whoever welcomes me welcomes the one who sent me. For he who is least among you all—he is the greatest."

THE COST OF DISCIPLESHIP

Luke 9:57b-10:20

A man said to him, "I will follow you wherever you go." {58} Jesus replied, "Foxes have holes and birds of the air have nests, but the Son of Man has no place to lay his head." {59} He said to another man, "Follow me." But the man replied, "Lord, first let me go and bury my father." {60} Jesus said to him, "Let the dead bury their own dead, but you go and proclaim the kingdom of God." {61} Still another said, "I will follow you, Lord; but first let me go back and say good-by to my family." {62} Jesus replied, "No one who puts his hand to the plow and looks back is fit for service in the kingdom of God." {10:1} After this the Lord appointed seventy-two others and sent them two by two ahead of him to every town and place where he was about to go. {2} He told them, "The harvest is plentiful, but the workers are few. Ask the Lord of the harvest, therefore, to send out workers into his harvest field. {3} Go! I am sending you out like lambs among wolves. {4} Do not take a purse or bag or sandals; and do not greet anyone on the road. {5} "When you enter a house, first say, 'Peace to this house.' {6} If a man of peace is there, your peace will rest on him; if not, it will return to you. {7} Stay in that house, eating and drinking whatever they give you, for the worker deserves his wages. Do not move around from house to house. {8} "When you enter a town and are welcomed, eat what is set before you. {9} Heal the sick who are there and tell them, 'The kingdom of God is near you.' {10} But when you enter a town and are not welcomed, go into its streets and say, {11} 'Even the dust of your town that sticks to our feet we wipe off against you. Yet be sure of this: The kingdom of God is near.' {12} I tell you, it will be more bearable on that day for Sodom than for that town. {13} "Woe to you, Korazin! Woe to you, Bethsaida! For if the miracles that were performed in you had been performed in Tyre and Sidon, they would have repented long ago, sitting in sackcloth and ashes. {14} But it will be more bearable for Tyre and Sidon at the judgment than for you. {15} And you, Capernaum, will you be lifted up to the skies? No, you will go down to the depths. {16} "He who listens to you listens to me; he who rejects you rejects me; but he who rejects me rejects him who sent me." {17} The seventy-two returned with joy and said, "Lord, even the demons submit to us in your name." {18} He replied, "I saw Satan fall like lightning from heaven. {19} I have given you authority to trample on snakes and scorpions and to overcome all the power of the enemy; nothing will harm you. {20} However , do not rejoice that the spirits submit to you, but rejoice that your names are written in heaven."

THE GOOD SAMARITAN; MARY AND MARTHA

Luke 10:25-42

On one occasion an expert in the law stood up to test Jesus. "Teacher," he asked, "what must I do to inherit eternal life?" {26} "What is written in the Law?" he replied. "How do you read it?" {27} He answered: "'Love the Lord your God with all your heart and with all your soul and with all your strength and with all your mind'; and, 'Love your neighbor as yourself.'" {28} "You have answered correctly," Jesus replied. "Do this and you will live." {29} But he wanted to justify himself, so he asked Jesus, "And who is my neighbor?" {30} In reply Jesus said: "A man was going down from Jerusalem to Jericho, when he fell into the hands of robbers. They stripped him of his clothes, beat him and went away, leaving him half dead. {31} A priest happened to be going down the same road, and when he saw the man, he passed by on the other side. {32} So too, a Levite, when he came to the place and saw him, passed by on the other side. {33} But a Samaritan, as he traveled, came where the man was; and when he saw him, he took pity on him. {34} He went to him and bandaged his wounds, pouring on oil and wine. Then he put the man on his own donkey, took him to an inn and took care of him. {35} The next day he took out two silver coins and gave them to the innkeeper. 'Look after him,' he said, 'and when I return, I will reimburse you for any extra expense you may have.' {36} "Which of these three do you think was a neighbor to the man who fell into the hands of robbers?" {37} The expert in the law replied, "The one who had mercy on him." Jesus told him, "Go and do likewise."

{38} As Jesus and his disciples were on their way, he came to a village where a woman named Martha opened her home to him. {39} She had a sister called Mary, who sat at the Lord's feet listening to what he said. {40} But Martha was distracted by all the preparations that had to be made. She came to him and asked, "Lord, don't you care that my sister has left me to do the work by myself? Tell her to help me!" {41} "Martha, Martha," the Lord answered, "you are worried and upset about many things, {42} but only one thing is needed. Mary has chosen what is better, and it will not be taken away from her."

JESUS COMMENTS ON PRAYER; A LAMP ON A STAND

Luke 11:1-10

One day Jesus was praying in a certain place. When he finished, one of his disciples said to him, "Lord, teach us to pray, just as John taught his disciples." {2} He said to them, "When you pray, say: "'Father, hallowed be your name, your kingdom come. {3} Give us each day our daily bread. {4} Forgive us our sins, for we also forgive everyone who sins against us. And lead us not into temptation. '" {5} Then he said to them, "Suppose one of you has a friend, and he goes to him at midnight and says, 'Friend, lend me three loaves of bread, {6} because a friend of mine on a journey has come to me, and I have nothing to set before him.' {7} "Then the one inside answers, 'Don't bother me. The door is already locked, and my children are with me in bed. I can't get up and give you anything.' {8} I tell you, though he will not get up and give him the bread because he is his friend, yet because of the man's boldness he will get up and give him as much as he needs. {9} "So I say to you: Ask and it will be given to you; seek and you will find; knock and the door will be opened to you. {10} For everyone who asks receives; he who seeks finds; and to him who knocks, the door will be opened.

Luke 11:33-36

"No one lights a lamp and puts it in a place where it will be hidden, or under a bowl. Instead he puts it on its stand, so that those who come in may see the light. {34} Your eye is the lamp of your body. When your eyes are good, your whole body also is full of light. But when they are bad, your body also is full of darkness. {35} See to it, then, that the light within you is not darkness. {36} Therefore , if your whole body is full of light, and no part of it dark, it will be completely lighted, as when the light of a lamp shines on you."

WARNINGS ON HYPOCRISY

Luke 11:37-12:2

When Jesus had finished speaking, a Pharisee invited him to eat with him; so he went in and reclined at the table. {38} But the Pharisee, noticing that Jesus did not first wash before the meal, was surprised. {39} Then the Lord said to him, "Now then, you Pharisees clean the outside of the cup and dish, but inside you are full of greed and wickedness. {40} You foolish people! Did not the one who made the outside make the inside also? {41} But give what is inside <the dish> to the poor, and everything will be clean for you. {42} "Woe to you Pharisees, because you give God a tenth of your mint, rue and all other kinds of garden herbs, but you neglect justice and the love of God. You should have practiced the latter without leaving the former undone. {43} "Woe to you Pharisees, because you love the most important seats in the synagogues and greetings in the marketplaces. {44} "Woe to you, because you are like unmarked graves, which men walk over without knowing it." {45} One of the experts in the law answered him, "Teacher, when you say these things, you insult us also." {46} Jesus replied, "And you experts in the law, woe to you, because you load people down with burdens they can hardly carry, and you yourselves will not lift one finger to help them. {47} "Woe to you, because you build tombs for the prophets, and it was your forefathers who killed them. {48} So you testify that you approve of what your forefathers did; they killed the prophets, and you build their tombs. {49} Because of this, God in his wisdom said, 'I will send them prophets and apostles, some of whom they will kill and others they will persecute.' {50} Therefore this generation will be held responsible for the blood of all the prophets that has been shed since the beginning of the world, {51} from the blood of Abel to the blood of Zechariah, who was killed between the altar and the sanctuary. Yes, I tell you, this generation will be held responsible for it all. {52} "Woe to you experts in the law, because you have taken away the key to knowledge. You yourselves have not entered, and you have hindered those who were entering." {53} When Jesus left there, the Pharisees and the teachers of the law began to oppose him fiercely and to besiege him with questions, {54} waiting to catch him in something he might say. {12:1} Meanwhile, when a crowd of many thousands had gathered, so that they were trampling on one another, Jesus began to speak first to his disciples, saying: "Be on your guard against the yeast of the Pharisees, which is hypocrisy. {2} There is nothing concealed that will not be disclosed, or hidden that will not be made known.

THE FOOLISH RICH MAN; CAST YOUR CARES ON GOD

Luke 12:13-35

Someone in the crowd said to him, "Teacher, tell my brother to divide the inheritance with me." {14} Jesus replied, "Man, who appointed me a judge or an arbiter between you?" {15} Then he said to them, "Watch out! Be on your guard against all kinds of greed; a man's life does not consist in the abundance of his possessions." {16} And he told them this parable: "The ground of a certain rich man produced a good crop. {17} He thought to himself, 'What shall I do? I have no place to store my crops.' {18} "Then he said, 'This is what I'll do. I will tear down my barns and build bigger ones, and there I will store all my grain and my goods. {19} And I'll say to myself, "You have plenty of good things laid up for many years. Take life easy; eat, drink and be merry."' {20} "But God said to him, 'You fool! This very night your life will be demanded from you. Then who will get what you have prepared for yourself?' {21} "This is how it will be with anyone who stores up things for himself but is not rich toward God."

{22} Then Jesus said to his disciples: "Therefore I tell you, do not worry about your life, what you will eat; or about your body, what you will wear. {23} Life is more than food, and the body more than clothes. {24} Consider the ravens: They do not sow or reap, they have no storeroom or barn; yet God feeds them. And how much more valuable you are than birds! {25} Who of you by worrying can add a single hour to his life ? {26} Since you cannot do this very little thing, why do you worry about the rest? {27} "Consider how the lilies grow. They do not labor or spin. Yet I tell you, not even Solomon in all his splendor was dressed like one of these. {28} If that is how God clothes the grass of the field, which is here today, and tomorrow is thrown into the fire, how much more will he clothe you, O you of little faith! {29} And do not set your heart on what you will eat or drink; do not worry about it. {30} For the pagan world runs after all such things, and your Father knows that you need them. {31} But seek his kingdom, and these things will be given to you as well. {32} "Do not be afraid, little flock, for your Father has been pleased to give you the kingdom. {33} Sell your possessions and give to the poor. Provide purses for yourselves that will not wear out, a treasure in heaven that will not be exhausted, where no thief comes near and no moth destroys. {34} For where your treasure is, there your heart will be also. {35} "Be dressed ready for service and keep your lamps burning,

REPENT!

Luke 13:1-8

Now there were some present at that time who told Jesus about the Galileans whose blood Pilate had mixed with their sacrifices. {2} Jesus answered, "Do you think that these Galileans were worse sinners than all the other Galileans because they suffered this way? {3} I tell you, no! But unless you repent, you too will all perish. {4} Or those eighteen who died when the tower in Siloam fell on them—do you think they were more guilty than all the others living in Jerusalem? {5} I tell you, no! But unless you repent, you too will all perish." {6} Then he told this parable: "A man had a fig tree, planted in his vineyard, and he went to look for fruit on it, but did not find any. {7} So he said to the man who took care of the vineyard, 'For three years now I've been coming to look for fruit on this fig tree and haven't found any. Cut it down! Why should it use up the soil?' {8} "'Sir,' the man replied, 'leave it alone for one more year, and I'll dig around it and fertilize it.

OF MUSTARD SEED, YEAST, AND THE NARROW DOOR

Luke 13:18-29

Then Jesus asked, "What is the kingdom of God like? What shall I compare it to? {19} It is like a mustard seed, which a man took and planted in his garden. It grew and became a tree, and the birds of the air perched in its branches." {20} Again he asked, "What shall I compare the kingdom of God to? {21} It is like yeast that a woman took and mixed into a large amount of flour until it worked all through the dough." {22} Then Jesus went through the towns and villages, teaching as he made his way to Jerusalem. {23} Someone asked him, "Lord, are only a few people going to be saved?" He said to them, {24} "Make every effort to enter through the narrow door, because many, I tell you, will try to enter and will not be able to. {25} Once the owner of the house gets up and closes the door, you will stand outside knocking and pleading, 'Sir, open the door for us.' "But he will answer, 'I don't know you or where you come from.' {26} "Then you will say, 'We ate and drank with you, and you taught in our streets.' {27} "But he will reply, 'I don't know you or where you come from. Away from me, all you evildoers!' {28} "There will be weeping there, and gnashing of teeth, when you see Abraham, Isaac and Jacob and all the prophets in the kingdom of God, but you yourselves thrown out. {29} People will come from east and west and north and south, and will take their places at the feast in the kingdom of God.

PARABLE OF THE BANQUET;
ON THE COST OF DISCIPLESHIP

Luke 14:13-35a
But when you give a banquet, invite the poor, the crippled, the lame, the blind, {14} and you will be blessed. Although they cannot repay you, you will be repaid at the resurrection of the righteous." {15} When one of those at the table with him heard this, he said to Jesus, "Blessed is the man who will eat at the feast in the kingdom of God." {16} Jesus replied: "A certain man was preparing a great banquet and invited many guests. {17} At the time of the banquet he sent his servant to tell those who had been invited, 'Come, for everything is now ready.' {18} "But they all alike began to make excuses. The first said, 'I have just bought a field, and I must go and see it. Please excuse me.' {19} "Another said, 'I have just bought five yoke of oxen, and I'm on my way to try them out. Please excuse me.' {20} "Still another said, 'I just got married, so I can't come.' {21} "The servant came back and reported this to his master. Then the owner of the house became angry and ordered his servant, 'Go out quickly into the streets and alleys of the town and bring in the poor, the crippled, the blind and the lame.' {22} "'Sir,' the servant said, 'what you ordered has been done, but there is still room.' {23} "Then the master told his servant, 'Go out to the roads and country lanes and make them come in, so that my house will be full. {24} I tell you, not one of those men who were invited will get a taste of my banquet.'"

{25} Large crowds were traveling with Jesus, and turning to them he said: {26} "If anyone comes to me and does not hate his father and mother, his wife and children, his brothers and sisters–yes, even his own life–he cannot be my disciple. {27} And anyone who does not carry his cross and follow me cannot be my disciple. {28} "Suppose one of you wants to build a tower. Will he not first sit down and estimate the cost to see if he has enough money to complete it? {29} For if he lays the foundation and is not able to finish it, everyone who sees it will ridicule him, {30} saying , 'This fellow began to build and was not able to finish.' {31} "Or suppose a king is about to go to war against another king. Will he not first sit down and consider whether he is able with ten thousand men to oppose the one coming against him with twenty thousand? {32} If he is not able, he will send a delegation while the other is still a long way off and will ask for terms of peace. {33} In the same way, any of you who does not give up everything he has cannot be my disciple. {34} "Salt is good, but if it loses its saltiness, how can it be made salty again? {35} It is fit neither for the soil nor for the manure pile....

THE LOST SON

Luke 15:11-32

Jesus continued: "There was a man who had two sons. {12} The younger one said to his father, 'Father, give me my share of the estate.' So he divided his property between them. {13} "Not long after that, the younger son got together all he had, set off for a distant country and there squandered his wealth in wild living. {14} After he had spent everything, there was a severe famine in that whole country, and he began to be in need. {15} So he went and hired himself out to a citizen of that country, who sent him to his fields to feed pigs. {16} He longed to fill his stomach with the pods that the pigs were eating, but no one gave him anything. {17} "When he came to his senses, he said, 'How many of my father's hired men have food to spare, and here I am starving to death! {18} I will set out and go back to my father and say to him: Father, I have sinned against heaven and against you. {19} I am no longer worthy to be called your son; make me like one of your hired men.' {20} So he got up and went to his father. "But while he was still a long way off, his father saw him and was filled with compassion for him; he ran to his son, threw his arms around him and kissed him. {21} "The son said to him, 'Father, I have sinned against heaven and against you. I am no longer worthy to be called your son.' {22} "But the father said to his servants, 'Quick! Bring the best robe and put it on him. Put a ring on his finger and sandals on his feet. {23} Bring the fattened calf and kill it. Let's have a feast and celebrate. {24} For this son of mine was dead and is alive again; he was lost and is found.' So they began to celebrate. {25} "Meanwhile, the older son was in the field. When he came near the house, he heard music and dancing. {26} So he called one of the servants and asked him what was going on. {27} 'Your brother has come,' he replied, 'and your father has killed the fattened calf because he has him back safe and sound.' {28} "The older brother became angry and refused to go in. So his father went out and pleaded with him. {29} But he answered his father, 'Look! All these years I've been slaving for you and never disobeyed your orders. Yet you never gave me even a young goat so I could celebrate with my friends. {30} But when this son of yours who has squandered your property with prostitutes comes home, you kill the fattened calf for him!' {31} "'My son,' the father said, 'you are always with me, and everything I have is yours. {32} But we had to celebrate and be glad, because this brother of yours was dead and is alive again; he was lost and is found.'"

PARABLE OF THE GOOD MANAGER;
THE RICH MAN AND LAZARUS

Luke 16:1-8a

Jesus told his disciples: "There was a rich man whose manager was accused of wasting his possessions. {2} So he called him in and asked him, 'What is this I hear about you? Give an account of your management, because you cannot be manager any longer.' {3} "The manager said to himself, 'What shall I do now? My master is taking away my job. I'm not strong enough to dig, and I'm ashamed to beg– {4} I know what I'll do so that, when I lose my job here, people will welcome me into their houses.' {5} "So he called in each one of his master's debtors. He asked the first, 'How much do you owe my master?' {6} "'Eight hundred gallons of olive oil,' he replied. "The manager told him, 'Take your bill, sit down quickly, and make it four hundred.' {7} "Then he asked the second, 'And how much do you owe?' "'A thousand bushels of wheat,' he replied. "He told him, 'Take your bill and make it eight hundred.' {8} "The master commended the dishonest manager because he had acted shrewdly.

Luke 16:19-31

"There was a rich man who was dressed in purple and fine linen and lived in luxury every day. {20} At his gate was laid a beggar named Lazarus, covered with sores {21} and longing to eat what fell from the rich man's table. Even the dogs came and licked his sores. {22} "The time came when the beggar died and the angels carried him to Abraham's side. The rich man also died and was buried. {23} In hell, where he was in torment, he looked up and saw Abraham far away, with Lazarus by his side. {24} So he called to him, 'Father Abraham, have pity on me and send Lazarus to dip the tip of his finger in water and cool my tongue, because I am in agony in this fire.' {25} "But Abraham replied, 'Son, remember that in your lifetime you received your good things, while Lazarus received bad things, but now he is comforted here and you are in agony. {26} And besides all this, between us and you a great chasm has been fixed, so that those who want to go from here to you cannot, nor can anyone cross over from there to us.' {27} "He answered, 'Then I beg you, father, send Lazarus to my father's house, {28} for I have five brothers. Let him warn them, so that they will not also come to this place of torment.' {29} "Abraham replied, 'They have Moses and the Prophets; let them listen to them.' {30} "'No, father Abraham,' he said, 'but if someone from the dead goes to them, they will repent.' {31} "He said to him, 'If they do not listen to Moses and the Prophets, they will not be convinced even if someone rises from the dead.'"

TEN LEPERS HEALED;
PARABLE OF THE PERSISTENT WIDOW; THE TAX COLLECTOR

Luke 17:11-19

Now on his way to Jerusalem, Jesus traveled along the border between Samaria and Galilee. {12} As he was going into a village, ten men who had leprosy met him. They stood at a distance {13} and called out in a loud voice, "Jesus, Master, have pity on us!" {14} When he saw them, he said, "Go, show yourselves to the priests." And as they went, they were cleansed. {15} One of them, when he saw he was healed, came back, praising God in a loud voice. {16} He threw himself at Jesus' feet and thanked him—and he was a Samaritan. {17} Jesus asked, "Were not all ten cleansed? Where are the other nine? {18} Was no one found to return and give praise to God except this foreigner?" {19} Then he said to him, "Rise and go; your faith has made you well."

Luke 18:1-14

Then Jesus told his disciples a parable to show them that they should always pray and not give up. {2} He said: "In a certain town there was a judge who neither feared God nor cared about men. {3} And there was a widow in that town who kept coming to him with the plea, 'Grant me justice against my adversary.' {4} "For some time he refused. But finally he said to himself, 'Even though I don't fear God or care about men, {5} yet because this widow keeps bothering me, I will see that she gets justice, so that she won't eventually wear me out with her coming!'" {6} And the Lord said, "Listen to what the unjust judge says. {7} And will not God bring about justice for his chosen ones, who cry out to him day and night? Will he keep putting them off? {8} I tell you, he will see that they get justice, and quickly. However, when the Son of Man comes, will he find faith on the earth?"

{9} To some who were confident of their own righteousness and looked down on everybody else, Jesus told this parable: {10} "Two men went up to the temple to pray, one a Pharisee and the other a tax collector. {11} The Pharisee stood up and prayed about himself: 'God, I thank you that I am not like other men—robbers, evildoers, adulterers—or even like this tax collector. {12} I fast twice a week and give a tenth of all I get.' {13} "But the tax collector stood at a distance. He would not even look up to heaven, but beat his breast and said, 'God, have mercy on me, a sinner.' {14} "I tell you that this man, rather than the other, went home justified before God. For everyone who exalts himself will be humbled, and he who humbles himself will be exalted."

ZACCHAEUS THE TAX COLLECTOR;
PARABLE ON STEWARDSHIP

Luke 19:1-23

Jesus entered Jericho and was passing through. {2} A man was there by the name of Zacchaeus; he was a chief tax collector and was wealthy. {3} He wanted to see who Jesus was, but being a short man he could not, because of the crowd. {4} So he ran ahead and climbed a sycamore-fig tree to see him, since Jesus was coming that way. {5} When Jesus reached the spot, he looked up and said to him, "Zacchaeus, come down immediately. I must stay at your house today." {6} So he came down at once and welcomed him gladly. {7} All the people saw this and began to mutter, "He has gone to be the guest of a 'sinner.'" {8} But Zacchaeus stood up and said to the Lord, "Look, Lord! Here and now I give half of my possessions to the poor, and if I have cheated anybody out of anything, I will pay back four times the amount." {9} Jesus said to him, "Today salvation has come to this house, because this man, too, is a son of Abraham. {10} For the Son of Man came to seek and to save what was lost."

{11} While they were listening to this, he went on to tell them a parable, because he was near Jerusalem and the people thought that the kingdom of God was going to appear at once. {12} He said: "A man of noble birth went to a distant country to have himself appointed king and then to return. {13} So he called ten of his servants and gave them ten minas. 'Put this money to work,' he said, 'until I come back.' {14} "But his subjects hated him and sent a delegation after him to say, 'We don't want this man to be our king.' {15} "He was made king, however, and returned home. Then he sent for the servants to whom he had given the money, in order to find out what they had gained with it. {16} "The first one came and said, 'Sir, your mina has earned ten more.' {17} "'Well done, my good servant!' his master replied. 'Because you have been trustworthy in a very small matter, take charge of ten cities.' {18} "The second came and said, 'Sir, your mina has earned five more.' {19} "His master answered, 'You take charge of five cities.' {20} "Then another servant came and said, 'Sir, here is your mina; I have kept it laid away in a piece of cloth. {21} I was afraid of you, because you are a hard man. You take out what you did not put in and reap what you did not sow.' {22} "His master replied, 'I will judge you by your own words, you wicked servant! You knew, did you, that I am a hard man, taking out what I did not put in, and reaping what I did not sow? {23} Why then didn't you put my money on deposit, so that when I came back, I could have collected it with interest?'

JESUS' TRIUMPHAL ENTRY INTO JERUSALEM; JESUS' AUTHORITY IS QUESTIONED

Luke 19:32-20:8

Those who were sent ahead went and found it just as he had told them. {33} As they were untying the colt, its owners asked them, "Why are you untying the colt?" {34} They replied, "The Lord needs it." {35} They brought it to Jesus, threw their cloaks on the colt and put Jesus on it. {36} As he went along, people spread their cloaks on the road. {37} When he came near the place where the road goes down the Mount of Olives, the whole crowd of disciples began joyfully to praise God in loud voices for all the miracles they had seen: {38} "Blessed is the king who comes in the name of the Lord!" "Peace in heaven and glory in the highest!" {39} Some of the Pharisees in the crowd said to Jesus, "Teacher, rebuke your disciples!" {40} "I tell you," he replied, "if they keep quiet, the stones will cry out." {41} As he approached Jerusalem and saw the city, he wept over it {42} and said, "If you, even you, had only known on this day what would bring you peace—but now it is hidden from your eyes. {43} The days will come upon you when your enemies will build an embankment against you and encircle you and hem you in on every side. {44} They will dash you to the ground, you and the children within your walls. They will not leave one stone on another, because you did not recognize the time of God's coming to you." {45} Then he entered the temple area and began driving out those who were selling. {46} "It is written," he said to them, "'My house will be a house of prayer'; but you have made it 'a den of robbers.'" {47} Every day he was teaching at the temple.

But the chief priests, the teachers of the law and the leaders among the people were trying to kill him. {48} Yet they could not find any way to do it, because all the people hung on his words. {20:1} One day as he was teaching the people in the temple courts and preaching the gospel, the chief priests and the teachers of the law, together with the elders, came up to him. {2} "Tell us by what authority you are doing these things," they said. "Who gave you this authority?" {3} He replied, "I will also ask you a question. Tell me, {4} John's baptism—was it from heaven, or from men?" {5} They discussed it among themselves and said, "If we say, 'From heaven,' he will ask, 'Why didn't you believe him?' {6} But if we say, 'From men,' all the people will stone us, because they are persuaded that John was a prophet." {7} So they answered, "We don't know where it was from." {8} Jesus said, "Neither will I tell you by what authority I am doing these things."

PARABLE OF TENANTS; ON PAYING TAXES

Luke 20:9-26

He went on to tell the people this parable: "A man planted a vineyard, rented it to some farmers and went away for a long time. {10} At harvest time he sent a servant to the tenants so they would give him some of the fruit of the vineyard. But the tenants beat him and sent him away empty-handed. {11} He sent another servant, but that one also they beat and treated shamefully and sent away empty-handed. {12} He sent still a third, and they wounded him and threw him out. {13} "Then the owner of the vineyard said, 'What shall I do? I will send my son, whom I love; perhaps they will respect him.' {14} "But when the tenants saw him, they talked the matter over. 'This is the heir,' they said. 'Let's kill him, and the inheritance will be ours.' {15} So they threw him out of the vineyard and killed him. "What then will the owner of the vineyard do to them? {16} He will come and kill those tenants and give the vineyard to others." When the people heard this, they said, "May this never be!" {17} Jesus looked directly at them and asked, "Then what is the meaning of that which is written: "'The stone the builders rejected has become the capstone'? {18} Everyone who falls on that stone will be broken to pieces, but he on whom it falls will be crushed."

{19} The teachers of the law and the chief priests looked for a way to arrest him immediately, because they knew he had spoken this parable against them. But they were afraid of the people. {20} Keeping a close watch on him, they sent spies, who pretended to be honest. They hoped to catch Jesus in something he said so that they might hand him over to the power and authority of the governor. {21} So the spies questioned him: "Teacher, we know that you speak and teach what is right, and that you do not show partiality but teach the way of God in accordance with the truth. {22} Is it right for us to pay taxes to Caesar or not?" {23} He saw through their duplicity and said to them, {24} "Show me a denarius. Whose portrait and inscription are on it?" {25} "Caesar's," they replied. He said to them, "Then give to Caesar what is Caesar's, and to God what is God's." {26} They were unable to trap him in what he had said there in public. And astonished by his answer, they became silent.

SIGNS OF THE END

Luke 21:8-31

"Watch out that you are not deceived. For many will come in my name, claiming, 'I am he,' and, 'The time is near.' Do not follow them. {9} When you hear of wars and revolutions, do not be frightened. These things must happen first, but the end will not come right away." {10} Then he said to them: "Nation will rise against nation, and kingdom against kingdom. {11} There will be great earthquakes, famines and pestilences in various places, and fearful events and great signs from heaven. {12} "But before all this, they will lay hands on you and persecute you. They will deliver you to synagogues and prisons, and you will be brought before kings and governors, and all on account of my name. {13} This will result in your being witnesses to them. {14} But make up your mind not to worry beforehand how you will defend yourselves. {15} For I will give you words and wisdom that none of your adversaries will be able to resist or contradict. {16} You will be betrayed even by parents, brothers, relatives and friends, and they will put some of you to death. {17} All men will hate you because of me. {18} But not a hair of your head will perish. {19} By standing firm you will gain life. {20} "When you see Jerusalem being surrounded by armies, you will know that its desolation is near. {21} Then let those who are in Judea flee to the mountains, let those in the city get out, and let those in the country not enter the city. {22} For this is the time of punishment in fulfillment of all that has been written. {23} How dreadful it will be in those days for pregnant women and nursing mothers! There will be great distress in the land and wrath against this people. {24} They will fall by the sword and will be taken as prisoners to all the nations. Jerusalem will be trampled on by the Gentiles until the times of the Gentiles are fulfilled. {25} "There will be signs in the sun, moon and stars. On the earth, nations will be in anguish and perplexity at the roaring and tossing of the sea. {26} Men will faint from terror, apprehensive of what is coming on the world, for the heavenly bodies will be shaken. {27} At that time they will see the Son of Man coming in a cloud with power and great glory. {28} When these things begin to take place, stand up and lift up your heads, because your redemption is drawing near." {29} He told them this parable: "Look at the fig tree and all the trees. {30} When they sprout leaves, you can see for yourselves and know that summer is near. {31} Even so, when you see these things happening, you know that the kingdom of God is near.

THE LAST SUPPER

Luke 22:13b-38

So they prepared the Passover. {14} When the hour came, Jesus and his apostles reclined at the table. {15} And he said to them, "I have eagerly desired to eat this Passover with you before I suffer. {16} For I tell you, I will not eat it again until it finds fulfillment in the kingdom of God." {17} After taking the cup, he gave thanks and said, "Take this and divide it among you. {18} For I tell you I will not drink again of the fruit of the vine until the kingdom of God comes." {19} And he took bread, gave thanks and broke it, and gave it to them, saying, "This is my body given for you; do this in remembrance of me." {20} In the same way, after the supper he took the cup, saying, "This cup is the new covenant in my blood, which is poured out for you. {21} But the hand of him who is going to betray me is with mine on the table. {22} The Son of Man will go as it has been decreed, but woe to that man who betrays him." {23} They began to question among themselves which of them it might be who would do this. {24} Also a dispute arose among them as to which of them was considered to be greatest. {25} Jesus said to them, "The kings of the Gentiles lord it over them; and those who exercise authority over them call themselves Benefactors. {26} But you are not to be like that. Instead, the greatest among you should be like the youngest, and the one who rules like the one who serves. {27} For who is greater, the one who is at the table or the one who serves? Is it not the one who is at the table? But I am among you as one who serves. {28} You are those who have stood by me in my trials. {29} And I confer on you a kingdom, just as my Father conferred one on me, {30} so that you may eat and drink at my table in my kingdom and sit on thrones, judging the twelve tribes of Israel. {31} "Simon , Simon, Satan has asked to sift you as wheat. {32} But I have prayed for you, Simon, that your faith may not fail. And when you have turned back, strengthen your brothers." {33} But he replied, "Lord, I am ready to go with you to prison and to death." {34} Jesus answered, "I tell you, Peter, before the rooster crows today, you will deny three times that you know me." {35} Then Jesus asked them, "When I sent you without purse, bag or sandals, did you lack anything?" "Nothing," they answered. {36} He said to them, "But now if you have a purse, take it, and also a bag; and if you don't have a sword, sell your cloak and buy one. {37} It is written: 'And he was numbered with the transgressors'; and I tell you that this must be fulfilled in me. Yes, what is written about me is reaching its fulfillment." {38} The disciples said, "See, Lord, here are two swords." "That is enough," he replied.

JESUS ON THE MOUNT OF OLIVES; BETRAYAL BY PETER

Luke 22:39-62

Jesus went out as usual to the Mount of Olives, and his disciples followed him. {40} On reaching the place, he said to them, "Pray that you will not fall into temptation." {41} He withdrew about a stone's throw beyond them, knelt down and prayed, {42} "Father, if you are willing, take this cup from me; yet not my will, but yours be done." {43} An angel from heaven appeared to him and strengthened him. {44} And being in anguish, he prayed more earnestly, and his sweat was like drops of blood falling to the ground. {45} When he rose from prayer and went back to the disciples, he found them asleep, exhausted from sorrow. {46} "Why are you sleeping?" he asked them. "Get up and pray so that you will not fall into temptation." {47} While he was still speaking a crowd came up, and the man who was called Judas, one of the Twelve, was leading them. He approached Jesus to kiss him, {48} but Jesus asked him, "Judas, are you betraying the Son of Man with a kiss?" {49} When Jesus' followers saw what was going to happen, they said, "Lord, should we strike with our swords?" {50} And one of them struck the servant of the high priest, cutting off his right ear. {51} But Jesus answered, "No more of this!" And he touched the man's ear and healed him. {52} Then Jesus said to the chief priests, the officers of the temple guard, and the elders, who had come for him, "Am I leading a rebellion, that you have come with swords and clubs? {53} Every day I was with you in the temple courts, and you did not lay a hand on me. But this is your hour—when darkness reigns." {54} Then seizing him, they led him away and took him into the house of the high priest. Peter followed at a distance.

{55} But when they had kindled a fire in the middle of the courtyard and had sat down together, Peter sat down with them. {56} A servant girl saw him seated there in the firelight. She looked closely at him and said, "This man was with him." {57} But he denied it. "Woman, I don't know him," he said. {58} A little later someone else saw him and said, "You also are one of them." "Man, I am not!" Peter replied. {59} About an hour later another asserted, "Certainly this fellow was with him, for he is a Galilean." {60} Peter replied, "Man, I don't know what you're talking about!" Just as he was speaking, the rooster crowed. {61} The Lord turned and looked straight at Peter. Then Peter remembered the word the Lord had spoken to him: "Before the rooster crows today, you will disown me three times." {62} And he went outside and wept bitterly.

JESUS BEFORE PILATE

Luke 22:70-23:25

They all asked, "Are you then the Son of God?" He replied, "You are right in saying I am." {71} Then they said, "Why do we need any more testimony? We have heard it from his own lips." {23:1} Then the whole assembly rose and led him off to Pilate. {2} And they began to accuse him, saying, "We have found this man subverting our nation. He opposes payment of taxes to Caesar and claims to be Christ, a king." {3} So Pilate asked Jesus, "Are you the king of the Jews?" "Yes , it is as you say," Jesus replied. {4} Then Pilate announced to the chief priests and the crowd, "I find no basis for a charge against this man." {5} But they insisted, "He stirs up the people all over Judea by his teaching. He started in Galilee and has come all the way here." {6} On hearing this, Pilate asked if the man was a Galilean. {7} When he learned that Jesus was under Herod's jurisdiction, he sent him to Herod, who was also in Jerusalem at that time. {8} When Herod saw Jesus, he was greatly pleased, because for a long time he had been wanting to see him. From what he had heard about him, he hoped to see him perform some miracle. {9} He plied him with many questions, but Jesus gave him no answer. {10} The chief priests and the teachers of the law were standing there, vehemently accusing him. {11} Then Herod and his soldiers ridiculed and mocked him. Dressing him in an elegant robe, they sent him back to Pilate. {12} That day Herod and Pilate became friends—before this they had been enemies. {13} Pilate called together the chief priests, the rulers and the people, {14} and said to them, "You brought me this man as one who was inciting the people to rebellion. I have examined him in your presence and have found no basis for your charges against him. {15} Neither has Herod, for he sent him back to us; as you can see, he has done nothing to deserve death. {16} Therefore, I will punish him and then release him." {17} {18} With one voice they cried out, "Away with this man! Release Barabbas to us!" {19} (Barabbas had been thrown into prison for an insurrection in the city, and for murder.) {20} Wanting to release Jesus, Pilate appealed to them again. {21} But they kept shouting, "Crucify him! Crucify him!" {22} For the third time he spoke to them: "Why? What crime has this man committed? I have found in him no grounds for the death penalty. Therefore I will have him punished and then release him." {23} But with loud shouts they insistently demanded that he be crucified, and their shouts prevailed. {24} So Pilate decided to grant their demand. {25} He released the man who had been thrown into prison for insurrection and murder, the one they asked for, and surrendered Jesus to their will.

JESUS' CRUCIFIXION, DEATH AND BURIAL

Luke 23:32-56

Two other men, both criminals, were also led out with him to be executed. {33} When they came to the place called the Skull, there they crucified him, along with the criminals—one on his right, the other on his left. {34} Jesus said, "Father, forgive them, for they do not know what they are doing." And they divided up his clothes by casting lots. {35} The people stood watching, and the rulers even sneered at him. They said, "He saved others; let him save himself if he is the Christ of God, the Chosen One." {36} The soldiers also came up and mocked him. They offered him wine vinegar {37} and said, "If you are the king of the Jews, save yourself." {38} There was a written notice above him, which read: THIS IS THE KING OF THE JEWS. {39} One of the criminals who hung there hurled insults at him: "Aren't you the Christ? Save yourself and us!" {40} But the other criminal rebuked him. "Don't you fear God," he said, "since you are under the same sentence? {41} We are punished justly, for we are getting what our deeds deserve. But this man has done nothing wrong." {42} Then he said, "Jesus, remember me when you come into your kingdom." {43} Jesus answered him, "I tell you the truth, today you will be with me in paradise." {44} It was now about the sixth hour, and darkness came over the whole land until the ninth hour, {45} for the sun stopped shining. And the curtain of the temple was torn in two. {46} Jesus called out with a loud voice, "Father, into your hands I commit my spirit." When he had said this, he breathed his last. {47} The centurion, seeing what had happened, praised God and said, "Surely this was a righteous man." {48} When all the people who had gathered to witness this sight saw what took place, they beat their breasts and went away. {49} But all those who knew him, including the women who had followed him from Galilee, stood at a distance, watching these things. {50} Now there was a man named Joseph, a member of the Council, a good and upright man, {51} who had not consented to their decision and action. He came from the Judean town of Arimathea and he was waiting for the kingdom of God. {52} Going to Pilate, he asked for Jesus' body. {53} Then he took it down, wrapped it in linen cloth and placed it in a tomb cut in the rock, one in which no one had yet been laid. {54} It was Preparation Day, and the Sabbath was about to begin. {55} The women who had come with Jesus from Galilee followed Joseph and saw the tomb and how his body was laid in it. {56} Then they went home and prepared spices and perfumes. But they rested on the Sabbath in obedience to the commandment.

JESUS' RESURRECTION; APPEARS TO HIS DISCIPLES; HIS ASCENSION

Luke 24:1-16

On the first day of the week, very early in the morning, the women took the spices they had prepared and went to the tomb. {2} They found the stone rolled away from the tomb, {3} but when they entered, they did not find the body of the Lord Jesus. {4} While they were wondering about this, suddenly two men in clothes that gleamed like lightning stood beside them. {5} In their fright the women bowed down with their faces to the ground, but the men said to them, "Why do you look for the living among the dead? {6} He is not here; he has risen! Remember how he told you, while he was still with you in Galilee: {7} 'The Son of Man must be delivered into the hands of sinful men, be crucified and on the third day be raised again.'" {8} Then they remembered his words. {9} When they came back from the tomb, they told all these things to the Eleven and to all the others. {10} It was Mary Magdalene, Joanna, Mary the mother of James, and the others with them who told this to the apostles. {11} But they did not believe the women, because their words seemed to them like nonsense. {12} Peter, however, got up and ran to the tomb. Bending over, he saw the strips of linen lying by themselves, and he went away, wondering to himself what had happened. {13} Now that same day two of them were going to a village called Emmaus, about seven miles from Jerusalem. {14} They were talking with each other about everything that had happened. {15} As they talked and discussed these things with each other, Jesus himself came up and walked along with them; {16} but they were kept from recognizing him.

Luke 24:30-32

When he was at the table with them, he took bread, gave thanks, broke it and began to give it to them. {31} Then their eyes were opened and they recognized him, and he disappeared from their sight. {32} They asked each other, "Were not our hearts burning within us while he talked with us on the road and opened the Scriptures to us?"

Luke 24:48-53

You are witnesses of these things. {49} I am going to send you what my Father has promised; but stay in the city until you have been clothed with power from on high." {50} When he had led them out to the vicinity of Bethany, he lifted up his hands and blessed them. {51} While he was blessing them, he left them and was taken up into heaven. {52} Then they worshiped him and returned to Jerusalem with great joy. {53} And they stayed continually at the temple, praising God.

PAUL CALLED TO PREACH TO JEWS AND GENTILES

Rom 1:1-20

Paul, a servant of Christ Jesus, called to be an apostle and set apart for the gospel of God– {2} the gospel he promised beforehand through his prophets in the Holy Scriptures {3} regarding his Son, who as to his human nature was a descendant of David, {4} and who through the Spirit of holiness was declared with power to be the Son of God by his resurrection from the dead: Jesus Christ our Lord. {5} Through him and for his name's sake, we received grace and apostleship to call people from among all the Gentiles to the obedience that comes from faith. {6} And you also are among those who are called to belong to Jesus Christ. {7} To all in Rome who are loved by God and called to be saints: Grace and peace to you from God our Father and from the Lord Jesus Christ. {8} First, I thank my God through Jesus Christ for all of you, because your faith is being reported all over the world. {9} God, whom I serve with my whole heart in preaching the gospel of his Son, is my witness how constantly I remember you {10} in my prayers at all times; and I pray that now at last by God's will the way may be opened for me to come to you. {11} I long to see you so that I may impart to you some spiritual gift to make you strong– {12} that is, that you and I may be mutually encouraged by each other's faith. {13} I do not want you to be unaware, brothers, that I planned many times to come to you (but have been prevented from doing so until now) in order that I might have a harvest among you, just as I have had among the other Gentiles. {14} I am obligated both to Greeks and non-Greeks, both to the wise and the foolish. {15} That is why I am so eager to preach the gospel also to you who are at Rome. {16} I am not ashamed of the gospel, because it is the power of God for the salvation of everyone who believes: first for the Jew, then for the Gentile. {17} For in the gospel a righteousness from God is revealed, a righteousness that is by faith from first to last, just as it is written: "The righteous will live by faith." {18} The wrath of God is being revealed from heaven against all the godlessness and wickedness of men who suppress the truth by their wickedness, {19} since what may be known about God is plain to them, because God has made it plain to them. {20} For since the creation of the world God's invisible qualities– his eternal power and divine nature–have been clearly seen, being understood from what has been made, so that men are without excuse.

ALL MEN HAVE A KNOWLEDGE OF GOD

Rom 1:21-2:8

For although they knew God, they neither glorified him as God nor gave thanks to him, but their thinking became futile and their foolish hearts were darkened. {22} Although they claimed to be wise, they became fools {23} and exchanged the glory of the immortal God for images made to look like mortal man and birds and animals and reptiles. {24} Therefore God gave them over in the sinful desires of their hearts to sexual impurity for the degrading of their bodies with one another. {25} They exchanged the truth of God for a lie, and worshiped and served created things rather than the Creator—who is forever praised. Amen. {26} Because of this, God gave them over to shameful lusts. Even their women exchanged natural relations for unnatural ones. {27} In the same way the men also abandoned natural relations with women and were inflamed with lust for one another. Men committed indecent acts with other men, and received in themselves the due penalty for their perversion. {28} Furthermore, since they did not think it worthwhile to retain the knowledge of God, he gave them over to a depraved mind, to do what ought not to be done. {29} They have become filled with every kind of wickedness, evil, greed and depravity. They are full of envy, murder, strife, deceit and malice. They are gossips, {30} slanderers, God-haters, insolent, arrogant and boastful; they invent ways of doing evil; they disobey their parents; {31} they are senseless, faithless, heartless, ruthless. {32} Although they know God's righteous decree that those who do such things deserve death, they not only continue to do these very things but also approve of those who practice them. {2:1} You, therefore, have no excuse, you who pass judgment on someone else, for at whatever point you judge the other, you are condemning yourself, because you who pass judgment do the same things. {2} Now we know that God's judgment against those who do such things is based on truth. {3} So when you, a mere man, pass judgment on them and yet do the same things, do you think you will escape God's judgment? {4} Or do you show contempt for the riches of his kindness, tolerance and patience, not realizing that God's kindness leads you toward repentance? {5} But because of your stubbornness and your unrepentant heart, you are storing up wrath against yourself for the day of God's wrath, when his righteous judgment will be revealed. {6} God "will give to each person according to what he has done." {7} To those who by persistence in doing good seek glory, honor and immortality, he will give eternal life. {8} But for those who are self-seeking and who reject the truth and follow evil, there will be wrath and anger.

BELIEVERS ARE JUSTIFIED BY FAITH

Rom 3:9-31

What shall we conclude then? Are we any better ? Not at all! We have already made the charge that Jews and Gentiles alike are all under sin. {10} As it is written: "There is no one righteous, not even one; {11} there is no one who understands, no one who seeks God. {12} All have turned away, they have together become worthless; there is no one who does good, not even one." {13} "Their throats are open graves; their tongues practice deceit." "The poison of vipers is on their lips." {14} "Their mouths are full of cursing and bitterness." {15} "Their feet are swift to shed blood; {16} ruin and misery mark their ways, {17} and the way of peace they do not know." {18} "There is no fear of God before their eyes." {19} Now we know that whatever the law says, it says to those who are under the law, so that every mouth may be silenced and the whole world held accountable to God. {20} Therefore no one will be declared righteous in his sight by observing the law; rather, through the law we become conscious of sin. {21} But now a righteousness from God, apart from law, has been made known, to which the Law and the Prophets testify. {22} This righteousness from God comes through faith in Jesus Christ to all who believe. There is no difference, {23} for all have sinned and fall short of the glory of God, {24} and are justified freely by his grace through the redemption that came by Christ Jesus. {25} God presented him as a sacrifice of atonement, through faith in his blood. He did this to demonstrate his justice, because in his forbearance he had left the sins committed beforehand unpunished– {26} he did it to demonstrate his justice at the present time, so as to be just and the one who justifies those who have faith in Jesus. {27} Where, then, is boasting? It is excluded. On what principle? On that of observing the law? No, but on that of faith. {28} For we maintain that a man is justified by faith apart from observing the law. {29} Is God the God of Jews only? Is he not the God of Gentiles too? Yes, of Gentiles too, {30} since there is only one God, who will justify the circumcised by faith and the uncircumcised through that same faith. {31} Do we, then, nullify the law by this faith? Not at all! Rather, we uphold the law.

ABRAHAM WAS JUSTIFIED BY FAITH

Rom 4:3-22

What does the Scripture say? "Abraham believed God, and it was credited to him as righteousness." {4} Now when a man works, his wages are not credited to him as a gift, but as an obligation. {5} However, to the man who does not work but trusts God who justifies the wicked, his faith is credited as righteousness. {6} David says the same thing when he speaks of the blessedness of the man to whom God credits righteousness apart from works: {7} "Blessed are they whose transgressions are forgiven, whose sins are covered. {8} Blessed is the man whose sin the Lord will never count against him." {9} Is this blessedness only for the circumcised, or also for the uncircumcised? We have been saying that Abraham's faith was credited to him as righteousness. {10} Under what circumstances was it credited? Was it after he was circumcised, or before? It was not after, but before! {11} And he received the sign of circumcision, a seal of the righteousness that he had by faith while he was still uncircumcised. So then, he is the father of all who believe but have not been circumcised, in order that righteousness might be credited to them. {12} And he is also the father of the circumcised who not only are circumcised but who also walk in the footsteps of the faith that our father Abraham had before he was circumcised. {13} It was not through law that Abraham and his offspring received the promise that he would be heir of the world, but through the righteousness that comes by faith. {14} For if those who live by law are heirs, faith has no value and the promise is worthless, {15} because law brings wrath. And where there is no law there is no transgression. {16} Therefore, the promise comes by faith, so that it may be by grace and may be guaranteed to all Abraham's offspring—not only to those who are of the law but also to those who are of the faith of Abraham. He is the father of us all. {17} As it is written: "I have made you a father of many nations." He is our father in the sight of God, in whom he believed—the God who gives life to the dead and calls things that are not as though they were. {18} Against all hope, Abraham in hope believed and so became the father of many nations, just as it had been said to him, "So shall your offspring be." {19} Without weakening in his faith, he faced the fact that his body was as good as dead—since he was about a hundred years old—and that Sarah's womb was also dead. {20} Yet he did not waver through unbelief regarding the promise of God, but was strengthened in his faith and gave glory to God, {21} being fully persuaded that God had power to do what he had promised. {22} This is why "it was credited to him as righteousness."

AS BY ONE MAN CAME DEATH, SO BY CHRIST CAME LIFE

Rom 5:1-19

Therefore, since we have been justified through faith, we have peace with God through our Lord Jesus Christ, {2} through whom we have gained access by faith into this grace in which we now stand. And we rejoice in the hope of the glory of God. {3} Not only so, but we also rejoice in our sufferings, because we know that suffering produces perseverance; {4} perseverance, character; and character, hope. {5} And hope does not disappoint us, because God has poured out his love into our hearts by the Holy Spirit, whom he has given us. {6} You see, at just the right time, when we were still powerless, Christ died for the ungodly. {7} Very rarely will anyone die for a righteous man, though for a good man someone might possibly dare to die. {8} But God demonstrates his own love for us in this: While we were still sinners, Christ died for us. {9} Since we have now been justified by his blood, how much more shall we be saved from God's wrath through him! {10} For if, when we were God's enemies, we were reconciled to him through the death of his Son, how much more, having been reconciled, shall we be saved through his life! {11} Not only is this so, but we also rejoice in God through our Lord Jesus Christ, through whom we have now received reconciliation. {12} Therefore, just as sin entered the world through one man, and death through sin, and in this way death came to all men, because all sinned– {13} for before the law was given, sin was in the world. But sin is not taken into account when there is no law. {14} Nevertheless, death reigned from the time of Adam to the time of Moses, even over those who did not sin by breaking a command, as did Adam, who was a pattern of the one to come. {15} But the gift is not like the trespass. For if the many died by the trespass of the one man, how much more did God's grace and the gift that came by the grace of the one man, Jesus Christ, overflow to the many! {16} Again, the gift of God is not like the result of the one man's sin: The judgment followed one sin and brought condemnation, but the gift followed many trespasses and brought justification. {17} For if, by the trespass of the one man, death reigned through that one man, how much more will those who receive God's abundant provision of grace and of the gift of righteousness reign in life through the one man, Jesus Christ. {18} Consequently, just as the result of one trespass was condemnation for all men, so also the result of one act of righteousness was justification that brings life for all men. {19} For just as through the disobedience of the one man the many were made sinners, so also through the obedience of the one man the many will be made righteous.

THE CHRISTIAN'S STRUGGLE WITH SIN

Rom 7:7b-8:3a

For I would not have known what coveting really was if the law had not said, "Do not covet." {8} But sin, seizing the opportunity afforded by the commandment, produced in me every kind of covetous desire. For apart from law, sin is dead. {9} Once I was alive apart from law; but when the commandment came, sin sprang to life and I died. {10} I found that the very commandment that was intended to bring life actually brought death. {11} For sin, seizing the opportunity afforded by the commandment, deceived me, and through the commandment put me to death. {12} So then, the law is holy, and the commandment is holy, righteous and good. {13} Did that which is good, then, become death to me? By no means! But in order that sin might be recognized as sin, it produced death in me through what was good, so that through the commandment sin might become utterly sinful. {14} We know that the law is spiritual; but I am unspiritual, sold as a slave to sin. {15} I do not understand what I do. For what I want to do I do not do, but what I hate I do. {16} And if I do what I do not want to do, I agree that the law is good. {17} As it is, it is no longer I myself who do it, but it is sin living in me. {18} I know that nothing good lives in me, that is, in my sinful nature. For I have the desire to do what is good, but I cannot carry it out. {19} For what I do is not the good I want to do; no, the evil I do not want to do—this I keep on doing. {20} Now if I do what I do not want to do, it is no longer I who do it, but it is sin living in me that does it. {21} So I find this law at work: When I want to do good, evil is right there with me. {22} For in my inner being I delight in God's law; {23} but I see another law at work in the members of my body, waging war against the law of my mind and making me a prisoner of the law of sin at work within my members. {24} What a wretched man I am! Who will rescue me from this body of death? {25} Thanks be to God—through Jesus Christ our Lord! So then, I myself in my mind am a slave to God's law, but in the sinful nature a slave to the law of sin. {8:1} Therefore, there is now no condemnation for those who are in Christ Jesus, {2} because through Christ Jesus the law of the Spirit of life set me free from the law of sin and death. {3} For what the law was powerless to do in that it was weakened by the sinful nature, God did by sending his own Son in the likeness of sinful man to be a sin offering.

CHRISTIANS WILL OVERCOME

Rom 8:18,22-39

I consider that our present sufferings are not worth comparing with the glory that will be revealed in us.

{22} We know that the whole creation has been groaning as in the pains of childbirth right up to the present time. {23} Not only so, but we ourselves, who have the firstfruits of the Spirit, groan inwardly as we wait eagerly for our adoption as sons, the redemption of our bodies. {24} For in this hope we were saved. But hope that is seen is no hope at all. Who hopes for what he already has? {25} But if we hope for what we do not yet have, we wait for it patiently. {26} In the same way, the Spirit helps us in our weakness. We do not know what we ought to pray for, but the Spirit himself intercedes for us with groans that words cannot express. {27} And he who searches our hearts knows the mind of the Spirit, because the Spirit intercedes for the saints in accordance with God's will. {28} And we know that in all things God works for the good of those who love him, who have been called according to his purpose. {29} For those God foreknew he also predestined to be conformed to the likeness of his Son, that he might be the firstborn among many brothers. {30} And those he predestined, he also called; those he called, he also justified; those he justified, he also glorified. {31} What, then, shall we say in response to this? If God is for us, who can be against us? {32} He who did not spare his own Son, but gave him up for us all–how will he not also, along with him, graciously give us all things? {33} Who will bring any charge against those whom God has chosen? It is God who justifies. {34} Who is he that condemns? Christ Jesus, who died–more than that, who was raised to life–is at the right hand of God and is also interceding for us. {35} Who shall separate us from the love of Christ? Shall trouble or hardship or persecution or famine or nakedness or danger or sword? {36} As it is written: "For your sake we face death all day long; we are considered as sheep to be slaughtered." {37} No, in all these things we are more than conquerors through him who loved us. {38} For I am convinced that neither death nor life, neither angels nor demons, neither the present nor the future, nor any powers, {39} neither height nor depth, nor anything else in all creation, will be able to separate us from the love of God that is in Christ Jesus our Lord.

GOD HAS MERCY ON HIS CHOSEN PEOPLE

Rom 9:1-21

I speak the truth in Christ–I am not lying, my conscience confirms it in the Holy Spirit– {2} I have great sorrow and unceasing anguish in my heart. {3} For I could wish that I myself were cursed and cut off from Christ for the sake of my brothers, those of my own race, {4} the people of Israel. Theirs is the adoption as sons; theirs the divine glory, the covenants, the receiving of the law, the temple worship and the promises. {5} Theirs are the patriarchs, and from them is traced the human ancestry of Christ, who is God over all, forever praised! Amen. {6} It is not as though God's word had failed. For not all who are descended from Israel are Israel. {7} Nor because they are his descendants are they all Abraham's children. On the contrary, "It is through Isaac that your offspring will be reckoned." {8} In other words, it is not the natural children who are God's children, but it is the children of the promise who are regarded as Abraham's offspring. {9} For this was how the promise was stated: "At the appointed time I will return, and Sarah will have a son." {10} Not only that, but Rebekah's children had one and the same father, our father Isaac. {11} Yet, before the twins were born or had done anything good or bad–in order that God's purpose in election might stand: {12} not by works but by him who calls–she was told, "The older will serve the younger." {13} Just as it is written: "Jacob I loved, but Esau I hated." {14} What then shall we say? Is God unjust? Not at all! {15} For he says to Moses, "I will have mercy on whom I have mercy, and I will have compassion on whom I have compassion." {16} It does not, therefore, depend on man's desire or effort, but on God's mercy. {17} For the Scripture says to Pharaoh: "I raised you up for this very purpose, that I might display my power in you and that my name might be proclaimed in all the earth." {18} Therefore God has mercy on whom he wants to have mercy, and he hardens whom he wants to harden. {19} One of you will say to me: "Then why does God still blame us? For who resists his will?" {20} But who are you, O man, to talk back to God? "Shall what is formed say to him who formed it, 'Why did you make me like this?'" {21} Does not the potter have the right to make out of the same lump of clay some pottery for noble purposes and some for common use?

GENTILE BELIEVERS ARE ALSO HEIRS OF GOD'S PROMISE

Rom 9:22-33

What if God, choosing to show his wrath and make his power known, bore with great patience the objects of his wrath–prepared for destruction? {23} What if he did this to make the riches of his glory known to the objects of his mercy, whom he prepared in advance for glory– {24} even us, whom he also called, not only from the Jews but also from the Gentiles? {25} As he says in Hosea: "I will call them 'my people' who are not my people; and I will call her 'my loved one' who is not my loved one," {26} and, "It will happen that in the very place where it was said to them, 'You are not my people,' they will be called 'sons of the living God.'" {27} Isaiah cries out concerning Israel: "Though the number of the Israelites be like the sand by the sea, only the remnant will be saved. {28} For the Lord will carry out his sentence on earth with speed and finality." {29} It is just as Isaiah said previously: "Unless the Lord Almighty had left us descendants, we would have become like Sodom, we would have been like Gomorrah." {30} What then shall we say? That the Gentiles, who did not pursue righteousness, have obtained it, a righteousness that is by faith; {31} but Israel, who pursued a law of righteousness, has not attained it. {32} Why not? Because they pursued it not by faith but as if it were by works. They stumbled over the "stumbling stone." {33} As it is written: "See, I lay in Zion a stone that causes men to stumble and a rock that makes them fall, and the one who trusts in him will never be put to shame."

CHRIST IS THE END OF THE LAW

Rom 10:1-21

Brothers, my heart's desire and prayer to God for the Israelites is that they may be saved. {2} For I can testify about them that they are zealous for God, but their zeal is not based on knowledge. {3} Since they did not know the righteousness that comes from God and sought to establish their own, they did not submit to God's righteousness. {4} Christ is the end of the law so that there may be righteousness for everyone who believes. {5} Moses describes in this way the righteousness that is by the law: "The man who does these things will live by them." {6} But the righteousness that is by faith says: "Do not say in your heart, 'Who will ascend into heaven?' " (that is, to bring Christ down) {7} "or 'Who will descend into the deep?' " (that is, to bring Christ up from the dead). {8} But what does it say? "The word is near you; it is in your mouth and in your heart," that is, the word of faith we are proclaiming: {9} That if you confess with your mouth, "Jesus is Lord," and believe in your heart that God raised him from the dead, you will be saved. {10} For it is with your heart that you believe and are justified, and it is with your mouth that you confess and are saved. {11} As the Scripture says, "Anyone who trusts in him will never be put to shame." {12} For there is no difference between Jew and Gentile–the same Lord is Lord of all and richly blesses all who call on him, {13} for, "Everyone who calls on the name of the Lord will be saved." {14} How, then, can they call on the one they have not believed in? And how can they believe in the one of whom they have not heard? And how can they hear without someone preaching to them? {15} And how can they preach unless they are sent? As it is written, "How beautiful are the feet of those who bring good news!" {16} But not all the Israelites accepted the good news. For Isaiah says, "Lord, who has believed our message?" {17} Consequently, faith comes from hearing the message, and the message is heard through the word of Christ. {18} But I ask: Did they not hear? Of course they did: "Their voice has gone out into all the earth, their words to the ends of the world." {19} Again I ask: Did Israel not understand? First, Moses says, "I will make you envious by those who are not a nation; I will make you angry by a nation that has no understanding." {20} And Isaiah boldly says, "I was found by those who did not seek me; I revealed myself to those who did not ask for me." {21} But concerning Israel he says, "All day long I have held out my hands to a disobedient and obstinate people."

GENTILES ARE BLESSED THROUGH ISRAEL

Rom 11:1-21

I ask then: Did God reject his people? By no means! I am an Israelite myself, a descendant of Abraham, from the tribe of Benjamin. {2} God did not reject his people, whom he foreknew. Don't you know what the Scripture says in the passage about Elijah–how he appealed to God against Israel: {3} "Lord, they have killed your prophets and torn down your altars; I am the only one left, and they are trying to kill me"? {4} And what was God's answer to him? "I have reserved for myself seven thousand who have not bowed the knee to Baal." {5} So too, at the present time there is a remnant chosen by grace. {6} And if by grace, then it is no longer by works; if it were, grace would no longer be grace. {7} What then? What Israel sought so earnestly it did not obtain, but the elect did. The others were hardened, {8} as it is written: "God gave them a spirit of stupor, eyes so that they could not see and ears so that they could not hear, to this very day." {9} And David says: "May their table become a snare and a trap, a stumbling block and a retribution for them. {10} May their eyes be darkened so they cannot see, and their backs be bent forever." {11} Again I ask: Did they stumble so as to fall beyond recovery? Not at all! Rather, because of their transgression, salvation has come to the Gentiles to make Israel envious. {12} But if their transgression means riches for the world, and their loss means riches for the Gentiles, how much greater riches will their fullness bring! {13} I am talking to you Gentiles. Inasmuch as I am the apostle to the Gentiles, I make much of my ministry {14} in the hope that I may somehow arouse my own people to envy and save some of them. {15} For if their rejection is the reconciliation of the world, what will their acceptance be but life from the dead? {16} If the part of the dough offered as firstfruits is holy, then the whole batch is holy; if the root is holy, so are the branches. {17} If some of the branches have been broken off, and you, though a wild olive shoot, have been grafted in among the others and now share in the nourishing sap from the olive root, {18} do not boast over those branches. If you do, consider this: You do not support the root, but the root supports you. {19} You will say then, "Branches were broken off so that I could be grafted in." {20} Granted. But they were broken off because of unbelief, and you stand by faith. Do not be arrogant, but be afraid. {21} For if God did not spare the natural branches, he will not spare you either.

BOTH GENTILES AND ISRAEL ARE BLESSED
BY A SOVEREIGN GOD

Rom 11:22-36

Consider therefore the kindness and sternness of God: sternness to those who fell, but kindness to you, provided that you continue in his kindness. Otherwise, you also will be cut off. {23} And if they do not persist in unbelief, they will be grafted in, for God is able to graft them in again. {24} After all, if you were cut out of an olive tree that is wild by nature, and contrary to nature were grafted into a cultivated olive tree, how much more readily will these, the natural branches, be grafted into their own olive tree! {25} I do not want you to be ignorant of this mystery, brothers, so that you may not be conceited: Israel has experienced a hardening in part until the full number of the Gentiles has come in. {26} And so all Israel will be saved, as it is written: "The deliverer will come from Zion; he will turn godlessness away from Jacob. {27} And this is my covenant with them when I take away their sins." {28} As far as the gospel is concerned, they are enemies on your account; but as far as election is concerned, they are loved on account of the patriarchs, {29} for God's gifts and his call are irrevocable. {30} Just as you who were at one time disobedient to God have now received mercy as a result of their disobedience, {31} so they too have now become disobedient in order that they too may now receive mercy as a result of God's mercy to you. {32} For God has bound all men over to disobedience so that he may have mercy on them all. {33} Oh, the depth of the riches of the wisdom and knowledge of God! How unsearchable his judgments, and his paths beyond tracing out! {34} "Who has known the mind of the Lord? Or who has been his counselor?" {35} "Who has ever given to God, that God should repay him?" {36} For from him and through him and to him are all things. To him be the glory forever! Amen.

PAUL CALLS FOR LIVING SACRIFICES

Rom 12:1-21

Therefore, I urge you, brothers, in view of God's mercy, to offer your bodies as living sacrifices, holy and pleasing to God–this is your spiritual act of worship. {2} Do not conform any longer to the pattern of this world, but be transformed by the renewing of your mind. Then you will be able to test and approve what God's will is–his good, pleasing and perfect will. {3} For by the grace given me I say to every one of you: Do not think of yourself more highly than you ought, but rather think of yourself with sober judgment, in accordance with the measure of faith God has given you. {4} Just as each of us has one body with many members, and these members do not all have the same function, {5} so in Christ we who are many form one body, and each member belongs to all the others. {6} We have different gifts, according to the grace given us. If a man's gift is prophesying, let him use it in proportion to his faith. {7} If it is serving, let him serve; if it is teaching, let him teach; {8} if it is encouraging, let him encourage; if it is contributing to the needs of others, let him give generously; if it is leadership, let him govern diligently; if it is showing mercy, let him do it cheerfully. {9} Love must be sincere. Hate what is evil; cling to what is good. {10} Be devoted to one another in brotherly love. Honor one another above yourselves. {11} Never be lacking in zeal, but keep your spiritual fervor, serving the Lord. {12} Be joyful in hope, patient in affliction, faithful in prayer. {13} Share with God's people who are in need. Practice hospitality. {14} Bless those who persecute you; bless and do not curse. {15} Rejoice with those who rejoice; mourn with those who mourn. {16} Live in harmony with one another. Do not be proud, but be willing to associate with people of low position. Do not be conceited. {17} Do not repay anyone evil for evil. Be careful to do what is right in the eyes of everybody. {18} If it is possible, as far as it depends on you, live at peace with everyone. {19} Do not take revenge, my friends, but leave room for God's wrath, for it is written: "It is mine to avenge; I will repay," says the Lord. {20} On the contrary: "If your enemy is hungry, feed him; if he is thirsty, give him something to drink. In doing this, you will heap burning coals on his head." {21} Do not be overcome by evil, but overcome evil with good.

SUBMIT TO AUTHORITIES; DO NOT JUDGE

Rom 13:1-14:1

Everyone must submit himself to the governing authorities, for there is no authority except that which God has established. The authorities that exist have been established by God. {2} Consequently, he who rebels against the authority is rebelling against what God has instituted, and those who do so will bring judgment on themselves. {3} For rulers hold no terror for those who do right, but for those who do wrong. Do you want to be free from fear of the one in authority? Then do what is right and he will commend you. {4} For he is God's servant to do you good. But if you do wrong, be afraid, for he does not bear the sword for nothing. He is God's servant, an agent of wrath to bring punishment on the wrongdoer. {5} Therefore, it is necessary to submit to the authorities, not only because of possible punishment but also because of conscience. {6} This is also why you pay taxes, for the authorities are God's servants, who give their full time to governing. {7} Give everyone what you owe him: If you owe taxes, pay taxes; if revenue, then revenue; if respect, then respect; if honor, then honor. {8} Let no debt remain outstanding, except the continuing debt to love one another, for he who loves his fellowman has fulfilled the law. {9} The commandments, "Do not commit adultery," "Do not murder," "Do not steal," "Do not covet," and whatever other commandment there may be, are summed up in this one rule: "Love your neighbor as yourself." {10} Love does no harm to its neighbor. Therefore love is the fulfillment of the law. {11} And do this, understanding the present time. The hour has come for you to wake up from your slumber, because our salvation is nearer now than when we first believed. {12} The night is nearly over; the day is almost here. So let us put aside the deeds of darkness and put on the armor of light. {13} Let us behave decently, as in the daytime, not in orgies and drunkenness, not in sexual immorality and debauchery, not in dissension and jealousy. {14} Rather, clothe yourselves with the Lord Jesus Christ, and do not think about how to gratify the desires of the sinful nature. {14:1} Accept him whose faith is weak, without passing judgment on disputable matters.

Rom 14:13

Therefore let us stop passing judgment on one another. Instead, make up your mind not to put any stumbling block or obstacle in your brother's way.

LET THERE BE NO DIVISIONS AMONG CHRISTIANS

1 Cor 1:10-31

I appeal to you, brothers, in the name of our Lord Jesus Christ, that all of you agree with one another so that there may be no divisions among you and that you may be perfectly united in mind and thought. {11} My brothers, some from Chloe's household have informed me that there are quarrels among you. {12} What I mean is this: One of you says, "I follow Paul"; another, "I follow Apollos"; another, "I follow Cephas"; still another, "I follow Christ." {13} Is Christ divided? Was Paul crucified for you? Were you baptized into the name of Paul? {14} I am thankful that I did not baptize any of you except Crispus and Gaius, {15} so no one can say that you were baptized into my name. {16} (Yes, I also baptized the household of Stephanas; beyond that, I don't remember if I baptized anyone else.) {17} For Christ did not send me to baptize, but to preach the gospel–not with words of human wisdom, lest the cross of Christ be emptied of its power. {18} For the message of the cross is foolishness to those who are perishing, but to us who are being saved it is the power of God. {19} For it is written: "I will destroy the wisdom of the wise; the intelligence of the intelligent I will frustrate." {20} Where is the wise man? Where is the scholar? Where is the philosopher of this age? Has not God made foolish the wisdom of the world? {21} For since in the wisdom of God the world through its wisdom did not know him, God was pleased through the foolishness of what was preached to save those who believe. {22} Jews demand miraculous signs and Greeks look for wisdom, {23} but we preach Christ crucified: a stumbling block to Jews and foolishness to Gentiles, {24} but to those whom God has called, both Jews and Greeks, Christ the power of God and the wisdom of God. {25} For the foolishness of God is wiser than man's wisdom, and the weakness of God is stronger than man's strength. {26} Brothers, think of what you were when you were called. Not many of you were wise by human standards; not many were influential; not many were of noble birth. {27} But God chose the foolish things of the world to shame the wise; God chose the weak things of the world to shame the strong. {28} He chose the lowly things of this world and the despised things–and the things that are not– to nullify the things that are, {29} so that no one may boast before him. {30} It is because of him that you are in Christ Jesus, who has become for us wisdom from God–that is, our righteousness, holiness and redemption. {31} Therefore, as it is written: "Let him who boasts boast in the Lord."

CHRISTIANS ARE TEMPLES OF GOD'S SPIRIT

1 Cor 3:16-23

Don't you know that you yourselves are God's temple and that God's Spirit lives in you? {17} If anyone destroys God's temple, God will destroy him; for God's temple is sacred, and you are that temple. {18} Do not deceive yourselves. If any one of you thinks he is wise by the standards of this age, he should become a "fool" so that he may become wise. {19} For the wisdom of this world is foolishness in God's sight. As it is written: "He catches the wise in their craftiness"; {20} and again, "The Lord knows that the thoughts of the wise are futile." {21} So then, no more boasting about men! All things are yours, {22} whether Paul or Apollos or Cephas or the world or life or death or the present or the future—all are yours, {23} and you are of Christ, and Christ is of God.

DO NOT TAKE A BROTHER TO COURT

1 Cor 5:9-6:9a

I have written you in my letter not to associate with sexually immoral people— {10} not at all meaning the people of this world who are immoral, or the greedy and swindlers, or idolaters. In that case you would have to leave this world. {11} But now I am writing you that you must not associate with anyone who calls himself a brother but is sexually immoral or greedy, an idolater or a slanderer, a drunkard or a swindler. With such a man do not even eat. {12} What business is it of mine to judge those outside the church? Are you not to judge those inside? {13} God will judge those outside. "Expel the wicked man from among you." {6:1} If any of you has a dispute with another, dare he take it before the ungodly for judgment instead of before the saints? {2} Do you not know that the saints will judge the world? And if you are to judge the world, are you not competent to judge trivial cases? {3} Do you not know that we will judge angels? How much more the things of this life! {4} Therefore, if you have disputes about such matters, appoint as judges even men of little account in the church! {5} I say this to shame you. Is it possible that there is nobody among you wise enough to judge a dispute between believers? {6} But instead, one brother goes to law against another—and this in front of unbelievers! {7} The very fact that you have lawsuits among you means you have been completely defeated already. Why not rather be wronged? Why not rather be cheated? {8} Instead, you yourselves cheat and do wrong, and you do this to your brothers. {9} Do you not know that the wicked will not inherit the kingdom of God?

ON SEX AND MARRIAGE

1 Cor 6:12-7:13

"Everything is permissible for me"–but not everything is beneficial. "Everything is permissible for me"–but I will not be mastered by anything. {13} "Food for the stomach and the stomach for food"–but God will destroy them both. The body is not meant for sexual immorality, but for the Lord, and the Lord for the body. {14} By his power God raised the Lord from the dead, and he will raise us also. {15} Do you not know that your bodies are members of Christ himself? Shall I then take the members of Christ and unite them with a prostitute? Never! {16} Do you not know that he who unites himself with a prostitute is one with her in body? For it is said, "The two will become one flesh." {17} But he who unites himself with the Lord is one with him in spirit. {18} Flee from sexual immorality. All other sins a man commits are outside his body, but he who sins sexually sins against his own body. {19} Do you not know that your body is a temple of the Holy Spirit, who is in you, whom you have received from God? You are not your own; {20} you were bought at a price. Therefore honor God with your body. {7:1} Now for the matters you wrote about: It is good for a man not to marry. {2} But since there is so much immorality, each man should have his own wife, and each woman her own husband. {3} The husband should fulfill his marital duty to his wife, and likewise the wife to her husband. {4} The wife's body does not belong to her alone but also to her husband. In the same way, the husband's body does not belong to him alone but also to his wife. {5} Do not deprive each other except by mutual consent and for a time, so that you may devote yourselves to prayer. Then come together again so that Satan will not tempt you because of your lack of self-control. {6} I say this as a concession, not as a command. {7} I wish that all men were as I am. But each man has his own gift from God; one has this gift, another has that. {8} Now to the unmarried and the widows I say: It is good for them to stay unmarried, as I am. {9} But if they cannot control themselves, they should marry, for it is better to marry than to burn with passion. {10} To the married I give this command (not I, but the Lord): A wife must not separate from her husband. {11} But if she does, she must remain unmarried or else be reconciled to her husband. And a husband must not divorce his wife. {12} To the rest I say this (I, not the Lord): If any brother has a wife who is not a believer and she is willing to live with him, he must not divorce her. {13} And if a woman has a husband who is not a believer and he is willing to live with her, she must not divorce him.

ON MARRIAGE

1 Cor 7:15-35

But if the unbeliever leaves, let him do so. A believing man or woman is not bound in such circumstances; God has called us to live in peace. {16} How do you know, wife, whether you will save your husband? Or, how do you know, husband, whether you will save your wife? {17} Nevertheless, each one should retain the place in life that the Lord assigned to him and to which God has called him. This is the rule I lay down in all the churches. {18} Was a man already circumcised when he was called? He should not become uncircumcised. Was a man uncircumcised when he was called? He should not be circumcised. {19} Circumcision is nothing and uncircumcision is nothing. Keeping God's commands is what counts. {20} Each one should remain in the situation which he was in when God called him. {21} Were you a slave when you were called? Don't let it trouble you–although if you can gain your freedom, do so. {22} For he who was a slave when he was called by the Lord is the Lord's freedman; similarly, he who was a free man when he was called is Christ's slave. {23} You were bought at a price; do not become slaves of men. {24} Brothers, each man, as responsible to God, should remain in the situation God called him to. {25} Now about virgins: I have no command from the Lord, but I give a judgment as one who by the Lord's mercy is trustworthy. {26} Because of the present crisis, I think that it is good for you to remain as you are. {27} Are you married? Do not seek a divorce. Are you unmarried? Do not look for a wife. {28} But if you do marry, you have not sinned; and if a virgin marries, she has not sinned. But those who marry will face many troubles in this life, and I want to spare you this. {29} What I mean, brothers, is that the time is short. From now on those who have wives should live as if they had none; {30} those who mourn, as if they did not; those who are happy, as if they were not; those who buy something, as if it were not theirs to keep; {31} those who use the things of the world, as if not engrossed in them. For this world in its present form is passing away. {32} I would like you to be free from concern. An unmarried man is concerned about the Lord's affairs– how he can please the Lord. {33} But a married man is concerned about the affairs of this world–how he can please his wife– {34} and his interests are divided. An unmarried woman or virgin is concerned about the Lord's affairs: Her aim is to be devoted to the Lord in both body and spirit. But a married woman is concerned about the affairs of this world– how she can please her husband. {35} I am saying this for your own good, not to restrict you, but that you may live in a right way in undivided devotion to the Lord.

LESSONS FROM ISRAEL; THE EARTH IS THE LORD'S

1 Cor 10:9-33a

We should not test the Lord, as some of them did—and were killed by snakes. {10} And do not grumble, as some of them did—and were killed by the destroying angel. {11} These things happened to them as examples and were written down as warnings for us, on whom the fulfillment of the ages has come. {12} So, if you think you are standing firm, be careful that you don't fall! {13} No temptation has seized you except what is common to man. And God is faithful; he will not let you be tempted beyond what you can bear. But when you are tempted, he will also provide a way out so that you can stand up under it. {14} Therefore, my dear friends, flee from idolatry. {15} I speak to sensible people; judge for yourselves what I say. {16} Is not the cup of thanksgiving for which we give thanks a participation in the blood of Christ? And is not the bread that we break a participation in the body of Christ? {17} Because there is one loaf, we, who are many, are one body, for we all partake of the one loaf. {18} Consider the people of Israel: Do not those who eat the sacrifices participate in the altar? {19} Do I mean then that a sacrifice offered to an idol is anything, or that an idol is anything? {20} No, but the sacrifices of pagans are offered to demons, not to God, and I do not want you to be participants with demons. {21} You cannot drink the cup of the Lord and the cup of demons too; you cannot have a part in both the Lord's table and the table of demons. {22} Are we trying to arouse the Lord's jealousy? Are we stronger than he?

{23} "Everything is permissible"—but not everything is beneficial. "Everything is permissible"—but not everything is constructive. {24} Nobody should seek his own good, but the good of others. {25} Eat anything sold in the meat market without raising questions of conscience, {26} for, "The earth is the Lord's, and everything in it." {27} If some unbeliever invites you to a meal and you want to go, eat whatever is put before you without raising questions of conscience. {28} But if anyone says to you, "This has been offered in sacrifice," then do not eat it, both for the sake of the man who told you and for conscience' sake – {29} the other man's conscience, I mean, not yours. For why should my freedom be judged by another's conscience? {30} If I take part in the meal with thankfulness, why am I denounced because of something I thank God for? {31} So whether you eat or drink or whatever you do, do it all for the glory of God. {32} Do not cause anyone to stumble, whether Jews, Greeks or the church of God– {33} even as I try to please everybody in every way.

ON THE LORD'S SUPPER

1 Cor 11:17-34

In the following directives I have no praise for you, for your meetings do more harm than good. {18} In the first place, I hear that when you come together as a church, there are divisions among you, and to some extent I believe it. {19} No doubt there have to be differences among you to show which of you have God's approval. {20} When you come together, it is not the Lord's Supper you eat, {21} for as you eat, each of you goes ahead without waiting for anybody else. One remains hungry, another gets drunk. {22} Don't you have homes to eat and drink in? Or do you despise the church of God and humiliate those who have nothing? What shall I say to you? Shall I praise you for this? Certainly not! {23} For I received from the Lord what I also passed on to you: The Lord Jesus, on the night he was betrayed, took bread, {24} and when he had given thanks, he broke it and said, "This is my body, which is for you; do this in remembrance of me." {25} In the same way, after supper he took the cup, saying, "This cup is the new covenant in my blood; do this, whenever you drink it, in remembrance of me." {26} For whenever you eat this bread and drink this cup, you proclaim the Lord's death until he comes. {27} Therefore, whoever eats the bread or drinks the cup of the Lord in an unworthy manner will be guilty of sinning against the body and blood of the Lord. {28} A man ought to examine himself before he eats of the bread and drinks of the cup. {29} For anyone who eats and drinks without recognizing the body of the Lord eats and drinks judgment on himself. {30} That is why many among you are weak and sick, and a number of you have fallen asleep. {31} But if we judged ourselves, we would not come under judgment. {32} When we are judged by the Lord, we are being disciplined so that we will not be condemned with the world. {33} So then, my brothers, when you come together to eat, wait for each other. {34} If anyone is hungry, he should eat at home, so that when you meet together it may not result in judgment. And when I come I will give further directions.

DIFFERENT GIFTS

1 Cor 12:1-24

Now about spiritual gifts, brothers, I do not want you to be ignorant. {2} You know that when you were pagans, somehow or other you were influenced and led astray to mute idols. {3} Therefore I tell you that no one who is speaking by the Spirit of God says, "Jesus be cursed," and no one can say, "Jesus is Lord," except by the Holy Spirit. {4} There are different kinds of gifts, but the same Spirit. {5} There are different kinds of service, but the same Lord. {6} There are different kinds of working, but the same God works all of them in all men. {7} Now to each one the manifestation of the Spirit is given for the common good. {8} To one there is given through the Spirit the message of wisdom, to another the message of knowledge by means of the same Spirit, {9} to another faith by the same Spirit, to another gifts of healing by that one Spirit, {10} to another miraculous powers, to another prophecy, to another distinguishing between spirits, to another speaking in different kinds of tongues, and to still another the interpretation of tongues. {11} All these are the work of one and the same Spirit, and he gives them to each one, just as he determines. {12} The body is a unit, though it is made up of many parts; and though all its parts are many, they form one body. So it is with Christ. {13} For we were all baptized by one Spirit into one body—whether Jews or Greeks, slave or free—and we were all given the one Spirit to drink. {14} Now the body is not made up of one part but of many. {15} If the foot should say, "Because I am not a hand, I do not belong to the body," it would not for that reason cease to be part of the body. {16} And if the ear should say, "Because I am not an eye, I do not belong to the body," it would not for that reason cease to be part of the body. {17} If the whole body were an eye, where would the sense of hearing be? If the whole body were an ear, where would the sense of smell be? {18} But in fact God has arranged the parts in the body, every one of them, just as he wanted them to be. {19} If they were all one part, where would the body be? {20} As it is, there are many parts, but one body. {21} The eye cannot say to the hand, "I don't need you!" And the head cannot say to the feet, "I don't need you!" {22} On the contrary, those parts of the body that seem to be weaker are indispensable, {23} and the parts that we think are less honorable we treat with special honor. And the parts that are unpresentable are treated with special modesty, {24} while our presentable parts need no special treatment. But God has combined the members of the body and has given greater honor to the parts that lacked it....

LOVE, THE PERFECT WAY

1 Cor 13:1-13

If I speak in the tongues of men and of angels, but have not love, I am only a resounding gong or a clanging cymbal. {2} If I have the gift of prophecy and can fathom all mysteries and all knowledge, and if I have a faith that can move mountains, but have not love, I am nothing. {3} If I give all I possess to the poor and surrender my body to the flames, but have not love, I gain nothing. {4} Love is patient, love is kind. It does not envy, it does not boast, it is not proud. {5} It is not rude, it is not self-seeking, it is not easily angered, it keeps no record of wrongs. {6} Love does not delight in evil but rejoices with the truth. {7} It always protects, always trusts, always hopes, always perseveres. {8} Love never fails. But where there are prophecies, they will cease; where there are tongues, they will be stilled; where there is knowledge, it will pass away. {9} For we know in part and we prophesy in part, {10} but when perfection comes, the imperfect disappears. {11} When I was a child, I talked like a child, I thought like a child, I reasoned like a child. When I became a man, I put childish ways behind me. {12} Now we see but a poor reflection as in a mirror; then we shall see face to face. Now I know in part; then I shall know fully, even as I am fully known. {13} And now these three remain: faith, hope and love. But the greatest of these is love.

SPEAKING IN TONGUES

1 Cor 14:2-22

For anyone who speaks in a tongue does not speak to men but to God. Indeed, no one understands him; he utters mysteries with his spirit. {3} But everyone who prophesies speaks to men for their strengthening, encouragement and comfort. {4} He who speaks in a tongue edifies himself, but he who prophesies edifies the church. {5} I would like every one of you to speak in tongues, but I would rather have you prophesy. He who prophesies is greater than one who speaks in tongues, unless he interprets, so that the church may be edified. {6} Now, brothers, if I come to you and speak in tongues, what good will I be to you, unless I bring you some revelation or knowledge or prophecy or word of instruction? {7} Even in the case of lifeless things that make sounds, such as the flute or harp, how will anyone know what tune is being played unless there is a distinction in the notes? {8} Again, if the trumpet does not sound a clear call, who will get ready for battle? {9} So it is with you. Unless you speak intelligible words with your tongue, how will anyone know what you are saying? You will just be speaking into the air. {10} Undoubtedly there are all sorts of languages in the world, yet none of them is without meaning. {11} If then I do not grasp the meaning of what someone is saying, I am a foreigner to the speaker, and he is a foreigner to me. {12} So it is with you. Since you are eager to have spiritual gifts, try to excel in gifts that build up the church. {13} For this reason anyone who speaks in a tongue should pray that he may interpret what he says. {14} For if I pray in a tongue, my spirit prays, but my mind is unfruitful. {15} So what shall I do? I will pray with my spirit, but I will also pray with my mind; I will sing with my spirit, but I will also sing with my mind. {16} If you are praising God with your spirit, how can one who finds himself among those who do not understand say "Amen" to your thanksgiving, since he does not know what you are saying? {17} You may be giving thanks well enough, but the other man is not edified. {18} I thank God that I speak in tongues more than all of you. {19} But in the church I would rather speak five intelligible words to instruct others than ten thousand words in a tongue. {20} Brothers, stop thinking like children. In regard to evil be infants, but in your thinking be adults. {21} In the Law it is written: "Through men of strange tongues and through the lips of foreigners I will speak to this people, but even then they will not listen to me," says the Lord. {22} Tongues, then, are a sign, not for believers but for unbelievers; prophecy, however, is for believers, not for unbelievers.

CHRIST IS RISEN

1 Cor 15:3-27a

For what I received I passed on to you as of first importance : that Christ died for our sins according to the Scriptures, {4} that he was buried, that he was raised on the third day according to the Scriptures, {5} and that he appeared to Peter, and then to the Twelve. {6} After that, he appeared to more than five hundred of the brothers at the same time, most of whom are still living, though some have fallen asleep. {7} Then he appeared to James, then to all the apostles, {8} and last of all he appeared to me also, as to one abnormally born. {9} For I am the least of the apostles and do not even deserve to be called an apostle, because I persecuted the church of God. {10} But by the grace of God I am what I am, and his grace to me was not without effect. No, I worked harder than all of them—yet not I, but the grace of God that was with me. {11} Whether, then, it was I or they, this is what we preach, and this is what you believed. {12} But if it is preached that Christ has been raised from the dead, how can some of you say that there is no resurrection of the dead? {13} If there is no resurrection of the dead, then not even Christ has been raised. {14} And if Christ has not been raised, our preaching is useless and so is your faith. {15} More than that, we are then found to be false witnesses about God, for we have testified about God that he raised Christ from the dead. But he did not raise him if in fact the dead are not raised. {16} For if the dead are not raised, then Christ has not been raised either. {17} And if Christ has not been raised, your faith is futile; you are still in your sins. {18} Then those also who have fallen asleep in Christ are lost. {19} If only for this life we have hope in Christ, we are to be pitied more than all men. {20} But Christ has indeed been raised from the dead, the firstfruits of those who have fallen asleep. {21} For since death came through a man, the resurrection of the dead comes also through a man. {22} For as in Adam all die, so in Christ all will be made alive. {23} But each in his own turn: Christ, the firstfruits; then, when he comes, those who belong to him. {24} Then the end will come, when he hands over the kingdom to God the Father after he has destroyed all dominion, authority and power. {25} For he must reign until he has put all his enemies under his feet. {26} The last enemy to be destroyed is death. {27} For he "has put everything under his feet."

THE DEAD WILL BE RAISED

1 Cor 15:35-58

But someone may ask, "How are the dead raised? With what kind of body will they come?" {36} How foolish! What you sow does not come to life unless it dies. {37} When you sow, you do not plant the body that will be, but just a seed, perhaps of wheat or of something else. {38} But God gives it a body as he has determined, and to each kind of seed he gives its own body. {39} All flesh is not the same: Men have one kind of flesh, animals have another, birds another and fish another. {40} There are also heavenly bodies and there are earthly bodies; but the splendor of the heavenly bodies is one kind, and the splendor of the earthly bodies is another. {41} The sun has one kind of splendor, the moon another and the stars another; and star differs from star in splendor. {42} So will it be with the resurrection of the dead. The body that is sown is perishable, it is raised imperishable; {43} it is sown in dishonor, it is raised in glory; it is sown in weakness, it is raised in power; {44} it is sown a natural body, it is raised a spiritual body. If there is a natural body, there is also a spiritual body. {45} So it is written: "The first man Adam became a living being" ; the last Adam, a life-giving spirit. {46} The spiritual did not come first, but the natural, and after that the spiritual. {47} The first man was of the dust of the earth, the second man from heaven. {48} As was the earthly man, so are those who are of the earth; and as is the man from heaven, so also are those who are of heaven. {49} And just as we have borne the likeness of the earthly man, so shall we bear the likeness of the man from heaven. {50} I declare to you, brothers, that flesh and blood cannot inherit the kingdom of God, nor does the perishable inherit the imperishable. {51} Listen, I tell you a mystery: We will not all sleep, but we will all be changed– {52} in a flash, in the twinkling of an eye, at the last trumpet. For the trumpet will sound, the dead will be raised imperishable, and we will be changed. {53} For the perishable must clothe itself with the imperishable, and the mortal with immortality. {54} When the perishable has been clothed with the imperishable, and the mortal with immortality, then the saying that is written will come true: "Death has been swallowed up in victory." {55} "Where, O death, is your victory? Where, O death, is your sting?" {56} The sting of death is sin, and the power of sin is the law. {57} But thanks be to God! He gives us the victory through our Lord Jesus Christ. {58} Therefore, my dear brothers, stand firm. Let nothing move you. Always give yourselves fully to the work of the Lord, because you know that your labor in the Lord is not in vain.

A TREASURE IN EARTHEN VESSELS

2 Cor 4:6-5:10

For God, who said, "Let light shine out of darkness," made his light shine in our hearts to give us the light of the knowledge of the glory of God in the face of Christ. {7} But we have this treasure in jars of clay to show that this all-surpassing power is from God and not from us. {8} We are hard pressed on every side, but not crushed; perplexed, but not in despair; {9} persecuted, but not abandoned; struck down, but not destroyed. {10} We always carry around in our body the death of Jesus, so that the life of Jesus may also be revealed in our body. {11} For we who are alive are always being given over to death for Jesus' sake, so that his life may be revealed in our mortal body. {12} So then, death is at work in us, but life is at work in you. {13} It is written: "I believed; therefore I have spoken." With that same spirit of faith we also believe and therefore speak, {14} because we know that the one who raised the Lord Jesus from the dead will also raise us with Jesus and present us with you in his presence. {15} All this is for your benefit, so that the grace that is reaching more and more people may cause thanksgiving to overflow to the glory of God. {16} Therefore we do not lose heart. Though outwardly we are wasting away, yet inwardly we are being renewed day by day. {17} For our light and momentary troubles are achieving for us an eternal glory that far outweighs them all. {18} So we fix our eyes not on what is seen, but on what is unseen. For what is seen is temporary, but what is unseen is eternal. {5:1} Now we know that if the earthly tent we live in is destroyed, we have a building from God, an eternal house in heaven, not built by human hands. {2} Meanwhile we groan, longing to be clothed with our heavenly dwelling, {3} because when we are clothed, we will not be found naked. {4} For while we are in this tent, we groan and are burdened, because we do not wish to be unclothed but to be clothed with our heavenly dwelling, so that what is mortal may be swallowed up by life. {5} Now it is God who has made us for this very purpose and has given us the Spirit as a deposit, guaranteeing what is to come. {6} Therefore we are always confident and know that as long as we are at home in the body we are away from the Lord. {7} We live by faith, not by sight. {8} We are confident, I say, and would prefer to be away from the body and at home with the Lord. {9} So we make it our goal to please him, whether we are at home in the body or away from it. {10} For we must all appear before the judgment seat of Christ, that each one may receive what is due him for the things done while in the body, whether good or bad.

A MINISTRY OF RECONCILIATION

2 Cor 5:11-6:2

Since, then, we know what it is to fear the Lord, we try to persuade men. What we are is plain to God, and I hope it is also plain to your conscience. {12} We are not trying to commend ourselves to you again, but are giving you an opportunity to take pride in us, so that you can answer those who take pride in what is seen rather than in what is in the heart. {13} If we are out of our mind, it is for the sake of God; if we are in our right mind, it is for you. {14} For Christ's love compels us, because we are convinced that one died for all, and therefore all died. {15} And he died for all, that those who live should no longer live for themselves but for him who died for them and was raised again. {16} So from now on we regard no one from a worldly point of view. Though we once regarded Christ in this way, we do so no longer. {17} Therefore, if anyone is in Christ, he is a new creation; the old has gone, the new has come! {18} All this is from God, who reconciled us to himself through Christ and gave us the ministry of reconciliation: {19} that God was reconciling the world to himself in Christ, not counting men's sins against them. And he has committed to us the message of reconciliation. {20} We are therefore Christ's ambassadors, as though God were making his appeal through us. We implore you on Christ's behalf: Be reconciled to God. {21} God made him who had no sin to be sin for us, so that in him we might become the righteousness of God. {6:1} As God's fellow workers we urge you not to receive God's grace in vain. {2} For he says, "In the time of my favor I heard you, and in the day of salvation I helped you." I tell you, now is the time of God's favor, now is the day of salvation.

BE NOT YOKED WITH UNBELIEVERS

2 Cor 6:14-18

Do not be yoked together with unbelievers. For what do righteousness and wickedness have in common? Or what fellowship can light have with darkness? {15} What harmony is there between Christ and Belial ? What does a believer have in common with an unbeliever? {16} What agreement is there between the temple of God and idols? For we are the temple of the living God. As God has said: "I will live with them and walk among them, and I will be their God, and they will be my people." {17} "Therefore come out from them and be separate, says the Lord. Touch no unclean thing, and I will receive you." {18} "I will be a Father to you, and you will be my sons and daughters, says the Lord Almighty."

BELIEVERS TO BE GENEROUS

2 Cor 8:1-15

And now, brothers, we want you to know about the grace that God has given the Macedonian churches. {2} Out of the most severe trial, their overflowing joy and their extreme poverty welled up in rich generosity. {3} For I testify that they gave as much as they were able, and even beyond their ability. Entirely on their own, {4} they urgently pleaded with us for the privilege of sharing in this service to the saints. {5} And they did not do as we expected, but they gave themselves first to the Lord and then to us in keeping with God's will. {6} So we urged Titus, since he had earlier made a beginning, to bring also to completion this act of grace on your part. {7} But just as you excel in everything–in faith, in speech, in knowledge, in complete earnestness and in your love for us –see that you also excel in this grace of giving. {8} I am not commanding you, but I want to test the sincerity of your love by comparing it with the earnestness of others. {9} For you know the grace of our Lord Jesus Christ, that though he was rich, yet for your sakes he became poor, so that you through his poverty might become rich. {10} And here is my advice about what is best for you in this matter: Last year you were the first not only to give but also to have the desire to do so. {11} Now finish the work, so that your eager willingness to do it may be matched by your completion of it, according to your means. {12} For if the willingness is there, the gift is acceptable according to what one has, not according to what he does not have. {13} Our desire is not that others might be relieved while you are hard pressed, but that there might be equality. {14} At the present time your plenty will supply what they need, so that in turn their plenty will supply what you need. Then there will be equality, {15} as it is written: "He who gathered much did not have too much, and he who gathered little did not have too little."

2 Cor 9:6-10

Remember this: Whoever sows sparingly will also reap sparingly, and whoever sows generously will also reap generously. {7} Each man should give what he has decided in his heart to give, not reluctantly or under compulsion, for God loves a cheerful giver. {8} And God is able to make all grace abound to you, so that in all things at all times, having all that you need, you will abound in every good work. {9} As it is written: "He has scattered abroad his gifts to the poor; his righteousness endures forever." {10} Now he who supplies seed to the sower and bread for food will also supply and increase your store of seed and will enlarge the harvest of your righteousness.

WARNING ABOUT FALSE TEACHERS

2 Cor 11:1-13

I hope you will put up with a little of my foolishness; but you are already doing that. {2} I am jealous for you with a godly jealousy. I promised you to one husband, to Christ, so that I might present you as a pure virgin to him. {3} But I am afraid that just as Eve was deceived by the serpent's cunning, your minds may somehow be led astray from your sincere and pure devotion to Christ. {4} For if someone comes to you and preaches a Jesus other than the Jesus we preached, or if you receive a different spirit from the one you received, or a different gospel from the one you accepted, you put up with it easily enough. {5} But I do not think I am in the least inferior to those "super-apostles." {6} I may not be a trained speaker, but I do have knowledge. We have made this perfectly clear to you in every way. {7} Was it a sin for me to lower myself in order to elevate you by preaching the gospel of God to you free of charge? {8} I robbed other churches by receiving support from them so as to serve you. {9} And when I was with you and needed something, I was not a burden to anyone, for the brothers who came from Macedonia supplied what I needed. I have kept myself from being a burden to you in any way, and will continue to do so. {10} As surely as the truth of Christ is in me, nobody in the regions of Achaia will stop this boasting of mine. {11} Why? Because I do not love you? God knows I do! {12} And I will keep on doing what I am doing in order to cut the ground from under those who want an opportunity to be considered equal with us in the things they boast about. {13} For such men are false apostles, deceitful workmen, masquerading as apostles of Christ.

2 Cor 11:23-28

Are they servants of Christ? (I am out of my mind to talk like this.) I am more. I have worked much harder, been in prison more frequently, been flogged more severely, and been exposed to death again and again. {24} Five times I received from the Jews the forty lashes minus one. {25} Three times I was beaten with rods, once I was stoned, three times I was shipwrecked, I spent a night and a day in the open sea, {26} I have been constantly on the move. I have been in danger from rivers, in danger from bandits, in danger from my own countrymen, in danger from Gentiles; in danger in the city, in danger in the country, in danger at sea; and in danger from false brothers. {27} I have labored and toiled and have often gone without sleep; I have known hunger and thirst and have often gone without food; I have been cold and naked. {28} Besides everything else, I face daily the pressure of my concern for all the churches.

PAUL'S CONCERN FOR CORINTHIAN BELIEVERS

2 Cor 12:15-13:11

So I will very gladly spend for you everything I have and expend myself as well. If I love you more, will you love me less? {16} Be that as it may, I have not been a burden to you. Yet, crafty fellow that I am, I caught you by trickery! {17} Did I exploit you through any of the men I sent you? {18} I urged Titus to go to you and I sent our brother with him. Titus did not exploit you, did he? Did we not act in the same spirit and follow the same course? {19} Have you been thinking all along that we have been defending ourselves to you? We have been speaking in the sight of God as those in Christ; and everything we do, dear friends, is for your strengthening. {20} For I am afraid that when I come I may not find you as I want you to be, and you may not find me as you want me to be. I fear that there may be quarreling, jealousy, outbursts of anger, factions, slander, gossip, arrogance and disorder. {21} I am afraid that when I come again my God will humble me before you, and I will be grieved over many who have sinned earlier and have not repented of the impurity, sexual sin and debauchery in which they have indulged. {13:1} This will be my third visit to you. "Every matter must be established by the testimony of two or three witnesses." {2} I already gave you a warning when I was with you the second time. I now repeat it while absent: On my return I will not spare those who sinned earlier or any of the others, {3} since you are demanding proof that Christ is speaking through me. He is not weak in dealing with you, but is powerful among you. {4} For to be sure, he was crucified in weakness, yet he lives by God's power. Likewise, we are weak in him, yet by God's power we will live with him to serve you. {5} Examine yourselves to see whether you are in the faith; test yourselves. Do you not realize that Christ Jesus is in you–unless, of course, you fail the test? {6} And I trust that you will discover that we have not failed the test. {7} Now we pray to God that you will not do anything wrong. Not that people will see that we have stood the test but that you will do what is right even though we may seem to have failed. {8} For we cannot do anything against the truth, but only for the truth. {9} We are glad whenever we are weak but you are strong; and our prayer is for your perfection. {10} This is why I write these things when I am absent, that when I come I may not have to be harsh in my use of authority–the authority the Lord gave me for building you up, not for tearing you down. {11} Finally, brothers, good-by. Aim for perfection, listen to my appeal, be of one mind, live in peace. And the God of love and peace will be with you.

PAUL'S MESSAGE FROM GOD

Gal 1:11-2:2

I want you to know, brothers, that the gospel I preached is not something that man made up. {12} I did not receive it from any man, nor was I taught it; rather, I received it by revelation from Jesus Christ. {13} For you have heard of my previous way of life in Judaism, how intensely I persecuted the church of God and tried to destroy it. {14} I was advancing in Judaism beyond many Jews of my own age and was extremely zealous for the traditions of my fathers. {15} But when God, who set me apart from birth and called me by his grace, was pleased {16} to reveal his Son in me so that I might preach him among the Gentiles, I did not consult any man, {17} nor did I go up to Jerusalem to see those who were apostles before I was, but I went immediately into Arabia and later returned to Damascus. {18} Then after three years, I went up to Jerusalem to get acquainted with Peter and stayed with him fifteen days. {19} I saw none of the other apostles—only James, the Lord's brother. {20} I assure you before God that what I am writing you is no lie. {21} Later I went to Syria and Cilicia. {22} I was personally unknown to the churches of Judea that are in Christ. {23} They only heard the report: "The man who formerly persecuted us is now preaching the faith he once tried to destroy." {24} And they praised God because of me. {2:1} Fourteen years later I went up again to Jerusalem, this time with Barnabas. I took Titus along also. {2} I went in response to a revelation and set before them the gospel that I preach among the Gentiles. But I did this privately to those who seemed to be leaders, for fear that I was running or had run my race in vain.

Gal 2:15-21

"We who are Jews by birth and not 'Gentile sinners' {16} know that a man is not justified by observing the law, but by faith in Jesus Christ. So we, too, have put our faith in Christ Jesus that we may be justified by faith in Christ and not by observing the law, because by observing the law no one will be justified. {17} "If, while we seek to be justified in Christ, it becomes evident that we ourselves are sinners, does that mean that Christ promotes sin? Absolutely not! {18} If I rebuild what I destroyed, I prove that I am a lawbreaker. {19} For through the law I died to the law so that I might live for God. {20} I have been crucified with Christ and I no longer live, but Christ lives in me. The life I live in the body, I live by faith in the Son of God, who loved me and gave himself for me. {21} I do not set aside the grace of God, for if righteousness could be gained through the law, Christ died for nothing!"

OF FAITH AND THE LAW

Gal 3:6-25

Consider Abraham: "He believed God, and it was credited to him as righteousness." {7} Understand, then, that those who believe are children of Abraham. {8} The Scripture foresaw that God would justify the Gentiles by faith, and announced the gospel in advance to Abraham: "All nations will be blessed through you." {9} So those who have faith are blessed along with Abraham, the man of faith. {10} All who rely on observing the law are under a curse, for it is written: "Cursed is everyone who does not continue to do everything written in the Book of the Law." {11} Clearly no one is justified before God by the law, because, "The righteous will live by faith." {12} The law is not based on faith; on the contrary, "The man who does these things will live by them." {13} Christ redeemed us from the curse of the law by becoming a curse for us, for it is written: "Cursed is everyone who is hung on a tree." {14} He redeemed us in order that the blessing given to Abraham might come to the Gentiles through Christ Jesus, so that by faith we might receive the promise of the Spirit. {15} Brothers, let me take an example from everyday life. Just as no one can set aside or add to a human covenant that has been duly established, so it is in this case. {16} The promises were spoken to Abraham and to his seed. The Scripture does not say "and to seeds," meaning many people, but "and to your seed," meaning one person, who is Christ. {17} What I mean is this: The law, introduced 430 years later, does not set aside the covenant previously established by God and thus do away with the promise. {18} For if the inheritance depends on the law, then it no longer depends on a promise; but God in his grace gave it to Abraham through a promise. {19} What, then, was the purpose of the law? It was added because of transgressions until the Seed to whom the promise referred had come. The law was put into effect through angels by a mediator. {20} A mediator, however, does not represent just one party; but God is one. {21} Is the law, therefore, opposed to the promises of God? Absolutely not! For if a law had been given that could impart life, then righteousness would certainly have come by the law. {22} But the Scripture declares that the whole world is a prisoner of sin, so that what was promised, being given through faith in Jesus Christ, might be given to those who believe. {23} Before this faith came, we were held prisoners by the law, locked up until faith should be revealed. {24} So the law was put in charge to lead us to Christ that we might be justified by faith. {25} Now that faith has come, we are no longer under the supervision of the law.

HEIRS OF GOD

Gal 3:26-4:7

You are all sons of God through faith in Christ Jesus, {27} for all of you who were baptized into Christ have clothed yourselves with Christ. {28} There is neither Jew nor Greek, slave nor free, male nor female, for you are all one in Christ Jesus. {29} If you belong to Christ, then you are Abraham's seed, and heirs according to the promise. {4:1} What I am saying is that as long as the heir is a child, he is no different from a slave, although he owns the whole estate. {2} He is subject to guardians and trustees until the time set by his father. {3} So also, when we were children, we were in slavery under the basic principles of the world. {4} But when the time had fully come, God sent his Son, born of a woman, born under law, {5} to redeem those under law, that we might receive the full rights of sons. {6} Because you are sons, God sent the Spirit of his Son into our hearts, the Spirit who calls out, <"Abba>, Father." {7} So you are no longer a slave, but a son; and since you are a son, God has made you also an heir.

Gal 4:21-31

Tell me, you who want to be under the law, are you not aware of what the law says? {22} For it is written that Abraham had two sons, one by the slave woman and the other by the free woman. {23} His son by the slave woman was born in the ordinary way; but his son by the free woman was born as the result of a promise. {24} These things may be taken figuratively, for the women represent two covenants. One covenant is from Mount Sinai and bears children who are to be slaves: This is Hagar. {25} Now Hagar stands for Mount Sinai in Arabia and corresponds to the present city of Jerusalem, because she is in slavery with her children. {26} But the Jerusalem that is above is free, and she is our mother. {27} For it is written: "Be glad, O barren woman, who bears no children; break forth and cry aloud, you who have no labor pains; because more are the children of the desolate woman than of her who has a husband." {28} Now you, brothers, like Isaac, are children of promise. {29} At that time the son born in the ordinary way persecuted the son born by the power of the Spirit. It is the same now. {30} But what does the Scripture say? "Get rid of the slave woman and her son, for the slave woman's son will never share in the inheritance with the free woman's son." {31} Therefore, brothers, we are not children of the slave woman, but of the free woman.

FREEDOM IN CHRIST

Gal 5:1-25

It is for freedom that Christ has set us free. Stand firm, then, and do not let yourselves be burdened again by a yoke of slavery. {2} Mark my words! I, Paul, tell you that if you let yourselves be circumcised, Christ will be of no value to you at all. {3} Again I declare to every man who lets himself be circumcised that he is obligated to obey the whole law. {4} You who are trying to be justified by law have been alienated from Christ; you have fallen away from grace. {5} But by faith we eagerly await through the Spirit the righteousness for which we hope. {6} For in Christ Jesus neither circumcision nor uncircumcision has any value. The only thing that counts is faith expressing itself through love. {7} You were running a good race. Who cut in on you and kept you from obeying the truth? {8} That kind of persuasion does not come from the one who calls you. {9} "A little yeast works through the whole batch of dough." {10} I am confident in the Lord that you will take no other view. The one who is throwing you into confusion will pay the penalty, whoever he may be. {11} Brothers, if I am still preaching circumcision, why am I still being persecuted? In that case the offense of the cross has been abolished. {12} As for those agitators, I wish they would go the whole way and emasculate themselves! {13} You, my brothers, were called to be free. But do not use your freedom to indulge the sinful nature ; rather, serve one another in love. {14} The entire law is summed up in a single command: "Love your neighbor as yourself." {15} If you keep on biting and devouring each other, watch out or you will be destroyed by each other. {16} So I say, live by the Spirit, and you will not gratify the desires of the sinful nature. {17} For the sinful nature desires what is contrary to the Spirit, and the Spirit what is contrary to the sinful nature. They are in conflict with each other, so that you do not do what you want. {18} But if you are led by the Spirit, you are not under law. {19} The acts of the sinful nature are obvious: sexual immorality, impurity and debauchery; {20} idolatry and witchcraft; hatred, discord, jealousy, fits of rage, selfish ambition, dissensions, factions {21} and envy; drunkenness, orgies, and the like. I warn you, as I did before, that those who live like this will not inherit the kingdom of God. {22} But the fruit of the Spirit is love, joy, peace, patience, kindness, goodness, faithfulness, {23} gentleness and self-control. Against such things there is no law. {24} Those who belong to Christ Jesus have crucified the sinful nature with its passions and desires. {25} Since we live by the Spirit, let us keep in step with the Spirit.

BLESSINGS IN CHRIST

Eph 1:3-23

Praise be to the God and Father of our Lord Jesus Christ, who has blessed us in the heavenly realms with every spiritual blessing in Christ. {4} For he chose us in him before the creation of the world to be holy and blameless in his sight. In love {5} he predestined us to be adopted as his sons through Jesus Christ, in accordance with his pleasure and will– {6} to the praise of his glorious grace, which he has freely given us in the One he loves. {7} In him we have redemption through his blood, the forgiveness of sins, in accordance with the riches of God's grace {8} that he lavished on us with all wisdom and understanding. {9} And he made known to us the mystery of his will according to his good pleasure, which he purposed in Christ, {10} to be put into effect when the times will have reached their fulfillment–to bring all things in heaven and on earth together under one head, even Christ. {11} In him we were also chosen, having been predestined according to the plan of him who works out everything in conformity with the purpose of his will, {12} in order that we, who were the first to hope in Christ, might be for the praise of his glory. {13} And you also were included in Christ when you heard the word of truth, the gospel of your salvation. Having believed, you were marked in him with a seal, the promised Holy Spirit, {14} who is a deposit guaranteeing our inheritance until the redemption of those who are God's possession–to the praise of his glory. {15} For this reason, ever since I heard about your faith in the Lord Jesus and your love for all the saints, {16} I have not stopped giving thanks for you, remembering you in my prayers. {17} I keep asking that the God of our Lord Jesus Christ, the glorious Father, may give you the Spirit of wisdom and revelation, so that you may know him better. {18} I pray also that the eyes of your heart may be enlightened in order that you may know the hope to which he has called you, the riches of his glorious inheritance in the saints, {19} and his incomparably great power for us who believe. That power is like the working of his mighty strength, {20} which he exerted in Christ when he raised him from the dead and seated him at his right hand in the heavenly realms, {21} far above all rule and authority, power and dominion, and every title that can be given, not only in the present age but also in the one to come. {22} And God placed all things under his feet and appointed him to be head over everything for the church, {23} which is his body, the fullness of him who fills everything in every way.

CHRIST IS OUR PEACE

Eph 2:1-22

As for you, you were dead in your transgressions and sins, {2} in which you used to live when you followed the ways of this world and of the ruler of the kingdom of the air, the spirit who is now at work in those who are disobedient. {3} All of us also lived among them at one time, gratifying the cravings of our sinful nature and following its desires and thoughts. Like the rest, we were by nature objects of wrath. {4} But because of his great love for us, God, who is rich in mercy, {5} made us alive with Christ even when we were dead in transgressions–it is by grace you have been saved. {6} And God raised us up with Christ and seated us with him in the heavenly realms in Christ Jesus, {7} in order that in the coming ages he might show the incomparable riches of his grace, expressed in his kindness to us in Christ Jesus. {8} For it is by grace you have been saved, through faith–and this not from yourselves, it is the gift of God– {9} not by works, so that no one can boast. {10} For we are God's workmanship, created in Christ Jesus to do good works, which God prepared in advance for us to do. {11} Therefore, remember that formerly you who are Gentiles by birth and called "uncircumcised" by those who call themselves "the circumcision" (that done in the body by the hands of men)– {12} remember that at that time you were separate from Christ, excluded from citizenship in Israel and foreigners to the covenants of the promise, without hope and without God in the world. {13} But now in Christ Jesus you who once were far away have been brought near through the blood of Christ. {14} For he himself is our peace, who has made the two one and has destroyed the barrier, the dividing wall of hostility, {15} by abolishing in his flesh the law with its commandments and regulations. His purpose was to create in himself one new man out of the two, thus making peace, {16} and in this one body to reconcile both of them to God through the cross, by which he put to death their hostility. {17} He came and preached peace to you who were far away and peace to those who were near. {18} For through him we both have access to the Father by one Spirit. {19} Consequently, you are no longer foreigners and aliens, but fellow citizens with God's people and members of God's household, {20} built on the foundation of the apostles and prophets, with Christ Jesus himself as the chief cornerstone. {21} In him the whole building is joined together and rises to become a holy temple in the Lord. {22} And in him you too are being built together to become a dwelling in which God lives by his Spirit.

ONE BODY AND ONE SPIRIT

Eph 4:4-28a

There is one body and one Spirit– just as you were called to one hope when you were called– {5} one Lord, one faith, one baptism; {6} one God and Father of all, who is over all and through all and in all. {7} But to each one of us grace has been given as Christ apportioned it. {8} This is why it says: "When he ascended on high, he led captives in his train and gave gifts to men." {9} (What does "he ascended" mean except that he also descended to the lower, earthly regions ? {10} He who descended is the very one who ascended higher than all the heavens, in order to fill the whole universe.) {11} It was he who gave some to be apostles, some to be prophets, some to be evangelists, and some to be pastors and teachers, {12} to prepare God's people for works of service, so that the body of Christ may be built up {13} until we all reach unity in the faith and in the knowledge of the Son of God and become mature, attaining to the whole measure of the fullness of Christ. {14} Then we will no longer be infants, tossed back and forth by the waves, and blown here and there by every wind of teaching and by the cunning and craftiness of men in their deceitful scheming. {15} Instead, speaking the truth in love, we will in all things grow up into him who is the Head, that is, Christ. {16} From him the whole body, joined and held together by every supporting ligament, grows and builds itself up in love, as each part does its work. {17} So I tell you this, and insist on it in the Lord, that you must no longer live as the Gentiles do, in the futility of their thinking. {18} They are darkened in their understanding and separated from the life of God because of the ignorance that is in them due to the hardening of their hearts. {19} Having lost all sensitivity, they have given themselves over to sensuality so as to indulge in every kind of impurity, with a continual lust for more. {20} You, however, did not come to know Christ that way. {21} Surely you heard of him and were taught in him in accordance with the truth that is in Jesus. {22} You were taught, with regard to your former way of life, to put off your old self, which is being corrupted by its deceitful desires; {23} to be made new in the attitude of your minds; {24} and to put on the new self, created to be like God in true righteousness and holiness. {25} Therefore each of you must put off falsehood and speak truthfully to his neighbor, for we are all members of one body. {26} "In your anger do not sin": Do not let the sun go down while you are still angry, {27} and do not give the devil a foothold. {28} He who has been stealing must steal no longer, but must work, doing something useful with his own hands....

OF WIVES, HUSBANDS AND CHILDREN;
SERVANTS AND MASTERS

Eph 5:22-6:9

Wives, submit to your husbands as to the Lord. {23} For the husband is the head of the wife as Christ is the head of the church, his body, of which he is the Savior. {24} Now as the church submits to Christ, so also wives should submit to their husbands in everything. {25} Husbands, love your wives, just as Christ loved the church and gave himself up for her {26} to make her holy, cleansing her by the washing with water through the word, {27} and to present her to himself as a radiant church, without stain or wrinkle or any other blemish, but holy and blameless. {28} In this same way, husbands ought to love their wives as their own bodies. He who loves his wife loves himself. {29} After all, no one ever hated his own body, but he feeds and cares for it, just as Christ does the church– {30} for we are members of his body. {31} "For this reason a man will leave his father and mother and be united to his wife, and the two will become one flesh." {32} This is a profound mystery–but I am talking about Christ and the church. {33} However, each one of you also must love his wife as he loves himself, and the wife must respect her husband. {6:1} Children, obey your parents in the Lord, for this is right. {2} "Honor your father and mother"–which is the first commandment with a promise– {3} "that it may go well with you and that you may enjoy long life on the earth." {4} Fathers, do not exasperate your children; instead, bring them up in the training and instruction of the Lord.

{5} Slaves, obey your earthly masters with respect and fear, and with sincerity of heart, just as you would obey Christ. {6} Obey them not only to win their favor when their eye is on you, but like slaves of Christ, doing the will of God from your heart. {7} Serve wholeheartedly, as if you were serving the Lord, not men, {8} because you know that the Lord will reward everyone for whatever good he does, whether he is slave or free. {9} And masters, treat your slaves in the same way. Do not threaten them, since you know that he who is both their Master and yours is in heaven, and there is no favoritism with him.

PUT ON THE ARMOUR OF GOD

Eph 6:10-18

Finally, be strong in the Lord and in his mighty power. {11} Put on the full armor of God so that you can take your stand against the devil's schemes. {12} For our struggle is not against flesh and blood, but against the rulers, against the authorities, against the powers of this dark world and against the spiritual forces of evil in the heavenly realms. {13} Therefore put on the full armor of God, so that when the day of evil comes, you may be able to stand your ground, and after you have done everything, to stand. {14} Stand firm then, with the belt of truth buckled around your waist, with the breastplate of righteousness in place, {15} and with your feet fitted with the readiness that comes from the gospel of peace. {16} In addition to all this, take up the shield of faith, with which you can extinguish all the flaming arrows of the evil one. {17} Take the helmet of salvation and the sword of the Spirit, which is the word of God. {18} And pray in the Spirit on all occasions with all kinds of prayers and requests. With this in mind, be alert and always keep on praying for all the saints.

CONSIDER OTHERS BETTER THAN YOURSELVES

Phil 2:1-18

If you have any encouragement from being united with Christ, if any comfort from his love, if any fellowship with the Spirit, if any tenderness and compassion, {2} then make my joy complete by being like-minded, having the same love, being one in spirit and purpose. {3} Do nothing out of selfish ambition or vain conceit, but in humility consider others better than yourselves. {4} Each of you should look not only to your own interests, but also to the interests of others. {5} Your attitude should be the same as that of Christ Jesus: {6} Who, being in very nature God, did not consider equality with God something to be grasped, {7} but made himself nothing, taking the very nature of a servant, being made in human likeness. {8} And being found in appearance as a man, he humbled himself and became obedient to death– even death on a cross! {9} Therefore God exalted him to the highest place and gave him the name that is above every name, {10} that at the name of Jesus every knee should bow, in heaven and on earth and under the earth, {11} and every tongue confess that Jesus Christ is Lord, to the glory of God the Father. {12} Therefore, my dear friends, as you have always obeyed–not only in my presence, but now much more in my absence–continue to work out your salvation with fear and trembling, {13} for it is God who works in you to will and to act according to his good purpose. {14} Do everything without complaining or arguing, {15} so that you may become blameless and pure, children of God without fault in a crooked and depraved generation, in which you shine like stars in the universe {16} as you hold out the word of life–in order that I may boast on the day of Christ that I did not run or labor for nothing. {17} But even if I am being poured out like a drink offering on the sacrifice and service coming from your faith, I am glad and rejoice with all of you. {18} So you too should be glad and rejoice with me.

PRESS ON TOWARD THE GOAL IN CHRIST JESUS

Phil 3:2-4:1

Watch out for those dogs, those men who do evil, those mutilators of the flesh. {3} For it is we who are the circumcision, we who worship by the Spirit of God, who glory in Christ Jesus, and who put no confidence in the flesh– {4} though I myself have reasons for such confidence. If anyone else thinks he has reasons to put confidence in the flesh, I have more: {5} circumcised on the eighth day, of the people of Israel, of the tribe of Benjamin, a Hebrew of Hebrews; in regard to the law, a Pharisee; {6} as for zeal, persecuting the church; as for legalistic righteousness, faultless. {7} But whatever was to my profit I now consider loss for the sake of Christ. {8} What is more, I consider everything a loss compared to the surpassing greatness of knowing Christ Jesus my Lord, for whose sake I have lost all things. I consider them rubbish, that I may gain Christ {9} and be found in him, not having a righteousness of my own that comes from the law, but that which is through faith in Christ–the righteousness that comes from God and is by faith. {10} I want to know Christ and the power of his resurrection and the fellowship of sharing in his sufferings, becoming like him in his death, {11} and so, somehow, to attain to the resurrection from the dead. {12} Not that I have already obtained all this, or have already been made perfect, but I press on to take hold of that for which Christ Jesus took hold of me. {13} Brothers, I do not consider myself yet to have taken hold of it. But one thing I do: Forgetting what is behind and straining toward what is ahead, {14} I press on toward the goal to win the prize for which God has called me heavenward in Christ Jesus. {15} All of us who are mature should take such a view of things. And if on some point you think differently, that too God will make clear to you. {16} Only let us live up to what we have already attained. {17} Join with others in following my example, brothers, and take note of those who live according to the pattern we gave you. {18} For, as I have often told you before and now say again even with tears, many live as enemies of the cross of Christ. {19} Their destiny is destruction, their god is their stomach, and their glory is in their shame. Their mind is on earthly things. {20} But our citizenship is in heaven. And we eagerly await a Savior from there, the Lord Jesus Christ, {21} who, by the power that enables him to bring everything under his control, will transform our lowly bodies so that they will be like his glorious body. {4:1} Therefore, my brothers, you whom I love and long for, my joy and crown, that is how you should stand firm in the Lord, dear friends!

REJOICE IN THE LORD, AND SHARE WITH OTHERS

Phil 4:4-20

Rejoice in the Lord always. I will say it again: Rejoice! {5} Let your gentleness be evident to all. The Lord is near. {6} Do not be anxious about anything, but in everything, by prayer and petition, with thanksgiving, present your requests to God. {7} And the peace of God, which transcends all understanding, will guard your hearts and your minds in Christ Jesus. {8} Finally, brothers, whatever is true, whatever is noble, whatever is right, whatever is pure, whatever is lovely, whatever is admirable–if anything is excellent or praiseworthy–think about such things. {9} Whatever you have learned or received or heard from me, or seen in me–put it into practice. And the God of peace will be with you.

{10} I rejoice greatly in the Lord that at last you have renewed your concern for me. Indeed, you have been concerned, but you had no opportunity to show it. {11} I am not saying this because I am in need, for I have learned to be content whatever the circumstances. {12} I know what it is to be in need, and I know what it is to have plenty. I have learned the secret of being content in any and every situation, whether well fed or hungry, whether living in plenty or in want. {13} I can do everything through him who gives me strength. {14} Yet it was good of you to share in my troubles. {15} Moreover, as you Philippians know, in the early days of your acquaintance with the gospel, when I set out from Macedonia, not one church shared with me in the matter of giving and receiving, except you only; {16} for even when I was in Thessalonica, you sent me aid again and again when I was in need. {17} Not that I am looking for a gift, but I am looking for what may be credited to your account. {18} I have received full payment and even more; I am amply supplied, now that I have received from Epaphroditus the gifts you sent. They are a fragrant offering, an acceptable sacrifice, pleasing to God. {19} And my God will meet all your needs according to his glorious riches in Christ Jesus. {20} To our God and Father be glory for ever and ever. Amen.

ALL THE FULNESS OF GOD IS IN CHRIST;
LIVE IN THE FREEDOM OF CHRIST

Col 1:19-23

For God was pleased to have all his fullness dwell in him, {20} and through him to reconcile to himself all things, whether things on earth or things in heaven, by making peace through his blood, shed on the cross. {21} Once you were alienated from God and were enemies in your minds because of your evil behavior. {22} But now he has reconciled you by Christ's physical body through death to present you holy in his sight, without blemish and free from accusation– {23} if you continue in your faith, established and firm, not moved from the hope held out in the gospel. This is the gospel that you heard and that has been proclaimed to every creature under heaven, and of which I, Paul, have become a servant.

Col 2:6-18

So then, just as you received Christ Jesus as Lord, continue to live in him, {7} rooted and built up in him, strengthened in the faith as you were taught, and overflowing with thankfulness. {8} See to it that no one takes you captive through hollow and deceptive philosophy, which depends on human tradition and the basic principles of this world rather than on Christ. {9} For in Christ all the fullness of the Deity lives in bodily form, {10} and you have been given fullness in Christ, who is the head over every power and authority. {11} In him you were also circumcised, in the putting off of the sinful nature, not with a circumcision done by the hands of men but with the circumcision done by Christ, {12} having been buried with him in baptism and raised with him through your faith in the power of God, who raised him from the dead. {13} When you were dead in your sins and in the uncircumcision of your sinful nature, God made you alive with Christ. He forgave us all our sins, {14} having canceled the written code, with its regulations, that was against us and that stood opposed to us; he took it away, nailing it to the cross. {15} And having disarmed the powers and authorities, he made a public spectacle of them, triumphing over them by the cross. {16} Therefore do not let anyone judge you by what you eat or drink, or with regard to a religious festival, a New Moon celebration or a Sabbath day. {17} These are a shadow of the things that were to come; the reality, however, is found in Christ. {18} Do not let anyone who delights in false humility and the worship of angels disqualify you for the prize. Such a person goes into great detail about what he has seen, and his unspiritual mind puffs him up with idle notions.

SET YOUR AFFECTION ON THINGS ABOVE;
WIVES SUBMIT, HUSBANDS LOVE, CHILDREN OBEY;

Col 3:1-24

Since, then, you have been raised with Christ, set your hearts on things above, where Christ is seated at the right hand of God. {2} Set your minds on things above, not on earthly things. {3} For you died, and your life is now hidden with Christ in God. {4} When Christ, who is your life, appears, then you also will appear with him in glory. {5} Put to death, therefore, whatever belongs to your earthly nature: sexual immorality, impurity, lust, evil desires and greed, which is idolatry. {6} Because of these, the wrath of God is coming. {7} You used to walk in these ways, in the life you once lived. {8} But now you must rid yourselves of all such things as these: anger, rage, malice, slander, and filthy language from your lips. {9} Do not lie to each other, since you have taken off your old self with its practices {10} and have put on the new self, which is being renewed in knowledge in the image of its Creator. {11} Here there is no Greek or Jew, circumcised or uncircumcised, barbarian, Scythian, slave or free, but Christ is all, and is in all. {12} Therefore, as God's chosen people, holy and dearly loved, clothe yourselves with compassion, kindness, humility, gentleness and patience. {13} Bear with each other and forgive whatever grievances you may have against one another. Forgive as the Lord forgave you. {14} And over all these virtues put on love, which binds them all together in perfect unity. {15} Let the peace of Christ rule in your hearts, since as members of one body you were called to peace. And be thankful. {16} Let the word of Christ dwell in you richly as you teach and admonish one another with all wisdom, and as you sing psalms, hymns and spiritual songs with gratitude in your hearts to God. {17} And whatever you do, whether in word or deed, do it all in the name of the Lord Jesus, giving thanks to God the Father through him.

{18} Wives, submit to your husbands, as is fitting in the Lord. {19} Husbands, love your wives and do not be harsh with them. {20} Children, obey your parents in everything, for this pleases the Lord. {21} Fathers, do not embitter your children, or they will become discouraged. {22} Slaves, obey your earthly masters in everything; and do it, not only when their eye is on you and to win their favor, but with sincerity of heart and reverence for the Lord. {23} Whatever you do, work at it with all your heart, as working for the Lord, not for men, {24} since you know that you will receive an inheritance from the Lord as a reward. It is the Lord Christ you are serving.

LIVING TO GOD'S GLORY

1 Th 1:2-10

We always thank God for all of you, mentioning you in our prayers. {3} We continually remember before our God and Father your work produced by faith, your labor prompted by love, and your endurance inspired by hope in our Lord Jesus Christ. {4} For we know, brothers loved by God, that he has chosen you, {5} because our gospel came to you not simply with words, but also with power, with the Holy Spirit and with deep conviction. You know how we lived among you for your sake. {6} You became imitators of us and of the Lord; in spite of severe suffering, you welcomed the message with the joy given by the Holy Spirit. {7} And so you became a model to all the believers in Macedonia and Achaia. {8} The Lord's message rang out from you not only in Macedonia and Achaia—your faith in God has become known everywhere. Therefore we do not need to say anything about it, {9} for they themselves report what kind of reception you gave us. They tell how you turned to God from idols to serve the living and true God, {10} and to wait for his Son from heaven, whom he raised from the dead—Jesus, who rescues us from the coming wrath.

1 Th 4:1-12

Finally, brothers, we instructed you how to live in order to please God, as in fact you are living. Now we ask you and urge you in the Lord Jesus to do this more and more. {2} For you know what instructions we gave you by the authority of the Lord Jesus. {3} It is God's will that you should be sanctified: that you should avoid sexual immorality; {4} that each of you should learn to control his own body in a way that is holy and honorable, {5} not in passionate lust like the heathen, who do not know God; {6} and that in this matter no one should wrong his brother or take advantage of him. The Lord will punish men for all such sins, as we have already told you and warned you. {7} For God did not call us to be impure, but to live a holy life. {8} Therefore, he who rejects this instruction does not reject man but God, who gives you his Holy Spirit. {9} Now about brotherly love we do not need to write to you, for you yourselves have been taught by God to love each other. {10} And in fact, you do love all the brothers throughout Macedonia. Yet we urge you, brothers, to do so more and more. {11} Make it your ambition to lead a quiet life, to mind your own business and to work with your hands, just as we told you, {12} so that your daily life may win the respect of outsiders and so that you will not be dependent on anybody.

WORK, FOR THE LORD IS COMING

1 Th 4:15-5:24

According to the Lord's own word, we tell you that we who are still alive, who are left till the coming of the Lord, will certainly not precede those who have fallen asleep. {16} For the Lord himself will come down from heaven, with a loud command, with the voice of the archangel and with the trumpet call of God, and the dead in Christ will rise first. {17} After that, we who are still alive and are left will be caught up together with them in the clouds to meet the Lord in the air. And so we will be with the Lord forever. {18} Therefore encourage each other with these words. {5:1} Now, brothers, about times and dates we do not need to write to you, {2} for you know very well that the day of the Lord will come like a thief in the night. {3} While people are saying, "Peace and safety," destruction will come on them suddenly, as labor pains on a pregnant woman, and they will not escape. {4} But you, brothers, are not in darkness so that this day should surprise you like a thief. {5} You are all sons of the light and sons of the day. We do not belong to the night or to the darkness. {6} So then, let us not be like others, who are asleep, but let us be alert and self-controlled. {7} For those who sleep, sleep at night, and those who get drunk, get drunk at night. {8} But since we belong to the day, let us be self-controlled, putting on faith and love as a breastplate, and the hope of salvation as a helmet. {9} For God did not appoint us to suffer wrath but to receive salvation through our Lord Jesus Christ. {10} He died for us so that, whether we are awake or asleep, we may live together with him. {11} Therefore encourage one another and build each other up, just as in fact you are doing. {12} Now we ask you, brothers, to respect those who work hard among you, who are over you in the Lord and who admonish you. {13} Hold them in the highest regard in love because of their work. Live in peace with each other. {14} And we urge you, brothers, warn those who are idle, encourage the timid, help the weak, be patient with everyone. {15} Make sure that nobody pays back wrong for wrong, but always try to be kind to each other and to everyone else. {16} Be joyful always; {17} pray continually; {18} give thanks in all circumstances, for this is God's will for you in Christ Jesus. {19} Do not put out the Spirit's fire; {20} do not treat prophecies with contempt. {21} Test everything. Hold on to the good. {22} Avoid every kind of evil. {23} May God himself, the God of peace, sanctify you through and through. May your whole spirit, soul and body be kept blameless at the coming of our Lord Jesus Christ. {24} The one who calls you is faithful and he will do it.

WORK AND KEEP THE FAITH

2 Th 1:5b-2:12

And as a result you will be counted worthy of the kingdom of God, for which you are suffering. {6} God is just: He will pay back trouble to those who trouble you {7} and give relief to you who are troubled, and to us as well. This will happen when the Lord Jesus is revealed from heaven in blazing fire with his powerful angels. {8} He will punish those who do not know God and do not obey the gospel of our Lord Jesus. {9} They will be punished with everlasting destruction and shut out from the presence of the Lord and from the majesty of his power {10} on the day he comes to be glorified in his holy people and to be marveled at among all those who have believed. This includes you, because you believed our testimony to you. {11} With this in mind, we constantly pray for you, that our God may count you worthy of his calling, and that by his power he may fulfill every good purpose of yours and every act prompted by your faith. {12} We pray this so that the name of our Lord Jesus may be glorified in you, and you in him, according to the grace of our God and the Lord Jesus Christ. {2:1} Concerning the coming of our Lord Jesus Christ and our being gathered to him, we ask you, brothers, {2} not to become easily unsettled or alarmed by some prophecy, report or letter supposed to have come from us, saying that the day of the Lord has already come. {3} Don't let anyone deceive you in any way, for that day will not come until the rebellion occurs and the man of lawlessness is revealed, the man doomed to destruction. {4} He will oppose and will exalt himself over everything that is called God or is worshiped, so that he sets himself up in God's temple, proclaiming himself to be God. {5} Don't you remember that when I was with you I used to tell you these things? {6} And now you know what is holding him back, so that he may be revealed at the proper time. {7} For the secret power of lawlessness is already at work; but the one who now holds it back will continue to do so till he is taken out of the way. {8} And then the lawless one will be revealed, whom the Lord Jesus will overthrow with the breath of his mouth and destroy by the splendor of his coming. {9} The coming of the lawless one will be in accordance with the work of Satan displayed in all kinds of counterfeit miracles, signs and wonders, {10} and in every sort of evil that deceives those who are perishing. They perish because they refused to love the truth and so be saved. {11} For this reason God sends them a powerful delusion so that they will believe the lie {12} and so that all will be condemned who have not believed the truth but have delighted in wickedness.

KEEP THE FAITH AND WORK

2 Th 2:13-3:16

But we ought always to thank God for you, brothers loved by the Lord, because from the beginning God chose you to be saved through the sanctifying work of the Spirit and through belief in the truth. {14} He called you to this through our gospel, that you might share in the glory of our Lord Jesus Christ. {15} So then, brothers, stand firm and hold to the teachings we passed on to you, whether by word of mouth or by letter. {16} May our Lord Jesus Christ himself and God our Father, who loved us and by his grace gave us eternal encouragement and good hope, {17} encourage your hearts and strengthen you in every good deed and word. {3:1} Finally, brothers, pray for us that the message of the Lord may spread rapidly and be honored, just as it was with you. {2} And pray that we may be delivered from wicked and evil men, for not everyone has faith. {3} But the Lord is faithful, and he will strengthen and protect you from the evil one. {4} We have confidence in the Lord that you are doing and will continue to do the things we command. {5} May the Lord direct your hearts into God's love and Christ's perseverance. {6} In the name of the Lord Jesus Christ, we command you, brothers, to keep away from every brother who is idle and does not live according to the teaching you received from us. {7} For you yourselves know how you ought to follow our example. We were not idle when we were with you, {8} nor did we eat anyone's food without paying for it. On the contrary, we worked night and day, laboring and toiling so that we would not be a burden to any of you. {9} We did this, not because we do not have the right to such help, but in order to make ourselves a model for you to follow. {10} For even when we were with you, we gave you this rule: "If a man will not work, he shall not eat." {11} We hear that some among you are idle. They are not busy; they are busybodies. {12} Such people we command and urge in the Lord Jesus Christ to settle down and earn the bread they eat. {13} And as for you, brothers, never tire of doing what is right. {14} If anyone does not obey our instruction in this letter, take special note of him. Do not associate with him, in order that he may feel ashamed. {15} Yet do not regard him as an enemy, but warn him as a brother. {16} Now may the Lord of peace himself give you peace at all times and in every way. The Lord be with all of you.

HOW TO SELECT CHURCH LEADERS

1 Tim 2:2b-3:13

That we may live peaceful and quiet lives in all godliness and holiness. {3} This is good, and pleases God our Savior, {4} who wants all men to be saved and to come to a knowledge of the truth. {5} For there is one God and one mediator between God and men, the man Christ Jesus, {6} who gave himself as a ransom for all men–the testimony given in its proper time. {7} And for this purpose I was appointed a herald and an apostle–I am telling the truth, I am not lying–and a teacher of the true faith to the Gentiles. {8} I want men everywhere to lift up holy hands in prayer, without anger or disputing. {9} I also want women to dress modestly, with decency and propriety, not with braided hair or gold or pearls or expensive clothes, {10} but with good deeds, appropriate for women who profess to worship God. {11} A woman should learn in quietness and full submission. {12} I do not permit a woman to teach or to have authority over a man; she must be silent. {13} For Adam was formed first, then Eve. {14} And Adam was not the one deceived; it was the woman who was deceived and became a sinner. {15} But women will be saved through childbearing–if they continue in faith, love and holiness with propriety. {3:1} Here is a trustworthy saying: If anyone sets his heart on being an overseer, he desires a noble task. {2} Now the overseer must be above reproach, the husband of but one wife, temperate, self-controlled, respectable, hospitable, able to teach, {3} not given to drunkenness, not violent but gentle, not quarrelsome, not a lover of money. {4} He must manage his own family well and see that his children obey him with proper respect. {5} (If anyone does not know how to manage his own family, how can he take care of God's church?) {6} He must not be a recent convert, or he may become conceited and fall under the same judgment as the devil. {7} He must also have a good reputation with outsiders, so that he will not fall into disgrace and into the devil's trap. {8} Deacons, likewise, are to be men worthy of respect, sincere, not indulging in much wine, and not pursuing dishonest gain. {9} They must keep hold of the deep truths of the faith with a clear conscience. {10} They must first be tested; and then if there is nothing against them, let them serve as deacons. {11} In the same way, their wives are to be women worthy of respect, not malicious talkers but temperate and trustworthy in everything. {12} A deacon must be the husband of but one wife and must manage his children and his household well. {13} Those who have served well gain an excellent standing and great assurance in their faith in Christ Jesus.

OF WIDOWS AND ELDERS

1 Tim 5:1-20

Do not rebuke an older man harshly, but exhort him as if he were your father. Treat younger men as brothers, {2} older women as mothers, and younger women as sisters, with absolute purity. {3} Give proper recognition to those widows who are really in need. {4} But if a widow has children or grandchildren, these should learn first of all to put their religion into practice by caring for their own family and so repaying their parents and grandparents, for this is pleasing to God. {5} The widow who is really in need and left all alone puts her hope in God and continues night and day to pray and to ask God for help. {6} But the widow who lives for pleasure is dead even while she lives. {7} Give the people these instructions, too, so that no one may be open to blame. {8} If anyone does not provide for his relatives, and especially for his immediate family, he has denied the faith and is worse than an unbeliever. {9} No widow may be put on the list of widows unless she is over sixty, has been faithful to her husband, {10} and is well known for her good deeds, such as bringing up children, showing hospitality, washing the feet of the saints, helping those in trouble and devoting herself to all kinds of good deeds. {11} As for younger widows, do not put them on such a list. For when their sensual desires overcome their dedication to Christ, they want to marry. {12} Thus they bring judgment on themselves, because they have broken their first pledge. {13} Besides, they get into the habit of being idle and going about from house to house. And not only do they become idlers, but also gossips and busybodies, saying things they ought not to. {14} So I counsel younger widows to marry, to have children, to manage their homes and to give the enemy no opportunity for slander. {15} Some have in fact already turned away to follow Satan. {16} If any woman who is a believer has widows in her family, she should help them and not let the church be burdened with them, so that the church can help those widows who are really in need.

{17} The elders who direct the affairs of the church well are worthy of double honor, especially those whose work is preaching and teaching. {18} For the Scripture says, "Do not muzzle the ox while it is treading out the grain," and "The worker deserves his wages." {19} Do not entertain an accusation against an elder unless it is brought by two or three witnesses. {20} Those who sin are to be rebuked publicly, so that the others may take warning.

GODLINESS WITH CONTENTMENT

1 Tim 6:3-21

If anyone teaches false doctrines and does not agree to the sound instruction of our Lord Jesus Christ and to godly teaching, {4} he is conceited and understands nothing. He has an unhealthy interest in controversies and quarrels about words that result in envy, strife, malicious talk, evil suspicions {5} and constant friction between men of corrupt mind, who have been robbed of the truth and who think that godliness is a means to financial gain. {6} But godliness with contentment is great gain. {7} For we brought nothing into the world, and we can take nothing out of it. {8} But if we have food and clothing, we will be content with that. {9} People who want to get rich fall into temptation and a trap and into many foolish and harmful desires that plunge men into ruin and destruction. {10} For the love of money is a root of all kinds of evil. Some people, eager for money, have wandered from the faith and pierced themselves with many griefs. {11} But you, man of God, flee from all this, and pursue righteousness, godliness, faith, love, endurance and gentleness. {12} Fight the good fight of the faith. Take hold of the eternal life to which you were called when you made your good confession in the presence of many witnesses. {13} In the sight of God, who gives life to everything, and of Christ Jesus, who while testifying before Pontius Pilate made the good confession, I charge you {14} to keep this command without spot or blame until the appearing of our Lord Jesus Christ, {15} which God will bring about in his own time— God, the blessed and only Ruler, the King of kings and Lord of lords, {16} who alone is immortal and who lives in unapproachable light, whom no one has seen or can see. To him be honor and might forever. Amen. {17} Command those who are rich in this present world not to be arrogant nor to put their hope in wealth, which is so uncertain, but to put their hope in God, who richly provides us with everything for our enjoyment. {18} Command them to do good, to be rich in good deeds, and to be generous and willing to share. {19} In this way they will lay up treasure for themselves as a firm foundation for the coming age, so that they may take hold of the life that is truly life. {20} Timothy, guard what has been entrusted to your care. Turn away from godless chatter and the opposing ideas of what is falsely called knowledge, {21} which some have professed and in so doing have wandered from the faith. Grace be with you.

BE STRONG IN GOD'S GRACE

2 Tim 1:3-2:6

I thank God, whom I serve, as my forefathers did, with a clear conscience, as night and day I constantly remember you in my prayers. {4} Recalling your tears, I long to see you, so that I may be filled with joy. {5} I have been reminded of your sincere faith, which first lived in your grandmother Lois and in your mother Eunice and, I am persuaded, now lives in you also. {6} For this reason I remind you to fan into flame the gift of God, which is in you through the laying on of my hands. {7} For God did not give us a spirit of timidity, but a spirit of power, of love and of self-discipline. {8} So do not be ashamed to testify about our Lord, or ashamed of me his prisoner. But join with me in suffering for the gospel, by the power of God, {9} who has saved us and called us to a holy life—not because of anything we have done but because of his own purpose and grace. This grace was given us in Christ Jesus before the beginning of time, {10} but it has now been revealed through the appearing of our Savior, Christ Jesus, who has destroyed death and has brought life and immortality to light through the gospel. {11} And of this gospel I was appointed a herald and an apostle and a teacher. {12} That is why I am suffering as I am. Yet I am not ashamed, because I know whom I have believed, and am convinced that he is able to guard what I have entrusted to him for that day. {13} What you heard from me, keep as the pattern of sound teaching, with faith and love in Christ Jesus. {14} Guard the good deposit that was entrusted to you—guard it with the help of the Holy Spirit who lives in us. {15} You know that everyone in the province of Asia has deserted me, including Phygelus and Hermogenes. {16} May the Lord show mercy to the household of Onesiphorus, because he often refreshed me and was not ashamed of my chains. {17} On the contrary, when he was in Rome, he searched hard for me until he found me. {18} May the Lord grant that he will find mercy from the Lord on that day! You know very well in how many ways he helped me in Ephesus. {2:1} You then, my son, be strong in the grace that is in Christ Jesus. {2} And the things you have heard me say in the presence of many witnesses entrust to reliable men who will also be qualified to teach others. {3} Endure hardship with us like a good soldier of Christ Jesus. {4} No one serving as a soldier gets involved in civilian affairs—he wants to please his commanding officer. {5} Similarly, if anyone competes as an athlete, he does not receive the victor's crown unless he competes according to the rules. {6} The hardworking farmer should be the first to receive a share of the crops.

A WORKMAN APPROVED OF GOD

2 Tim 2:15-26

Do your best to present yourself to God as one approved, a workman who does not need to be ashamed and who correctly handles the word of truth. {16} Avoid godless chatter, because those who indulge in it will become more and more ungodly. {17} Their teaching will spread like gangrene. Among them are Hymenaeus and Philetus, {18} who have wandered away from the truth. They say that the resurrection has already taken place, and they destroy the faith of some. {19} Nevertheless, God's solid foundation stands firm, sealed with this inscription: "The Lord knows those who are his," and, "Everyone who confesses the name of the Lord must turn away from wickedness." {20} In a large house there are articles not only of gold and silver, but also of wood and clay; some are for noble purposes and some for ignoble. {21} If a man cleanses himself from the latter, he will be an instrument for noble purposes, made holy, useful to the Master and prepared to do any good work. {22} Flee the evil desires of youth, and pursue righteousness, faith, love and peace, along with those who call on the Lord out of a pure heart. {23} Don't have anything to do with foolish and stupid arguments, because you know they produce quarrels. {24} And the Lord's servant must not quarrel; instead, he must be kind to everyone, able to teach, not resentful. {25} Those who oppose him he must gently instruct, in the hope that God will grant them repentance leading them to a knowledge of the truth, {26} and that they will come to their senses and escape from the trap of the devil, who has taken them captive to do his will.

2 Tim 3:10-17

You, however, know all about my teaching, my way of life, my purpose, faith, patience, love, endurance, {11} persecutions, sufferings– what kinds of things happened to me in Antioch, Iconium and Lystra, the persecutions I endured. Yet the Lord rescued me from all of them. {12} In fact, everyone who wants to live a godly life in Christ Jesus will be persecuted, {13} while evil men and impostors will go from bad to worse, deceiving and being deceived. {14} But as for you, continue in what you have learned and have become convinced of, because you know those from whom you learned it, {15} and how from infancy you have known the holy Scriptures, which are able to make you wise for salvation through faith in Christ Jesus. {16} All Scripture is God-breathed and is useful for teaching, rebuking, correcting and training in righteousness, {17} so that the man of God may be thoroughly equipped for every good work.

CONDUCT OF THE BELIEVERS

Titus 2:1-3:7

You must teach what is in accord with sound doctrine. {2} Teach the older men to be temperate, worthy of respect, self-controlled, and sound in faith, in love and in endurance. {3} Likewise, teach the older women to be reverent in the way they live, not to be slanderers or addicted to much wine, but to teach what is good. {4} Then they can train the younger women to love their husbands and children, {5} to be self-controlled and pure, to be busy at home, to be kind, and to be subject to their husbands, so that no one will malign the word of God. {6} Similarly, encourage the young men to be self-controlled. {7} In everything set them an example by doing what is good. In your teaching show integrity, seriousness {8} and soundness of speech that cannot be condemned, so that those who oppose you may be ashamed because they have nothing bad to say about us. {9} Teach slaves to be subject to their masters in everything, to try to please them, not to talk back to them, {10} and not to steal from them, but to show that they can be fully trusted, so that in every way they will make the teaching about God our Savior attractive. {11} For the grace of God that brings salvation has appeared to all men. {12} It teaches us to say "No" to ungodliness and worldly passions, and to live self-controlled, upright and godly lives in this present age, {13} while we wait for the blessed hope–the glorious appearing of our great God and Savior, Jesus Christ, {14} who gave himself for us to redeem us from all wickedness and to purify for himself a people that are his very own, eager to do what is good. {15} These, then, are the things you should teach. Encourage and rebuke with all authority. Do not let anyone despise you. {3:1} Remind the people to be subject to rulers and authorities, to be obedient, to be ready to do whatever is good, {2} to slander no one, to be peaceable and considerate, and to show true humility toward all men. {3} At one time we too were foolish, disobedient, deceived and enslaved by all kinds of passions and pleasures. We lived in malice and envy, being hated and hating one another. {4} But when the kindness and love of God our Savior appeared, {5} he saved us, not because of righteous things we had done, but because of his mercy. He saved us through the washing of rebirth and renewal by the Holy Spirit, {6} whom he poured out on us generously through Jesus Christ our Savior, {7} so that, having been justified by his grace, we might become heirs having the hope of eternal life.

PAUL'S PLEA FOR HIS FRIEND

Phile 1:1-25

Paul, a prisoner of Christ Jesus, and Timothy our brother, To Philemon our dear friend and fellow worker, {2} to Apphia our sister, to Archippus our fellow soldier and to the church that meets in your home: {3} Grace to you and peace from God our Father and the Lord Jesus Christ. {4} I always thank my God as I remember you in my prayers, {5} because I hear about your faith in the Lord Jesus and your love for all the saints. {6} I pray that you may be active in sharing your faith, so that you will have a full understanding of every good thing we have in Christ. {7} Your love has given me great joy and encouragement, because you, brother, have refreshed the hearts of the saints. {8} Therefore, although in Christ I could be bold and order you to do what you ought to do, {9} yet I appeal to you on the basis of love. I then, as Paul–an old man and now also a prisoner of Christ Jesus– {10} I appeal to you for my son Onesimus, who became my son while I was in chains. {11} Formerly he was useless to you, but now he has become useful both to you and to me. {12} I am sending him–who is my very heart–back to you. {13} I would have liked to keep him with me so that he could take your place in helping me while I am in chains for the gospel. {14} But I did not want to do anything without your consent, so that any favor you do will be spontaneous and not forced. {15} Perhaps the reason he was separated from you for a little while was that you might have him back for good– {16} no longer as a slave, but better than a slave, as a dear brother. He is very dear to me but even dearer to you, both as a man and as a brother in the Lord. {17} So if you consider me a partner, welcome him as you would welcome me. {18} If he has done you any wrong or owes you anything, charge it to me. {19} I, Paul, am writing this with my own hand. I will pay it back–not to mention that you owe me your very self. {20} I do wish, brother, that I may have some benefit from you in the Lord; refresh my heart in Christ. {21} Confident of your obedience, I write to you, knowing that you will do even more than I ask. {22} And one thing more: Prepare a guest room for me, because I hope to be restored to you in answer to your prayers. {23} Epaphras, my fellow prisoner in Christ Jesus, sends you greetings. {24} And so do Mark, Aristarchus, Demas and Luke, my fellow workers. {25} The grace of the Lord Jesus Christ be with your spirit.

CHRISTIANS SHOULD ACT ON WHAT THEY KNOW

James 1:5-27

If any of you lacks wisdom, he should ask God, who gives generously to all without finding fault, and it will be given to him. {6} But when he asks, he must believe and not doubt, because he who doubts is like a wave of the sea, blown and tossed by the wind. {7} That man should not think he will receive anything from the Lord; {8} he is a double-minded man, unstable in all he does. {9} The brother in humble circumstances ought to take pride in his high position. {10} But the one who is rich should take pride in his low position, because he will pass away like a wild flower. {11} For the sun rises with scorching heat and withers the plant; its blossom falls and its beauty is destroyed. In the same way, the rich man will fade away even while he goes about his business. {12} Blessed is the man who perseveres under trial, because when he has stood the test, he will receive the crown of life that God has promised to those who love him. {13} When tempted, no one should say, "God is tempting me." For God cannot be tempted by evil, nor does he tempt anyone; {14} but each one is tempted when, by his own evil desire, he is dragged away and enticed. {15} Then, after desire has conceived, it gives birth to sin; and sin, when it is full-grown, gives birth to death. {16} Don't be deceived, my dear brothers. {17} Every good and perfect gift is from above, coming down from the Father of the heavenly lights, who does not change like shifting shadows. {18} He chose to give us birth through the word of truth, that we might be a kind of firstfruits of all he created. {19} My dear brothers, take note of this: Everyone should be quick to listen, slow to speak and slow to become angry, {20} for man's anger does not bring about the righteous life that God desires. {21} Therefore, get rid of all moral filth and the evil that is so prevalent and humbly accept the word planted in you, which can save you. {22} Do not merely listen to the word, and so deceive yourselves. Do what it says. {23} Anyone who listens to the word but does not do what it says is like a man who looks at his face in a mirror {24} and, after looking at himself, goes away and immediately forgets what he looks like. {25} But the man who looks intently into the perfect law that gives freedom, and continues to do this, not forgetting what he has heard, but doing it–he will be blessed in what he does. {26} If anyone considers himself religious and yet does not keep a tight rein on his tongue, he deceives himself and his religion is worthless. {27} Religion that God our Father accepts as pure and faultless is this: to look after orphans and widows in their distress and to keep oneself from being polluted by the world.

DEEDS MUST BE CONSISTENT WITH CONFESSION OF FAITH

James 2:1-24

My brothers, as believers in our glorious Lord Jesus Christ, don't show favoritism. {2} Suppose a man comes into your meeting wearing a gold ring and fine clothes, and a poor man in shabby clothes also comes in. {3} If you show special attention to the man wearing fine clothes and say, "Here's a good seat for you," but say to the poor man, "You stand there" or "Sit on the floor by my feet," {4} have you not discriminated among yourselves and become judges with evil thoughts? {5} Listen, my dear brothers: Has not God chosen those who are poor in the eyes of the world to be rich in faith and to inherit the kingdom he promised those who love him? {6} But you have insulted the poor. Is it not the rich who are exploiting you? Are they not the ones who are dragging you into court? {7} Are they not the ones who are slandering the noble name of him to whom you belong? {8} If you really keep the royal law found in Scripture, "Love your neighbor as yourself," you are doing right. {9} But if you show favoritism, you sin and are convicted by the law as lawbreakers. {10} For whoever keeps the whole law and yet stumbles at just one point is guilty of breaking all of it. {11} For he who said, "Do not commit adultery," also said, "Do not murder." If you do not commit adultery but do commit murder, you have become a lawbreaker. {12} Speak and act as those who are going to be judged by the law that gives freedom, {13} because judgment without mercy will be shown to anyone who has not been merciful. Mercy triumphs over judgment! {14} What good is it, my brothers, if a man claims to have faith but has no deeds? Can such faith save him? {15} Suppose a brother or sister is without clothes and daily food. {16} If one of you says to him, "Go, I wish you well; keep warm and well fed," but does nothing about his physical needs, what good is it? {17} In the same way, faith by itself, if it is not accompanied by action, is dead. {18} But someone will say, "You have faith; I have deeds." Show me your faith without deeds, and I will show you my faith by what I do. {19} You believe that there is one God. Good! Even the demons believe that—and shudder. {20} You foolish man, do you want evidence that faith without deeds is useless ? {21} Was not our ancestor Abraham considered righteous for what he did when he offered his son Isaac on the altar? {22} You see that his faith and his actions were working together, and his faith was made complete by what he did. {23} And the scripture was fulfilled that says, "Abraham believed God, and it was credited to him as righteousness," and he was called God's friend. {24} You see that a person is justified by what he does and not by faith alone.

THE TONGUE CAN BE BOTH CURSE AND PRAISE

James 3:1-18

Not many of you should presume to be teachers, my brothers, because you know that we who teach will be judged more strictly. {2} We all stumble in many ways. If anyone is never at fault in what he says, he is a perfect man, able to keep his whole body in check. {3} When we put bits into the mouths of horses to make them obey us, we can turn the whole animal. {4} Or take ships as an example. Although they are so large and are driven by strong winds, they are steered by a very small rudder wherever the pilot wants to go. {5} Likewise the tongue is a small part of the body, but it makes great boasts. Consider what a great forest is set on fire by a small spark. {6} The tongue also is a fire, a world of evil among the parts of the body. It corrupts the whole person, sets the whole course of his life on fire, and is itself set on fire by hell. {7} All kinds of animals, birds, reptiles and creatures of the sea are being tamed and have been tamed by man, {8} but no man can tame the tongue. It is a restless evil, full of deadly poison. {9} With the tongue we praise our Lord and Father, and with it we curse men, who have been made in God's likeness. {10} Out of the same mouth come praise and cursing. My brothers, this should not be. {11} Can both fresh water and salt water flow from the same spring? {12} My brothers, can a fig tree bear olives, or a grapevine bear figs? Neither can a salt spring produce fresh water. {13} Who is wise and understanding among you? Let him show it by his good life, by deeds done in the humility that comes from wisdom. {14} But if you harbor bitter envy and selfish ambition in your hearts, do not boast about it or deny the truth. {15} Such "wisdom" does not come down from heaven but is earthly, unspiritual, of the devil. {16} For where you have envy and selfish ambition, there you find disorder and every evil practice. {17} But the wisdom that comes from heaven is first of all pure; then peace-loving, considerate, submissive, full of mercy and good fruit, impartial and sincere. {18} Peacemakers who sow in peace raise a harvest of righteousness.

NO ONE KNOWS ABOUT TOMORROW

James 4:1-17

What causes fights and quarrels among you? Don't they come from your desires that battle within you? {2} You want something but don't get it. You kill and covet, but you cannot have what you want. You quarrel and fight. You do not have, because you do not ask God. {3} When you ask, you do not receive, because you ask with wrong motives, that you may spend what you get on your pleasures. {4} You adulterous people, don't you know that friendship with the world is hatred toward God? Anyone who chooses to be a friend of the world becomes an enemy of God. {5} Or do you think Scripture says without reason that the spirit he caused to live in us envies intensely? {6} But he gives us more grace. That is why Scripture says: "God opposes the proud but gives grace to the humble." {7} Submit yourselves, then, to God. Resist the devil, and he will flee from you. {8} Come near to God and he will come near to you. Wash your hands, you sinners, and purify your hearts, you double-minded. {9} Grieve, mourn and wail. Change your laughter to mourning and your joy to gloom. {10} Humble yourselves before the Lord, and he will lift you up. {11} Brothers, do not slander one another. Anyone who speaks against his brother or judges him speaks against the law and judges it. When you judge the law, you are not keeping it, but sitting in judgment on it. {12} There is only one Lawgiver and Judge, the one who is able to save and destroy. But you—who are you to judge your neighbor? {13} Now listen, you who say, "Today or tomorrow we will go to this or that city, spend a year there, carry on business and make money." {14} Why, you do not even know what will happen tomorrow. What is your life? You are a mist that appears for a little while and then vanishes. {15} Instead, you ought to say, "If it is the Lord's will, we will live and do this or that." {16} As it is, you boast and brag. All such boasting is evil. {17} Anyone, then, who knows the good he ought to do and doesn't do it, sins.

WARNING TO THE RICH; PRAY FOR ONE ANOTHER

James 5:1-20

Now listen, you rich people, weep and wail because of the misery that is coming upon you. {2} Your wealth has rotted, and moths have eaten your clothes. {3} Your gold and silver are corroded. Their corrosion will testify against you and eat your flesh like fire. You have hoarded wealth in the last days. {4} Look! The wages you failed to pay the workmen who mowed your fields are crying out against you. The cries of the harvesters have reached the ears of the Lord Almighty. {5} You have lived on earth in luxury and self-indulgence. You have fattened yourselves in the day of slaughter. {6} You have condemned and murdered innocent men, who were not opposing you. {7} Be patient, then, brothers, until the Lord's coming. See how the farmer waits for the land to yield its valuable crop and how patient he is for the autumn and spring rains. {8} You too, be patient and stand firm, because the Lord's coming is near. {9} Don't grumble against each other, brothers, or you will be judged. The Judge is standing at the door! {10} Brothers, as an example of patience in the face of suffering, take the prophets who spoke in the name of the Lord. {11} As you know, we consider blessed those who have persevered. You have heard of Job's perseverance and have seen what the Lord finally brought about. The Lord is full of compassion and mercy. {12} Above all, my brothers, do not swear—not by heaven or by earth or by anything else. Let your "Yes" be yes, and your "No," no, or you will be condemned.

{13} Is any one of you in trouble? He should pray. Is anyone happy? Let him sing songs of praise. {14} Is any one of you sick? He should call the elders of the church to pray over him and anoint him with oil in the name of the Lord. {15} And the prayer offered in faith will make the sick person well; the Lord will raise him up. If he has sinned, he will be forgiven. {16} Therefore confess your sins to each other and pray for each other so that you may be healed. The prayer of a righteous man is powerful and effective. {17} Elijah was a man just like us. He prayed earnestly that it would not rain, and it did not rain on the land for three and a half years. {18} Again he prayed, and the heavens gave rain, and the earth produced its crops. {19} My brothers, if one of you should wander from the truth and someone should bring him back, {20} remember this: Whoever turns a sinner from the error of his way will save him from death and cover over a multitude of sins.

BE HOLY IN ALL YOU DO

1 Pet 1:6-25

In this you greatly rejoice, though now for a little while you may have had to suffer grief in all kinds of trials. {7} These have come so that your faith–of greater worth than gold, which perishes even though refined by fire–may be proved genuine and may result in praise, glory and honor when Jesus Christ is revealed. {8} Though you have not seen him, you love him; and even though you do not see him now, you believe in him and are filled with an inexpressible and glorious joy, {9} for you are receiving the goal of your faith, the salvation of your souls. {10} Concerning this salvation, the prophets, who spoke of the grace that was to come to you, searched intently and with the greatest care, {11} trying to find out the time and circumstances to which the Spirit of Christ in them was pointing when he predicted the sufferings of Christ and the glories that would follow. {12} It was revealed to them that they were not serving themselves but you, when they spoke of the things that have now been told you by those who have preached the gospel to you by the Holy Spirit sent from heaven. Even angels long to look into these things. {13} Therefore, prepare your minds for action; be self-controlled; set your hope fully on the grace to be given you when Jesus Christ is revealed. {14} As obedient children, do not conform to the evil desires you had when you lived in ignorance. {15} But just as he who called you is holy, so be holy in all you do; {16} for it is written: "Be holy, because I am holy." {17} Since you call on a Father who judges each man's work impartially, live your lives as strangers here in reverent fear. {18} For you know that it was not with perishable things such as silver or gold that you were redeemed from the empty way of life handed down to you from your forefathers, {19} but with the precious blood of Christ, a lamb without blemish or defect. {20} He was chosen before the creation of the world, but was revealed in these last times for your sake. {21} Through him you believe in God, who raised him from the dead and glorified him, and so your faith and hope are in God. {22} Now that you have purified yourselves by obeying the truth so that you have sincere love for your brothers, love one another deeply, from the heart. {23} For you have been born again, not of perishable seed, but of imperishable, through the living and enduring word of God. {24} For, "All men are like grass, and all their glory is like the flowers of the field; the grass withers and the flowers fall, {25} but the word of the Lord stands forever." And this is the word that was preached to you.

YOU ARE A CHOSEN PEOPLE

1 Pet 2:6-25

For in Scripture it says: "See, I lay a stone in Zion, a chosen and precious cornerstone, and the one who trusts in him will never be put to shame." {7} Now to you who believe, this stone is precious. But to those who do not believe, "The stone the builders rejected has become the capstone, " {8} and, "A stone that causes men to stumble and a rock that makes them fall." They stumble because they disobey the message—which is also what they were destined for. {9} But you are a chosen people, a royal priesthood, a holy nation, a people belonging to God, that you may declare the praises of him who called you out of darkness into his wonderful light. {10} Once you were not a people, but now you are the people of God; once you had not received mercy, but now you have received mercy. {11} Dear friends, I urge you, as aliens and strangers in the world, to abstain from sinful desires, which war against your soul. {12} Live such good lives among the pagans that, though they accuse you of doing wrong, they may see your good deeds and glorify God on the day he visits us. {13} Submit yourselves for the Lord's sake to every authority instituted among men: whether to the king, as the supreme authority, {14} or to governors, who are sent by him to punish those who do wrong and to commend those who do right. {15} For it is God's will that by doing good you should silence the ignorant talk of foolish men. {16} Live as free men, but do not use your freedom as a cover-up for evil; live as servants of God. {17} Show proper respect to everyone: Love the brotherhood of believers, fear God, honor the king. {18} Slaves, submit yourselves to your masters with all respect, not only to those who are good and considerate, but also to those who are harsh. {19} For it is commendable if a man bears up under the pain of unjust suffering because he is conscious of God. {20} But how is it to your credit if you receive a beating for doing wrong and endure it? But if you suffer for doing good and you endure it, this is commendable before God. {21} To this you were called, because Christ suffered for you, leaving you an example, that you should follow in his steps. {22} "He committed no sin, and no deceit was found in his mouth." {23} When they hurled their insults at him, he did not retaliate; when he suffered, he made no threats. Instead, he entrusted himself to him who judges justly. {24} He himself bore our sins in his body on the tree, so that we might die to sins and live for righteousness; by his wounds you have been healed. {25} For you were like sheep going astray, but now you have returned to the Shepherd and Overseer of your souls.

WIVES SUBMIT, HUSBANDS BE CONSIDERATE;
REPAY EVIL WITH BLESSING

1 Pet 3:1-18

Wives, in the same way be submissive to your husbands so that, if any of them do not believe the word, they may be won over without words by the behavior of their wives, {2} when they see the purity and reverence of your lives. {3} Your beauty should not come from outward adornment, such as braided hair and the wearing of gold jewelry and fine clothes. {4} Instead, it should be that of your inner self, the unfading beauty of a gentle and quiet spirit, which is of great worth in God's sight. {5} For this is the way the holy women of the past who put their hope in God used to make themselves beautiful. They were submissive to their own husbands, {6} like Sarah, who obeyed Abraham and called him her master. You are her daughters if you do what is right and do not give way to fear. {7} Husbands, in the same way be considerate as you live with your wives, and treat them with respect as the weaker partner and as heirs with you of the gracious gift of life, so that nothing will hinder your prayers. {8} Finally, all of you, live in harmony with one another; be sympathetic, love as brothers, be compassionate and humble.

{9} Do not repay evil with evil or insult with insult, but with blessing, because to this you were called so that you may inherit a blessing. {10} For, "Whoever would love life and see good days must keep his tongue from evil and his lips from deceitful speech. {11} He must turn from evil and do good; he must seek peace and pursue it. {12} For the eyes of the Lord are on the righteous and his ears are attentive to their prayer, but the face of the Lord is against those who do evil." {13} Who is going to harm you if you are eager to do good? {14} But even if you should suffer for what is right, you are blessed. "Do not fear what they fear; do not be frightened." {15} But in your hearts set apart Christ as Lord. Always be prepared to give an answer to everyone who asks you to give the reason for the hope that you have. But do this with gentleness and respect, {16} keeping a clear conscience, so that those who speak maliciously against your good behavior in Christ may be ashamed of their slander. {17} It is better, if it is God's will, to suffer for doing good than for doing evil. {18} For Christ died for sins once for all, the righteous for the unrighteous, to bring you to God. He was put to death in the body but made alive by the Spirit,

LIVE FOR GOD'S GLORY

1 Pet 4:1-19

Therefore, since Christ suffered in his body, arm yourselves also with the same attitude, because he who has suffered in his body is done with sin. {2} As a result, he does not live the rest of his earthly life for evil human desires, but rather for the will of God. {3} For you have spent enough time in the past doing what pagans choose to do–living in debauchery, lust, drunkenness, orgies, carousing and detestable idolatry. {4} They think it strange that you do not plunge with them into the same flood of dissipation, and they heap abuse on you. {5} But they will have to give account to him who is ready to judge the living and the dead. {6} For this is the reason the gospel was preached even to those who are now dead, so that they might be judged according to men in regard to the body, but live according to God in regard to the spirit. {7} The end of all things is near. Therefore be clear minded and self-controlled so that you can pray. {8} Above all, love each other deeply, because love covers over a multitude of sins. {9} Offer hospitality to one another without grumbling. {10} Each one should use whatever gift he has received to serve others, faithfully administering God's grace in its various forms. {11} If anyone speaks, he should do it as one speaking the very words of God. If anyone serves, he should do it with the strength God provides, so that in all things God may be praised through Jesus Christ. To him be the glory and the power for ever and ever. Amen. {12} Dear friends, do not be surprised at the painful trial you are suffering, as though something strange were happening to you. {13} But rejoice that you participate in the sufferings of Christ, so that you may be overjoyed when his glory is revealed. {14} If you are insulted because of the name of Christ, you are blessed, for the Spirit of glory and of God rests on you. {15} If you suffer, it should not be as a murderer or thief or any other kind of criminal, or even as a meddler. {16} However, if you suffer as a Christian, do not be ashamed, but praise God that you bear that name. {17} For it is time for judgment to begin with the family of God; and if it begins with us, what will the outcome be for those who do not obey the gospel of God? {18} And, "If it is hard for the righteous to be saved, what will become of the ungodly and the sinner?" {19} So then, those who suffer according to God's will should commit themselves to their faithful Creator and continue to do good.

ELDERS, EAGER TO SERVE; YOUNG MEN, SUBMISSIVE

1 Pet 5:1-12

To the elders among you, I appeal as a fellow elder, a witness of Christ's sufferings and one who also will share in the glory to be revealed: {2} Be shepherds of God's flock that is under your care, serving as overseers—not because you must, but because you are willing, as God wants you to be; not greedy for money, but eager to serve; {3} not lording it over those entrusted to you, but being examples to the flock. {4} And when the Chief Shepherd appears, you will receive the crown of glory that will never fade away. {5} Young men, in the same way be submissive to those who are older. All of you, clothe yourselves with humility toward one another, because, "God opposes the proud but gives grace to the humble." {6} Humble yourselves, therefore, under God's mighty hand, that he may lift you up in due time. {7} Cast all your anxiety on him because he cares for you. {8} Be self-controlled and alert. Your enemy the devil prowls around like a roaring lion looking for someone to devour. {9} Resist him, standing firm in the faith, because you know that your brothers throughout the world are undergoing the same kind of sufferings. {10} And the God of all grace, who called you to his eternal glory in Christ, after you have suffered a little while, will himself restore you and make you strong, firm and steadfast. {11} To him be the power for ever and ever. Amen. {12} With the help of Silas, whom I regard as a faithful brother, I have written to you briefly, encouraging you and testifying that this is the true grace of God. Stand fast in it.

MAKE YOUR SALVATION SURE;
PROPHETS SPEAK GOD'S WORD

2 Pet 1:3-21

His divine power has given us everything we need for life and godliness through our knowledge of him who called us by his own glory and goodness. {4} Through these he has given us his very great and precious promises, so that through them you may participate in the divine nature and escape the corruption in the world caused by evil desires. {5} For this very reason, make every effort to add to your faith goodness; and to goodness, knowledge; {6} and to knowledge, self-control; and to self-control, perseverance; and to perseverance, godliness; {7} and to godliness, brotherly kindness; and to brotherly kindness, love. {8} For if you possess these qualities in increasing measure, they will keep you from being ineffective and unproductive in your knowledge of our Lord Jesus Christ. {9} But if anyone does not have them, he is nearsighted and blind, and has forgotten that he has been cleansed from his past sins. {10} Therefore, my brothers, be all the more eager to make your calling and election sure. For if you do these things, you will never fall, {11} and you will receive a rich welcome into the eternal kingdom of our Lord and Savior Jesus Christ. {12} So I will always remind you of these things, even though you know them and are firmly established in the truth you now have. {13} I think it is right to refresh your memory as long as I live in the tent of this body, {14} because I know that I will soon put it aside, as our Lord Jesus Christ has made clear to me. {15} And I will make every effort to see that after my departure you will always be able to remember these things. {16} We did not follow cleverly invented stories when we told you about the power and coming of our Lord Jesus Christ, but we were eyewitnesses of his majesty. {17} For he received honor and glory from God the Father when the voice came to him from the Majestic Glory, saying, "This is my Son, whom I love; with him I am well pleased." {18} We ourselves heard this voice that came from heaven when we were with him on the sacred mountain. {19} And we have the word of the prophets made more certain, and you will do well to pay attention to it, as to a light shining in a dark place, until the day dawns and the morning star rises in your hearts. {20} Above all, you must understand that no prophecy of Scripture came about by the prophet's own interpretation. {21} For prophecy never had its origin in the will of man, but men spoke from God as they were carried along by the Holy Spirit.

FALSE TEACHERS WILL BE DESTROYED

2 Pet 2:3-19

In their greed these teachers will exploit you with stories they have made up. Their condemnation has long been hanging over them, and their destruction has not been sleeping. {4} For if God did not spare angels when they sinned, but sent them to hell, putting them into gloomy dungeons to be held for judgment; {5} if he did not spare the ancient world when he brought the flood on its ungodly people, but protected Noah, a preacher of righteousness, and seven others; {6} if he condemned the cities of Sodom and Gomorrah by burning them to ashes, and made them an example of what is going to happen to the ungodly; {7} and if he rescued Lot, a righteous man, who was distressed by the filthy lives of lawless men {8} (for that righteous man, living among them day after day, was tormented in his righteous soul by the lawless deeds he saw and heard)– {9} if this is so, then the Lord knows how to rescue godly men from trials and to hold the unrighteous for the day of judgment, while continuing their punishment. {10} This is especially true of those who follow the corrupt desire of the sinful nature and despise authority. Bold and arrogant, these men are not afraid to slander celestial beings; {11} yet even angels, although they are stronger and more powerful, do not bring slanderous accusations against such beings in the presence of the Lord. {12} But these men blaspheme in matters they do not understand. They are like brute beasts, creatures of instinct, born only to be caught and destroyed, and like beasts they too will perish. {13} They will be paid back with harm for the harm they have done. Their idea of pleasure is to carouse in broad daylight. They are blots and blemishes, reveling in their pleasures while they feast with you. {14} With eyes full of adultery, they never stop sinning; they seduce the unstable; they are experts in greed–an accursed brood! {15} They have left the straight way and wandered off to follow the way of Balaam son of Beor, who loved the wages of wickedness. {16} But he was rebuked for his wrongdoing by a donkey–a beast without speech–who spoke with a man's voice and restrained the prophet's madness. {17} These men are springs without water and mists driven by a storm. Blackest darkness is reserved for them. {18} For they mouth empty, boastful words and, by appealing to the lustful desires of sinful human nature, they entice people who are just escaping from those who live in error. {19} They promise them freedom, while they themselves are slaves of depravity–for a man is a slave to whatever has mastered him.

SCOFFERS WILL COME IN THE LAST DAYS

2 Pet 3:1-18

Dear friends, this is now my second letter to you. I have written both of them as reminders to stimulate you to wholesome thinking. {2} I want you to recall the words spoken in the past by the holy prophets and the command given by our Lord and Savior through your apostles. {3} First of all, you must understand that in the last days scoffers will come, scoffing and following their own evil desires. {4} They will say, "Where is this 'coming' he promised? Ever since our fathers died, everything goes on as it has since the beginning of creation." {5} But they deliberately forget that long ago by God's word the heavens existed and the earth was formed out of water and by water. {6} By these waters also the world of that time was deluged and destroyed. {7} By the same word the present heavens and earth are reserved for fire, being kept for the day of judgment and destruction of ungodly men. {8} But do not forget this one thing, dear friends: With the Lord a day is like a thousand years, and a thousand years are like a day. {9} The Lord is not slow in keeping his promise, as some understand slowness. He is patient with you, not wanting anyone to perish, but everyone to come to repentance. {10} But the day of the Lord will come like a thief. The heavens will disappear with a roar; the elements will be destroyed by fire, and the earth and everything in it will be laid bare. {11} Since everything will be destroyed in this way, what kind of people ought you to be? You ought to live holy and godly lives {12} as you look forward to the day of God and speed its coming. That day will bring about the destruction of the heavens by fire, and the elements will melt in the heat. {13} But in keeping with his promise we are looking forward to a new heaven and a new earth, the home of righteousness. {14} So then, dear friends, since you are looking forward to this, make every effort to be found spotless, blameless and at peace with him. {15} Bear in mind that our Lord's patience means salvation, just as our dear brother Paul also wrote you with the wisdom that God gave him. {16} He writes the same way in all his letters, speaking in them of these matters. His letters contain some things that are hard to understand, which ignorant and unstable people distort, as they do the other Scriptures, to their own destruction. {17} Therefore, dear friends, since you already know this, be on your guard so that you may not be carried away by the error of lawless men and fall from your secure position. {18} But grow in the grace and knowledge of our Lord and Savior Jesus Christ. To him be glory both now and forever! Amen.

THE WORD OF LIFE WAS FROM THE BEGINNING; THOSE IN THE LIGHT HAVE FELLOWSHIP

1 John 1:1-2:12

That which was from the beginning, which we have heard, which we have seen with our eyes, which we have looked at and our hands have touched–this we proclaim concerning the Word of life. {2} The life appeared; we have seen it and testify to it, and we proclaim to you the eternal life, which was with the Father and has appeared to us. {3} We proclaim to you what we have seen and heard, so that you also may have fellowship with us. And our fellowship is with the Father and with his Son, Jesus Christ. {4} We write this to make our joy complete.

{5} This is the message we have heard from him and declare to you: God is light; in him there is no darkness at all. {6} If we claim to have fellowship with him yet walk in the darkness, we lie and do not live by the truth. {7} But if we walk in the light, as he is in the light, we have fellowship with one another, and the blood of Jesus, his Son, purifies us from all sin. {8} If we claim to be without sin, we deceive ourselves and the truth is not in us. {9} If we confess our sins, he is faithful and just and will forgive us our sins and purify us from all unrighteousness. {10} If we claim we have not sinned, we make him out to be a liar and his word has no place in our lives. {2:1} My dear children, I write this to you so that you will not sin. But if anybody does sin, we have one who speaks to the Father in our defense–Jesus Christ, the Righteous One. {2} He is the atoning sacrifice for our sins, and not only for ours but also for the sins of the whole world. {3} We know that we have come to know him if we obey his commands. {4} The man who says, "I know him," but does not do what he commands is a liar, and the truth is not in him. {5} But if anyone obeys his word, God's love is truly made complete in him. This is how we know we are in him: {6} Whoever claims to live in him must walk as Jesus did. {7} Dear friends, I am not writing you a new command but an old one, which you have had since the beginning. This old command is the message you have heard. {8} Yet I am writing you a new command; its truth is seen in him and you, because the darkness is passing and the true light is already shining. {9} Anyone who claims to be in the light but hates his brother is still in the darkness. {10} Whoever loves his brother lives in the light, and there is nothing in him to make him stumble. {11} But whoever hates his brother is in the darkness and walks around in the darkness; he does not know where he is going, because the darkness has blinded him. {12} I write to you, dear children, because your sins have been forgiven on account of his name.

BE NOT LED ASTRAY

1 John 2:15-3:7a

Do not love the world or anything in the world. If anyone loves the world, the love of the Father is not in him. {16} For everything in the world–the cravings of sinful man, the lust of his eyes and the boasting of what he has and does–comes not from the Father but from the world. {17} The world and its desires pass away, but the man who does the will of God lives forever. {18} Dear children, this is the last hour; and as you have heard that the antichrist is coming, even now many antichrists have come. This is how we know it is the last hour. {19} They went out from us, but they did not really belong to us. For if they had belonged to us, they would have remained with us; but their going showed that none of them belonged to us. {20} But you have an anointing from the Holy One, and all of you know the truth. {21} I do not write to you because you do not know the truth, but because you do know it and because no lie comes from the truth. {22} Who is the liar? It is the man who denies that Jesus is the Christ. Such a man is the antichrist–he denies the Father and the Son. {23} No one who denies the Son has the Father; whoever acknowledges the Son has the Father also. {24} See that what you have heard from the beginning remains in you. If it does, you also will remain in the Son and in the Father. {25} And this is what he promised us–even eternal life. {26} I am writing these things to you about those who are trying to lead you astray. {27} As for you, the anointing you received from him remains in you, and you do not need anyone to teach you. But as his anointing teaches you about all things and as that anointing is real, not counterfeit–just as it has taught you, remain in him. {28} And now, dear children, continue in him, so that when he appears we may be confident and unashamed before him at his coming. {29} If you know that he is righteous, you know that everyone who does what is right has been born of him. {3:1} How great is the love the Father has lavished on us, that we should be called children of God! And that is what we are! The reason the world does not know us is that it did not know him. {2} Dear friends, now we are children of God, and what we will be has not yet been made known. But we know that when he appears, we shall be like him, for we shall see him as he is. {3} Everyone who has this hope in him purifies himself, just as he is pure. {4} Everyone who sins breaks the law; in fact, sin is lawlessness. {5} But you know that he appeared so that he might take away our sins. And in him is no sin. {6} No one who lives in him keeps on sinning. No one who continues to sin has either seen him or known him. {7} Dear children, do not let anyone lead you astray.

LOVE ONE ANOTHER

1 John 3:11-24

This is the message you heard from the beginning: We should love one another. {12} Do not be like Cain, who belonged to the evil one and murdered his brother. And why did he murder him? Because his own actions were evil and his brother's were righteous. {13} Do not be surprised, my brothers, if the world hates you. {14} We know that we have passed from death to life, because we love our brothers. Anyone who does not love remains in death. {15} Anyone who hates his brother is a murderer, and you know that no murderer has eternal life in him. {16} This is how we know what love is: Jesus Christ laid down his life for us. And we ought to lay down our lives for our brothers. {17} If anyone has material possessions and sees his brother in need but has no pity on him, how can the love of God be in him? {18} Dear children, let us not love with words or tongue but with actions and in truth. {19} This then is how we know that we belong to the truth, and how we set our hearts at rest in his presence {20} whenever our hearts condemn us. For God is greater than our hearts, and he knows everything. {21} Dear friends, if our hearts do not condemn us, we have confidence before God {22} and receive from him anything we ask, because we obey his commands and do what pleases him. {23} And this is his command: to believe in the name of his Son, Jesus Christ, and to love one another as he commanded us. {24} Those who obey his commands live in him, and he in them. And this is how we know that he lives in us: We know it by the Spirit he gave us.

1 John 4:7-16

Dear friends, let us love one another, for love comes from God. Everyone who loves has been born of God and knows God. {8} Whoever does not love does not know God, because God is love. {9} This is how God showed his love among us: He sent his one and only Son into the world that we might live through him. {10} This is love: not that we loved God, but that he loved us and sent his Son as an atoning sacrifice for our sins. {11} Dear friends, since God so loved us, we also ought to love one another. {12} No one has ever seen God; but if we love one another, God lives in us and his love is made complete in us. {13} We know that we live in him and he in us, because he has given us of his Spirit. {14} And we have seen and testify that the Father has sent his Son to be the Savior of the world. {15} If anyone acknowledges that Jesus is the Son of God, God lives in him and he in God. {16} And so we know and rely on the love God has for us. God is love. Whoever lives in love lives in God, and God in him.

TO LOVE GOD IS TO OBEY HIM

1 John 5:1-21

Everyone who believes that Jesus is the Christ is born of God, and everyone who loves the father loves his child as well. {2} This is how we know that we love the children of God: by loving God and carrying out his commands. {3} This is love for God: to obey his commands. And his commands are not burdensome, {4} for everyone born of God overcomes the world. This is the victory that has overcome the world, even our faith. {5} Who is it that overcomes the world? Only he who believes that Jesus is the Son of God. {6} This is the one who came by water and blood– Jesus Christ. He did not come by water only, but by water and blood. And it is the Spirit who testifies, because the Spirit is the truth. {7} For there are three that testify: {8} the Spirit, the water and the blood; and the three are in agreement. {9} We accept man's testimony, but God's testimony is greater because it is the testimony of God, which he has given about his Son. {10} Anyone who believes in the Son of God has this testimony in his heart. Anyone who does not believe God has made him out to be a liar, because he has not believed the testimony God has given about his Son. {11} And this is the testimony: God has given us eternal life, and this life is in his Son. {12} He who has the Son has life; he who does not have the Son of God does not have life. {13} I write these things to you who believe in the name of the Son of God so that you may know that you have eternal life. {14} This is the confidence we have in approaching God: that if we ask anything according to his will, he hears us. {15} And if we know that he hears us–whatever we ask–we know that we have what we asked of him. {16} If anyone sees his brother commit a sin that does not lead to death, he should pray and God will give him life. I refer to those whose sin does not lead to death. There is a sin that leads to death. I am not saying that he should pray about that. {17} All wrongdoing is sin, and there is sin that does not lead to death. {18} We know that anyone born of God does not continue to sin; the one who was born of God keeps him safe, and the evil one cannot harm him. {19} We know that we are children of God, and that the whole world is under the control of the evil one. {20} We know also that the Son of God has come and has given us understanding, so that we may know him who is true. And we are in him who is true–even in his Son Jesus Christ. He is the true God and eternal life. {21} Dear children, keep yourselves from idols.

WALK IN LOVE

2 John

The elder, To the chosen lady and her children, whom I love in the truth—and not I only, but also all who know the truth— {2} because of the truth, which lives in us and will be with us forever: {3} Grace, mercy and peace from God the Father and from Jesus Christ, the Father's Son, will be with us in truth and love. {4} It has given me great joy to find some of your children walking in the truth, just as the Father commanded us. {5} And now, dear lady, I am not writing you a new command but one we have had from the beginning. I ask that we love one another. {6} And this is love: that we walk in obedience to his commands. As you have heard from the beginning, his command is that you walk in love. {7} Many deceivers, who do not acknowledge Jesus Christ as coming in the flesh, have gone out into the world. Any such person is the deceiver and the antichrist. {8} Watch out that you do not lose what you have worked for, but that you may be rewarded fully. {9} Anyone who runs ahead and does not continue in the teaching of Christ does not have God; whoever continues in the teaching has both the Father and the Son. {10} If anyone comes to you and does not bring this teaching, do not take him into your house or welcome him. {11} Anyone who welcomes him shares in his wicked work. {12} I have much to write to you, but I do not want to use paper and ink. Instead, I hope to visit you and talk with you face to face, so that our joy may be complete. {13} The children of your chosen sister send their greetings.

IMITATE THE GOOD

3 John

The elder, To my dear friend Gaius, whom I love in the truth. {2} Dear friend, I pray that you may enjoy good health and that all may go well with you, even as your soul is getting along well. {3} It gave me great joy to have some brothers come and tell about your faithfulness to the truth and how you continue to walk in the truth. {4} I have no greater joy than to hear that my children are walking in the truth. {5} Dear friend, you are faithful in what you are doing for the brothers, even though they are strangers to you. {6} They have told the church about your love. You will do well to send them on their way in a manner worthy of God. {7} It was for the sake of the Name that they went out, receiving no help from the pagans. {8} We ought therefore to show hospitality to such men so that we may work together for the truth. {9} I wrote to the church, but Diotrephes, who loves to be first, will have nothing to do with us. {10} So if I come, I will call attention to what he is doing, gossiping maliciously about us. Not satisfied with that, he refuses to welcome the brothers. He also stops those who want to do so and puts them out of the church. {11} Dear friend, do not imitate what is evil but what is good. Anyone who does what is good is from God. Anyone who does what is evil has not seen God. {12} Demetrius is well spoken of by everyone–and even by the truth itself. We also speak well of him, and you know that our testimony is true. {13} I have much to write you, but I do not want to do so with pen and ink. {14} I hope to see you soon, and we will talk face to face. Peace to you. The friends here send their greetings. Greet the friends there by name.

GODLESS MEN ARE CONDEMNED;
GOD CAN KEEP US FROM FALLING

Jude 1:8-25

In the very same way, these dreamers pollute their own bodies, reject authority and slander celestial beings. {9} But even the archangel Michael, when he was disputing with the devil about the body of Moses, did not dare to bring a slanderous accusation against him, but said, "The Lord rebuke you!" {10} Yet these men speak abusively against whatever they do not understand; and what things they do understand by instinct, like unreasoning animals—these are the very things that destroy them. {11} Woe to them! They have taken the way of Cain; they have rushed for profit into Balaam's error; they have been destroyed in Korah's rebellion. {12} These men are blemishes at your love feasts, eating with you without the slightest qualm—shepherds who feed only themselves. They are clouds without rain, blown along by the wind; autumn trees, without fruit and uprooted—twice dead. {13} They are wild waves of the sea, foaming up their shame; wandering stars, for whom blackest darkness has been reserved forever. {14} Enoch, the seventh from Adam, prophesied about these men: "See, the Lord is coming with thousands upon thousands of his holy ones {15} to judge everyone, and to convict all the ungodly of all the ungodly acts they have done in the ungodly way, and of all the harsh words ungodly sinners have spoken against him." {16} These men are grumblers and faultfinders; they follow their own evil desires; they boast about themselves and flatter others for their own advantage. {17} But, dear friends, remember what the apostles of our Lord Jesus Christ foretold. {18} They said to you, "In the last times there will be scoffers who will follow their own ungodly desires." {19} These are the men who divide you, who follow mere natural instincts and do not have the Spirit. {20} But you, dear friends, build yourselves up in your most holy faith and pray in the Holy Spirit. {21} Keep yourselves in God's love as you wait for the mercy of our Lord Jesus Christ to bring you to eternal life. {22} Be merciful to those who doubt; {23} snatch others from the fire and save them; to others show mercy, mixed with fear—hating even the clothing stained by corrupted flesh. {24} To him who is able to keep you from falling and to present you before his glorious presence without fault and with great joy— {25} to the only God our Savior be glory, majesty, power and authority, through Jesus Christ our Lord, before all ages, now and forevermore! Amen.

I HEARD A LOUD VOICE LIKE A TRUMPET

Rev 1:1-16

The revelation of Jesus Christ, which God gave him to show his servants what must soon take place. He made it known by sending his angel to his servant John, {2} who testifies to everything he saw–that is, the word of God and the testimony of Jesus Christ. {3} Blessed is the one who reads the words of this prophecy, and blessed are those who hear it and take to heart what is written in it, because the time is near. {4} John, To the seven churches in the province of Asia: Grace and peace to you from him who is, and who was, and who is to come, and from the seven spirits before his throne, {5} and from Jesus Christ, who is the faithful witness, the firstborn from the dead, and the ruler of the kings of the earth. To him who loves us and has freed us from our sins by his blood, {6} and has made us to be a kingdom and priests to serve his God and Father–to him be glory and power for ever and ever! Amen. {7} Look, he is coming with the clouds, and every eye will see him, even those who pierced him; and all the peoples of the earth will mourn because of him. So shall it be! Amen. {8} "I am the Alpha and the Omega," says the Lord God, "who is, and who was, and who is to come, the Almighty." {9} I, John, your brother and companion in the suffering and kingdom and patient endurance that are ours in Jesus, was on the island of Patmos because of the word of God and the testimony of Jesus. {10} On the Lord's Day I was in the Spirit, and I heard behind me a loud voice like a trumpet, {11} which said: "Write on a scroll what you see and send it to the seven churches: to Ephesus, Smyrna, Pergamum, Thyatira, Sardis, Philadelphia and Laodicea." {12} I turned around to see the voice that was speaking to me. And when I turned I saw seven golden lampstands, {13} and among the lampstands was someone "like a son of man," dressed in a robe reaching down to his feet and with a golden sash around his chest. {14} His head and hair were white like wool, as white as snow, and his eyes were like blazing fire. {15} His feet were like bronze glowing in a furnace, and his voice was like the sound of rushing waters. {16} In his right hand he held seven stars, and out of his mouth came a sharp double-edged sword. His face was like the sun shining in all its brilliance.

MESSAGES TO EPHESUS AND SMYRNA

Rev 1:17-2:11

When I saw him, I fell at his feet as though dead. Then he placed his right hand on me and said: "Do not be afraid. I am the First and the Last. {18} I am the Living One; I was dead, and behold I am alive for ever and ever! And I hold the keys of death and Hades. {19} "Write , therefore, what you have seen, what is now and what will take place later. {20} The mystery of the seven stars that you saw in my right hand and of the seven golden lampstands is this: The seven stars are the angels of the seven churches, and the seven lampstands are the seven churches. {2:1} "To the angel of the church in Ephesus write: These are the words of him who holds the seven stars in his right hand and walks among the seven golden lampstands: {2} I know your deeds, your hard work and your perseverance. I know that you cannot tolerate wicked men, that you have tested those who claim to be apostles but are not, and have found them false. {3} You have persevered and have endured hardships for my name, and have not grown weary. {4} Yet I hold this against you: You have forsaken your first love. {5} Remember the height from which you have fallen! Repent and do the things you did at first. If you do not repent, I will come to you and remove your lampstand from its place. {6} But you have this in your favor: You hate the practices of the Nicolaitans, which I also hate. {7} He who has an ear, let him hear what the Spirit says to the churches. To him who overcomes, I will give the right to eat from the tree of life, which is in the paradise of God.

{8} "To the angel of the church in Smyrna write: These are the words of him who is the First and the Last, who died and came to life again. {9} I know your afflictions and your poverty–yet you are rich! I know the slander of those who say they are Jews and are not, but are a synagogue of Satan. {10} Do not be afraid of what you are about to suffer. I tell you, the devil will put some of you in prison to test you, and you will suffer persecution for ten days. Be faithful, even to the point of death, and I will give you the crown of life. {11} He who has an ear, let him hear what the Spirit says to the churches. He who overcomes will not be hurt at all by the second death.

MESSAGES TO PERGAMUM AND THYATIRA

Rev 2:12-29

"To the angel of the church in Pergamum write: These are the words of him who has the sharp, double-edged sword. {13} I know where you live–where Satan has his throne. Yet you remain true to my name. You did not renounce your faith in me, even in the days of Antipas, my faithful witness, who was put to death in your city–where Satan lives. {14} Nevertheless , I have a few things against you: You have people there who hold to the teaching of Balaam, who taught Balak to entice the Israelites to sin by eating food sacrificed to idols and by committing sexual immorality. {15} Likewise you also have those who hold to the teaching of the Nicolaitans. {16} Repent therefore! Otherwise, I will soon come to you and will fight against them with the sword of my mouth. {17} He who has an ear, let him hear what the Spirit says to the churches. To him who overcomes, I will give some of the hidden manna. I will also give him a white stone with a new name written on it, known only to him who receives it.

{18} "To the angel of the church in Thyatira write: These are the words of the Son of God, whose eyes are like blazing fire and whose feet are like burnished bronze. {19} I know your deeds, your love and faith, your service and perseverance, and that you are now doing more than you did at first. {20} Nevertheless, I have this against you: You tolerate that woman Jezebel, who calls herself a prophetess. By her teaching she misleads my servants into sexual immorality and the eating of food sacrificed to idols. {21} I have given her time to repent of her immorality, but she is unwilling. {22} So I will cast her on a bed of suffering, and I will make those who commit adultery with her suffer intensely, unless they repent of her ways. {23} I will strike her children dead. Then all the churches will know that I am he who searches hearts and minds, and I will repay each of you according to your deeds. {24} Now I say to the rest of you in Thyatira, to you who do not hold to her teaching and have not learned Satan's so-called deep secrets (I will not impose any other burden on you): {25} Only hold on to what you have until I come. {26} To him who overcomes and does my will to the end, I will give authority over the nations– {27} 'He will rule them with an iron scepter; he will dash them to pieces like pottery' – just as I have received authority from my Father. {28} I will also give him the morning star. {29} He who has an ear, let him hear what the Spirit says to the churches.

MESSAGES TO SARDIS, PHILADELPHIA AND LAODICEA

Rev 3:1-17

"To the angel of the church in Sardis write: These are the words of
him who holds the seven spirits of God and the seven stars. I know your
deeds; you have a reputation of being alive, but you are dead. {2} Wake
up! Strengthen what remains and is about to die, for I have not found
your deeds complete in the sight of my God. {3} Remember , therefore,
what you have received and heard; obey it, and repent. But if you do not
wake up, I will come like a thief, and you will not know at what time I
will come to you. {4} Yet you have a few people in Sardis who have not
soiled their clothes. They will walk with me, dressed in white, for they
are worthy. {5} He who overcomes will, like them, be dressed in white. I
will never blot out his name from the book of life, but will acknowledge
his name before my Father and his angels. {6} He who has an ear, let
him hear what the Spirit says to the churches.

{7} "To the angel of the church in Philadelphia write: These are
the words of him who is holy and true, who holds the key of David. What
he opens no one can shut, and what he shuts no one can open. {8} I
know your deeds. See, I have placed before you an open door that no
one can shut. I know that you have little strength, yet you have kept my
word and have not denied my name. {9} I will make those who are of
the synagogue of Satan, who claim to be Jews though they are not, but
are liars–I will make them come and fall down at your feet and
acknowledge that I have loved you. {10} Since you have kept my
command to endure patiently, I will also keep you from the hour of trial
that is going to come upon the whole world to test those who live on the
earth. {11} I am coming soon. Hold on to what you have, so that no one
will take your crown. {12} Him who overcomes I will make a pillar in the
temple of my God. Never again will he leave it. I will write on him the
name of my God and the name of the city of my God, the new Jerusalem,
which is coming down out of heaven from my God; and I will also write
on him my new name. {13} He who has an ear, let him hear what the
Spirit says to the churches.

{14} "To the angel of the church in Laodicea write: These are the
words of the Amen, the faithful and true witness, the ruler of God's
creation. {15} I know your deeds, that you are neither cold nor hot. I
wish you were either one or the other! {16} So , because you are
lukewarm–neither hot nor cold–I am about to spit you out of my mouth.
{17} You say, 'I am rich; I have acquired wealth and do not need a thing.'
But you do not realize that you are wretched, pitiful, poor, blind and
naked.

I WILL TELL YOU WHAT WILL HAPPEN

Rev 4:6-5:10

Also before the throne there was what looked like a sea of glass, clear as crystal. In the center, around the throne, were four living creatures, and they were covered with eyes, in front and in back. {7} The first living creature was like a lion, the second was like an ox, the third had a face like a man, the fourth was like a flying eagle. {8} Each of the four living creatures had six wings and was covered with eyes all around, even under his wings. Day and night they never stop saying: "Holy, holy, holy is the Lord God Almighty, who was, and is, and is to come." {9} Whenever the living creatures give glory, honor and thanks to him who sits on the throne and who lives for ever and ever, {10} the twenty-four elders fall down before him who sits on the throne, and worship him who lives for ever and ever. They lay their crowns before the throne and say: {11} "You are worthy, our Lord and God, to receive glory and honor and power, for you created all things, and by your will they were created and have their being." {5:1} Then I saw in the right hand of him who sat on the throne a scroll with writing on both sides and sealed with seven seals. {2} And I saw a mighty angel proclaiming in a loud voice, "Who is worthy to break the seals and open the scroll?" {3} But no one in heaven or on earth or under the earth could open the scroll or even look inside it. {4} I wept and wept because no one was found who was worthy to open the scroll or look inside. {5} Then one of the elders said to me, "Do not weep! See, the Lion of the tribe of Judah, the Root of David, has triumphed. He is able to open the scroll and its seven seals." {6} Then I saw a Lamb, looking as if it had been slain, standing in the center of the throne, encircled by the four living creatures and the elders. He had seven horns and seven eyes, which are the seven spirits of God sent out into all the earth. {7} He came and took the scroll from the right hand of him who sat on the throne. {8} And when he had taken it, the four living creatures and the twenty-four elders fell down before the Lamb. Each one had a harp and they were holding golden bowls full of incense, which are the prayers of the saints. {9} And they sang a new song: "You are worthy to take the scroll and to open its seals, because you were slain, and with your blood you purchased men for God from every tribe and language and people and nation. {10} You have made them to be a kingdom and priests to serve our God, and they will reign on the earth."

A GREAT MULTITUDE IN WHITE ROBES

Rev 7:1-4

After this I saw four angels standing at the four corners of the earth, holding back the four winds of the earth to prevent any wind from blowing on the land or on the sea or on any tree. {2} Then I saw another angel coming up from the east, having the seal of the living God. He called out in a loud voice to the four angels who had been given power to harm the land and the sea: {3} "Do not harm the land or the sea or the trees until we put a seal on the foreheads of the servants of our God." {4} Then I heard the number of those who were sealed: 144,000 from all the tribes of Israel.

Rev 7:9-17

After this I looked and there before me was a great multitude that no one could count, from every nation, tribe, people and language, standing before the throne and in front of the Lamb. They were wearing white robes and were holding palm branches in their hands. {10} And they cried out in a loud voice: "Salvation belongs to our God, who sits on the throne, and to the Lamb." {11} All the angels were standing around the throne and around the elders and the four living creatures. They fell down on their faces before the throne and worshiped God, {12} saying: "Amen! Praise and glory and wisdom and thanks and honor and power and strength be to our God for ever and ever. Amen!" {13} Then one of the elders asked me, "These in white robes–who are they, and where did they come from?" {14} I answered, "Sir, you know." And he said, "These are they who have come out of the great tribulation; they have washed their robes and made them white in the blood of the Lamb. {15} Therefore, "they are before the throne of God and serve him day and night in his temple; and he who sits on the throne will spread his tent over them. {16} Never again will they hunger; never again will they thirst. The sun will not beat upon them, nor any scorching heat. {17} For the Lamb at the center of the throne will be their shepherd; he will lead them to springs of living water. And God will wipe away every tear from their eyes."

THE SEVENTH ANGEL SOUNDS THE TRUMPET

Rev 11:15-19

The seventh angel sounded his trumpet, and there were loud voices in heaven, which said: "The kingdom of the world has become the kingdom of our Lord and of his Christ, and he will reign for ever and ever." {16} And the twenty-four elders, who were seated on their thrones before God, fell on their faces and worshiped God, {17} saying: "We give thanks to you, Lord God Almighty, the One who is and who was, because you have taken your great power and have begun to reign. {18} The nations were angry; and your wrath has come. The time has come for judging the dead, and for rewarding your servants the prophets and your saints and those who reverence your name, both small and great– and for destroying those who destroy the earth." {19} Then God's temple in heaven was opened, and within his temple was seen the ark of his covenant. And there came flashes of lightning, rumblings, peals of thunder, an earthquake and a great hailstorm.

Rev 12:7-12

And there was war in heaven. Michael and his angels fought against the dragon, and the dragon and his angels fought back. {8} But he was not strong enough, and they lost their place in heaven. {9} The great dragon was hurled down–that ancient serpent called the devil, or Satan, who leads the whole world astray. He was hurled to the earth, and his angels with him. {10} Then I heard a loud voice in heaven say: "Now have come the salvation and the power and the kingdom of our God, and the authority of his Christ. For the accuser of our brothers, who accuses them before our God day and night, has been hurled down. {11} They overcame him by the blood of the Lamb and by the word of their testimony; they did not love their lives so much as to shrink from death. {12} Therefore rejoice, you heavens and you who dwell in them! But woe to the earth and the sea, because the devil has gone down to you! He is filled with fury, because he knows that his time is short."

OUR LORD GOD ALMIGHTY REIGNS

Rev 19:6-21

Then I heard what sounded like a great multitude, like the roar of rushing waters and like loud peals of thunder, shouting: "Hallelujah! For our Lord God Almighty reigns. {7} Let us rejoice and be glad and give him glory! For the wedding of the Lamb has come, and his bride has made herself ready. {8} Fine linen, bright and clean, was given her to wear." (Fine linen stands for the righteous acts of the saints.) {9} Then the angel said to me, "Write: 'Blessed are those who are invited to the wedding supper of the Lamb!'" And he added, "These are the true words of God." {10} At this I fell at his feet to worship him. But he said to me, "Do not do it! I am a fellow servant with you and with your brothers who hold to the testimony of Jesus. Worship God! For the testimony of Jesus is the spirit of prophecy." {11} I saw heaven standing open and there before me was a white horse, whose rider is called Faithful and True. With justice he judges and makes war. {12} His eyes are like blazing fire, and on his head are many crowns. He has a name written on him that no one knows but he himself. {13} He is dressed in a robe dipped in blood, and his name is the Word of God. {14} The armies of heaven were following him, riding on white horses and dressed in fine linen, white and clean. {15} Out of his mouth comes a sharp sword with which to strike down the nations. "He will rule them with an iron scepter." He treads the winepress of the fury of the wrath of God Almighty. {16} On his robe and on his thigh he has this name written: KING OF KINGS AND LORD OF LORDS. {17} And I saw an angel standing in the sun, who cried in a loud voice to all the birds flying in midair, "Come, gather together for the great supper of God, {18} so that you may eat the flesh of kings, generals, and mighty men, of horses and their riders, and the flesh of all people, free and slave, small and great." {19} Then I saw the beast and the kings of the earth and their armies gathered together to make war against the rider on the horse and his army. {20} But the beast was captured, and with him the false prophet who had performed the miraculous signs on his behalf. With these signs he had deluded those who had received the mark of the beast and worshiped his image. The two of them were thrown alive into the fiery lake of burning sulfur. {21} The rest of them were killed with the sword that came out of the mouth of the rider on the horse, and all the birds gorged themselves on their flesh.

THE RIGHTEOUS WILL REIGN WITH CHRIST FOR A THOUSAND YEARS; SATAN IS DOOMED; THE BOOKS ARE OPENED

Rev 20:1-15

And I saw an angel coming down out of heaven, having the key to the Abyss and holding in his hand a great chain. {2} He seized the dragon, that ancient serpent, who is the devil, or Satan, and bound him for a thousand years. {3} He threw him into the Abyss, and locked and sealed it over him, to keep him from deceiving the nations anymore until the thousand years were ended. After that, he must be set free for a short time. {4} I saw thrones on which were seated those who had been given authority to judge. And I saw the souls of those who had been beheaded because of their testimony for Jesus and because of the word of God. They had not worshiped the beast or his image and had not received his mark on their foreheads or their hands. They came to life and reigned with Christ a thousand years. {5} (The rest of the dead did not come to life until the thousand years were ended.) This is the first resurrection. {6} Blessed and holy are those who have part in the first resurrection. The second death has no power over them, but they will be priests of God and of Christ and will reign with him for a thousand years. {7} When the thousand years are over, Satan will be released from his prison {8} and will go out to deceive the nations in the four corners of the earth–Gog and Magog–to gather them for battle. In number they are like the sand on the seashore. {9} They marched across the breadth of the earth and surrounded the camp of God's people, the city he loves. But fire came down from heaven and devoured them. {10} And the devil, who deceived them, was thrown into the lake of burning sulfur, where the beast and the false prophet had been thrown. They will be tormented day and night for ever and ever. {11} Then I saw a great white throne and him who was seated on it. Earth and sky fled from his presence, and there was no place for them. {12} And I saw the dead, great and small, standing before the throne, and books were opened. Another book was opened, which is the book of life. The dead were judged according to what they had done as recorded in the books. {13} The sea gave up the dead that were in it, and death and Hades gave up the dead that were in them, and each person was judged according to what he had done. {14} Then death and Hades were thrown into the lake of fire. The lake of fire is the second death. {15} If anyone's name was not found written in the book of life, he was thrown into the lake of fire.

THEN I SAW A NEW HEAVEN AND A NEW EARTH

Rev 21:6-25

He said to me: "It is done. I am the Alpha and the Omega, the Beginning and the End. To him who is thirsty I will give to drink without cost from the spring of the water of life. {7} He who overcomes will inherit all this, and I will be his God and he will be my son. {8} But the cowardly, the unbelieving, the vile, the murderers, the sexually immoral, those who practice magic arts, the idolaters and all liars–their place will be in the fiery lake of burning sulfur. This is the second death." {9} One of the seven angels who had the seven bowls full of the seven last plagues came and said to me, "Come, I will show you the bride, the wife of the Lamb." {10} And he carried me away in the Spirit to a mountain great and high, and showed me the Holy City, Jerusalem, coming down out of heaven from God. {11} It shone with the glory of God, and its brilliance was like that of a very precious jewel, like a jasper, clear as crystal. {12} It had a great, high wall with twelve gates, and with twelve angels at the gates. On the gates were written the names of the twelve tribes of Israel. {13} There were three gates on the east, three on the north, three on the south and three on the west. {14} The wall of the city had twelve foundations, and on them were the names of the twelve apostles of the Lamb. {15} The angel who talked with me had a measuring rod of gold to measure the city, its gates and its walls. {16} The city was laid out like a square, as long as it was wide. He measured the city with the rod and found it to be 12,000 stadia in length, and as wide and high as it is long. {17} He measured its wall and it was 144 cubits thick, by man's measurement, which the angel was using. {18} The wall was made of jasper, and the city of pure gold, as pure as glass. {19} The foundations of the city walls were decorated with every kind of precious stone. The first foundation was jasper, the second sapphire, the third chalcedony, the fourth emerald, {20} the fifth sardonyx, the sixth carnelian, the seventh chrysolite, the eighth beryl, the ninth topaz, the tenth chrysoprase, the eleventh jacinth, and the twelfth amethyst. {21} The twelve gates were twelve pearls, each gate made of a single pearl. The great street of the city was of pure gold, like transparent glass. {22} I did not see a temple in the city, because the Lord God Almighty and the Lamb are its temple. {23} The city does not need the sun or the moon to shine on it, for the glory of God gives it light, and the Lamb is its lamp. {24} The nations will walk by its light, and the kings of the earth will bring their splendor into it. {25} On no day will its gates ever be shut, for there will be no night there.

THE SPIRIT AND THE BRIDE SAY, "COME."

Rev 22:3-21

No longer will there be any curse. The throne of God and of the Lamb will be in the city, and his servants will serve him. {4} They will see his face, and his name will be on their foreheads. {5} There will be no more night. They will not need the light of a lamp or the light of the sun, for the Lord God will give them light. And they will reign for ever and ever. {6} The angel said to me, "These words are trustworthy and true. The Lord, the God of the spirits of the prophets, sent his angel to show his servants the things that must soon take place." {7} "Behold, I am coming soon! Blessed is he who keeps the words of the prophecy in this book." {8} I, John, am the one who heard and saw these things. And when I had heard and seen them, I fell down to worship at the feet of the angel who had been showing them to me. {9} But he said to me, "Do not do it! I am a fellow servant with you and with your brothers the prophets and of all who keep the words of this book. Worship God!" {10} Then he told me, "Do not seal up the words of the prophecy of this book, because the time is near. {11} Let him who does wrong continue to do wrong; let him who is vile continue to be vile; let him who does right continue to do right; and let him who is holy continue to be holy." {12} "Behold, I am coming soon! My reward is with me, and I will give to everyone according to what he has done. {13} I am the Alpha and the Omega, the First and the Last, the Beginning and the End. {14} "Blessed are those who wash their robes, that they may have the right to the tree of life and may go through the gates into the city. {15} Outside are the dogs, those who practice magic arts, the sexually immoral, the murderers, the idolaters and everyone who loves and practices falsehood. {16} "I, Jesus, have sent my angel to give you this testimony for the churches. I am the Root and the Offspring of David, and the bright Morning Star." {17} The Spirit and the bride say, "Come!" And let him who hears say, "Come!" Whoever is thirsty, let him come; and whoever wishes, let him take the free gift of the water of life. {18} I warn everyone who hears the words of the prophecy of this book: If anyone adds anything to them, God will add to him the plagues described in this book. {19} And if anyone takes words away from this book of prophecy, God will take away from him his share in the tree of life and in the holy city, which are described in this book. {20} He who testifies to these things says, "Yes, I am coming soon." Amen. Come, Lord Jesus. {21} The grace of the Lord Jesus be with God's people. Amen.

NOTES

NOTES

NOTES